DON'T WORRY
ABOUT THE MONEY NOW

'Sandy Gall has become better known as a newscaster recently. By writing this book, which is entertaining and serious by turns, he has shown he is more than a face on the box and has had, and is having a worthwhile, not to say, enjoyable, alternative career.'

The Financial Times

'Perhaps better than anyone, Sandy Gall explains the hard work that goes into reporting a war – the agonies of being unable to pass on vital information or cans of film because airports are closed or telex lines not functioning. Many of his stories are excellent and it is wonderful to see the picture that Evelyn Waugh painted in *Scoop* still seems true.'

The Daily Telegraph

'The autobiography of ITN reporter and newsreader Sandy Gall is a journalist's memoir: disasters, wars, scoops, misadventures – an action-packed confection liberally sprinkled with anecdotes. *Don't Worry About the Money Now* is an engaging account of reporting around the world by a man who comes over as genially as he does on the small screen.'

Ion Trewin, *Hampstead & Highgate Express*

D0257175

DON'T WORRY ABOUT THE MONEY NOW

Sandy Gall

NEW ENGLISH LIBRARY

For Johnny Bett, without whose generous encouragement I would probably never have started, Sheila, Rory and my godson, Hamish; for the long-suffering Gall tribe – Eleanor, Fiona, Alexander, Carlotta and Michaela; and all the splendid chums of the ghastlier assignments who lend the book what distinction it has.

Penshurst, November, 1982

First published in Great Britain in 1983 by Hamish Hamilton Ltd

First NEL Paperback Edition June 1984
Reprinted March, August 1985

NEL Books are published by
New English Library,
Mill Road, Dunton Green,
Sevenoaks, Kent.
Editorial office: 47 Bedford Square, London WC1B 3DP

Typeset by Fleet Graphics, Enfield, Middlesex

Printed and bound in Great Britain by
Cox & Wyman Ltd, Reading

Gall, Sandy
   Don't worry about the money now.
   1. Foreign correspondents
   I. Title
   070.4′33′0924   PN4784.F6

ISBN 0–450–05682–1

CONTENTS

CHAPTER 1

REUTERS: the World at my Feet

Reuters Ltd. is housed at 85 Fleet Street, opposite the *Express* and the *Telegraph*, in a handsome 1920s building it shares with the Press Association. I knew very little about Reuters that spring morning in 1953 as I entered the swing doors through which so many dashing and distinguished correspondents had passed. I knew simply that it was a worldwide organisation started by a German Jew called Reuter in the nineteenth century and that it was a synonym for speed, accuracy and impartiality. I also knew that along its wires had hummed many scoops and sensations, from the relief of Mafeking to the outbreak of World War Two. I therefore expected to be put through a testing and exhaustive series of interviews in which my knowledge of world events would be examined in minute detail. I trembled slightly as I went up into the lift to the office of the Secretary, W.S. Carter. He turned out to be a gentle, almost withdrawn man who spoke in the accents of Oxbridge. Instead of the searching questions I dreaded, we had a friendly chat about my sporting interests and not much else, and then I was taken along to see the deputy Editor, Doon Campbell. Doon was a striking figure in that he had only one arm (the other ended in a slightly sinister black glove). He had reported the assassination of Mahatma Gandhi from India in 1948.

Doon wanted to know about my French and German, which I had with great confidence claimed to speak fluently, but he did not, thank God actually make me say anything in a foreign tongue. He also wanted to know about my politics. I said truthfully that I did not belong to any political party and, since I spoke in the accents of a well-known Scottish public school, I got the impression that I was acceptable. Certainly when Doon walked me to the door he held me under the arm with his black-gloved hand in a gesture that combined a hint of authoritarianism with a touch of friendly familiarity. They would let me know, he said and sure enough a week later a letter arrived bearing the copperplate heading of Reuters Ltd.

It was from the Secretary, dated May 1, 1953, and told me that Reuters had decided to give me a trial of from three to six months at a weekly salary of £6.16s.6d. plus a cost of living bonus of 18s, which worked out at the princely sum of £401.13s.2d. a year. I was overjoyed and impatient to start, but I had to give notice to the *Aberdeen Press and Journal*, for which I had worked as a trainee sub for a few months, and did not make my way finally to London until the summer. I had a week in London meeting various Reuters luminaries, including the Editor, Walter 'Tony' Cole, a huge rather intimidating Scotsman, and, very briefly, Christopher Chancellor, the General Manager, who possessed a diplomat's smoothness of manner.

As a new boy I merely glimpsed these important personages. I spent most of the time being briefed by Doon Campbell and the Chief News Editor, Sidney Mason, a hard-working, hard-swearing, hard-bitten journalist of the old school. He could be a devastatingly tough taskmaster, until you realised that underneath that fierce manner throbbed the kindest of hearts. He was also intensely loyal to his 'boys' in the field, sometimes I suspect to his own detriment. The sad decline of his career with Reuters was to hurt me deeply, but that was still a long way in the future: when I first met him

Sid was the God of all foreign correspondents, which meant most of us.

I also had to pay my respects to the formidable Muriel Penn, an intimidatingly bespectacled old spinster who ran the Situationer Service, a news feature service which went out to newspapers across the world with the correspondent's by-line at the top of the story. This was a considerable attraction because, as I was soon to discover, working for Reuters was an extraordinarily anonymous occupation. Unless you had a scoop or something quite exceptional, Reuters would not give you a by-line, and, even if they did, the chances of a newspaper using it were very remote indeed. Situationers could be about virtually anything and in due course I was to derive a lot of fun from writing them.

Then I spent a somewhat disconsolate day or two sitting on Central Desk, which was like a mere mortal being invited to Mount Olympus. All stories filed by Reuters correspondents across the world came to Central Desk, where they would be weighed by hard-eyed men who had seen it all before, judged by the most exacting standards and either pencil-subbed and, if they were important enough, fed out straight away to the teleprinters and thence to newspapers and radio stations all over the world, or, if they failed to meet the required standard, rewritten or even – worst of all – spiked. I sat bemused, at the bottom of the desk, watching the words come pouring in like a tide – they handled a million a day – and, after a few dexterous adjustments, pour out again in torrents of well-honed Reuters prose. I was thrown a scrap or two to sub or re-write, but I do not think I was expected to make a very valuable contribution and I certainly did not do so. Central Desk was the centre of the Reuters solar system, but there were all sorts of lesser suns scattered around the huge room: next to Central Desk was the Diplomatic Desk, then the Home Desk with a handful of reporters, then Sid Mason and his small empire. Opposite, at the far end of the room, was the Asian Desk, then the North American Desk staffed by Americans and Canadians, the Africa Desk, and finally the European Desk run by John Bonham, whose real name before he changed it by deed poll had been, as everyone was anxious to tell me, Pigg. He was not at all like his animal namesake, but a thin, bespectacled, schoolmaster-ish man with whom I never felt a great deal of rapport.

Reuters decided, luckily for me, that Head Office was too big and impersonal a place for trainees and had hit on the idea of sending us, depending on the languages we could speak, to Paris, Rome or, in my case, Frankfurt. Paris would have been marvellous, I thought, until I heard that the Reuters boss there was a holy terror called Harold King. Rome would have been truly wonderful, since the Chief Correspondent there, Patrick Cross, was one of the nicest men in Reuters, but unfortunately, I spoke no Italian.

So, after a week in head office, with lots of advice and a little money, I was despatched to Frankfurt by plane and the great adventure had begun. It was summer, the sun was shining, I was twenty-five. The world was at my feet . . .

After three months' probation in Frankfurt under a pipe-smoking Yorkshireman called Bob Petty, I was formally accepted by Reuters as a trainee and posted to Berlin. The former German capital was then very much in the front line of the Cold War and nothing could have demonstrated this better than the recent defection of John Peet, Reuters' Chief Correspondent in West Berlin. He had, everyone agreed, staged it beautifully, telephoning the office before the start of his own press conference in East Berlin and dictating the story of his own defection to a startled German colleague called Herbert Sternberg.

I got my first scoop while in Berlin, although it actually occurred in Leipzig. Every year the East German Govern-ment ran a big industrial fair in Leipzig and Reuters sent me to cover it in the summer of 1954. At first sight there was not much excitement to be had among all the tractors and tur-bines, but, during a reception given by the British Motor Corporation, as it then was, I picked up the merest whiff of a story. One of the senior sales staff let slip that they had had a remarkable coup that day.

'A big deal?' I asked. 'Worth how much?'

'I honestly can't tell you . . . I'd get shot if I told you . . . here, have another drink.' A lot of drinks later, he suddenly cracked. 'All right,' he succumbed. 'What the hell! Why shouldn't I tell you?' I waited, swaying slightly on my feet.

'We've just sold an MG to one of the top East Germans.'

'Really. An MG sports?'

'Yes.'

'What colour?'

He chuckled. 'Red.'

'What could be more suitable,' I agreed. 'And who's bought it?'

He shook his head. 'That I really can't tell you.'

'There's no story if I can't say who bought it,' I pointed out.

The tray of drinks came round again and we helped ourselves. Finally, out of sheer exhaustion, I think, he gave in. Lowering his voice, he said, 'You won't believe this but we sold it to the Prime Minister himself, Otto Grotewohl.'

I was amazed. How could such a paragon of Communist rectitude, a prim ideologue if ever I saw one, with his rimless pince-nez, bring himself to buy such a frivolous, decadent, capitalist toy as a red MG sports car. I said so to my sales friend.

'Ah well,' he said, 'you see, it's for his twenty-year-old daughter.'

My story made the front page of every British paper next morning – with one exception: *The Times*. That was odd enough. What made it doubly strange was that I was then acting as the *Times* 'stringer' in Berlin and I had filed a separate report to them. But it did not matter. The Reuters wire carried fulsome praise of my scoop.

My first real break came when, early in 1955, Reuters posted me to Nairobi as their East African correspondent. This was a big promotion and I was as excited as a child. I came back to London for a few weeks and was fully briefed about the situation there. The final accolade was delivered by the Editor, Tony Cole, who sat me down and started talking very fast in a honey-smooth, deep Scots brogue with a suggestion of a mid-Atlantic drawl. Cole was a master of the intellectual bear-hug and the conversation went something like this.

'Okay, Sandy. Sit down, ole boy. You fit? You're looking well. Let's see, how old are you now, twenty-eight? Well, this is a big new responsibility we're giving you, sending you to East Africa. You talked to Doon and Sid and Muriel Penn? Very important to keep the Situationers flowing. Mau Mau's been a very big story as you know and Ronnie Batchelor [my predecessor] has done a great job. Story's gone a bit down page now of course, but we want to maintain continuity and keep our relations with the [East African] *Standard* on a friendly basis. You know all about that? Okay, that's fine. Best of luck.'

At this point the huge figure rose and propelled me by apparent force of personality towards the door. I tried to say something about a rise in pay, but he brushed my feeble attempt aside with what I discovered later was his standard and classic phrase. 'Don't worry about the money now, old boy,' he drawled, towering over me, although I was just as tall as he was. 'Keep in touch, ole boy . . . so long.' I felt my hand being squeezed in one of Tony's mammoth fists and the heavy door closed behind me. I felt outmanoeuvred, but not entirely defeated. The magic phrase – 'don't worry about the money now, old boy' – rang in my ears, suggesting that although Reuters could not afford to be generous at the moment, since things were particularly tight, the prospects for the future were rosier. I returned to the newsroom where Alex Valentine, a cynical smile on his face, was waiting to disabuse me. 'Don't worry about the money now, ole boy,' he teased. 'Did he give you that? He did? Better men than you, Gunga Din, have fallen for that old chestnut,' Alex chortled (he's the only man I have ever known who actually did chortle). I knew I had been done. My salary was only a pittance – I had only discovered on my return from Berlin that I was being paid less than the union minimum. On the other hand, I was going to East Africa at Reuters' expense and that in itself was a fabulous bonus.

On the way to Nairobi I stopped off for a couple of days in Cairo where I was met by the Reuters man, Gilbert Sedbon. Cairo has not changed, and in 1955 the street scene was much as it is today: the traffic a snarl of cars, horns blaring, swerving past camels and donkey carts, buses careering along with as many people clinging to the outside as inside, the sun pitiless and only the Nile itself, broad and mysterious, lending a grandeur to the city that nothing will ever diminish. I saw my first felucca, white sails filling, gliding gracefully up the river, and in the delta we drove past blindfolded oxen turning endlessly in a circle as they pumped water for irrigation in a method unchanged since Pharaonic times. Gilbert, the perfect host and guide, took me to the Pyramids and the Sphinx. We clambered up into the central chamber of the Great Pyramid where the guide demonstrated the echo with a deafening shout, and in the chokingly close atmosphere I knew for a few moments something of the excitement that must have possessed the first Egyptologists. The Pyramids were exactly as one had been led to expect and yet more, much more. The desert stretched away behind them and we stood on the very threshold of Africa. Even the importunities of the Egyptian touts – 'You like ride camel? You want change money, mister? You like my sister? You like boy, yes?' then, on a more threatening note, 'you give me baksheesh, mister!' – could not rob the moment of its magic.

Next day I flew to Nairobi. It was the first time I had ever been in black Africa and I found the landscape and culture so alien that I experienced for the only time in my life what the psychologists call 'culture shock', although I prefer the French word '*dépaysement*'. I felt quite simply lost. The sky was too vast, the distances too great, and Africa too different. Mau Mau was almost over but not quite. On arrival, I walked into the long bar of the New Stanley and found myself standing next to a pretty blonde girl. She was dressed in well-cut bush shirt and trousers and I noticed with a gulp of innocent surprise that on her hip she was wearing a revolver in a leopardskin holster.

Kenya was then in the final hectic stage of its colonial history. Mau Mau had imposed a long reign of terror on the rural whites in their remote upcountry farms and people were only just starting to move about normally. One farmer told me that, until very recently, he had not left his farm at night for four years. Now, with Mau Mau virtually defeated, the

Kenya settlers were determined to have a last fling. Kenya had always attracted exotic and unusual characters. In the early days, when it was still a pioneer country and there was real danger and hardship, the club was very exclusive. People like Baroness Blixen set a style and a standard that few who followed were able to maintain. One of her friends, Denys Finch Hatton, remarked that, at the age of forty, life was too short to drink anything but the best claret and smoke anything but the best cigars. He drove a vintage Rolls-Royce and would read poetry to her after a day spent in the bush stalking a wounded lion. The people who came later were also characters, but more in the Sunday newspaper tradition.

Even in 1956 there were still a number of eccentric English aristocrats about, for example the famous Lady . . . who, celebrating one night at the Equator Club in Nairobi, had taken a dislike to a tune the band was playing, pulled out her pistol and shot the drummer through the leg.

One of my first friends in Nairobi, Ned Kelly, had had a hair-raising escape from Mau Mau. He lived ten or twelve miles from Nairobi and was driving home from the office one night when he ran into an ambush. The car was riddled with bullets and he was wounded in the leg and arm. He managed, however, to get out of the car and crawl clear. He lay in the bush just off the road listening to the Mau Mau hunting for him. Somehow they failed to find him and, after what seemed an eternity, they gave up and silence returned. Ned lay not daring to move in case they were still waiting for him. Finally he crept off through the bush and walked home.

There were many other horror stories, but one that happened soon after I arrived made a particularly chilling impression on me. There were two distinguished Leakey brothers in Kenya, Dr. Louis Leakey who was Curator of the Coryndon Museum, and David who was a farmer. Louis Leakey had been the official interpreter at the much-publicised trial of Jomo Kenyatta, who was found guilty of managing Mau Mau and jailed for seven years. (All the time I was in Kenya, Jomo was in prison in the remote and barren Northern Frontier District, where it was said he was given a bottle of brandy a day in the hope that he would drink himself to death. He disappointed his captors and emerged from jail hale and hearty to become President of an independent Kenya.) The Leakey brothers were the sons of missionaries, they had been brought up with the Kikuyu, spoke the language fluently and were blood brothers of the tribe. As such they had great influence on the Kikuyu and were therefore considered a potential threat by the Mau Mau organisers. One night, a gang of Mau Mau burst in through the back door of David Leakey's farm just as the family were sitting down for supper. In the savagery that followed Mrs. Leakey and some of the servants were butchered to death, but one of the Leakeys' daughters managed to scramble up into the loft where she remained hidden, hearing the screams and sounds of killing below. She was the only survivor. When the gang left they took Leakey with them. Although he was a diabetic, they forced him to walk through the night to the foot of Mount Kenya, where the Kikuyu believe their gods reside. There, after various bestialities, they carried out his ritual murder, burying him head down with a spear through his heart. Even among the hardened settlers of Kenya, the cold-blooded brutality of that murder sent a shiver down their spines.

I spent three months in the New Stanley which was noisy and inefficient but very central. Above all, it was one of the great meeting places. There was a little courtyard where one could sit and get gently plastered in the sun at lunchtime, which is what we usually did. There were really only two proper London-employed foreign correspondents at the time, Donald Wise of the *Daily Express* and myself. Though there had of course been a dozen or more in the heyday of Mau Mau, there were still always one or two people coming through, either from London or more frequently from South Africa which had superseded Kenya as the more prolific dateline. People like Eric Downton and Douglas Brown of the *Daily Telegraph,* James Cameron of the *News Chronicle*, Roy Lewis of *The Times*, Len Ingalls of the *New York Times* and a host of other transient 'firemen' came and went. So there was always an opportunity for lunch at the New Stanley and much discussion of events in and outside Kenya before

15

these far-travelled wanderers went away to sleep it off and file their copy. I would go off to the *East African Standard* and consult the Chief Reporter, an oracle called Ken Meadows, who was a fund of information on Kenya and its various happenings. Ken always, in or out of the office, wore a rather battered brown trilby on the back of his head, only taking it off to scratch his pate in bewilderment at the stupidity of some government official.

He would often be cross-examining one of his reporters.

'What did he say? The government is not aware of the situation? Not aware . . . ?' he would repeat, his voice full of contempt and his homespun Birmingham accent cutting through the noise in the room like a buzz saw.

The reporter who was relaying the result of his enquiries would elaborate. The hat would be pushed further back.

'What the hell does the government think it's supposed to be doing if it's not being aware of the situation . . . ? Who had the temerity to tell you such a load of balls?'

The reporter would mention a name.

'Oh, him! That cunt! In that case I'm not surprised, not surprised one bloody bit.' And Ken would roll out his 'I've-seen-it-all-before' laugh, the scorn in his voice enough to wither the leaves of the trees in Delamere Avenue.

The *Standard* was the leading paper in the colony, read by all the whites and most of the politically-conscious Africans – at least those of them who were not being detained at His Majesty's pleasure, or as they put it in the quaint pidgin of Kenya 'in the King Georgy Hotely' – but it was rather establishment. Ken Meadows was the perfect foil. He was a thoroughly professional no-nonsense provincial journalist who was concerned with the facts and a good shorthand note of what the man had said.

'Did he actually say that?' he would ask disbelievingly. 'Did you get it down? What's the quote then?' And when the reporter confirmed the words from his notebook he would tilt his hat back, scratch his head and laugh. 'Jesus Christ,' Ken would say, 'I knew he was daft but I didn't know he was that bloody daft.' Pushing his typewriter away, he would rise to his feet. 'Let's go and have a beer,' he would say with relish, 'and forget about these silly buggers. They don't know what the hell they're doing anyway.' And, settling his hat once more firmly on his head, he would lead the way to the Long Bar in the New Stanley.

Donald Wise has always been my idea of the ideal foreign correspondent: tall, dashing, distinguished, with an unfailing sense of humour. He enlivened many a dull story and imparted a *joie de vivre* to even the most unpleasant assignment as if he had just uncorked a bottle of champagne. He had had an amazing career which, to a wide-eyed innocent like me, seemed little short of miraculous. He was born in South Africa, where his father was a wealthy business man, had been up at Oxford, and done a spell as a cub reporter on the *Daily Mirror* before the war, then joined up and been sent to the Far East. He was captured by the Japanese when Singapore fell and locked up in the notorious Changi prison camp where for three years he watched his companions die and his own youth waste away. He still bore the scars when I first knew him and I suppose he still carries them, though they have faded a bit with time. With the end of the war and his release from Changi, Donald returned to Britain and his young wife whom he had married only a few months before joining up. There was a terrible shock in store for him. He discovered that she had given him up for dead – in fact he had been posted missing, presumed dead, by the War Office – and married an American.

With celebration turned to ashes in his mouth, Donald headed straight back to the Far East, to Malaya, where he got a job as a trainee rubber planter. When the Emergency started a year or two later, he led a tracker team of headhunters in the jungle, looking for Chinese Communist terrorists. But he was still restless and decided to go back to South Africa. There, he turned to journalism and worked for a while on the *Rand Daily Mail*, the chief English-language daily in South Africa, famous for its uncompromising belief in democracy and its courage in standing up to the Nationalist Government. Soon, Donald's talents attracted bigger fish and he was enrolled as local 'stringer' by the *Daily Express*. The rest followed from there. When I met him in Nairobi in

1955 he was a fulltime 'fireman' for the *Express*, based in Kenya but travelling far and wide, to Johannesburg and Cape Town in the south, to Cairo in the north, literally from the Cape to Cairo, with side trips to Turkey and other hot spots.

He took me under his wing, introduced me to everyone who mattered, and was generous with advice and ideas for stories. Donald, his new wife Bridget, who was South African, and I all lived by this time in a smaller residential hotel, the Grosvenor, on the outskirts of Nairobi. It was run by an extraordinary Greek Cypriot called Stelleonides. 'Stelleo' looked like a professional wrestler, a huge, beetle-browed bruiser with whom it would have been extremely foolish to tangle. Occasionally he would lose his temper with the staff and the walls used to tremble as Stelleo shouted Greek curses at the top of his voice.

There was also a very beautiful English girl called Lynn with whom I fell madly in love. She had a rather weepy mother who also lived in the Grosvenor and who, after a few drinks, would always put on the same record. 'You men,' she would say, accepting another gin and tonic. 'You always kill the thing you love, always.' I found this pessimism irritating as well as untrue, but I was nice to her because of my designs on her daughter. These were successful but alas short-lived; the period of bliss was both extreme and extremely brief.

A friend of Donald's soon to become a friend of mine, Lucy Hoare, was PRO to the Kenya Police and truly the journalist's saviour. She knew everyone and was marvellously clever at arranging things if she liked you – and she liked almost everyone. She lived in a charming cottage in Muthaiga and was waited on hand and foot by a gentle and devoted character called Boniface. Lucy told me that he was the youngest son of a tribal chief, which explained his perfect manners and air of distinction, but that because of lack of tribal prospects he had taken it upon himself to look after Lucy until the chieftainship called.

One weekend Lucy took me to stay with some people called Shaw who had a big farm about fifty miles east of Nairobi, near Machakos, where the green uplands start to give way to the dry plains that extend halfway to Mombasa and the scrub around Tsavo. I was to write a feature on the farm and we were to stay for a big dance on the Saturday night. The house was an adaptation of an English country house, a big rambling affair, built of huge wooden beams and covered with thatch. It was both attractive and practical and the thatch, which was cut on the farm, kept the rooms cool in the heat of the summer. Our host, Sir Robert Shaw, then about seventy, was a Kenya pioneer who had played an important role in introducing broadcasting to the colony. He had also hacked out his 20,000 acres from virgin bush, drilled for water, made roads and now ran several hundred beef cattle on the arid-looking pastures that stretched almost as far as the eye could see. We sat on his verandah one evening, sipping our whiskies, and Sir Robert pointed out the summer lightning flickering on Mount Kilimanjaro a hundred miles away. The dance, given to celebrate his birthday, was a great success. Hundreds of people came from all over Kenya and we roistered into the small hours. At the end of it, as the band played the last bars of the last waltz, the old patriarch and his major domo, a handsome, grey-haired African in a white uniform with an imposing red sash to show he was head man, threw their arms around each other and danced round the room to general applause.

One weekend Lucy and I went to stay with a District Commissioner who ran the NFD (Northern Frontier District), an area about half the size of Scotland bordering on Somalia. Somali raiders known as *shifta* continually came across the border, stealing cattle and sometimes killing the owners so it was hardly surprising that the NFD was a closed area and you had to have special permission to go there. With her connections, there was no obstacle to Lucy. We drove north from Nairobi, past Mount Kenya over 17,000 feet and wrapped in cloud, the country getting steadily drier and emptier, until we reached Isiolo, the administrative centre, where the DC lived.

The three of us started off on a long sight-seeing tour by Landrover, going for miles across the barren landscape which becomes semi-desert just north of Isiolo. At one point we went hurtling over a ridge on the dirt road. As we came crashing down on the other side the DC spun the wheel wildly and we narrowly missed the bulky, bleached skeleton of a camel which had thoughtlessly chosen to die in the middle of the road. Then we suddenly came upon a small family of tribesmen walking along by the side of the road. 'Turkana,' the DC explained and stopped to speak to them in their own language. There was a thin old man carrying a spear and a very pretty young woman carrying a baby, and two other young children, straight and slim and naked with shy eyes. Their skin had an almost apricot sheen over the blackness, and as they smiled happily they showed brilliant white teeth. As we drove off I watched them walking away quite happily into what to me was a total wilderness.

Lucy arranged for me to see the legendary Police Commissioner, Richard Catling, a tough little customer who sat behind his desk tight-lipped and yet somehow demure. He did not have much to say to me, in fact he gave the impression that he thought the press, if you recognized them at all, ought to be kept at arm's length. When Lucy asked me how I had got on and I told her, she laughed. 'You'd never think that demure little man, as you call him, was up all night at a mess party and it got so wild they threw him through a wall as part of the fun.'

'Threw him through a wall?' I said in disbelief. 'Hold on, Lucy, are we talking about the same person?'

'No, it's true,' she giggled. 'They were so tight they grabbed old Catling by the legs and arms and swung him backwards and forwards like this, you know. They let him go by mistake and he went right through the mess wall, one of those plaster-board things. Luckily he wasn't hurt, but there was quite a mess . . .'

Catling's PA at that time was Jim Orr. I met him briefly when he ushered me in to see his master, but I only got to know him well much later. He had had an amazing career. After leaving Gordonstoun where he had been a contemporary of Prince Philip's and head boy – 'Only because I was older than everyone else,' he used to say deprecatingly – he decided to go into the British South Africa Police in Rhodesia. But he did not care for the BSAP – 'they were too fascist,' he said – so he moved to Kenya where he was accepted into the Kenya Police and posted to Nyeri. Nyeri is in the heart of Kikuyuland and had been one of the hottest Mau Mau areas. Jim, for some reason he never explained, fell foul of the Nyeri police chief and was continually in trouble. One day the Commissioner, Catling, arrived on a tour of inspection and was told about Jim and his misdemeanours. Catling decided to find out what was going on so he called Jim in and they had a long heart to heart. At the end of it, Catling asked Jim to come to Nairobi and be his PA.

A few months later, Prince Philip and Princess Elizabeth, as she then was, arrived in Mombasa aboard the Royal Yacht on their honeymoon. Jim had been sent down to Mombasa to give a hand and Prince Philip spotted his old school chum.

'Good God, Orr, what the hell are you doing here?'

'In the Kenya Police, sir,' Orr replied, saluting.

'Well, come and have a drink on *Britannia* tonight,' Prince Philip said and strolled away. A few months later, Jim Orr got a call from Buckingham Palace. Prince Philip wanted a new Private Secretary. Would he come and do the job? He replied that he would and did so, for ten self-effacing, devoted years.

On one memorable occasion, the army took me out on patrol. Trackers had reported a Mau Mau camp in the forest above Nyeri and the patrol was going in at dawn in an attempt to capture the gang. We started at about four and drove up through the forest to the tree line. It was very cold at 8,000 feet. Then we walked through the forest for several miles. The patrol was quite small, a young British officer and a couple of British soldiers and half a dozen Africans from the King's African Rifles on whose forest lore and tracking skill we all depended. I was nervous, jumping at every sound. At one point, when we were getting near the camp, there was a sudden crashing in the bush just ahead of us. We could sense the direction of the movement rather than see it and I immediately thought we had run into a band of Mau Mau. 'It's all right,' the officer whispered. 'We just disturbed a herd of buffalo.' Any Mau Mau for miles around would also have heard the crashing noises and taken off in a hurry. Whether

21

that was the case we never found out. When we reached the camp, just as the sky was getting light, it was empty.

The Mau Mau had many camps in the forest and moved between them as they felt inclined. Their senses were as finely tuned as a wild animal's. They could smell the smoke of a cigarette, for example, half a mile away, and read the sights and sounds of the forest as accurately as anyone else could read a book. The most successful Mau Mau leaders, like Dedan Kimathi, developed a kind of sixth sense which kept them out of trouble right to the end, despite the odds steadily worsening against them. Kimathi was finally shot down, hungry and with only a handful of followers left, as he crawled out of the forest to raid a field of mealies. He was dressed in a leopard-skin and the soldier who shot him thought in the half-light that he was indeed a leopard.

General China was another slippery customer who eluded the security forces time after time. Donald Wise and I once spent a couple of days watching five hundred soldiers and police fruitlessly sweeping the papyrus swamp round Lake Naivasha in which General China and his gang were supposed to be trapped. But none of us ever caught sight of him. If he had been there at all, he must have slipped away the first night when the soldiers were all in their tents, apart that is from the guards posted round the edge of the lake. But there were just not enough of them to seal off the whole vast area.

The hard-core Mau Mau prisoners were kept in the old prison on Lamu island just off the coast. The Kenya Government flew a few of us down there one day to counter reports that they were being badly treated. Naturally everything looked fine on the day in question, but the overriding impression was not of the lush tropical setting of Lamu with palm trees nodding against the deep blue of the Indian Ocean, but the feeling of pure hatred for the British, the colonial oppressor, that emanated from the group of prisoners as we walked past them. I do not think I have ever felt such an intensity of emotion generated by men who did not actually do or say anything, except stare at us with sullen malevolence.

*   *   *

One day London send me a telegram instructing me to go to Kampala, the capital of Uganda, which lies due west of Kenya and, with Tanganyika, was once part of British East Africa. Nairobi to Kampala is about 300 miles and would take seven or eight hours' driving. I filled up my Ford Zephyr and set out early on the road to Nakuru. As nearly always in Kenya, the morning had a sense of vastness and promise about it. I was soon humming along at seventy miles an hour, reeling off the by now familiar landmarks: Longonot, the Great Rift Valley, Lake Naivasha, Lake Elmenteita with its pink necklace of flamingoes – time only for a lingering glance on this occasion – then I was slowing down to cruise along the wide main street of Nakuru. Ahead of me, as I picked up speed, the road rose smoothly between vast green fields of summer wheat that sloped up on either side to the skyline. I sang as I drove, full of the joys of youth and adventure. The story that awaited me at the other end was an intriguing one. The Kabaka, the hereditary ruler of the biggest Ugandan tribe, the Baganda, who had been exiled by the governor, Sir Andrew Cohen, a few years before for obstructing British policy, had just been allowed back. He was returning in some triumph and Sir Andrew had to welcome him.

I stopped for a beer and a sandwich at Kisumu, on the shores of Lake Victoria, and had my first view of the world's largest inland sheet of water, a blue sea dotted with islands. From Kisumu the road to Kampala roughly follows the shoreline, running through lush, verdant vegetation such as I had never seen before, with thick groves of banana trees carrying small hands of reddish fruit and plantations of pawpaws. It is beautiful country and at that time, under the final stages of benevolent British colonial rule, was a terrestrial paradise in which it seemed anything would grow with the minimum of cultivation. Life was easy and good and this was reflected most obviously in the flashing smiles of the Ugandan women and in the gay colours of their clothes. Kampala was *en fête* for the return of the prodigal son, the Kabaka. When I arrived at the Imperial Hotel, however, a nasty little scene was in progress. A buxom blonde in tears was halfway down the stairs, being harangued by Colin

Legum of the *Observer*. Apparently, when he was in exile in London, the Kabaka had had little else to do except make the round of the night clubs and had become a particular habitué of Churchill's. The young lady on the stairs was one of the attractions there, I was told, and in a moment of gallantry the Kabaka had invited her to attend the celebrations as his guest. That, however, was precisely the point at issue. She claimed she was present by royal appointment, as it were, whereas Legum seemed to think that she had no business to be there and was giving the whole place a bad name. He was therefore urging her with some force to pack her bags and go and she was responding with tears. Some of us, including Douglas Brown of the *Daily Telegraph* and myself, sympathised with the lady and thought it was none of Legum's business, but he won the day and the poor girl was on the next plane out. Honour had been saved.

Next day, as part of his reinstatement, the Kabaka attended a full-scale ceremonial parade. Resplendent in the dress uniform of the Grenadier Guards, in which he held an honorary commission, the Kabaka inspected the troops. Equally resplendent in full regalia, including a cocked hat with plumes and sword, Sir Andrew Cohen trailed round behind King Freddy (as the Kabaka was known to Fleet Street), fuming as he was repeatedly upstaged. The Governor was a severe-looking intellectual autocrat and it was easy to see that he had absolutely nothing in common with the pleasure-loving Freddy: in fact the two men detested each other. Sir Andrew was another of the 'keep the press at arm's length' school and in the subsequent propaganda battle he was easily outmanoeuvred by the Kabaka. Immediately after the parade, the Kabaka made a beeline for Douglas and myself, a conspicuous white island, in our lightweight, foreign correspondents' suits, in that sea of negritude. He knew Douglas, who in turn introduced me as the new Reuters correspondent.

'I'm furious,' said the Kabaka.

'Why, Sir?' asked Douglas, 'The parade seemed to go off very well.'

'Because of the behaviour of Sir Andrew,' the Kabaka said

in his best Guards accent. 'He really will have to be taught a lesson.' Then, aware that a host of people were pressing around him, eager for a word, he checked himself. 'Come and have a drink at the Palace in half an hour and we'll talk then.'

I felt the excitement bubbling up in me like champagne. I had never met a king before, albeit an African king, and I had never had a drink with one in a palace. We strolled slowly through the throng of Bagandans. The women were particularly striking, mostly tall and strapping, swathed in voluminous lengths of brightly-coloured cloth, like Roman dowagers, and wearing tall brocaded hats on their heads. They walked with a swagger, their voices soaring in laughter and declamation, their eyes gleaming and their teeth brilliantly white against their dark skin. They were alive and vital and I found them tremendously attractive, much more so than the rather dour and ill-favoured Kikuyu in Kenya.

As we walked I went over in my mind what little I knew of the Kabaka and his country. The kingdom was Buganda, the people were the Baganda, someone was a Muganda and the language was Luganda. But, if the terminology was tricky, the history was horrific. One of Freddy's ancestors, Mwanga, was the bloodthirsty tyrant who in the 1880s ordered the massacre of a group of young christian converts known as the Ugandan martyrs (they were canonized in 1978).

When the explorer John Hanning Speke visited Uganda in 1862, he met another ancestor, Mutesa I and, in order to ingratiate himself, gave him a string of presents including guns and a gold ring. After demonstrating the efficacy of a revolver by shooting four cows with five shots, Speke goes on: 'Great applause followed this *wonderful* feat and the cows were given to my men. The king now loaded one of the carbines I had given him with his own hands and, giving it full-cock to a page, told him to go out and shoot a man in the outer court; which was no sooner accomplished than the little urchin returned to announce his success, with a look of glee such as one would see in the face of a boy who had robbed a bird's nest, caught a trout, or done any other boyish trick.

25

The king said to him, "And did you do it well?" "Oh, yes, capitally." He spoke the truth no doubt, for he dared not have trifled with the King: but the affair created hardly any interest. I never heard and there appeared no curiosity to know what individual human being the urchin had deprived of life.'

Unfortunately the same disregard for human life has persisted in Uganda down the years, finding its most brutal expression in the reign of terror instituted from 1971 to 1979 by Idi Amin.

Freddy, Mutesa II, was on the face of it a very different person to his great-grandfather: educated at Cambridge and commissioned into the Guards, he had all the airs and graces of upper-class Englishmen. He was fond of the girls, but what king worth his salt is not? The Bishop of Uganda and Sir Andrew Cohen no doubt found him immoral and politically devious but, in retrospect, he was no better and no worse than many kings and most politicians. And, unlike so many of them, he had charm.

Entering the palace grounds, Douglas and I made our way through a series of large thatched houses linked by corridors. These were the outer buildings of the palace which stood on the Mengo hill overlooking the modern city of Kampala. Finally we were ushered into a stone-built central section which was the Kabaka's private quarters. There we waited in an ante-room while a courier took word that we had arrived. One of the Kabaka's nieces, a bright-eyed girl of about twenty, came and sat on the arm of my chair and told me she hoped to go to London soon to train as a nurse. She was natural and pretty and full of life.

'You've made a hit there, old boy,' Douglas teased as we were escorted down a long corridor to the Kabaka's rooms. The sitting-room was furnished in English style with chintz covers on the chairs and a sofa that might have come from a Senior Common Room. The Kabaka had changed into casual clothes and greeted us with a smile, dismissing the courtier, who backed out of the room in a respectful crouch. He was quite small and slender, good-looking in a slightly disreputable way, with delicate features and a pale smooth skin. The eyes were his most striking feature, large, dark and hooded in a way that sometimes gave his face a remote almost sinister expression. That was the dark side of the Mutesa character. But now he was all charm and Britishness. 'Have a drink,' he said, opening the cupboard and rummaging around. 'Sorry, there only seems to be whisky.'

He produced three tumblers, all different sizes, and poured generous tots. He apologised again for the lack of amenities, explaining that he had not had time to organise things since his return.

As we drank the Kabaka gave his side of the morning's row with Sir Andrew. It was really a storm in a teacup but the Kabaka was determined to make the most of it. He accused Sir Andrew of deliberately insulting him by his high-handed treatment, which had culminated in that morning's parade, and said that since the British Government had approved of his return, indeed were responsible for it, it was his right to be treated with the respect due not only to the King of Buganda, but to the political leader of the biggest tribe in Uganda. We had another glass of whisky and listened to more rebukes, all delivered in a smooth, civilised voice. But there was something venomous about the Kabaka and one sensed that he could be a dangerous opponent. It was obvious that he loathed Sir Andrew and was determined to get rid of him: it was to take some time, but he managed in the end. Finally, with a smile and a handshake, we were dispatched to write our stories quoting Freddy as saying that the Governor was no longer acceptable to the Bagandan nation. It was a minor scoop and Reuters and the *Daily Telegraph* were suitably grateful. Over the next few days, while the celebrations continued, and Kampala rang with ululations and drumming from Mengo Hill, Douglas and I were rung up several times by Freddy's English ADC, Captain Owen, and kept abreast of developments. In the background, Sir Andrew and his men fumed and fulminated but made little effort to tell their side of the story. The 'arm's length' policy was working well, or badly, whichever way you looked at it. A day or two later I drove Douglas back to Nairobi.

By now I had been in Kenya about eight months and,

27

although I did not know it, my time was running out. Lucy Hoare had gone on three months' leave to England and I had taken over her cottage in Muthaiga. It was both pretty and secluded, and the gentle Boniface in his long blue galabiyeh and fez was the perfect servant. I had two more trips to make, one which started as an office chore but turned out to be high office politics, and the other, my last major assignment, Princess Margaret's royal tour of East Africa and Mauritius.

The office chore involved Reuters' then boss, Sir Christopher Chancellor, who was on a visit to South Africa, where the Reuters service was the main source of world news. It had been a great success. He had met Dr. Verwoerd, the Prime Minister, and the South African Government had given a dinner for him in Cape Town, with the Foreign Minister, Dr. Eric Louw, in the chair. (Louw, although Jewish, was an ardent Nationalist. He was also of course an apostle of *apartheid* which he preached *ad nauseam* to anyone who would listen in the days when South Africa was still a member of the United Nations.) At any rate, the dinner went off well, with fulsome compliments paid by the South Africans to Chancellor and Reuters and vice-versa. Chancellor caught the ship home from Cape Town a day or so later in a glow of euphoria that was marred only at the very last moment. In an exhibition of gullibility so enormous as to be almost touching, Sir Christopher Chancellor, one time Reuters' chief correspondent in China, then Editor, then General Manager, knighted for his services to journalism, made a mistake so elementary that it virtually took my breath away. He started to talk off the record to an old friend, the editor of the local paper who had come to meet him when the ship put in briefly at Port Elizabeth, halfway between Cape Town and Durban. Standing on the deck, he was giving his old friend the benefit of his real thoughts about South Africa in general and *apartheid* in particular (as opposed to the diplomatic words of conciliation he had uttered at the Cape Town dinner) when, out of the corner of his eye, he noticed that an insignificant figure had sidled up and was busy taking notes. What I have never been able to understand – and, I have no doubt,

Sir Christopher felt the same when he looked back at his behaviour – was why he did not draw breath and stop right there. After all, his editor friend was not taking notes and they were talking off the record. But the young reporter from the rival evening paper – for that is who the other man turned out to be – had entered into no off-the-record agreement. Sir Christopher's explanation to me in Mombasa, where I had to meet him, was that he turned to his friend and said: 'Take care of that young man, would you, and see none of that gets into the paper.'

Now, it is just possible that the editor thought the young man was from his own paper, although it is unlikely. At any rate, when he tried to carry out his pledge to 'take care of it', he discovered to his amazement, and to Sir Christopher's subsequent fury, that the story, with ample quotes, was already on its way round South Africa and to London via SAPA, the South African Press Association. Because of the way the press worked and still works in South Africa, nearly all newspapers are members of SAPA and are supposed to make available to it any regional story of national import. These are fed to SAPA on a direct wire and then fed out by SAPA to all other member newspapers; and, if the story is big enough, to the world at large, at that time via Reuters. An additional irony was that Reuters had set up SAPA in the first place. It was Reuters' creature and here was the head of Reuters being hoist by his own SAPA petard. The reaction and recriminations were immediate and extremely unpleasant. Poor Sir Christopher must have thought he had restarted the Boer War. When I met him, I could see how it had happened. He was a very good talker, no doubt over-fond of his own voice but worth listening to, and he had enjoyed exploding the absurdities of *apartheid,* its manifest injustice and bogus intellectualism. No doubt it made extremely good listening; it certainly made devastating reading, catching the Nationalists on the raw, producing screams of anger from Eric Louw and smug homilies on the abuse of hospitality from the solidly pro-Government Afrikaans papers, which of course all took the Reuters world service via SAPA. SAPA itself was on the face of it hugely embarrassed but, being already half in the Government's pocket editorially, trotted the story out with, I suspect, a good deal of *schadenfreude* behind the 'tut-tuts' and 'how unfortunates'.

By then, of course, Sir Christopher was at sea on what should have been a halcyon passage to Dar-es-Salaam, the next port of call. Instead, he was disturbed by a flurry of cables. Up in Nairobi I was blissfully unaware of all this excitement, as naturally Reuters did not give Sir Christopher's intended off-the-record remarks any wider circulation. Suddenly I received a cable from Tony Cole in London telling me to go immediately to Dar-es-Salaam to meet the General Manager and render him all possible assistance. The contretemps was outlined briefly and the final instruction was: 'Take your typewriter.'

I flew down on the next plane, arriving in Dar in the afternoon. The heat rose to meet me off the tarmac as if the door of an oven had been opened and I sat sweating mutely as the bus bore me into town along the elegant avenue of palm trees to the old wooden hotel, its beams picked out in black against a white background. Like so much of the centre of Dar, it had been built by the Germans.

The great man had already arrived and was staying with Sir Edward Twining at Government House where I now went, typewriter in hand. Chancellor was a dapper figure in his tropical suit and faultlessly-ironed shirt, but not as relaxed as he should have been after a week at sea. The first thing I did was hand him a cable from our man in South Africa, Astley Hawkins, who had borne the brunt of the Nats' fury and who recommended as strongly as he could that Chancellor should do or say nothing more. The damage had been done, Hawkins said, the storm was already blowing over and any statement by Chancellor, however convincing, would simply serve to reopen the whole sorry business. London agreed with this assessment. But Chancellor was adamant. He had drafted in longhand his own account of the incident and he was determined to send it to South Africa. 'You see,' he said after reading the cables from London and South Africa, 'If you make a mistake, you must admit it. I made a mistake and I think the honourable thing now is to admit it. Here, this is what I have written,' he went on. 'Read it, tell me what you think of it and then type it up and send it to SAPA – urgent rate.'

I started to read the five-page message. Chancellor told his story as plausibly and well as it could be told, but at the end it was a *mea culpa*, no more no less, and no doubt the South Africans would read it as such and feel doubly infuriated. He was pleading guilty. 'Well?' he asked. I was both flattered and embarrassed at being asked for my opinion. As diplomatically as I knew how, I told him I thought it was very well put, but that for the reasons Astley Hawkins had given it was a mistake to send it and stir up the whole row again.

He did not agree. 'No,' he said very equably, 'I have made up my mind. I must make an apology and so off you go to Cable and Wireless.' I did as I was told, typing, checking and re-checking each page, marking it urgent press SAPA Johannesburg before handing it across the counter at Cable and Wireless and signing each sheet 'Chancellor more'.

That done, I sent a message to London reporting what Chancellor had done plus another covering message to Hawkins. Next day I went back to Nairobi while the Chancellors continued their royal progress up the coast to Mombasa, where they were to disembark and fly on to Nairobi to stay with Sir Evelyn and Lady Baring. I was to meet them there for further instructions.

Sir Evelyn Baring and his wife Lady Mary held court at Government House in splendid style. The building itself was in the best traditions of late-Raj: large, imposing, with white colonial pillars and porticoes and manicured gardens, yet inside it had the feel of an English country house. I had been invited to lunch soon after arriving in Nairobi and had met two or three daughters of the house, the youngest of whom was the prettiest. I had sat next to Lady Mary who was small and gracious, but steely, as upper-class English women of her generation often were; no doubt they had to be in order to carry their share of the white man's burden, and very often the white man as well. Lunch was served by deft, silent African waiters in immaculate white tunics with crested gold buttons and, during it, Sir Evelyn quizzed his family about

English history, at one point asking one of his daughters: 'What year did Van Tromp sail up the Thames?'

I was glad he had not asked me as I did not have the slightest idea. She made a stab at it, got it wrong, and amid shrieks of laughter, Sir Evelyn corrected her and pressed on to other matters. It was hard to believe that this very English way of life had survived Mau Mau and all its horrors. We hardly talked politics during the meal but at one point Lady Mary turned her china-blue eyes on me and said in a musical but firm voice: 'The important thing to remember, Mr Gall, is that the pace of change must not be too fast . . . ' 'On the other hand, there must be change eventually,' I objected cautiously. 'Yes,' she said firmly, 'but it must not be too fast or it will be disastrous.'

In fact, among white settlers, the pace of change was the great topic of conversation. Most Kenya settlers disliked the press and the British press especially. It was easy to understand why. We came out from Britain and sported our liberal ideas: that Africans were also human beings and that one day Kenya would be run by Kenya.

'But they're not fit to run a *shamba*, let alone a country, man,' the settlers would explode.

'Yes,' I would say, infuriatingly, 'but that's a matter of training. In a few years' time . . . '

'But, Jesus, man, you don't know the African. You just don't understand his mentality. These fellows were swinging from the trees when I first came here and now you want to dress them up in dinner jackets and make them run the country.'

'I'm not saying there should be independence overnight,' I would respond, trying very hard to keep cool. 'What I am saying is that the democratic process was started by the British, has been developed by successive governments and must inevitably lead to one man one vote . . . ' That phrase was like a red rag to a bull.

'When they can't read or write? They don't *know* what an election is, let alone a free election . . . '

And so the argument would go on, becoming more heated as the glasses were recharged by the ever-generous host, until in a final moment of rage and frustration my interlocutor would say: 'You must be a bloody Communist, that's what you must be.'

End of argument and possibly end of evening. Everyone of course was a Communist who did not approve of white rule for ever and ever. Eventually even that impeccable English Conservative Sir Evelyn Baring was suspected of being a Socialist.

The Chancellors were very much at home in this sort of colonial atmosphere. Both Sir Christopher and Lady Chancellor's fathers had been colonial governors, his in Mauritius, where he inhabited a splendid French château called 'Au bout du monde', and hers in Rhodesia. Soon after their arrival to stay with the Barings, I was bidden to dinner and it was as friendly and informal as had been my original lunch. I sat at the bottom of the table with the youngest, prettiest daughter and a young ADC who rejoiced in the Wodehousian name of Peregrine Pollen. We had a jolly time below the salt while the governing class exchanged anecdotes and enjoyed themselves in a restrained way at the top of the table. The silver was out, the candles gleamed and Sir Evelyn was at his best: tall, handsome, genial. After dinner, while the ladies retired, he got up and announced loudly: 'Who wants to water Africa?' It was more of a command than a question and we all trooped through the French windows into the garden and relieved ourselves on the Governor's roses. Chancellor was also at his best that evening, holding forth about South Africa, the strange personality of Dr. Verwoerd and the inconsistencies of *apartheid*. This time there was no danger of being quoted off the record.

I had only one row with Sir Evelyn Baring and that came towards the end of my stay. By this time, mid-1956, the rehabilitation of Mau Mau prisoners was in full swing, and even the hard-core members were being fed down the pipeline to freedom. I had a friend in the department which dealt with rehabilitation and after a particularly good dinner he told me that the Moral Rearmament people were playing an increasingly active role in the programme and that the whole thing had become a farce.

'What do you mean, a farce?' I asked, immediately alert to the prospect of a story.

'Well,' he said, 'you know the MRA have been given control of the Athi River Rehabilitation camp?'

'Vaguely.'

'Well, they have. Full control. And they're churning out the hard-core like nobody's business.'

'What's wrong with that?'

'They're just not rehabilitated, that's what's wrong with it. As long as the hard-core boys say that they've renounced Mau Mau and want to go back to being model citizens, they let them out.'

'But perhaps they do want to go back to being good citizens?'

He shook his head. 'They don't. We know from the local DOs that, as soon as they're back in the Reserve, they start spouting Mau Mau progaganda again. The Government knows it too, but they're doing damn all to stop it.' He was angry and perhaps over-reacting, but I could understand how a civil servant who had fought long and hard to eradicate Mau Mau must feel when a bunch of do-gooders breezed in and undid all the good work in a couple of months.

'Why don't you do down there and have a look and then we can talk again,' he concluded.

I arranged to visit Athi River a few days later. It was a big prison sprawled on the plain outside Nairobi and housing several hundred hard-core Mau Mau. I was met by the dynamic MRA boss of the camp, Major Anderson. He had the irritating urgency and belief in his own infallibility of a Billy Graham. We started off on a conducted tour and the first thing I noticed was that the place was plastered with signs. One in particular was unavoidable, a large hand with forefinger outstretched, rather like the Kitchener First World War posters, pointing at the passer-by. But, instead of announcing that your country needed you, the MRA version read: 'Every time you point your finger at someone else, three fingers are pointing back at you.' I tried it out and saw it was true.

Major Anderson was watching me. 'You see what we're

getting at?' Instead of accusing other people all the time, we ought to examine our own conduct first.'

We proceeded. The whole tone of the place, and of the Major's running commentary, struck me as being almost revivalist. Listening to him, I tried to analyse what exactly the MRA philosophy was, and I settled finally and no doubt over-simply for: Christianity without Christ. Here, at Athi River, the immediate policy seemed to be: forgive the Mau Mau sinners and they will see the light and be reformed. They did not exactly pray for them, but they lectured them and gave them the benefit of the doubt and then asked them: 'Are you reformed? Do you hereby renounce the devil Mau Mau and all his works?' And, on getting an answer in the affirmative, for the hard-core were not stupid, the gates swung open and the former Mau Mau leaders and oath-administrators stepped out into the Kenya sunshine, free men. And no doubt winked at one another and made the sign of the Mau Mau initiate.

I went back to Nairobi and wrote the story of what I had seen and heard in Athi River, topping it with the critical comments of my civil service friend. Naturally I did not name him, describing him only as a source in the ministry.

The story went off to Reuters in London and, as part of my agreement with the *East African Standard,* I gave a copy to Ken Meadows. He read it.

'Bloody good story, that,' he said. 'Who gave it to you?'

I told him and he nodded. 'That'll stir the buggers up,' he laughed.

He was prophetically accurate. The story appeared in the *Standard* next morning under the Reuters by-line and the repercussions were immediate. Reuters in London wanted to know how this story had reached print in Nairobi when it had been 'spiked' in London. This was the first I knew of my story being spiked. Letter follows, they said. Then the 'phone rang. Government House on the line. Would I come and see the Governor at 2 p.m. No invitation to lunch on this occasion.

I drove up and parked beside the imposing front door, was received by the major-domo and shown into an office. A few minutes later the Governor appeared. His manner was cool and his handshake perfunctory.

'Sit down, Gall,' he said. 'This Athi River story. Where did you get the information from?'

'I can't disclose the name of my informant, sir,' I said.

'I know who it is,' he said crossly. 'It's so and so, isn't it?' naming the very man who had given me the information. I looked straight into the haughty blue eyes.

'As a journalist I simply cannot divulge the name of my source,' I repeated rather pompously.

'Doesn't matter,' he snapped. 'I know it's him. He's disaffected and your loyalty is misplaced.' His patrician brow darkened. 'Look here, Gall, I can't have one of my officials who is pledged to carrying out Government policy turning round and disavowing that policy, can I?'

I tried another tack: 'One of the problems is that no one was prepared to give us any information originally about Athi River.'

I spoke of lack of information about Government activities generally and about the rehabilitation of Mau Mau in particular. If there had been more cooperation in the first place, I said, any misunderstandings, if indeed there had been any, might have been avoided.

The Governor did not like even implied criticism. 'Two blacks do not make a white, he told me loftily. I was dismissed.

I later discovered that Sir Evelyn was if not a member of MRA at least a sympathiser. But much more important, as far as I was concerned, was that Tony Cole, my boss in London, was a dedicated MRA man. That was where the real trouble lay. To give him his due, however, Tony Cole never held the episode against me.

The Chancellors duly departed by plane to London and I returned to more mundane matters. Except that Kenya was never mundane for very long. Part of its attraction to a journalist was that it seemed to contain more characters per square mile than any other place I had ever been in. One of the greatest characters of all, 'Grogs' Grogan eluded me until near the end of my assignment. He had come out to Kenya from England as a young man and walked – he was a great walker – up to Nairobi from the coast. Nairobi was then an Indian village, mostly swamp, and Grogan was able to buy land there for very little. Later, he was to sell bits of it for a great deal. Among his many properties was Torr's Hotel (now, alas, pulled down) right in the middle of the city. This was a favourite with the older settlers, Grogan's contemporaries. There they would foregather of a lunchtime, after doing their shopping, for a pink gin or two. By the time I met him, Grogan was about eighty but still spry and handsome with a mane of beautiful fine silvery hair, a silver goatee beard like General Smuts's and brilliant blue eyes. A famous orator in his day he had been one of the first elected members of Legco (the Parliament). He had also written a book many years before called *From the Cape to Cairo*, the record of an expedition he had made from one end of the Continent to the other. Popular rumour had it that Grogan had made his prodigious walk to win the hand of a girl in marriage. The girl's father was said to have imposed the condition, never expecting him to fulfil it. But, having successfully accomplished his mission, young Grogan decided he no longer wanted to marry the girl. That, in any case, was the story one heard in the bars of Nairobi.

One day Ken Meadows rang me from his office at the *Standard* and said he had finally wangled an interview with Grogan. Would I like to come along? I said that I certainly would, so we arranged to drive out together to Grogan's house in Muthaiga. We arrived to find the great man sitting at his ease surrounded by Pekingese dogs. After a few preliminaries Ken asked the question everyone had always wanted to ask. Was it true that he had walked from Cape to Cairo to win the hand of a girl?

There was a pause, a chuckle and 'Grogs' patted one of the Pekingese. 'Well, I suppose after all these years I can tell you the truth. No, it wasn't because of a girl at all. I was asked to do it by the British Secret Service. At that time the French were showing a keen interest in getting their hands on as much of Africa as possible and I was asked by the British to travel from the Cape to Cairo to find out just what was going on in all these places.' He chuckled again. 'That was the real reason but we had to make up the story about the girl to put the French off the scent.'

During one of the more difficult parts of the journey, Grogan said, he and his team of bearers ran out of food. Things were getting desperate when they were ambushed by hostile tribesmen. Grogan's men beat them off, killing many in the process and, turning their victory to doubly good account, dined off the fallen enemy. Had he, to keep body and soul together, also eaten human flesh? The bright blue eyes looked at us mischievously. 'What do you expect? I had no option.'

'What was it like?'

Another chuckle. 'Not bad, not bad at all. Quite tasty in fact.'

My last assignment in East Africa turned out to be Princess Margaret's tour, which started in the autumn of 1956 and included Kenya, Tanganyika and the Indian Ocean island of Mauritius, but not, because of recent political upheavals, Uganda. It was almost the apotheosis of the British colonial system, then on its last legs, and to do the Queen's sister proud the Governors and their ladies brought out their finest regalia and organised the African equivalent of a vice-regal Durbar.

The Press Corps, mostly from England but including a few locals like myself, was sent on ahead to Mauritius. Because of the distance, we had to spend the night in an old Portuguese fort on Mozambique Island and then fly east next day to Mauritius, refuelling at Madagascar. Mauritius is an island of such exotic beauty that it still reminds me irresistibly of a Douanier Rousseau painting. Port Louis, the capital, is hot and frantic, the food spicy, the local population a mélange of African, Malay, Indian and Arab, and the language is pidgin French, or Creole. Once you leave the curry house atmosphere of Port Louis and climb up into the hills, the landscape becomes what you might call a domesticated tropical forest: the huge trees are festooned with creepers, the warm scented air is bright with humming birds and giant butterflies, and here and there on the fringes of the forest, like jewels suspended in mid-air, you come across hanging gardens of wild orchids.

We were put up in a pretty hotel set in just such exotic surroundings at a place with the delicious name of Pamplemousse (French for grapefruit). There was another little town called Curepipe and a beautiful beach called Blue Bay where both Princess Margaret and the Press Corps swam, although not on the same day. We also went to a garden party at the Governor's mansion, 'Au bout du monde'. I could see why it had been called that. The house, a copy of a French country château, stood in a rather lonely spot with, behind it, a wild garden that fell away sharply, giving the impression that the house stood on a sort of precipice, at the very end of the world. But, although the French influence was so strong, we saw little of the local French settlers who owned most of the Mauritian sugar plantations. They were having some quarrel with the British – *plus ça change* – and boycotted the garden party. No doubt they considered Princess Margaret an upstart, for they were tremendously *snob*, most of them claiming descent from the old aristocracy who either avoided the Revolution in 1789 by being on Mauritius, or who managed to escape there afterwards. They expressed their displeasure at the fact that Mauritius had passed from French to British rule in 1810 by pretending that they could not speak English, although of course they could all do so perfectly well.

The Press Corps soon got the impression that, not surprisingly Princess Margaret became easily bored by the official pomp with which she was inevitably surrounded. The whole tour seemed to be designed to cater for a middle-aged monarch, not a beautiful and wilful young princess, and we all felt for her when at some dreary dinner party the Archbishop of Mauritius fell fast asleep at her side. No wonder the blue eyes flashed fire.

Just how stunningly blue they were I saw for myself when the Press Corps had a drink with the Princess at the start of the tour. She arrived alone, looking incredibly beautiful, and we were all introduced to her by an urbane fellow from the *Daily Express* called David Wynne Morgan who later went into public relations. There were others of the same ilk there too, including Alan Whicker, then an agency reporter like myself. He worked for Extel before his rise to television stardom, but he already displayed in those days a considerable talent for the sarcastic chuckle and the cutting phrase. Frank Barber was there for the old *News Chronicle*, a forthright Yorkshireman with a broad accent, and a large posse of royal photographers, led by the distinguished and apparently indestructible Freddy Reed, who took a picture of me strolling across some African field with a flower in my buttonhole, looking, I thought, incredibly dashing. It is one of the few photographs of myself I really like.

From Mauritius the Princess flew to Tanganyika where the Governor, Sir Edward Twining, a genial gin-drinking giant, had done his best to make the tour as unstuffy as possible. One obligatory trip was to the White Highlands in the south where a small British community was flourishing in the remote *bundu*. They staged a miniature garden party for her and it was all very English, with the tanned farmers in their grey suits and Old Etonian ties and the women in picture hats. The silver teapots gleamed and the Royal Worcester rattled away happily while behind the hedge the *m'totos* stood on one leg, their eyes like black marbles, solemnly watching this curious and impressive ritual of the white man.

We stayed for most of the time in the New Africa Hotel in Dar-es-Salaam. One night a few of us went to a restaurant a few miles out along the coast. It was a pleasant place, near the beach, with palm trees swaying in the breeze. Quite romantic in fact. As the evening wore on, I became aware that a rather attractive young lady had attached herself to our party and in particular to me. When it came to the time for us to go, she got into my taxi, but it was only when we reached the hotel that she said:

'By the way, I've nowhere to sleep.'

'Well,' I said, 'you're very welcome to come with me. There's only one snag.'

'What's that?' she said, slipping her arm through mine as I paid off the taxi.

'They're short of rooms and there are two other fellows sharing with me already.'

She thought about this for a moment and then said: 'But you've got separate beds, haven't you?'

'Of course,' I said. 'And it's a big room.'

'Well, that's all right,' she said casually. 'It doesn't worry me at all.'

It was pretty late, nearly three in the morning, and, as we tiptoed into the room, the other two were fast asleep. Nearest the door was Kenneth Ames, the *Daily Mail* man, and on the far side of the room a photographer for one of the London evening papers. We both got a fit of the giggles as we listened to the two of them snoring away obliviously. I took the girl by the hand and led her across to where my bed stood, draped in its mosquito net, right in the middle of the room. We undressed slowly, collapsing with laughter as one or other of the two sleepers gave a particularly loud snore or grunt. I thought at one point Ken was going to wake up. He turned over and muttered something and half-sat up. We both waited in suspense for the next move, but he gave another grunt, rolled over and went back to sleep. Still giggling, we crawled into bed under the mosquito net.

It was, alas, a very short night and, early next morning, the girl got up and started to dress. I asked her what the hurry was. She said she did not want the others to see her dressing and anyway she had to get home, which was somewhere miles away up country. Just as she was ready to leave and we were saying a fond farewell. Ken woke up and looked across the room.

'Good God,' he said. 'Who's that?'

'It's all right, Ken,' I said. 'A friend of mine. She's just leaving.'

Being a gentleman, he ostentatiously turned over to spare us further embarrassment.

The most magical part of the tour, certainly for us and almost certainly for Princess Margaret, was the visit to one of the great East African game reserves, the Ngorongoro Crater. It is, as the name implies, an extinct volcanic crater, a huge shallow bowl about ten to fifteen miles across, thick with

41

game. Huge herds of zebra, wildebeest, buffalo, Thomson's gazelle and antelope graze its rich grasslands; there are several prides of lion and cheetah, and elephant roam the forest round the crater rim. Princess Margaret disappeared down an almost vertical trail in a specially spruced-up Landrover from the Game Department, and we, after a suitable delay, were allowed to go on our own game-watching safari, but in another direction, so as not to disturb the royal visitor.

As the climax of the tour, Sir Edward Twining organised a superb *indaba*. Thousands of tribesmen came from all over the country, dancers, drummers, singers, witchdoctors and warriors carrying spears and shields. Thousands more turned up to see the show and, under a boiling sun, the noise and the excitement rose to fever pitch. By the time Princess Margaret arrived with her party, looking as if they were at Ascot, the crowd was almost out of control and, for one ugly moment, it seemed as if the royal party were going to be trampled under foot by the frenzied dancers. The heat, the beat of the drums and the cloud of dust which enveloped the whole huge arena like a fog added to the sense of near-panic. But Sir Edward, cool as an ice-cream in his white Governor's uniform and plumed hat, kept his head: the Tanganyika police moved in and Princess Margaret smilingly pushed her way through the throng. It all turned out well but it had been touch and go.

After the Kenya section of the tour was over, a couple of the women reporters and I decided to have a brief holiday at Malindi on the coast, north of Mombasa. Malindi now is overrun by tourists, especially Germans, a centre of the package tour industry, but then it was unspoiled and very simple. We chartered a small plane to fly us direct – it was not very expensive in those days – and landed on the strip right beside the hotel, which was built just above the beach.

We were having lunch in the dining-room, when the manager came up and said, 'Nairobi's on the phone.' My heart fell. I feared the worst and I was right. It was the *East African Standard* man who was looking after my interests in Nairobi.

'Sorry to disturb your holiday,' he began, 'but we've just

received a cable from London. It says they want you to go immediately to Aden.'

'Aden?' I demanded. 'What the hell's going on in Aden?'

'I dunno exactly,' he said. 'But there are rumours of an invasion of Egypt and I suppose it's connected with that. Anyway they want you to get on the first plane to Aden and that leaves first thing tomorrow.'

I swore, but I knew there was no way out. 'Okay,' I said. 'Tell London I'm on my way back and book me a seat on that flight tomorrow.'

I went back to the dining-room where the two girls were laughing and chatting.

They saw my long face.

'What's wrong?' they chirped. 'Been fired?'

'Worse than that. They want me to go to Aden.'

'Aden?' they both shrieked. 'What the hell is happening in Aden?'

'I'm damned if I know.' I said. 'But I've got to catch the plane tomorrow. First thing.'

Luckily our pilot was still there, also having lunch. 'I'll take you back,' he said. 'No extra charge.'

The girls did not want to stay on their own, so two hours after we arrived in Malindi we had packed, paid our bills, and were taking off. I looked back disappointed at the wonderful deep indigo of the Indian Ocean, broken by the white line of the coral reef, and at the pale turquoise of the lagoon. It was heart-breaking to be leaving it and so suddenly, and it was twenty-five years before I saw it again.

We were in Nairibo two hours later, and found out soon enough what was making London so excited. The long-awaited and not very secret British invasion of Egypt was said to be imminent and Reuters had been tipped off in London that some of the task force would be going up the Red Sea from Aden. They wanted me to go there immediately and report what was happening.

The tip about Aden turned out to be completely wrong, but it was, even so, the start of the ill-fated Suez operation.

CHAPTER II

Suez: A Miss and a Scoop

I had been to Aden several times before and it was the hottest and dreariest place I had ever visited. For many years the only hotel had been the Crescent, owned by a rich and civilised family called Besse, although the food at the Crescent was anything but civilised. The bar had about as much character as an air raid shelter and the limp air was beaten by large ceiling fans. Outside, the heat and the humidity were both intense and the physical structure of the place – a narrow strip of foreshore surrounded by bare, tortured, volcanic mountains – intensified the feeling of being shut in. The famous pipe tune, 'The Barren Rocks of Aden', which I had heard so often as a boy in Scotland, took on a fresh meaning. I thought of the poor Jocks who had sweated there, thinking longingly of the misty moors and cool peat streams of the Highlands.

There was not a blade of grass to be seen anywhere, except at Government House, perched on a rock high above the sea. Even on the apology for a golf course which the British had laid out on reclaimed land on the foreshore, the greens were 'browns', made of a mixture of sand and oil. In the cool of the early morning and in the evening you could walk along the main street past all the Indian shops, each one trying to sell you a watch or a radio as if their life depended on it, but during the heat of the day only those who did not have the price of a taxi fare risked their sanity by walking about in the sun. The Adeni taxis were, in any case, a law unto themselves. The style was casual Arab, the driver usually having one hand on the wheel and the other on the horn. They would drive as fast as possible on the narrow, winding roads, horn blaring, and swerve their way past other cars, lorries, camels and bicycles. Brakes were only used as a last resort. Things got really alarming when the drivers were high on *qat*, a green leaf imported from Ethiopia with strong narcotic properties, and when you saw your driver's jaw working and his eyes gleaming like a mad dog's you knew you would be in for a very rough ride.

As soon as I had booked in at the Crescent, I started ringing round my contacts. I soon discovered that there was a big security clamp on anything to do with the planned invasion and indeed on anything at all military. I made the rounds of the Army and Air Force PROs and got the same brush-off. I had lunch at the Aden club and went swimming behind the shark net at Goldmohur, where the Army often went, but drew a blank all round. 'Something's going on,' friends told me. 'But I'm not allowed to tell you anything. In fact I'm running a risk even being seen with you.'

Finally I hired a car and drove out to the airport to talk to a pal there. He was slightly more forthcoming and I did discover that there had been a lot of RAF activity in the past few days. I went back to the hotel and filed a despatch to Reuters saying that, although there was no sign of the Royal Navy, the RAF had been staging large numbers of troops through Aden, heading for an undisclosed destination. The inference was that they were in some way connected with the Suez invasion, then just starting.

Next morning I got an unexpected call from the RAF press office that the Air Officer Commanding Aden would like to see me at once. It was soon clear that the AOC was not in the friendliest of moods. He sat at the far end of a large room behind a big desk and did not bother to shake hands or ask me to take a seat. I was obviously in for a carpeting. He looked up and barked.

'You've been spying on my airfield. Don't deny it, I know you have!'

I was taken aback by the fury and, it seemed to me, unreasonableness of his onslaught. I protested that I had simply being going about my normal journalistic business. And I said I strongly resented the word spying. He repeated his accusations. I denied them. Although it was not exactly an agreeable occasion, I enjoyed the situation in which I, an ex-corporal in the RAF, was able, thanks to my Reuters position, to say 'Go to hell' to this objectionable and over-weening Air Vice-Marshal.

Finally be barked, 'I shall inform the Air Ministry and ask them to withdraw all accreditation from you as a correspondent.'

I said he could do as he pleased and left. Sure enough, he did carry out his threat and the consequences were to have a quite disproportionate effect.

But why was the Air Force so sensitive about air movements through Aden? It was only years later that I discovered that they had nothing to do with Suez at all. Unknown to the British public, there had been serious riots in Bahrein, then a British protectorate, a state of emergency had been declared and troops were flown in from East Africa via Aden. The story was hushed up but in any case the attention of the world was on Suez, not Bahrein. So the Air Vice-Marshal need not have got in such a state. No one would have really cared.

Immediately after my confrontation, Reuters cabled telling me to go to Khartoum in the Sudan, to which the Eygptians had apparently transferred part of their air force in order to escape the British bombing.

It was always difficult as a journalist to organise a visa to Khartoum and, since there was no time for even the minimum of formalities, I decided to risk getting it on arrival.

Just as I was boarding the Alitalia flight, a clerk came

running up with a telegram. London were getting cold feet. 'Do not proceed Khartoum unless you guaranteed visa on arrival.' I suppose I should have turned back there and then, but I thought: 'To hell with it.' I had had enough of Aden, which was obviously going to be a complete backwater for the rest of the war. I was eager for action. So I screwed up the cable, put it in my pocket and climbed aboard the plane.

When we landed in Khartoum I was soon in trouble. I was about the only passenger wishing to disembark and certainly the only one without a visa. A very fat Sudanese immigration officer eyed me with great suspicion. Why did I not have a visa? I explained I had not had time to get one. That was no excuse. No visa, no chance of entering the Sudan. I pleaded and then, getting angry, demanded to telephone the Reuters stringer. I found a number and rang but there was no reply. I then asked if I could ring the British Embassy but this was refused. More argument. Finally the fat Sudanese rose from his chair and screamed at me: 'There is a state of emergency in the Sudan. You must leave at once.' He then summoned the airport guard commander and I was marched across the tarmac under escort to the waiting plane. The Alitalia officials were furious. I had delayed the flight for half an hour and, they said, every minute on the ground was costing them money. They were clearly exaggerating but I suppose I was upsetting their plans by making them late into Rome, our next stop. The pasta would be getting cold and the mistresses impatient.

I ordered a large whisky from the stewardess and tried to face the future with equanimity. But it was not easy. Would I get fired, I asked myself, for disobeying Head Office's instructions? I ordered another whisky and tried to drown my fears.

We arrived in Rome on a Sunday morning and there to meet me was Reuters' Chief Correspondent in Italy, Patrick Cross. It was the first time I had met him and I immediately fell under his spell. He brushed aside the possible flouting of instructions, said that no one had reported the State of Emergency in Sudan, and whisked me off to the office to write the story and inform London of my arrival.

47

Then he took me home to a magnificent flat at the top of a medieval tower in the centre of Rome. We climbed up a flight of narrow stone stairs to a large living room with a spectacular view of the city on three sides, including the Colosseum. It was so high that you had the feeling of being in an eagle's eyrie. The flat belonged to an old aristocratic Italian family who refused to sell it, but I thought Patrick was lucky to be able to rent it.

Patrick's wife Jenny came in. She was bubbly, enthusiastic and friendly, a journalist in her own right and a daughter of Robert Graves. Her parents had split up soon after her birth, and she had kept her mother's name of Nicholson. She had previously been married to Alex Clifford, the *Daily Mail* war correspondent. She immediately made me feel at home and within ten minutes knew all about me. It was rather like meeting a whirlwind. Patrick then announced that they were going to lunch with a friend, Iris Tree, and that I was to come along as well. A lesser man would have packed me off to a hotel and left me to find my own lunch. That was not Patrick's and Jenny's way. Iris Tree, daughter of the famous actor-manager Beerbohm Tree, was a distinguished old lady living high up in another part of Rome. There was no lift and we had to toil up four or five flights of stairs, but when we got to the top it was worth it. The view was almost as spectacular as the one from the Crosses' tower, a cubist conglomeration of roof-tops and chimneys with a distant prospect of streets and squares below.

There was only one other guest, a rather pale quiet young man, who was almost literally back from the dead. He had been told by his doctors that he was suffering from some obscure disease and that he had only six months to live. The six months had just expired and he was very pleased to have proved the doctors wrong. He died about a year later. His story, retailed on the way quite matter-of-factly by Patrick, immediately gave the lunch a hallucinatory quality. This was heightened when Patrick started to tell us his own amazing story. As a young man he had been a TB suspect and was sent to a sanatorium in Switzerland just before the war. It turned out, he said, to be a sadistic prison and he hated it. So he and

48

another rebellious inmate decided to escape. It was not easy because security was extremely strict. The place was run on Gestapo-like lines and the guards, according to Patrick, could well have been drawn from the ranks of the SS.

The young escapees, however, perfected their plans, choosing a night with a full moon. They had managed to acquire somehow a duplicate of the key to their room and when the hour came they slipped out, stole across the snow to an outbuilding and quietly extracted the sledge which was to be their means of escape. They dragged it to the edge of the slope, climbed aboard, pushed off, gathering momentum quickly and within a few seconds were tobogganing at break-neck speed down the hill and away from the grim asylum. The dizzying descent, the rush of cold air, the speed, the silence and the shadows, made it a terrifying run. They nearly came to grief several times but, after a number of spills, they finally arrived at the foot of the mountains in some sleepy village where they were able to take shelter and revive themselves with hot coffee. They had got away with it.

After that lunch, I looked on Patrick with new admiration. I have always admired the man of action. When he told me that London wanted me to go immediately to Suez to help out our hard-pressed correspondent on the spot, I felt it was in some way a personal accolade. I left for Cyprus next day in high spirits.

Reuters had a remarkable correspondent in Nicosia, Shahe Gubenlian or 'Gubby' as everyone called him, an Armenian who was both a walking encyclopedia about Cyprus and an ambulant dictionary: he spoke Turkish, Greek, English, French and of course Armenian. He knew everyone in Cyprus, including EOKA, and every telephone line and messenger's run seemed to lead to his office-cum-flat. I spent about a week with him and saw just how skilled an operator he was. He had 'stringers' all over the island who kept him better informed than British intelligence.

One day the 'phone rang. After a brief conversation Gubby put the receiver down and explained. 'That was one of my Turkish stringers, a lawyer from the north. He just wanted to tell me that he'd been released from prison and is back in action. He will be tipping me off on anything that happens up there.' 'He rang you as soon as he came out?' I was impressed. Gubby chuckled. 'Actually I have been paying him something while he was in jail and he is suitably grateful.'

Gubby was like a very amiable spider, sitting at the centre of a web of information which came to him in a babel of languages and which he sifted and checked, translated into English or at least Reuterese and rattled off to London on his private teleprinter. Owing to his amazing contacts, he was invariably first with the news at a time when EOKA were killing British soldiers with sickening regularity. Now he had Suez on his hands as well.

Gubby put me in the famous Ledra Palace Hotel, where the barman made the best brandy sours in the business and the head porter, Savas, was a journalistic legend. Savas never forgot a face and had an intuitive understanding of how Fleet Street worked. Evelyn Waugh would have adored him. Savas kept a sharp eye on all cables coming in to the hotel from Fleet Street, so that favoured customers were always abreast of what the opposition was doing. Savas would also peruse all copy being sent to the post office for cabling to London. If the *Daily Express* man, say, had an exclusive story on a big Army hunt for General Grivas, the elusive EOKA leader, Savas would ring the *Daily Mail* man, get him out of bed and give him the story, often making a few inquiries himself among his excellent contacts so that the story was finally better researched and more colourful than it had been in the first place. Such services of course did not come cheap, but so indispensable was Savas that the correspondent was happy always to pay up. Ultimately everyone was Savas' client and so the next time the *Daily Mail* had a scoop, Savas would after a suitable delay tip off the *Express* man. In this way, he maintained a sense of security and a kind of balance among his large, grateful clientele.

Behind his desk at the Ledra Palace, Savas was like the captain of an ocean liner, completely in charge, never panicking, never at a loss. When my Reuters colleague, Alex Valentine, received a cable from London one day informing him that a head office mandarin, by the name of Valpy, was coming out to Cyprus to inspect our operation, Alex knew immediately what that meant. Valpy was coming to cast a critical eye over the cost of Valentine's high-powered and expensive coverage of the Suez and Cyprus stories.

Alex showed me the cable and swore. 'Come on,' he said. 'We'll have to talk to Savas.' Alex leaned over the desk conspiratorially. 'Look here, Savas,' he said in his rich Italo-Scottish brogue, 'we're in a spot of bother. This old fool is coming out from London to check up on our expenses so it's absolutely *vital*, vital do you understand, Savas, that he doesn't get any idea of what's really going on here. So when Mr. Valpy arrives tomorrow I want his bill to be made out exactly like mine and Mr. Gall's. Is that understood? Same rate, same everything.'

Savas's smooth, clever face smiled back at us reassuringly. 'Of course, Mr. Valentine, there is no problem. Mr. Valpy will be in . . . let me see . . . 402 . . . and his bill will be made out exactly like yours and Mr. Gall's.' He made a note on his pad and turned to take another telephone call.

'You can't be too careful,' Alex said as we walked to the bar. 'But, with a man like Savas behind the desk, you don't have to worry too much.'

The fiddle that Alex and willy-nilly I could not afford to have uncovered by Valpy or any other head office snoop was simple, but ingenious. The normal room charge was in those days say £10 a night, but we were charging Reuters £15 or £20. There were two sets of bills, the real ones which we paid, and the amended version which London received in our expenses. We pocketed the difference. Savas arranged all this, of course, in return for a suitable fee. What had made Alex tremble was the thought that Valpy might arrive and through an oversight be presented with a bill that differed markedly from the bills that Alex and I had been putting in. As it turned out, Valpy came and went a few days later, suitably impressed with the excellent job Alex was doing and none the wiser about the financial arrangements which he so nearly upset.

Most mornings I would take a taxi to Gubby's flat near

Ledra Street, better known as Murder Mile. It was here that most British soldiers were gunned down, usually as they were strolling along in civilian clothes, window shopping. I used to get out of the taxi and have an apprehensive look round before diving into the entrance. I was very conscious that I was tall and British-looking and therefore might be mistaken for a soldier off duty. Another frequent visitor to Gubby's flat was a young Scot called Angus MacDonald who had been working in London as a researcher for Randolph Churchill; Randolph, though, had gone to the United States and Angus had decided to come to Cyprus to see for himself what was going on. He was intensely interested, he said, in the possibilities of a political settlement between the Greek and Turkish Cypriots and the British, and to that end he was trying to sound out opinion on both sides. In the course of his investigations he talked to a number of Greek Cypriots, including a number of EOKA members or sympathisers. One day I arrived at the flat to find Gubby and his girl friend (later wife) Jill in a frightful state. Jill was in tears and I asked what was wrong.

'It's Angus,' she said, wiping her eyes. 'The bastards have shot him.'

I felt a sudden chill in the room.

'How? Where?' I heard myself stammering.

'In the street,' Gubby said, giving the exact spot. 'He was apparently talking to some Greek shopkeeper, you know how he talked to everyone, he was so interested in everything, and some bastard came up and shot him dead at point-blank range.'

'But who?' I said. 'Who could have done such a terrible thing? After all, he wasn't a soldier, he was a journalist.'

Gubby shrugged. 'I don't know who did it but I can make a guess.' He meant of course Nicos Sampson, an EOKA gunman who specialised in street killings and was credited with the murders of a dozen or more British soldiers. His speciality was to shoot his victims in the back. Later, incredible as it may seem, he became President of Cyprus for a few days after the Colonels' coup against Archbishop Makarios in 1974.

I had hardly known Angus but I had felt close to him. We were both about the same age and I admired his courage and enterprise in trying to do something positive about the Cyprus problem, even if he did go about it in a rather naive way. His death diminished and depressed us all. It also made me doubly aware of the hidden violence that lurked in the shadowy alleys of the old city of Nicosia. You did not walk about there, flaunting your Britishness, if you valued your life.

I was really in Cyprus, however, to be accredited to the British Expeditionary Force in Egypt and it was taking an unconscionably long time. I had been in Nicosia for nearly a week and, despite daily visits and calls to Headquarters, nothing seemed to be happening. This was infuriating to everyone concerned. Alex Valentine made frequent shuttles across to Port Said to help Sean Maynes, the Reuters man on the spot, and to pick up his copy and bring it back for transmission to London. I did so too a couple of times but was unable to stay because of lack of accreditation. Sean Maynes was desperate for permanent help on the spot, facing as he did strong opposition from the American agencies, AP and UPI, and the French agency, AFP, all of whom had more than one correspondent in Port Said. London kept bombarding us with demands to know why there was a delay in accreditation and all Gubby and I could do was to redouble our telephone calls and visits. Finally, after several days, the RAF public relations officer, a civilian, let us into the secret. Apologetically he explained that, as a result of my fracas with the Air Vice-Marshal in Aden, I had been blacklisted by the RAF and so there would be no accreditation for me for Suez.

Gubby and I were incredulous and angry that some obscure Air Vice-Marshal sitting in a backwater in Aden should be allowed seriously to hamper Reuters' on-the-spot coverage of Britain's biggest military operation since the Second World War. No wonder, we said, we were losing the propaganda war to the Egyptians and their allies. The PRO was obviously embarrassed. He suggested that, to cut the red tape and prevent further delays, we should switch my accreditation request to the Navy. This we did immediately, I was accredited that afternoon and left next morning for Port Said, flying in with a handful of other journalists and commuting officers.

I had been to Port Said once before, when I was four, on the way home from Malaya with my mother and, although I could remember nothing about the place, I did recall what she had told me about the bumboats, the importunities of the Egyptian traders, and the fun she had obviously had haggling with them over a camel-skin pouffe or a box of Turkish delight. There was a famous shop called Simon Artzt where everyone off the liners went to shop. I wondered what had happened to Simon Artzt now. Locked and shuttered like all the other shops, no doubt, and possibly with a few bullet holes through the windows. The whole town was closed down, the population sullen and hostile. The old oppressor had returned and was once more sitting on the necks of the Egyptians.

The British on the other hand bustled about, the young commandos and guardsmen enjoying a bit of action, although that was over now for them. It was almost like being on holiday, the weather warm and sunny, the canal like an ornamental lake, the sunken ships dotted across it decoratively.

Sean Maynes, a veteran of the Second World War, took me on a tour of the city. We called in at various Army offices where there were daily briefings, at the press centre which was the old Suez Canal Pilots' Association headquarters, and the International Press Club where we had a pre-lunch drink. It was full of Foreign Legion officers, Paras and other dashing types. The French, who had captured Port Fuad, the twin city to Port Said on the other side of the Canal, displayed as usual a delightfully cynical attitude to the whole affair. The fighting over, they were busy looting when I arrived, loading up all the flashier cars they could lay their hands on. I saw a white Mercedes and a couple of Chevrolets being hoisted aboard a supply ship, and anything else that took their fancy. The bulk of the French contingent was made up of the famous Legion and most of them seemed to be German. I went one day to write a feature on the Legion and, arriving at the checkpoint, asked in French for the Commandant. The sergeant on the gate, a blond giant of about thirty, turned and bawled in German. 'Wo ist der Herr Major?' Another legionnaire took up the cry, also in German, and so it went down the line.

Sean and I downed a couple of Pernods and went off to have lunch at a French restaurant which had survived, shakily, from the pre-war days. It was high up overlooking the canal, next to the Pilots' Association building, and served food that was ambrosia after British Army rations.

Over lunch, Sean told me what a terrible time he, and indeed most of the British correspondents had at the start of the operation. Communications were obviously going to be the key factor in the reporting of the Suez affair, and the planners, in their wisdom, had made arrangements for a radio transmitter to be loaded into one of the supply ships which sailed from Malta. Unfortunately the transmitter, jokingly nicknamed the Golden Arrow, was dropped into the bottom of the hold and damaged, and so was not in full working order when lifted out at Port Said. While the engineers struggled to repair it, correspondents had to ferry their copy back as best they could. Sean gave his first top priority copy on his landing by assault craft and the state of the fighting in the town to an officer who was flying back to Cyprus. The idiot left it in the aeroplane. Only hours later and after a frantic search did the message come to light.

Even when the Golden Arrow had been repaired, it still did not work very well. Frustrated journalists would be told: 'Sorry, we're doing a frequency change, no copy for a couple of hours.' It was explained to us that the Golden Arrow was built to transmit over a long distance, to London for example. But because it had to work to Cyprus instead, which was too short a 'throw', the signal was often poor and the messages frequently unreadable.

The man who bore the brunt of the journalists' anger was an extremely conventional career Major who had no real rapport with his charges, and was in fact absolutely the wrong man to have in the job of Chief PRO. This state of affairs happened so often in the Fifties and Sixties that I became convinced the British Services did their best to find the least suitable candidate for liaison with the Press. Commanding officers, for class and other reasons, disliked and distrusted the Press and, when compelled against their will to appoint a Press Officer, invariably selected someone who was considered a failure at everything else. As a result the officer had no self-confidence – he knew he was being given the lowest job in the regiment – and no influence; and the CO was making his own derogatory comment on these 'writing johnnies'. It was only when the Services suddenly realised that they needed public approval that they changed their tune. The Americans of course had always been as naturally gifted at public relations as we had been deplorably bad.

In Port Said, most of us avoided the Major at all costs and went instead to one of his two assistants, Michael Parkinson and Robin Esser, both of whom were then unassuming young National Service Officers with sympathy and understanding for the Press. They were almost the only two Army PROs I can remember in twenty years of being a foreign correspondent who knew what the Press wanted and were prepared to help them get it.

But the Major was not alone in having no idea of how the Press worked. No less a person than the Force Commander, General Hugh Stockwell, was just as ignorant. One day, Maynes and I were summoned to answer for something that had displeased Stockwell in the Reuters service, which somehow or other his office was managing to receive. We were ushered into the presence, and told to sit down.

'Look at this,' General Stockwell ordered sharply. 'What the hell does Reuters think it's doing?'

We both looked at the offending piece of paper. It was a minor news item, what we call a sidebar, a sort of footnote to the main story of the day, which was of course Suez. The message was date-lined London and quoted Tanjug, the Yugoslav news agency, for a slanted anti-British report of what was happening in Port Said.

'Absolute tripe,' snapped Stockwell. 'What on earth do you mean by putting out this kind of lies?'

Sean and I looked at each other disbelievingly. Did he really imagine that we were responsible? I took a deep breath.

'General,' I said, 'this had nothing to do with us. As you see, this story has a London dateline which means that they have monitored Tanjug, the Yugoslav news agency in London, and that is what Tanjug is saying. Reuters are simply carrying the story as a factual account of what the Yugoslavs are saying about Suez.'

It was as if I were speaking of the higher calculus. General Stockwell's brow wrinkled in thought.

'You mean that message wasn't sent from here?'

'No, sir,' Maynes's gravelly voice grated. 'As Mr Gall here says, it's a Tanjug report picked up in London by our Head Office. Nothing to do with us at all.'

More wrinkling of the General's brow.

'The whole story's a load of balls, anyway. What I can't understand is why Reuters, a British agency, should be putting out lies like this which can only help the enemy.'

That was it. The cat was out of the bag. Maynes now took a deep breath.

'Reuters is an impartial, world-wide agency, sir. We carry reports and statements emanating from all sorts of sources round the world as part of the service. It's got nothing to do with whether we believe them or not.'

This was too much for the General. He got up.

'Well, don't let me catch you putting out any rubbish about our operation from here. Otherwise . . . '

He let the threat trail in the air, but not very convincingly. Maynes and I walked out stiffly, to show that we had a job to do and that Reuters had an obligation to the truth that transcended the narrow political expediencies of the day. Sir Christopher Chancellor had instructed all staff at the start of Suez that Reuters would remain strictly neutral. As far as the British Government was concerned, the Egyptians were the enemy. But, as far as Reuters was concerned, there was no enemy. There were the British and the Egyptians, and both sides were equally entitled to their statements, claims and counter-claims, neither more nor less.

By the time I arrived, thanks to the delaying tactics of the RAF, the fighting was in fact over. There had not been all that much anyway, but the Egyptians had been reasonably well dug in and had fought better than the brass hats had expected. Instead of breaking out of the beach-head within twenty-four hours of landing, it took the assault group two days. This had all sorts of repercussions. A successful landing and quick capture of Port Said was supposed to have been followed by the rapid seizure of the whole of the Canal all the way down to Port Suez. It seemed that Anthony Eden had even grander designs, the capture of Cairo itself and the overthrow of Nasser. Stockwell let that slip one day. But, because of the slow break-out and the immense world outcry that followed the attack, with the Soviet Union to the fore, the invasion was stillborn. Under enormous pressure from the United States and in the face of Soviet threats, the Government in London, not surprisingly, got cold feet and capitulated. They agreed to the UN Security Council ceasefire at midnight on November 6, which effectively halted the British advance just as it was getting going. With any luck they would have taken the whole of the Canal by next morning. But as it turned out they had only reached Kilometre 22 when the order came through on their radios to stop. And there, to their fury and resentment, with the Canal and Port Suez within their grasp, the British and French had reluctantly to climb out of their armoured cars and dig themselves in. In New York a UN Emergency Force, consisting almost entirely of Swedes, was hastily organised and flown to Cairo.

They were expected at Kilometre 22 in a couple of days' time and Sean assigned me to the story. The Army put a Landrover at our disposal and a group of correspondents set off for the front line to await the arrival of the Swedes. We drove south through the suburbs of Port Said, the road running straight as a ruler between the Suez Canal on our left and the Sweet Water Canal on our right. It looked a bit of a misnomer, I thought, being both smelly and discoloured, but someone explained that it was called that simply to differentiate it from the Canal proper which is of course salt water.

The landscape was typical of Lower Egypt and the Nile Delta, a flat, rich alluvial plain still tilled by oxen and the hand plough. All along the road were signs of the British presence, groups of soldiers relaxing beside their guns and

armoured vehicles, who waved as we drove past. At the Kilometre 22 marker stone we were taken to forward HQ and
briefed by a nonchalant young Captain of the Grenadier
Guards. We crowded round him.

'Where are the Egyptians? Where's the front line? How
many men are there facing you?' and so on, the inevitable
questions.

The Captain slapped his leg with his swagger stick and
replied as casually as if he had been standing at the bar of the
Guards Club in Charles Street.

'Oh, the Gippos are about a couple of hundred yards up
the road – you can just see their flag between the trees. No,
they don't give us much trouble. Yes, they have laid a few
mines between our positions but they obviously don't keep a
record of where they put them, because some of their people
blew themselves up on a couple of their own mines the other
night.' The Captain grinned.

'But it's pretty quiet here on the whole. They just sit and
watch us and we just sit and watch them back. The only bit of
sport is on the other side of the Canal, the French side. The
French didn't advance as far as we did and so every night for
the past few nights they've been advancing their flag fifty
yards under cover of darkness. Every morning when the
Gippos wake up they rub their eyes and wonder if the
French flag really was on that telegraph post the night
before.'

He pointed across the Canal at a row of telegraph poles,
one of which was flying the Tricolour, and everyone laughed
at the thought of the foolishness of the Egyptians. I felt rather
sorry for them. What chance did they have against the devil-
may-care professionalism of the British and French regular
troops, especially the Legion, who were on the other side.

There was a commotion farther up the road and someone
said, 'Here they come.'

A convoy of white UN jeeps and lorries was driving slowly
along the empty road towards us, prominently flying the blue
and white UN flag. There was a slight stir of excitement but
nothing more. The British, I felt, were quite happy to see
them arrive. The Captain walked up to the first vehicle, a

jeep, and shook hands with a tall, serious-faced Swedish officer. They chattered for a few minutes and then the Swede went off with the Captain, to see the Colonel, I supposed. The Swedes got out and stretched their legs, looking rather as if they had been invited to a party and were wondering if they had come on the right day. I walked around, making notes, until perhaps ten minutes later, I suddenly thought, 'That's it, I must get back!'

I looked around and to my horror realised that my main rival, the Associated Press correspondent, had disappeared. Panic seized me. I had committed the unpardonable sin for an agency journalist, I had allowed myself to be beaten on an important development by a rival. He was on his way back to Port Said with the story – that the first men of the United Nations Force who were to relieve the British and French had actually arrived – and I was still sitting like an idiot at Kilometre 22, bereft of transport.

The rest of my colleagues, mainly newspaper men, were, of course, not at all in a hurry. It was still morning, they had all day to write their stories, and were interested in finding out exactly what the United Nations soldiers would do first, where they had come from, and what their precise role would be. So was I. But the wretched experienced AP man was off and running with the guts of the story. There were no telephones and nothing I could do until my colleagues were ready to get back into the Landrover and return to Port Said. I knew I would be up to an hour behind the opposition and I felt sick with annoyance and anger at my own incompetence all the way back.

Sean was waiting for me, swelling with rage.

'Where the hell have you been?' he grumbled. 'The AP's already got the arrival on the wire and London's screaming for our copy.' He looked me angrily in the eye, all five foot four of him, and I, all of six foot one and a half, felt very small.

'Sorry,' I apologised weakly. 'I couldn't get a lift back.' Sean sat down and started rattling the keys of his typewriter as I dictated the story. It was a good account, with lots of quotes and colour, but it had one irredeemable fault in the eyes of London: it was well behind the opposition. These details were all duly recorded by Head Office clerks and a log later circulated to all departments. This would say: 'The arrival of the first United Nations Swedish troops outside Port Said was a big story that claimed worldwide attention, specially in the United Kingdom and North America. We were badly beaten by AP on the arrival at Kilometre 22. AP 1140 Reuter 1217, although we recovered somewhat with a fuller and more colourful story with some good quotes and had good play in the mornings.'

But the message was clear. We had been left behind and it was my fault. Still, one good thing about journalism is that your failures as well as your triumphs are short-lived. There is always tomorrow's story and the chance to redeem yourself. Rather as in golf, each new round presents a different challenge and the opportunity for victory.

Next day, the main United Nations force entered Port Said itself for the formal take-over. They came by special train, several hundred blond Swedes, and were met at the station by General Stockwell. I was following him through the crowd of chanting Egyptians, who naturally construed the Swedes' arrival as a defeat for the British, when one Egyptian jumped out of the crowd and snatched off the General's red and gold braided hat.

To my admiration, General Stockwell without hesitation leaped into the crowd, swagger stick at the ready, and snatched his hat back from the man who was desperately trying to escape, but was held by the thickness of the crush. Red-faced but triumphant, 'Hughie' clapped his hat back on his head and strode purposefully to the station.

After the Swedes had shaken hands, got into their lorries and driven away, the crowd which had been building up all morning and which must now have been twenty thousand-strong, surged forward as if they were going to engulf us all. British troops with fixed bayonets made a single line round the station and, as the Egyptians pressed forward excitedly, the young National Servicemen, with admirable calm, forced them back, using their rifle butts when they had to but never anything more lethal.

The arrival of the Swedes had transformed the mood in Port Said and it began to get ugly as the last of the troops withdrew. I and some other British journalists were walking back to the city centre when a mob of Egyptians came racing down the street towards us. An Army Landrover happened to be cruising past. We flagged down the driver and ran towards it. I was the last to get in and, as my friends pulled me aboard, I was conscious of the crowd close at my back. Sitting on the tailboard, I turned and looked at them, waving their fists in the air and shouting abuse, and I suddenly realised that if they had got hold of us they would quite happily have kicked and beaten us to death, as happened to several Europeans who were unwise enough to be caught in the street during the Cairo riots of 1952, when the old Shepheards Hotel was burned down.

A few days later I atoned for my failure at Kilometre 22. I was making my daily rounds, calling in at various Army offices, including the main Military Police guardroom, to see if there had been any interesting overnight developments. The main outer office was empty except for a corporal on the desk and a couple of officers, one Military Police, who were talking in a corner. As I came in I overheard one of them saying: ' . . . young British officer failed to report in this morning . . . '

'What do you mean? He's missing?'

'Yes, and there's concern that he . . . ' He dropped his voice, ' . . . may have been kidnapped.'

They both looked over at me.

'Shh,' the MP officer said. 'Keep your voice down, we don't want the Press to hear about this.'

He spoke to me directly.

'Yes,' he said, 'what can I do for you?'

He could see from my uniform and the flash on my shoulder that I was a war correspondent.

'Reuters,' I said. 'Checking to see if anything happened overnight.'

'No,' he said, lying smoothly. 'Nothing at all.'

I hesitated, tempted to say, 'Well, what were you two discussing in that case?', but kept my peace and walked out.

They would only deny it and I was clear about what I had heard.

We had to go everywhere on foot in Port Said – there was no transport – and I raced back to the Press Centre where Sean was going through the handouts.

'Hey,' I said, 'British officer's missing, possibly kidnapped by the Gippos.'

'Shh,' Sean said, looking round anxiously. 'For God's sake, keep your voice down.' He led me to a side office. 'Now, tell me what the hell is going on.'

Two minutes later he was on the telephone to the Army PRO. They had nothing, they would check. In the meantime, though, Sean sent out the following message:

Officer Snap ex Gall Maynes
Port Said December . . . Reuter – A British officer is missing in Port Said after failing to report for duty this morning and may have been kidnapped by the Egyptians, Army sources said.

More

He tore it out of the typewriter and a few minutes later it was on its way to London. We had a scoop on our hands. Or did we? Had I got it right? We waited impatiently, and nervously.

An hour later the Army 'phoned back and said grudgingly, yes, it was true. Captain Geoffrey Moorhouse, of the 1st Battalion, West Yorkshire Regiment was missing, believed kidnapped. He had been walking down a street, on his way to the mess, when a car pulled up beside him and several men jumped out. There appeared to have been a struggle. Captain Moorhouse was bundled into the car and driven away at high speed. The report came from another British soldier who had been too far away to help, but had seen the incident.

With that the dam broke. The British Press went mad and the story was to dominate the headlines for the next few days. The Army immediately launched a full-scale hunt for Moorhouse, cordoning off the town, section by section, ordering everyone out of their houses and into the street.

63

Squads of National Servicemen went through the buildings, kicking a door down here, bursting open a lock there, searching for the missing man.

Some of the big blocks of flats were like rabbit warrens and we stood and watched amazed, as an apparently impossible number of Egyptians emerged to stand silent and sullen in the street. Some of the men looked like army officers in civilian clothes, which was quite possible since the Egyptian Army in Port Said had gone underground when the British invaded and it was undoubtedly an underground group which had kidnapped Moorhouse. The search went on for several days but drew a blank. In the end, Moorhouse's body was found in a box in an empty flat. He had apparently suffocated, possibly, it was thought, when the flat in which he had been hidden was being searched.

In the days that followed, the Swedes gradually took over more and more of the patrolling and policing duties that had been carried out by the British, and we withdrew to a small perimeter near the Canal. Troops began to leave and, since there was no point in having two correspondents on the ground, Reuters decided that I, being accredited to the Royal Navy, should transfer to the aircraft carrier *Ark Royal*. She was the flagship of the naval task force that would cover the withdrawal and, as soon as it started, I was to flash the news to London over the carrier's communication network.

So, one warm sunny day in mid-December, I said goodbye to Sean and flew fifty miles out over the Mediterranean to *Ark Royal*, steaming majestically in a big circle across the blue sea, a white wave like a bib at her bow, Vampire and Meteor jets on her decks, and the sun gleaming on the metal and glass of her bridge. She looked the very epitome of British Imperial power. It was in fact a swan song, the last time a full-size British carrier was to be used in an offensive role.

I was taken in tow by Jimmy, a jolly lieutenant who had hurt his back and was unfit for active flying duty. His job seemed to be to ply me with as many gins as possible and prevent me from finding out anything of real moment. But he did his best to entertain me, taking me up next day in a

Meteor fighter jet. I sat directly behind him and strapped myself tightly in against the hard upright seat. We watched a fighter take off in front of us with a heave and a clank as the catapult hurled it off the bow of the carrier at over a hundred miles an hour. It seemed to dip towards the sea for a moment and then climbed up and away. Jimmy had explained that that was the most dangerous time, immediately after launch, when the chances were greatest that you would come down in the drink. It was our turn next. The launch crew manhandled our jet into position, and hooked us on to the steam catapult launcher. The catapult runs along a narrow slit in the deck with only the launching hook visible. Wisps of steam curl upwards from this crevice rather as they do in the middle of the streets in New York. Now they were whipped away by the wind because we were steaming into it at ten or fifteen knots.

'Hold tight,' Jimmy said, 'and remember to sit absolutely straight.' He had cricked his back at the vital moment of launch when the G forces are at their greatest. I listened on the headset as the tower gave us wind speed and direction, cloud height and other information.

'Charlie Zulu, are you ready for take-off?' they crackled.

'Charlie Zulu to tower. Roger, we're all set,' Jimmy replied. Something hit me in the back with terrific force, driving the breath out of my body and pinning me against my seat from head to backside with amazing strength. Even if I had wanted to, I could not have moved a muscle. I was conscious of the carrier's deck receding in a blur and we were over the water, hanging in mid-air, it seemed, with a sensation almost of floating. Then the surge of the jet engine picked us up and lifted us in an easy climb away from the sea, which had been heaving just below us a moment ago. As I looked down, I could see *Ark Royal* steaming unconcernedly along.

We climbed to 30,000 feet, which gave us a perfect if rather distant view of the Egyptian coast and the city of Port Said. We could see the Canal running away to the south, with the Sinai Desert stretching off to the east. It was fascinating to observe how precisely the Canal marked the limit of civilisation, all trees and greenery to our right, the west, all sand and desolation to the left. After half an hour of sight-seeing we turned and flew back to the carrier, still cutting her imperial way through the blue seas, flanked and protected by a couple of narrow-hulled destroyers, patrolling like sheep-dogs. The landing was more nerve-racking than the launch. The carrier deck seemed very small and unstable as we circled and then we were lining up, the landing lights blazing brightly in front of us in the strong sunshine. We came down fast, wings waggling as gusts of wind caught us. I watched with utter concentration and slight tightness in the stomach as we closed the gap between us and the stern of the carrier. Would we make it, or would we just drop short? Jimmy applied a little more power and the jet lifted fractionally and suddenly the deck was coming to meet us with a rush, the three arrester wires criss-crossing the steel deck. Instead of dropping down, we seemed to rise slightly. I looked past Jimmy's shoulder and saw the end of the flight deck approaching with frightening speed. For one agonising moment I thought we were going to overshoot and then I was hurled forward in my harness so hard that once again the breath was knocked out of me. Just when the pull seemed intolerable it eased and we were actually rolling backwards. The middle arrester wire had caught us with unerring precision and yanked us to a dead stop in thirty or forty feet.

As the recovery crew came round the plane, Jimmy took off his helmet and grinned at me.

'Enjoy your first flight from a carrier?'

I swallowed and managed a shaky grin.

'You look a bit shaken,' he said. 'Come and have a gin in the mess. Do you good.'

But I had enjoyed it immensely. Who wouldn't? We had a gin and then another to celebrate the occasion. The great advantage British carriers and indeed the whole of the Royal Navy have over the American Navy is that they are not dry. Years later, in Vietnam, when we were filming the USS *Enterprise* launching round-the-clock strikes against the Communists, the pilots would occasionally ask us to their cabins for a quick one. But, since it was strictly illegal, it was all done in such a hole-in-the-corner, quick-drink-up-before-anyone-comes atmosphere, that there was no pleasure in it; it was somehow sordid and demeaning.

Although everyone on *Ark Royal* was extremely hospitable, I was getting restless. I had sent a couple of messages to London to test the communications but there was no news I could get my teeth into. We had the date for the final British withdrawal, but not the exact time, and I tried hard to establish a foolproof plan for finding out exactly when the last British soldier had left Egyptian soil. I reasoned that *Ark Royal* would get a signal from the shore and would pass it on to London. I asked to be told, whatever time the signal came in, and in fact left a specially prepared message with the duty officer to be sent off immediately the withdrawal was complete.

But the Navy won. The withdrawal took place around midnight, but no one woke me and no message was sent. Next morning, in answer to my angry remonstrations, the Navy maintained that they had received no message from Port Said, and therefore had not been officially informed.

'Don't worry old boy,' they said with a smile. 'Come and have a gin.'

A day later Jimmy wished me *bon voyage* and waved as I was catapulted off over the sea. This time it was a fixed wing plane, a slow old tortoise compared to the Meteor, but it got me to Cyprus and the plaudits of Gubby a few hours later. Apparently London thought Sean and I had done a great job, they were still purring about our scoop on Captain Moorhouse, and so everyone was happy. We went out to celebrate that evening in one of Gubby's favourite restaurants, behind the wire mesh, just round the corner from Murder Mile. Sean was still on the high seas, grumbling away, I imagined, in his cracked brogue.

CHAPTER III

Budapest after the Revolution: The Secret Police, a Defector and Romance

Suez was a disaster in nearly every sense. For a once great military power, deploying her armed might only eleven years after the end of the Second World War, Britain made a sorry showing, having difficulty even in quelling the Egyptians, who were not exactly noted for their military prowess. But it was, of course, mainly a political disaster and there can be no doubt that the blame must attach principally to the then Prime Minister, Sir Anthony Eden. Beyond all the arguments about collusion, which, however much it was denied, indubitably existed, there remained quite simply Eden's staggering loss of judgement. He let the public mask slip right at the beginning, in the famous broadcast when he announced the reasons for Britain's action and compared Nasser to Hitler. I heard it well before I actually arrived in Port Said and I thought as I listened to his words that anyone who could compare a tinpot conspirator like Nasser with a megalomaniac monster like Hitler must be unbalanced. Politicians often make claims that cannot be substantiated but I do not think that Eden was guilty of that sort of hyperbole. He really meant it. Nasser and his overthrow had become an obsession, the obsession of a sick man. That Eden was a very sick man at the time of Suez and that his illness clouded and confused his judgement was conclusively confirmed to me a couple of years later by Lord Evans, Physician to the Queen and perhaps the most famous GP of his day.

Horace Evans was a close friend of my father-in-law, Michael Smyth, himself a distinguished Harley Street surgeon. Over a glass of whisky one evening, standing in front of Michael's fireside in Elm Tree Road, Horace Evans told me that when Eden, whom he had attended, resigned after Suez, and went to the Mayo Clinic in America for a bile duct operation, the American doctors discovered that the tube that had been inserted during a previous operation in London was no longer there. I asked what had happened to it. 'He had passed it,' Evans said succinctly.

'What was the effect of that?'

Quite simple. All the waste matter that should have been eliminated via the intestines had remained in the body and had poisoned the system.

'And would that have had a serious effect on Eden's whole personality and behaviour?' I asked.

Oh yes, came the answer. The poisoning of the system over a period was bound to have a serious effect not only on his physical health, but on his mind as well. It was the cause of his recurrent fevers. Under those circumstances, nothing that Eden said or did was very surprising.

I did not ask Lord Evans if he had guessed at the truth, but knowing his reputation as a diagnostician I would be surprised if he had not had a very shrewd idea of what was wrong. What is certain, and what he told me that evening, is that he repeatedly urged Eden to go to America and have the operation. He finally did, but too late.

While the world was preoccupied with Suez, however, another event of the first magnitude was taking place in its shadow: the Hungarian Revolution. And it was to Hungary, a few months later, by way of Bonn, that I was next posted.

On October 23, 1956, eight days before the start of the

Suez invasion, a popular demonstration took place in Budapest. It began modestly enough on the anniversary of the birth of Hungary's most famous poet, Sandor Petöfi, and was led by writers and artists who were rebelling against the soulless degradation of art and literature by the Stalinist bureaucrats of the Rakosi régime. To everyone's surprise this essentially cultural protest touched off a tremendous explosion, as if someone had thrown a lighted match on to a bonfire soaked in petrol. The writers' march became a mass demonstration and by the end of the day the Hungarians were in revolt against their Communist masters. They pulled down and smashed Stalin's statue, the very symbol of Soviet domination, and then turned on the Interior Ministry. In the space of a few days the whole country had risen in revolt against the entire brutal, cynical system. The chief target for revenge was the most hated part of that system, the Hungarian secret police, the AVO.

One amazing series of stills taken by a *Life* photographer and showing the trapping and shooting of four AVO men in a Budapest street brilliantly caught this side of the Revolution. The first picture shows four secret policemen, in civilian clothes and raincoats, at the moment they are caught and lined up against the wall by the revolutionaries. In the next picture you see them raising their hands, fear flooding their faces as they realise what is coming. The next, most searing picture catches them at the very moment of being shot, the bullets tearing their bodies, the agony on their faces. The final picture has them slumped on the ground, the agony over. The crowd looks on approvingly, obviously feeling that they have got their just deserts.

A junior member of the Government, Imre Nagy, had replaced the hardliner Gerö as Prime Minister and he eventually joined the revolutionaries in their call for the withdrawal of Russian forces from Hungary. The revolutionaries went further, perhaps too far. They also wanted Hungary to leave the Warsaw Pact. Both these demands caused consternation in the Kremlin. They struck at the very root of Soviet power in Eastern Europe and raised what was, for the Russians, the appalling spectre of other satellites – Poland,

Czechoslovakia and, worst of all, East Germany – following suit.

For a few days it looked as if the revolutionaries might get away with it. The Russians agreed to withdraw and indeed were seen to drive their tanks eastwards over the border. But the respite was brief. A few days later, on November 4, Russian tanks rolled back into Budapest. Fierce battles followed. The Hungarian revolutionary army under the command of General Pal Máleter fought desperately. So did the street and factory militias. The freedom fighters were outstandingly brave: there were stories of teenage boys running up to tanks and throwing Molotov cocktails in their turrets. But in the end their barehanded courage was no match for the Russian weight of armour and superior fire-power. Máleter was captured and Nagy took refuge in the Yugoslav Embassy. Thousands of Hungarians started to flee the country, making for the one open border, with Austria in the west, in a race against the Russians. For those who either decided to stay or failed to get to the border in time, the future was going to be bleak indeed.

Retribution was swift. The Russians imposed martial law throughout Hungary and started a massive manhunt for any revolutionary leaders still at large. They appointed an unknown Communist Party official, János Kádár, as Prime Minister, and the Secret Police, the AVO, although badly shaken, were back in business. A year later when I left Bonn for Budapest, early on the morning of December 24, 1957, the Russian grip on Hungary was still total. I drove south all day through a wintry, grey German landscape to the Austrian border, arriving in Salzburg in time to eat a solitary dinner in the only restaurant that was open on Christmas Eve, the station buffet. A fountain played in the middle of the large half-empty marble *Saal*. I felt as if I were sitting on a stage.

Next day, Christmas morning, I left immediately after breakfast, driving to Vienna for brunch with the Reuters correspondent, 'Harry' Harrison, a Balkan veteran and a man of great charm and kindness, who lived in a spacious, elegant but slightly spartan flat on the Schwarzenberg Platz. All my copy would pass through Harry's wireroom, which

71

was part of the flat, but I was my own boss and took orders only from London. Harry and his wife gave me a glass of champagne and something to eat and sent me on my way just after midday. It was about an hour's drive to the border and another three hours after that to Budapest.

The Austrian border formalities were minimal and then, with a slight tightening of the stomach, I got back into my Opel to drive the mile or so across no-man's land to the Hungarian checkpoint at Hegyeshalom. Halfway across there was a wire fence, floodlit at night, a ditch and a minefield, and, as I looked along the smoothly-raked strip of earth which would show immediately if anyone had walked across it, I saw the watchtowers, sinister skeletons among the cabbage fields. Up there, the guards with their machine-guns and binoculars kept a day and night watch. The myth was that they were guarding against the possibility of an armed counter-revolution from the West, but in reality they were there to prevent any of their fellow-countrymen from voting with their feet and escaping to the West.

I immediately detected a totally different atmosphere at the Hungarian border post. First of all, there was a curious odour that I was to get to know so well over the next two years, a musty, stale smell that went with the heavy, ugly furniture and the propaganda pictures on the wall. Secondly, there was an air of grim bureaucracy, of the police jackboot under the desk, that was also to become very familiar. The formalities here took much longer although I was the only traveller, the border officials moving deliberately, ponderously. They came out and looked at the car, in the boot and under the bonnet, and finally waved me on my way. With a deep breath and feeling I had negotiated the first major hurdle successfully, I drove on in the gathering gloom of the afternoon, the first plains of Hungary stretching away endlessly in front of me. I passed the first straggling, one-street villages, bumped through the small town of Mosonmagyorovar, where several AVO men had been kicked and beaten to death during the Revolution and crossed the Danube at Györ, a big industrial town, following the signs to Budapest. The roads were bad, often narrow and winding and made hazardous in the failing

72

light by the peasants' ox carts. They never carried lights and they were almost impossible to see in the dusk. On Christmas Day, though, there was little traffic of any other kind and I had an almost unimpeded run, reaching Budapest just after dark. I drove over one of the many bridges, the lights reflecting off the broad sweep of the Danube which divides the two parts of the city, Buda and Pest, and crossed Parliament Square, a huge empty expanse with at one side the ornate neo-Gothic Parliament building, a copy of Westminster it was said. A few hundred yards farther on, a blue neon sign showed me where the Hotel Duna stood in splendid isolation right on the river bank.

The lights beckoned to me out of the gloom and I went in through the swing doors to take stock of my new home: a plain reception desk on the left, in front of me a small lobby with two lifts, opening into a large lounge furnished in heavy brown plush, a tiny bar – more like a hole in the wall – in the far left-hand corner and beyond the dining-room overlooking the Danube. This was the most attractive room, with the best view, in the whole hotel.

Before I had finished registering, the man I had come to replace, Ronnie Farquhar, appeared to greet me, warmly but not effusively. Ronnie was never effusive. I knew him slightly and liked him. We were both Scots, always a bond in a hostile world of Englishmen and other Sassenachs, and I enjoyed his wry sense of humour and his irreverence for any pomposity. For the next few days Ronnie guided me through the labyrinth that was Budapest and, if it had not been for the sense of adventure that a new assignment inevitably brings, I would have found the whole thing infinitely depressing. The sky was uniformly leaden with a hint of snow, a yellowish smog caught the back of the throat and, being so near the river, the air was damp and cold. We called on all the key places: the press section of the Foreign Ministry, run by an engaging French-speaking old Communist called Gyaros, but staffed by less engaging young bureaucrats; then the Hungarian News Agency, MTI, whose head, Sandor Barcs, was an unexpectedly helpful man, a non-party member and at heart, I was convinced, a democrat, but who had learned how to

73

survive in the arctic political conditions of post-Revolution Hungary; and, finally and very importantly, the British Legation. Each weekday, Ronnie and I in turn would walk or drive the quarter of a mile from the Duna to the Legation (one step below an Embassy) and pick up the daily translation of the Hungarian press which contained extracts from the provincial papers that we would not otherwise have seen. But the visit also gave us a chance to talk to the diplomats, all of whom were to become friends or at least good acquaintances in the months ahead. Since their sum total of knowledge of the Hungarian scene was infinitely greater than any lone correspondent could command, they were an invaluable source of information and background. We also made a daily run to MTI to pick up stencilled copies of their news service – in Hungarian – which our translators would then read for items of interest. As I had learned in Berlin, ninety per cent of the material put out by Communist news agencies is deadly dull unless you really want to know how a particular brigade in some factory or other has invented a new method of producing sparking plugs for tractors, or how many pigs were born at the Rosa Luxembourg collective in Debrecen last month. Most of MTI's interminable sheets, in the mumbo-jumbo of Communist jargon, yielded nothing, but occasionally, very occasionally, some vital nugget of news would be buried away at the bottom of a story and, when found, would cast a fitful light on the murky, secret world that was the Communist government of Hungary in the late Fifties.

Very few of the Communist officials I met ever displayed any sort of humour or individuality, but Gyaros, the Foreign Office spokesman, was a notable exception. To celebrate my arrival and Ronnie's departure, Gyaros invited us to dinner. He spoke excellent French from his days as a Comintern agent in Belgium and, since my French was also fairly fluent, we got on well from the start. He had a marvellously sardonic sense of humour which he enjoyed exercising at the expense of the West, but unlike most party members would take the return thrust with good grace and a smile. He was surprisingly undoctrinaire and affable and there was also the suggestion of an exciting past, heightened by the fact that he had lost two fingers of one hand in some unspecified accident. A bomb? A fight? The Gestapo? One simply did not know.

After a good dinner, Gyaros took us to the Moulin Rouge, famous in Hungary's capitalist days for its beautiful girls and glittering floor show. Now, however, the place was tawdry, the girls plain and the floor show pathetically bad. To make up for it Gyaros ordered *baracsk*, a fiery apricot brandy which Hungarians drink like water. After a few of those we were laughing at the feeblest jokes and applauding the dullest turns on the stage. When we staggered out into the empty streets in the early hours of the morning, I was in such a happy mood that I no longer felt constrained by the thought of being in a Communist police state. As a demonstration of my *joie de vivre* I picked Gyaros up and carried him halfway round the square. The *baracsk* had obviously done its work well on both of us for when I set him down again Gyaros was still laughing and we parted shortly afterwards with warm protestations of mutual respect.

Next morning, however, I woke with a sore head and acute feelings of remorse. I had appalling visions of being declared *persona non grata* and sent packing for insulting a high official of the Hungarian Communist Government. Reuters would be furious. My career was ruined. I went to find Ronnie and explained my fears to him.

'Away, Jock,' he said comfortingly. 'Just a wee bit of fun in Sauchiehall Street.'

And he was right. Gyaros never held it against me and we became in a curious way friends, although we rarely met except at one of his infrequent press conferences when he would deliver fearsome tirades against the policies of the West in general, and of the United States in particular.

For a Westerner, and especially a Western journalist who was automatically considered a spy, it was almost impossible to have a close relationship with Hungarians. Because of the recent past, the great majority were understandably scared and instinctively shied away from any contact. Anyone who frequented the enemy – and we were the enemy – was by definition an enemy himself, and in post-Revolution Hungary enemies got short shrift. Only the naivest did not know that the AVO kept an eye on all foreigners and thus on any Hungarians who were friendly with them; and that they would be pulled in, sooner or later, and either ordered to spy on the foreigner, if that is what the AVO wanted, or more probably warned off. For the vast majority of Hungarians, even the threat of a visit to the dreaded Interior Ministry was enough to make them shake in their shoes. It was only exceptional characters like my friend George Galfy, with little to lose, who were prepared to put up with the police harassment. But even with staunch friends like George – and here was the insidious infamy of the system – you were never completely sure that they were not reporting *something* to the police, if only to stay out of jail.

I inherited George from Ronnie. He was the son of a former mayor of Miskolc, the second biggest town in Hungary, a product of the old privileged class and had, I gathered, a revolutionary record from 1956 which made him doubly suspect to the authorities. At any rate, when we first met, he was driving a lorry from Miskolc, in north-eastern Hungary, not far from the Russian border, to Budapest and he said it was the only job he could get. Once a month or so he would come bouncing into the Duna, resplendent in what I imagined was his only suit, bringing with him something of the elegance and ease of the old Hungary. He did not actually click his heels but almost and, when he greeted a lady, he used the charming old Austro-Hungarian formula: '*Küss die Hand*' (I kiss your hand). We would go out to dinner together and George would be the perfect host, ordering the wine, tipping the gypsy band, and very often, to my embarrassment, insisting on paying, although I guessed that he had very little money. Behind the optimistic, brave façade, however, there lurked the other George, who would suddenly lean forward, lower his voice and say: 'Things are terrible, they cannot go on like this . . .'

His English was not very good, although he managed to maintain a conversation remarkably well.

'What do you mean?' I would ask, also keeping my voice down and not speaking when the waiter was actually hovering over us. 'What do you mean things are terrible?'

George would look round the room as if to reassure himself he was not being overheard. Very often, on occasions like these, a furtive-looking man would come along and sit down discreetly, as he thought, but to me very obviously, close by, take out a paper and pretend to be reading it. George and I knew perfectly well that he was one of the scores of petty police informers who worked the Budapest cafés and restaurants. If George spotted such a customer, he would roll a warning eye at me and pointedly change the conversation. Usually he did this with a grin, and I came to admire the spirit that could so gallantly circumnavigate the treacherous shoals of a police state.

If however there was no one there, George would tell me some story of persecution or arrest by the AVO; or, alternatively, he would declaim on the shortcomings of the régime, illustrating its failures with some anecdote but never, as I recall, giving me a precise example that I could use as a story. I do not know if this was intentional on his part, probably not, but if it was, then it was clever of him, because if he had told me something really damaging which had appeared on the Reuters service, they would have traced it back and stopped his trips to Budapest or, worse still, put him in jail.

Still, I got from George very much of the feel of what life in Hungary was like for many of the middle class. I discounted some of what he said because he was quite obviously, and he admitted it, completely hostile to the régime. But George had the courage, or the foolhardiness, to speak his mind, and that was rare in Hungary in 1957-58.

Which brings me to Eleanor. She was one of the first people I met, a day or two after my arrival, in Ronnie's office-cum-bedroom that I was soon to inherit.

Eleanor Smyth was an Irish-looking strawberry blonde with blue eyes and an infectious laugh that rang out joyously in the dark and dingy confines of Budapest. I fell for her immediately and, since she also lived in the Duna, sharing a room with another girl from the British Legation, Gillie Hayes-Newington, we saw each other almost daily. They both worked in the hush-hush Visa Section, their main job being to stop AVO agents from slipping into Britain in the guise of refugees.

Carl Hartman, the Associated Press correspondent, his wife Martha and their little daughter Jessica also lived in the Duna. Carl and I were the only permanent Western correspondents in Hungary and, although our organisations were in direct competition, we decided that we had all the competition we needed from the Hungarian authorities: so we cooperated wherever possible. This worked excellently in practice, particularly for me since Carl was a very experienced journalist and had been in Hungary for several months. We had a simple code of conduct. We would often go out on a story together, gather the facts, discuss it and then write it each in our own way. Run-of-the-mill stories we pooled automatically, one of us giving the other a 'black'. But, if there was a genuine exclusive, whoever got it would put it out first and only share it an hour or two later.

We worked together in other ways. Carl and Ronnie had used a Hungarian husband-and-wife team as interpreters and I took the arrangement over. Laci (pronounced Lotsy) Boros worked for Carl, and his wife Ilona for me. Laci had been a Hungarian newspaperman before the Revolution and had then been offered a job by AP which was both better paid and more satisfying than anything he could have found on a Hungarian paper. But it was also more dangerous and Laci would one day pay the price. Looking back, I realise that the shadow of this possibility always hung over the Boroses, and it was Ilona, who often had a hunted look, who felt it more acutely, or at least showed it more.

She was petite and pretty, with dark expressive eyes, rather pessimistic and fearful. Ilona was really too sensitive a person to be torn between the conflicting demands of the Hungarian Communist régime with its cynical disregard for the truth, and our Western determination to get the facts, cost what it may.

In the late winter, one of the British diplomats, Frank Hoyer-Miller, asked me if I would like to look after his house on the Var for a fortnight while he went ski-ing. This was an unexpected piece of luck because the Var was the oldest and most beautiful part of the city, set high up in Buda and dominated by the Gothic splendour of the Matyas Church, where Hungarian kings had traditionally been crowned, and the brooding bulk of the castle, badly damaged in the fighting at the end of the Second World War. The Var was full of the once-magnificent town houses of the aristocracy, and it was to one of these that Frank Hoyer-Miller gave me the key. Despite the ravages of the past seventeen years, it had wooden panelling, cut glass chandeliers, one or two sticks of rather battered but still elegant furniture, and very little heating. Frank's motives were not entirely altruistic. He knew better than most that if the house were left empty for a couple of weeks the AVO would soon be inside, inserting microphones in every available crevice. At least I was some guarantee that they would not have an entirely free run.

I invited Eleanor and Gillie to join me and we moved in to what, compared to the Duna, was absolute luxury. After my cramped, dreary room with the teleprinter beside the bed, the pleasure I got from this eighteenth-century house was almost childish. I would walk through the Var with the Danube glinting in the winter sunshine far below, open the massive wooden front door, climb the narrow, creaking staircase to the spacious drawing-room on the first floor where a log fire would burn, and pour myself a whisky in one of Frank's cut glass tumblers.

Microphones, of course, were a part of one's daily life. I knew perfectly well, for example, that my telephone in the Duna was tapped. When I dialled out I could hear the whine and click as the recording started. Ronnie had warned me that the room was probably bugged as well, so we never discussed anything sensitive there. When Carl and I wanted to talk something over which we did not want the AVO to hear, we used to go into the corridor and converse in hushed tones. People who were really concerned about security would only talk to you in the street. We even distrusted the privacy of our own cars. In theory, it was quite possible for the AVO to have planted a microphone in your car and so it was safer to presume that they had done so. Not that we had any secret information, but things that would have seemed quite innocuous in the West became incriminating in Hungary.

Understandably, Hungarians were even more aware of the dangers of careless talk. Ilona and Laci, knowing they were in an exposed position, were especially careful. If Ilona wanted to tip me off about something, she was always extremely careful to tell me either in the corridor, in the street, or in some other neutral place, always in a hurried whisper, but casually, so that it did not look as if she were passing on confidential information, and always with the proviso that the information had *not* come from her.

There were numerous stories of how brazenly the Hungarian Interior Ministry, which controlled the AVO, planted microphones under the noses of Western diplomats. One day, the British Legation was obliged to call in Hungarian post office engineers to repair a fault in one of the diplomats' telephones. When the security people carefully checked afterwards, they found a bug cleverly secreted in the telephone, in spite of the fact that someone had been in the room the whole time. But the best bugging story I heard concerned one of the American political officers, Cub Gardiner, a tall blond man known inevitably as Lion Cub. When he and his wife arrived in Budapest, the house on the Var which had been allocated to them by the Hungarian Foreign Ministry was still being restored. A team of workmen were employed on the job and Cub often used to go past on his way to and from the Embassy to see how they were getting on. What he saw pleased him. The Hungarians were good workers and before long the house was ready. The Hungarians were good workers and before long the house was ready. Before moving in, however, the Americans sent two of their experts from Vienna to run a microphone detector over the place.

'We nearly fainted,' Cub told me. 'The place was just alive with bugs. Every wall, every ceiling, even the closet. Every place you could think of and some you couldn't. We had to tear the goddam house to pieces to get the damned things out.'

The Americans in Budapest were a particular target for the AVO, because inside their Legation they had Eastern

Europe's best-known and most controversial political prisoner: Cardinal Mindszenty, the Primate of Hungary.

The Cardinal was one of the key figures in Hungarian post-war history. He was, interestingly, of humble peasant origin but from the beginning he was destined for high places. His devoutness and exceptional ability burned like a flame. But he also knew how to speak to ordinary Hungarians. As Primate, he had his see at Esztergom, north of Budapest. Hungary had always been a largely Catholic country and when, in 1948, a Communist Government was imposed on an unwilling but impotent population at the points of Soviet bayonets, conflict between Church and State was inevitable. Cardinal Mindszenty was at the centre of it, an implacable opponent of the new Communist régime.

Quite simply, the Cardinal defied the Communists to lay a finger on the Church and they took up the challenge very firmly by placing their hand on him. He was arrested at Esztergom in 1949 and, after months of interrogation, put on trial. It was a show trial in which he was made to admit a whole series of implausible crimes, such as illegal currency transactions. But the main charge was treason and on that Mindszenty was found guilty and sentenced to life imprisonment. He appeared in the dock a broken man and one wondered what intolerable pressures had been placed upon him. Even today, little is generally known of what happened to Mindszenty. No doubt there was the now routine psychological assault, sleep deprivation, disorientation and intensely hostile interrogation until even his proud spirit was broken. There was talk of drugs and there may even have been physical torture as well. Whatever they did to him, they did it well and, with Mindszenty out of the way, the rest of the Hungarian Church quickly caved in, despite the isolated opposition of one or two brave priests. After the trial, little was heard of Mindszenty until 1956 when a group of revolutionaries broke into the jail where he was being held and freed him and the other prisoners. The Cardinal returned to Budapest in triumph and made a much-publicised radio broadcast in which he appeared at one point to call for a return to the old order. He was probably ill-advised to make a

81

broadcast at all since he was completely out of touch with developments and had never had the political astuteness of someone like Cardinal Wyszinsky in Poland. On the other hand, he was the best-known victim of the régime and most Hungarians saw his liberation as another step on the road to freedom. Both, alas, turned out to be tragically brief and, when it became certain that the Russians were going to smash the Revolution and that the only prospect for him was jail again or the firing squad, Mindszenty fled to the safety of the American Legation.

There he would remain a prisoner, albeit a privileged one for the next twelve years, occupying a tiny flat on the first floor of the building, hardly seeing anyone apart from Gary Ackerson, the Chargé d'Affaires, and his closest colleagues, except for once a week when he celebrated mass in Ackerson's office and Catholics from other Western Legations were allowed to attend. I caught a glimpse of him only once in two years. I was calling on Ackerson and on the way into his office looked over the bannisters down into a sort of interior courtyard. A lonely figure in a cassock, head bowed and hands behind his back, was walking round the confined space. It was the only exercise the Cardinal ever got. His only visitor was his mother, then over ninety, who came from her village, every week, bringing some of her cooking and her peasant faith to comfort him.

In case he ever tried to leave, two AVO men in long leather coats stood on duty outside the front door of the Legation all the time, night and day, winter and summer. Next to them a police car was parked ostentatiously beside the kerb, its engine always running. If the Hungarians were worried that Mindszenty might try to escape, the Americans were equally concerned that the AVO might try to kidnap him. So every night, week in week out, an American diplomat sat on duty just outside the Cardinal's rooms from the time the Legation closed until it opened for business again next morning. There were only a dozen or so Americans with diplomatic status in the Legation so the chore came round with monotonous regularity. No doubt the Hungarians, who knew exactly what was going on, enjoyed the harassment they were able to cause the Americans and for years refused to let Mindszenty leave the country. All attempts to negotiate his release were met by the threat that the Cardinal would have to face court proceedings for his alleged misdeeds during the Revolution. In this way they kept the knife twisting in the wound. It was a very cold war in Budapest in those days.

But at least Mindszenty was luckier than the two other leaders of the Revolution: Imre Nagy, the Prime Minister, and General Pal Máleter. Máleter, a strikingly tall, dashing officer, was the first Hungarian general to side with the revolutionaries and made his headquarters at the Killian Barracks a centre of resistance. When the Russians agreed to withdraw their troops from Hungary in the early days of the Revolution, they invited Máleter to negotiate with them. It was a trick. Once they got him to the table, they arrested him. Nagy was tricked even more flagrantly. On November 2, when the Russian tanks were closing in again on Budapest and after making one last desperate appeal to the United Nations to come to Hungary's aid, Nagy took refuge in the Yugoslav Embassy. Three weeks later, after a safe-conduct had been negotiated with the new government of János Kádár, Nagy and various colleagues left the Embassy in a bus to go to their homes. On the way the Russians stopped the bus and despite the protests of the two accompanying Yugoslav diplomats, arrested Nagy and his friends. They were later deported to Rumania and never seen in public again. In fact nothing definite was known of their fate until June 17, 1958, when their secret trial and execution were announced *post facto* by the Hungarian Government. In their crushing of the Hungarian Revolution the Russians displayed a callousness and a ruthlessness that even they would find hard to improve on.

I spent the rest of the winter learning how to cope with the frustrations of a police state. It was remarkable how quickly one learned. And there were plenty of compensations. Spring finally came, the ice disappeared from the Danube, the birds started to sing on the Var, and the plane trees came into flower. There were endless diplomatic parties to which Carl and Martha and Eleanor and I were nearly always invited, given by the Swiss, the French (Madame Paul Boncourt with her clashing beads and deep contralto voice), the Italians, the Americans and, of course, the British, a genial lot led by the small, imperious figure of Sir Leslie Fry. The most sought-after invitation from our point of view was to lunch or dinner at the American residence. Gary Ackerson was a New England patrician of the old school and, despite the fact that he did not really approve of the Press, was charming to me. He had a twenty-year-old daughter called Rhoda who came for periodic visits from Vienna, but for the rest of the time he was alone and probably lonely. When we went to dinner, Fritz, the Viennese chef, would appear in his white jacket and take one's order for a drink: Old-fashioneds and Manhattans he made especially skilfully. Every morning Fritz would bring his master two menus, one for lunch and one for dinner, and Ackerson would simply write down how many guests there would be at each meal. On special occasions, when Rhoda was visiting, Fritz would do something special, like a Baked Alaska.

Life began to assume a pattern. George Galfy would appear out of the blue with a demijohn of wine under his arm, having parked his lorry outside. When asked where the wine came from, George would simply laugh and say, 'Mountain wine. Very good.' It was.

We explored the restaurants. There had been scores of them before the war, serving delicious Hungarian food, which tends to be rich, full of paprika and cream, but now there were only a handful that were worth going to. We liked the Sász Eves (Hundred Years), just round the corner from the Duna, not because the food was particularly good but because the manager was so friendly. He was called Ságodi and had been pre-war manager of the Gellert, one of Budapest's leading hotels. The Duke and Duchess of Windsor had stayed there shortly after the Abdication, and Ságodi would recount endlessly how he had to go up to their suite and take their orders for the day. The Duke was above criticism. But Ságodi did not approve of the Duchess. She had very ugly hands, he said, and a curt way with underlings. She may have been irritated by his bowing and scraping because even with us Ságodi's performance was almost out of a comic opera.

'Come in, come in, dear lady,' he would boom at Eleanor. 'How charmingly beautiful you are looking. What an exquisite pleasure to have the privilege of your patronage tonight.' The restaurant was very small and quite unchic, but Ságodi would sweep us to the table as if it had been Maxim's, arm outflung and with a profusion of deep bows. He would then rattle on in his heavily-accented and rather old-fashioned English, ignoring his other, lesser, Hungarian clients. The food was usually very ordinary, but Ságodi brought it on with such a flourish that we ate it up with a good grace. Occasionally he would look around, lower his voice and apologise.

'We can't get anything better,' he would shrug. 'We are only a second-class restaurant. All the best cuts go to . . . you know who I mean . . . ' He would nod his head to indicate the new ruling classes, the party bureaucrats and the secret policemen who had access to special shops where they could buy luxuries that never appeared on the open market.

Hungarian food, on the whole, I found fairly forgettable, except for one dish, the great national delicacy called *libamaj*, or goose liver. Wherever you went in Hungary, which was still extremely rural, you would see flocks of big white geese being prepared for the slaughter. They were force fed so that their livers would become distended and there were some nasty stories about how they were nailed to the floor by their feet to speed up the fattening process. To my shame I chose to disbelieve or ignore these stories and I must confess I found goose liver a great delicacy, on a par with caviar. You could either have it hot in slices – and this was how they would serve it at big government receptions – or else you had it cold, as pâté on toast. These receptions were about the only place we Western journalists could meet senior Hungarian Communist politicians. They seldom gave interviews or press conferences and the only time I really met János Kádár was at a big national day reception in the Parliament Building. It had no proper function as a Parliament, since all the real decisions were taken behind closed doors in Communist

Party headquarters, but it made an excellent place to hold receptions.

Carl Hartman and I and a handful of other journalists, Hungarians and other Eastern Europeans, were standing chatting at one of these receptions when Kádár appeared. I thought he would ignore us but he came over with a smile, making some snide remark about the Western Press. The Hungarian journalists standing beside us grinned in anticipation and one of them interpreted.

Carl was good at these situations. It probably helped that he looked more European than American and that he had a Hungarian grandfather. The questions ranged over the issues of the day, with Kádár giving short rather sarcastic replies, delivered with a smile and raising a laugh among the Hungarians who clustered round. He usually managed to give his answer a twist to make a questioner look slightly foolish. The conversation went like this:

Carl: 'When are Russian troops going to be withdrawn from Hungary?'

Kádár: 'They will stay here as long as we, the Hungarian government, want them to stay. And that will be as long as there is any threat of counter-revolutionary incursions from the West.' (Smile)

Carl: 'Have there been any incursions from the West?'

Kádár: 'One or two funny things have happened and we know from experience we always have to be on our guard.' (Murmurs of approval from sycophantic officials.)

Carl: 'There seem to be a lot of trials going on in secret of people accused of crimes in 1956 . . . '

Kádár: 'Secret? I don't think there are any secret trials . . . '

Carl: 'Well, they are difficult to get to know about and to get into. They don't exactly encourage the Western Press to attend.'

Kádár: 'I wonder why?' (More sycophantic laughter.) 'The trials are not secret. If they are it is a decision by the judiciary taken in accordance with the demands of State security.'

Me: 'We hear rumours about the case of Imre Nagy. Is he going to be brought to trial?'

Kádár: 'Ah, another one who likes to ask questions about

86

secret trials. (More laughter.) The case of Imre Nagy is being investigated in the proper way and, when the due processes of the law are complete, a statement will be made.'

Me: 'Can you give us any idea of when that may be?'

But Kádár was already turning away, remarking loudly to the group of Hungarian officials and journalists: 'The Western Press always ask the same kind of questions, always concentrating on the negative side of things. Why don't they ask a few positive questions?' The grin belied the real anger behind the question. 'But we have nothing to hide. Hungary is making progress and will continue to do so whatever the Western Press may say.' (Laughter and applause as Kádár made his exit.)

We were left feeling rather like the enemy, except that we knew at least some of the Hungarian journalists were on our side, even though they could not say so, and that they would have liked to have asked the same questions as we did.

'Hey,' I said to Carl, 'I forgot to look at his fingers.'

'So did I.'

This was a reference to the story that, when Kádár had been arrested in 1949 in one of Rákosi's Stalinist purges, he had been tortured and all his finger-nails pulled out. It was probably an apocryphal story, although it was known that Kádár had been in jail for several months and been subjected to the full rigours of Communist interrogation. For that reason he was always more acceptable to non-Communist Hungarians – the vast majority – than most of the other party leaders. He was an enigma because at one point he appeared to side with Imre Nagy and the revolutionaries, being briefly a member of Nagy's cabinet. Then he disappeared for several days at the crucial period when the Russians were planning their counter-attack, re-emerging as the Russian's new man and Nagy's replacement. Ever since, Hungarians have argued over whether he was a traitor or a rather shop-soiled saviour.

In the summer of 1958, two important events occurred. Eleanor and I were married – and Nikita Khrushchev, first Secretary of the Soviet Communist Party and Stalin's debunker, came to Hungary for the first time since 1956. Carl and I were both asked for extensive coverage and, beyond the obvious angles of where he would go and what he would say, we were interested to see the response of ordinary Hungarians to the man who had ordered the crushing of their Revolution. Khrushchev's first major trip outside Budapest was to the town of Stalinvaros, Stalin City (since renamed). Carl, Ilona and I set off in my car on the hundred-mile drive, arriving in good time at the huge steel works. The entire workforce was paraded outside the main building, and in due course the short, squat figure of Khrushchev appeared on the platform, draped in red and hung with the Soviet and Hungarian flags and banners that proclaimed 'undying friendship' between the two countries. There must have been two or three thousand people there, including dozens of security men, Russian and Hungarian. We were closely scrutinised, but to our surprise no one told us to go away. Khrushchev started to speak around eleven, and Ilona did a running translation. She had the advantage of speaking Russian, so she was able to listen first to Khrushchev and then to the interpreter.

Halfway through the speech, Khrushchev seemed to depart from his set text. His face became red with anger and he gripped the podium as if he would like to strangle it.

'Let me give you a warning,' he cried. 'If ever you have another crisis, like the business in 1956, don't expect the Soviet Union to come to your help. If you expect that, you will be wrong. The next time, you'll have to get yourselves out of your own mess.'

Not a murmur from the crowd. They stood there like so many dummies. This was straight talking, a far cry from the usual mealy-mouthed protestations of proletarian solidarity. Khrushchev did not take off his shoe and bang it on the table as on the celebrated occasion at the UN, but his tone and manner were the same.

After the speech we went back over the translation with Ilona, checking every word. Carl and I had both written down what she had said and we cross-checked our versions as well. We both knew instinctively that there would be trouble over this quote, and we wanted to be absolutely sure we had it right. I drove at speed to Budapest and we sent off our opening paragraphs as soon as we reached our separate offices on the fourth floor of the Duna.

London sent my story straight back, marked priority, a sign that they considered it of unusual interest. The Vienna correspondents jumped on it and incorporated our material into their own reports as usual without acknowledgement. That evening, Carl and I scrutinised the MTI (Hungarian news agency) version of the speech with special care. Not for the first time, their account bore little relation to what we had just heard. The whole passage about the Hungarians having to sort out their own mess in future was not just watered down, it was hardly recognisable as the same speech.

Next morning, all the serious British and American papers, and scores of others all over the world, printed our story prominently. At noon, the Hungarians denied that Khrushchev had ever said it. We stuck to our guns. He had said it. We had been there. Now, our presence at Stalinvaros was undoubtedly a surprise to the Communist authorities. We had not been officially told about the trip, and of course we had not been invited. Khrushchev, if he thought about it at all, would have presumed that he was speaking to a purely Communist audience. He could say what he liked, off the cuff, and it would be edited afterwards. But someone had slipped up. They had forgotten about Reuters and AP. The Hungarian Foreign Ministry's Press Department was angry, particularly when we rejected their denial. They started planning their revenge then, although they would not execute it until later.

Shortly after the Stalinvaros incident, Khrushchev was due to speak at another big industrial plant, the big Iron and Steel Works on Csepel Island in the Danube, in the southern part of the city. This time Carl and I took Laci with us. Csepel had been one of the strongholds of the Revolution and its workers had been behind Nagy almost to a man. But now, with the ringleaders of the revolutionary committee long ago rounded up and either shot or sentenced to heavy prison terms, that was all in the past, a bad dream. At least that was what Carl and I thought, as we made our way through the shabby, joyless back streets to the main gate of the works. There we were stopped, scores of uniformed and plain clothes police barring the way. We took up position about a hundred yards from the main gate and waited. Khrushchev and his party, we knew, were inside. About half an hour later, the factory hooter sounded and men started to come off shift. At the same time, someone started to talk over the loudspeaker in Hungarian, announcing that Khrushchev was visiting the plant and was about to address the comrades. A pause, a crackle, and then the ringing, irascible tones of the Soviet boss came over the loudspeakers, so clear that even we, two or three hundred yards away from the speaker, could hear every word. Laci translated. This time, the speech held no verbal surprises, but something much more unexpected now took place.

Clearly Khrushchev's speech had been timed to coincide with the end of the day shift and the workers must have been told they were expected to stay and listen. But they did not do so, quite the opposite, and since they could not heckle Khrushchev, they voted with their feet. As we stood there, they came towards us, a trickle at first, then a steady steam, and then, as the bulk of the shift clocked off, a veritable flood of Hungarian steel men marching through the main gate, ignoring the Russian voice booming in their ears. Mostly, they walked in silence, faces set, heads high, conscious that they were in the public eye, almost like an army on parade.

This remarkable exodus lasted for ten or fifteen minutes and then it was over and the gates closed. Khrushchev was still speaking, but hardly anyone was listening.

Carl and I looked at each other. We were both thinking the same thing. It was as clear a demonstration as you would ever get that, two years after the Revolution, the Csepel Iron and Steel workers had not changed their political views and that they were still prepared to demonstrate their opposition to the régime, even in front of Khrushchev. It also showed that the Communist authorities were powerless to stop the demonstration, angry as they must have been. We rushed off and filed our stories. Mine started: 'Workers in one of Budapest's biggest industrial plants, the Csepel Iron and Steel Works, turned their backs on Nikita Khrushchev, the Soviet Communist Party leader today, walking out while he made a speech . . . ' This time there was no denial from the Foreign Ministry, but they did not like it. It all went into the dossier, they would not forget.

In the late summer of 1958, I was the only Western correspondent in Hungary. Carl and his family had gone on holiday, and Kurt Neubauer, the UPI man, was also away. Eleanor and I had dined quietly and gone to bed about midnight. We were both fast asleep when someone started hammering on the door. I sat up in bed and inquired crossly who was there.

'Telefon,' a familiar voice said. 'London.'

I got up, switched the light on and opened the door a crack. It was the night porter.

'Schnell, Herr Gall,' he said. 'London am Telefon, unten.'

I put on a dressing gown and went down in the lift with him. At that time of night the switchboard was unmanned and I had to take the call at the desk in the lobby. It was Reuters – as I had suspected. The night editor from Central Desk was on the line.

'Sorry to wake you up,' he said. 'Moscow Radio has just announced that Imre Nagy has been executed.'

I was almost speechless.

'Nagy,' I stammered. 'Nothing's been announced here.'

'We got it from Green End ten minutes ago,' he added. Green End was the monitoring station that Reuters shared with the BBC. 'Moscow Radio, quoting MTI, says that after a full trial Nagy was sentenced to death for treason. The sentence has already been carried out.'

The chilling words buzzed in my sleepy brain. I tried to pull myself together.

'Quoting MTI? But I picked up the MTI file last thing last night and there was nothing in it at all.'

'Well,' he said. 'You had better chase it up.'

Back in my room I dressed feverishly, still unable to grasp

91

the enormity of the news. There had long been rumours that Nagy had been brought back from Rumania, and secretly put on trial. Some said he was being held in the Fö Utca, the grim, old-fashioned prison on the street of that name just over the river in Buda. I used to pass it regularly on my way to MTI, and it always gave me the creeps. But I had seen nothing to alert me and there had never been any confirmation, not even from the Western diplomatic corps, who usually picked up a whisper of something like that.

I dialled the Boros home and got Laci. He said he would get dressed immediately and I agreed to pick him up in fifteen minutes. I drove down over the Danube and up into Buda. Laci was waiting for me, his face shuttered.

'I can't believe it,' he said. 'We heard nothing at all about it.' We drove in silence to MTI. The lights were blazing and there was an unusual amount of activity. We asked for the material in the Reuters pigeonhole. There was nothing there. The Nagy material, we said, where is it? The man behind the desk muttered in embarrassment and disappeared. Five minutes later, one of the senior editors, a man I liked, called Remenyi, appeared with a sheaf of papers in his hand. He handed them over. It was the Nagy communiqué, twenty or thirty pages of it.

At the top of the first page, underlined in heavy black type, it said: 'Embargoed. Not to be published or broadcast before midnight . . . '

'What happened?' I asked. 'Why did Moscow Radio get the story and not Reuters?'

Remenyi was embarrassed. Lowering his voice he said: 'It was made available only to friendly Socialist news agencies, last night. We were told not to give it to you. I'm sorry.' In other words, it was not his but a top-level government decision. Whatever the reasons, the effect was the opposite of what they desired. By withholding it from Reuters, the only Western agency represented in Hungary that night, they ensured that the world heard the news first from Moscow Radio, with the inevitable suggestion that the Russians, however much they denied it, had tried and executed Nagy. Their propaganda had backfired.

But these were points that could be debated later. It was now after three. Laci and I drove back through the still, dark, deserted streets to the Duna and went to work. While I organised some coffee, Laci raced through the long turgid rigmarole of the trial. The point came on about page twenty. Nagy, after a full hearing, it said, had been found guilty of treason and sentenced to death. The death sentence had already been carried out. That chilling phrase again. It did not say where or when. It had been a shabby business from the start, and it had finished in the same mean, vindictive way. A secret trial. Legalised murder, I thought, but I could not say it. Reuters was an objective organisation. A few minutes later, my teleprinter chattered into life and I started to file the story. It was substantially the same as the Moscow Radio story and four hours behind. Too late for the morning papers but in time for the evenings, and for every radio station in the civilised world.

After filing the complete story, I had an early breakfast and went for a walk through the city. People were going to work in the normal way. I studied their faces, searching for some emotion – anger, grief, despair. Nothing. The Hungarians displayed the same watchful, non-committal expression that had become second nature. I returned to my typewriter to report – that there was nothing to report. Of course it would have been silly to expect anything else. There was nothing the Hungarians could do. The repression that followed the Revolution had been thorough. The best and the bravest had left, or been arrested, like Nagy. The others were cowed into submission. And they knew that Nagy could only finish a dead man. For not only had he defied the system and tried to take Hungary out of it. Not only had he preferred Western democracy to Eastern totalitarianism. Not only had he requested the Soviet Union to remove its fraternal, peace-loving troops, the true friends of the Hungarian workers and peasants, from Hungarian soil. All that was enough to merit a thousand deaths. But – and here was his supreme crime – he had done all this despite being a member of the Communist Party. He was, in the deepest and most painful sense, a traitor to the cause. As such, they pursued him with the same ruthlessness as Torquemada pursued the victims of the Spanish Inquisition.

After it was all over, the rumour-mongers were quick to say that they had known all along that Nagy was in the Fö Utca. But very few details ever came out. One story I heard from several sources, and which I believed, was that Nagy had protested his innocence to the end, resisting every attempt to make him 'confess'. That would certainly have been in character.

A month or two later, the blow fell. Carl and I were summoned to the Foreign Ministry and told that for various 'administrative reasons' changes were being made in the arrangements for interpreters. From now on, they would have to be registered with the Foreign Ministry. Carl and I both knew what they meant. They would provide us with an interpreter they wanted rather than one we wanted. Laci and Ilona were both pro-Western and anti-Communist. Their inside knowledge of what was really happening in Hungary – as opposed to what the Government claimed was happening – was as invaluable to us as it must have been infuriating to the Government. There was nothing new about that, but something had made them decide to act, and Carl and I both thought it must have been Ilona's translation of Khrushchev's speech at Stalinvaros. That was the last straw.

Shortly after our visit to the Foreign Ministry, Laci and Ilona were told that they were not going to be registered. And, if they were not registered, they could not work for us. Again, it did not come as much of a surprise, but both Carl and I tried to fight it. We protested to Gyaros, as head of the Foreign Ministry's Press Department, and to anyone else who would listen, but we both knew it was hopeless. The order had obviously come down from on high and was, ultimately, a Communist Party-cum-Interior Ministry decision. Laci and Ilona, with their much finer 'feel' for the workings of the system, urged us not to protest any more: it would be counter-productive if not actually dangerous. How right they were. Shortly afterwards, Laci was summoned to the Interior Ministry and told that, again for administrative reasons, he would have to leave Budapest and report to the police in a remote village on the Rumanian border. He had fourteen days to make arrangements.

Naturally, he was completely stunned. He had expected to lose his job, but to be exiled to the middle of the *puszta* was a terrible shock for both of them. What would he do when he got there, he asked. Report to the cooperative farm: they would tell him what to do. There was no question of refusing to comply – that would have brought down on himself the full weight of the system. This was a relatively mild measure to teach him a lesson. So Laci packed up and departed for the cooperative farm, leaving a distraught Ilona in tears in Budapest. She too was out of a job and she had a flat and a baby to look after.

She came to see me for the last time, very depressed and frightened. She did not want any help – Carl was paying Laci a pension – and she asked me not to try and keep in touch. It was better, she felt, to make a complete break, sever the Western connection which had brought them to grief, and try to make a new life for herself. We only heard occasional reports after that from Laci's mother, and it was nearly always bad news. Conditions in the village were extremely primitive, there was no intellectual stimulus of any kind, and Laci's eyesight had deteriorated alarmingly. A year or so later, after both Carl and I had left Hungary, we heard that Laci had been able to return to Budapest where he eventually got a job in a publishing house. Then Ilona, who was in her late thirties, suddenly died. I felt a tremendous sense of loss and guilt. She and Laci had both suffered because of us. We had made them translate the awkward questions to the Hungarian officials, exposing them at press conferences in front of everyone as servants of the Western press, often a term of abuse in a place like Hungary. We had taken them with us to Stalinvaros and to the Csepel Iron and Steel Works; we took them with us to the Ministry of Justice in the Fö Utca to check on political trials – two and a half years after the end of the Revolution, there were still up to a hundred people a week before the courts on 'counter-Revolutionary' charges – and their association with us finally branded them in the eyes of the Hungarian régime as enemies and traitors. Both Laci and Ilona paid the penalty. It did not endear me very much to the theory of class hatred that Marxism preaches. If that was 'democratic socialism', I did not want any part of it. How lucky, I was, I thought, to be a British subject, and how little most of my companions knew about what went on behind the Iron Curtain.

Most foreign visitors to Hungary – not that there were many – stayed at the Duna and I met most of them. Very often we would make one another's acquaintance over a glass of the dreadful *baracsk* in the tiny bar, squeezed in between one or two of the 'girls' who were allowed to operate as part of the service to foreign businessmen. Being a fellow resident, I knew most of the girls, but luckily was never obliged to sample their charms, although one or two like Judith, a dark-haired gipsy-looking girl, were particularly friendly. But we all knew that they were licensed by the AVO and had to report the names of their customers to the secret police, who were always looking for a suitable blackmail victim among the Western businessmen.

One day a small group arrived from the British Aircraft Corporation. We met in the hotel and had dinner together and became, for the space of two or three days, friends. One night rather late, in the bar, one of them, called Geoffrey, said to me: 'Sandy, I have a friend here, used to be in the Air Force, now in Malev [the Hungarian airline]. Nice chap. Seems he's in a spot of trouble and might even want to leave the country. I have taken the liberty of giving him your name. I hope you don't mind? Just in case he wants to get in touch.' This is what is known as a *fait accompli* and all I could say, rather reluctantly, was: 'Oh no, that's all right.'

Weeks went by and I had pretty well forgotten the incident when one day the 'phone rang in my office. 'There's a Hungarian gentleman on the line for you,' the operator said.

'Mr. Gall,' the unknown voice said. 'I'm a friend of Geoffrey's. I wondered if I might see you?'

I could hear the whir of the machine recording our conversation.

'You want to come to the Duna?' I asked.

'No,' the man said. 'Could we meet at the . . . ?' He mentioned a big café in the centre of Budapest.

'All right, when?'

'Tomorrow, at four?'

Damn, I thought, as I rang off, that bloody Geoffrey has lumbered me with this ruddy Hungarian who wants to defect. That's the last thing I need. For I had a nasty feeling that this man could cause me a lot of trouble.

Next day I walked to the café, feeling slightly nervous. It was very large, on two levels, and fairly full. I looked for the man I had come to meet. He said he would be reading a copy of an Austrian newspaper and I soon spotted him. We introduced ourselves and I ordered a coffee. He had the frank, open good looks of a fighter pilot, which he had been, although he now was, I reckoned, around forty. He was well dressed by Hungarian standards, in a Western suit and heavy overcoat. As we spoke, he kept glancing nervously around. Geoffrey had told me that Peter, as I shall call him, had been the golden boy of the Hungarian Air Force, their youngest fighter pilot and the protégé of Marshal Zhukov, hero of Stalingrad and Soviet Minister of Defence from 1955 to 1957. Peter had gone on to become head of the Hungarian Air Force, and then in 1956, during the Revolution, he had fallen from grace. Without openly backing the wrong side, he had shown himself unreliable, too sympathetic to the revolutionaries, and he had been sacked. Now he was deputy head of Malev, but still suspect and unhappy.

'In what way?' I asked.

He gestured nervously.

'They follow me all the time,' he said. 'Last night, I went out with my family and they followed us, two cars right behind us, so close I could not help seeing them. What are they trying to do?' He seemed to be extremely shaken by the experience.

Suddenly I spotted him. The tail. He was a big man in the long brown leather coat which was regulation wear for the AVO. He came in, not looking at us, and sat down about three tables away.

'I think we have a friend with us,' I said. 'Over there.'
Peter nodded without turning his head.

'Yes,' he said, 'they follow me all the time now. That's
why I want to leave the country.'

'I see, and your family?'

He looked uncomfortable. 'They will have to stay for the
time being. Maybe they can come on later.' I thought that
was highly unlikely but did not say so.

The AVO tail sat at his table, not looking in our direction
and too far away to overhear our conversation, but keeping
us under observation.

Peter leaned forward. 'Please,' he said. 'I need your help. I
can't go to the British Legation. It is too dangerous. They
would guess what I was going to do and arrest me. But you
could find out certain things for me.'

'What?' I asked.

'Would the British accept me? Would they guarantee to let
me in and allow me to stay?'

'I don't know,' I said. 'Maybe I can find out.' I did not
want to become involved. My natural inclination was to be
cautious, to shy away. I looked at the man opposite me. He
was likeable. He was almost certainly sincere. In a place like
Hungary you always have doubts about everyone, in case he
is setting a trap for you, but Peter had to be genuine. And I
was sorry for him. I tried to put myself in his place. He felt in
danger, he wanted to defect to the West. Did I not have a
duty, as a human being, to help him? Professionally, of
course, I knew the answer should be no. I could not use the
story either now or later, for Reuters would fire me if they
knew I was mixed up in the defection of a former head of the
Hungarian Air Force. Especially if it went wrong and exposed
them to retaliation from the Hungarians. But I felt the issues
were bigger than my professional career, bigger even than
Reuters' reputation. One man was appealing to another
across the abyss and he was saying: 'Save me. Help. Give me
your hand.' If I refused and withdrew my hand, would it not
be on my conscience for the rest of my life? That I had
spurned an appeal for help from a fellow human in his hour
of need?

Reluctantly I decided I had to help Peter.

'All right,' I said. 'I will ask my British friends and let you know what they say.'

He smiled, I think, for the first time. 'Thank you,' he said. 'I am very grateful.'

'Don't ring me at the Duna,' I instructed him. 'I'll meet you here at the same time a week from today.'

I left first and, on the way back to the Duna, I tried to see if the AVO man was following me, but I could not spot him and I concluded that he was probably tailing Peter. Still, he would report that Peter had met a foreigner, and it would be easy for them to find out who I was, if they did not know already. I felt just a little bit scared. But I was committed now.

A couple of days later I talked to a friend in the Legation about Peter and he directed me to another friend, who handled these matters.

I told him the story, adding: 'I think he really wants to be sure that we would give him political asylum. He doesn't want to defect and then find out that we won't let him into Britain.'

'That's very understandable,' my friend said. 'Personally, I wouldn't have thought there would be any difficulty, but I will ask London and let you know as soon as I have their reply. By the way, how does your chum intend to carry out his, ah, plan?'

'He often goes abroad on official trips. He'll wait until a suitable opportunity presents itself.' This meant in effect a trip to a Western or at least neutral country.

'All right, when you next see your chum, tell him that when he's ready to make his move, he should go to the British Embassy in whatever country he's in, tell them who he is, that he's been in touch with us here and that his case is on file in London. He'll have to wait until they check with London, which will be a mere formality, and then they'll arrange to have him flown out.'

'For debriefing.'

My friend smiled. 'He'll have to go through the normal processing, but he'll understand about that. I'll let you know as soon as I have word from London.'

A couple of days later, he had the answer. It was an unequivocal yes. So, a week after our first meeting, I walked for the second time from the Duna across to Vörösmarty Square. The café was as usual full of talkative Hungarian hausfraus, drinking coffee and eating cakes. Peter sat at a table by himself, apparently deep in the afternoon paper. He looked more distraught than at our first meeting. My eyes wandered round the room, searching for the usual AVO tail, but I could not identify him. I had no doubt, however, that he was there, somewhere.

'Have you talked to the British?' Peter asked anxiously.

I nodded. 'Yes, and they say it is all arranged. Now listen,' I tried not to look conspiratorial but it was difficult to pretend that we were merely having a casual conversation about girl friends. Peter leaned forward, his pale blue fighter-pilot eyes on mine.

'This is what you have to do. When you arrive in a Western capital, whichever one it may be, you slip away when you have the chance and go to the British Embassy. You ask to see one of the diplomats and you tell them who you are. You say you have been in contact with the Legation here, in Budapest, and that London has been informed. Then you wait while they check with London. They may be able to give you an answer straightaway, or you might have to go back next day. Once they have the message from London, they'll take care of everything.'

He still looked worried. His mind was searching for holes in the scheme. Finally he accepted it.

'All right,' he said. 'Thank you, thank you.'

'Have you any idea when you might go abroad?' I asked.

Peter shrugged. 'Maybe in a month or two with a delegation. They don't give you much warning.'

'Well, good luck, if you finally decide to go.'

'I must,' he said. 'It gets worse every day. They tap my telephone, they follow me all the time, usually two cars. They wait outside my house . . . ' He had the hunted look of the man who is near the end of his tether.

There was no more to be said. We both got up and shook hands. It was the last time I saw him. Shortly afterwards I went to Geneva to join the Reuters team covering the Foreign Ministers' conference on European security. Eleanor followed with our new baby, Fiona, and later we all went home to Scotland on holiday. It was autumn before I was back in Budapest. One day, shortly after my return, I ran into the man in the legation whom I had consulted about Peter.

'Did you hear about your friend Peter?' he asked. I shook my head.

'Well, he did defect. In Rome. It all went according to plan. He contacted the Embassy and they relayed word to London, who gave the okay, and that was that.'

'Oh,' I said. 'Well, I'm glad for him.' I felt quite excited. My friend gave me an odd look. 'But you haven't heard the end of the story. After a few weeks he decided he didn't want to stay, so he came back to Budapest.'

I was amazed and startled. 'You mean he's back here now? Why on earth did he do that?'

My friend shrugged. 'Apparently he's a pretty neurotic character. Having taken the plunge he changed his mind. He missed his family and friends, and decided his place was here in Hungary.'

I was completely flummoxed. Nothing Peter had said suggested in any way that he was in two minds about wanting to leave Hungary and live in the West. However, I did know that Hungarians are particularly attached to their homeland, maybe more than most races. Perhaps their curious language which is unlike any other and their history sets them apart. Many Hungarians who fled abroad during the Revolution found it extremely difficult to adjust to life in the West.

I asked what had happened to him, whether he had been arrested. After all a man with Peter's background does not just defect to the West and then change his mind and come home again and carry on as if nothing had happened. But my friend said he had not heard.

I walked back to the hotel in a sombre frame of mind. Undoubtedly Peter would have been debriefed by the AVO when he came back, and it would be very strange if my name had not been mentioned as the go-between. Even if Peter left me out of it, his AVO tail must surely have reported our meetings, so they would know about me anyway. Here surely was the perfect opportunity for the blackmail which was part of the AVO's stock-in-trade. There was nothing they liked more than information on what was going on inside a Western Legation. No doubt the risk of this happening was the reason the Legation had not allowed Eleanor to keep on working there after we married – a decision she resented very much and which made life more difficult in the early days of our marriage, but which was understandable.

Then I thought of what had happened to Kurt Neubauer, our UPI colleague. Kurt, an Austrian, was a slightly sinister figure, tall and dark with a scar across his cheek, a relic of his days in the Hitler Youth Werewolves. Kurt was accident-prone. He was also very susceptible to feminine charm. His first brush with the secret police came when a Hungarian 'friend', a local journalist, asked him if he would buy him a radio the next time he was in Vienna, Western radios being unobtainable in Hungary. Kurt agreed. The journalist would pay him in local currency. Kurt duly bought the radio and was handing it over to his friend, showing him how it worked, when the police burst into his flat and arrested both of them. Kurt was accused of illegal currency transactions. Kurt denied it but the journalist, whether he was in the plot from the start or to save his own skin, turned state evidence. Enter AVO Colonel. He was a very smooth operator, who spoke good German and English, Kurt said. What he wanted was very simple. The currency charges would be dropped, provided Kurt was cooperative. What did that mean? Well, nothing very much, just a bit of information about what was going on in the American Legation. For example, who was the CIA representative? What was the precise lay-out of the Legation, and so on.

Kurt said he had no idea who the CIA man was, and that he only knew the ground floor plan of the Legation. But sensibly he played for time. He did not want to be sentenced to a couple of years in a Hungarian jail.

However, the next time he was in Vienna he went to the American Embassy and told them the whole story. They flew down a CIA man from Germany who made sketches of the Colonel, under Kurt's guidance, until he had an almost exact likeness.

'We know him,' the CIA man then said. 'He calls himself so-and-so and he often visits West Germany, posing as a businessman. We've suspected him for some time.' So far so good, but for some reason the Legation in Budapest was upset, Kurt said, about the incident. At least the next time he joined the queue for the Legation cinema, which you entered through a side door, the American on duty barred the way and said Kurt could not come in: he was not a member of the Legation staff. Kurt remonstrated that he had often been before, but the man refused to let him in. Kurt left in some embarrassment, to the enjoyment of the regular AVO plain-clothesmen, and convinced it was all because of the business with the AVO Colonel.

About this time, Kurt met, became engaged to and then quickly married a stunning twenty-year-old Hungarian blonde. She was a violin student at the Academy of Music, but spoke almost no English or German. Kurt, I presumed, communicated basically by sign language. I thought Maria was quite the most beautiful Hungarian girl I had ever seen, but I was equally convinced she saw in Kurt merely a passport to the West.

The AVO Colonel, of course, soon knew all about the forthcoming marriage and proceeded to use the happy event to turn the screw. Kurt had a passion for photographing girls in the nude and he had persuaded the lovely Maria to pose for him. Somehow the AVO found out about this, raided Kurt's flat one night and stole the pictures. Now, the Colonel said, unless Kurt could do a little better with his information about the CIA set-up in the Legation, those pictures would be on sale outside the church when the happy couple emerged from their nuptials.

'What did that mean?' I asked, 'on sale outside the church?'

'Well,' Kurt said, 'one of the Colonel's men would be standing on the pavement as the bride's parents and everyone else came out of the church, touting a selection of portraits of

Maria in her birthday suit.' I did not go to the wedding, but apparently the threat was not carried out. The last encounter between Kurt and the Colonel occurred near the Austrian border, in a hut, when the Colonel threatened Kurt with a revolver. Somehow Kurt extricated himself. But after that he remained in Vienna, where alas, after a predictably short time, the beautiful Maria, now an Austrian citizen, deserted him.

All this went through my mind as I contemplated the results of Peter's redefection. For the next week or so I waited for the summons to the Interior Ministry, the knock on my door and the entry of the Colonel, or merely the expulsion order. I decided that, if there was any attempt at blackmail, I would immediately refuse. I went about my work with a strange queasy feeling but, to my amazement, nothing happened. Perhaps Peter loyally had kept my name out of it, and possibly the AVO were much less efficient than I thought. At any rate, I left Hungary a couple of months later scot free, although I expected a hand on my shoulder right up to the last minute.

I did not really feel safe until my plane touched down in Vienna. I took a taxi to the Hotel Bristol, where Eleanor and I always stayed, went straight to the American Bar and ordered a champagne cocktail. To arrive in Vienna from the grim, prison-like atmosphere of Hungary always made me feel deliriously happy. It was like having your birthday, the first day of spring and falling in love, all rolled into one.

CHAPTER IV

Johannesburg and the Congo: Mutiny in Léopoldville and Arrest at Bakwanga

We spent the next six months in a basement flat in Chelsea –
living in London certainly showed up Reuters pay for the
pittance it was. I worked on the Central Desk and, after a
refresher course in Reuters style, spent most of my time
writing 'night leads', summaries of major stories for the
morning papers, alongside Hubert Nicholson, a bearded
veteran who could fashion these two- or three-page items with
enviable ease and speed. I also took my turn on the overnight
'trick' under Trevor 'Digger' Blore, a wartime Merchant
Navy captain with a stentorian voice and the proverbial heart
of gold. This was really a killing shift, although Digger did it
regularly and seemed to enjoy it. We would come in at eleven
and, after 'reading in' all the copy that had been sent out by
Central Desk in the past twenty-four hours, sub-edit or
rewrite the flow of new stories breaking then, as well as
preparing 'dayleads' for the evening papers.

Soon after I started I was summoned to see Tony Cole,
who was by now General Manager. There was a small matter
of a few hundred pounds outstanding on my Budapest

accounts which I felt Reuters should pay but which they considered was my responsibility. After our marriage Eleanor and I had been forced to take another room in the Duna – we could not possibly manage in the single room-cum-office which had been my home until then. That of course doubled my expenditure and I had run into debt.

Cole made me sit down beside him on the sofa. As he was a very large man, his end of the sofa sank under his weight, while I was hoisted up at the other end as if on a see-saw. We then went through the argument, Cole taking the line that Reuters was not responsible for my matrimonial impulses, and I retorting that it was not my fault I was obliged to live in a hotel at inflated prices because the Communist authorities would not let me live in a flat.

The figure at issue was £1,500, which represented a year's imbalance.

'All right,' Cole said, 'you want us to write off £1,000?' As he spoke he suddenly shifted his great bulk across the sofa as if he were going to squash me.

'No,' I said, edging away but not giving in. '£1,500, Mr. Cole.'

He glared at me. 'All right. £1,500, we'll wipe the slate clean this time, but don't let it happen again.'

I got thankfully to my feet and beat a hasty retreat, wondering if the sofa trick was one of his negotiating ploys, a veiled threat of physical force, or simply the reflex action of a tough customer when thwarted. After all, he need not have made me sit on the sofa beside him. Perhaps he was testing me out.

Reuters had said they wanted me to spend about six months on the desk but that nothing was planned after that. Then, at the end of March 1960, South African police opened fire on a crowd of Africans at Sharpeville, a mining town not far from Johannesburg, killing 67 and wounding 186. That set the wires humming in Reuters and everywhere else and made headlines around the world. The results were electrifying. The bottom fell out of South African shares on the London Stock Exchange, there was a rush to move money out of South Africa and there was talk of a bloodbath and civil war between black and white. Reuters had had no full-time correspondent in South Africa since Astley Hawkins died, but a young reporter called Nigel Ryan, who was en route to an assignment in the Congo, was hastily diverted. He was too late for Sharpeville but moved on to Cape Town where fierce rioting had broken out in Langa and Nyanga townships and the police were indulging in further shooting.

Sharpeville was one of those occasions when popular feeling and official stupidity combine to produce an explosion. The day had begun with demonstrations which started peacefully enough. But the situation became tense and the police, who were outnumbered, panicked. Some of the young, untried constables opened fire without orders. Very often in these cases it is the word of the police against that of the demonstrators, but at Sharpeville Ian Berry, a gifted young British photographer, then working for *Drum Magazine,* happened to be present. Lying flat on the ground as the bullets whisled over his head, he recorded the whole incident in a brilliant series of pictures: the police opening fire, the Africans – men, women and children – fleeing in terror, and the dead.

Normally, this would have been the kind of story at which Reuters excelled, but Sharpeville was a disaster for Reuters as well as for the South African Government. Our reporting of Sharpeville came exclusively from SAPA, the South African Press Association, which had become so subservient to the government that it had proved incapable of putting out a factual account of events. In fact, so glaringly obvious was this that the BBC, which had its own man in South Africa, threatened to cancel its lucrative contract unless Reuters took prompt action. In other words, we would not only have to send out a full-time correspondent to provide accurate and impartial day-to-day reporting, but we would have to re-organise the SAPA connection as well. This was not going to be easy and, I was told later, several people turned down the job. When they came to me, I jumped at the idea. I was already fed up with living in a basement in London, on a paltry wage, but apart from that I have never turned down an assignment in my life.

I was to go out immediately, and Eleanor and our second baby, due to be born in June, would follow later. I was again summoned to the presence of Walton A. Cole. This time he was all smiles and I was not asked to sit on the sofa. Doon Campbell, now the Editor, was in attendance. Cole was jovial and flattering, saying at one point, 'Sandy, after all, you are one of us, ole boy, isn't that right, Doon?'

He explained briefly the Reuters-SAPA arrangement and how it had foundered, but without going into much detail. He was determined, however, that the Reuters service out of South Africa, which had already been improved, would never again be allowed to become the creature of the South African Government's propaganda machine.

There remained the question of money. Cole spoke generously.

'Sandy, I want you to do everything properly. You'll need a house, and a car, that sort of thing . . . '

'What about an allowance?' I asked.

'Don't worry about the money now, ole boy,' Cole said. 'We'll fix all that later. The important thing is to get you out there as fast as possible. We'll send your family out in due course. We'll be generous, don't worry about that, ole boy. Good luck and keep in touch.'

It was the classic send-off and the last as it happened. I was ushered out, Doon Campbell holding me under the arm with his black-gloved hand, giving me final instructions as we walked down the corridor.

I did not quite know what to expect at the other end – a sort of white man's Kenya, I imagined, bigger, richer, and now, people were saying, poised on the lip of the volcano.

I got my jabs for yellow fever and cholera, bought a couple of new suits, packed my kilt and my swimming trunks and collected my travellers' cheques from accounts. Equipped, I hoped, for every eventuality, I boarded a BOAC flight to Tripoli, Nairobi and Johannesburg. It was a much longer haul in those days and I had plenty of time to reflect on the difficulties of the assignment that faced me. For the first time in my short career I would have to be more than a reporter – I would have to be a diplomat as well. Although my first priority was to ensure the accuracy of the file coming out of South Africa, Reuters did not want to lose the SAPA connection. After all, SAPA was part of the Reuters story in Africa that went back to Rhodes and the days of Lord Milner's Kindergarten before the Boer War. It was a Reuters man – one of three white men – who accompanied Rhodes to the famous meeting with Chief Lobengula, which ended the Matabele Rebellion and laid the foundations for the state of Rhodesia. Reuters was first with the Relief of Mafeking, and it was the fortunes to be made from gold and diamonds that attracted the young Roderick Jones, Reuters correspondent after the Boer War. He built up the investment there which allowed him later to buy Reuters. It was, however, an anachronism that a British organisation should control South Africa's national news agency, and in 1938 Reuters had turned over its journalistic empire to the South African Press Association, formed under Reuters' auspices and embodying its ideals.

Apart from the commercial service, Comtel, which remained separate, SAPA had become synonomous with Reuters in South Africa, until Sharpeville that is. After that SAPA was a dirty word. The Reuters bosses, and in particular, Patrick Cross, were very tough with the Editor of SAPA, David Friedman, and the General Manager, Wilson. Patrick had told them, with the combination of devastating directness and politeness of which he was a master, that their story file was abysmally inferior in quality, and unacceptably biased politically: in short, a disgrace to the Reuters name. He arranged that a former Reuters and *Daily Mail* correspondent, Alan Humphries, who had emigrated to South Africa and joined SAPA, should be put in charge of the Reuters file on a nine-to-five basis. But Alan was only able to do a re-write job. The real reporting job, which meant getting our own untainted account of events, would fall to me. I would have to look at South Africa, I told myself, with as sceptical and critical an eye as I had applied to Hungary. A journalist, as an observer, has to be an outsider looking in and, once he loses that sort of independence, once he becomes, even slightly, part of the Establishment, he is in danger of losing his credibility. The art is to remain sufficiently on the inside to be well-informed and yet sufficiently apart to be able to take a detached view. It was quite clear to Reuters – and to me after a short time – that SAPA was no longer a free agent and the service would have to be treated with the same scepticism as any other government-controlled organ.

One could understand the pressures that brought about the politicising of SAPA, even if one could not condone them. The real trouble was that for years South African politics had been dominated by one party, the Afrikaner National Party, or Nats as they were called. White South Africans, whether Nats or not, felt misunderstood by the rest of the world, isolated, embattled even. Everything turned on colour, every political argument started there and finished there. Colour was the inescapable and only real issue. For example, anyone suggesting that black men should have equal rights with white men was automatically considered to be a Communist and, if he were a South African, a traitor as well. In the demonology of National South Africa, nearly all British and American journalists were crypto-Communists, bent on the overthrow of 'white civilisation' in South Africa. They were the enemy and, as such, had to be treated with great circumspection, if at all. Luckily, the English-language Press in South Africa was both healthy and healthily dependent and so, unlike Hungary, where there was no overt Opposition, it was easy to get an alternative point of view. In Parliament there was a small but active Progressive Party, of which Mrs Helen Suzman was the chief adornment, but when it came to African opinion, only the Opposition English-language papers showed any real inclination to discover it and report it.

In retrospect, it was probably an advantage to me that the bosses of SAPA cold-shouldered me so effectively when I arrived in Johannesburg. In my first three months David Friedman hardly spoke to me, let alone invited me to have a drink or a meal with him. Neither he nor Wilson showed the slightest sign of wishing to be friendly. They could not afford to ignore the wishes of Reuters in London, but they could and did ignore me. If they had showered me with kindness they might have suborned me but, by deliberately cutting me, they forced me to go elsewhere for friendship and information. I would have cultivated South African journalists anyway, but it made me do so more actively. In fact I was to infuriate SAPA by building up my own network of 'stringers' in various places like Cape Town and Durban.

I arrived in the lull that followed Sharpeville which was perhaps just as well, for another story was building up to the north – the Independence of the Belgian Congo on June 30, 1960. Nigel Ryan had flown to Léopoldville from Johannesburg and was filing alarming stories of how unprepared the country was for Independence. One statistic was on everybody's lips – there were only fourteen black graduates out of total population of fourteen million. The Congo was huge, covering half of central Africa. It stretched from the central spine of the continent – the Ruwenzori mountains and the great lakes, Albert, Edward, Kivu and Tanganyika – to the Atlantic. It was a thousand miles from east to west, and almost as far from north to south, and it contained the second longest river in Africa, the Congo. Stanley had crisscrossed it in his search for Livingstone, and it was populated by a bewildering array of savage tribes, some of them still cannibals. It was indeed darkest Africa, the 'Heart of Darkness', Conrad called it, the original for all those jokes in *Men Only* and the *New Yorker* about intrepid explorers being boiled alive in cooking-pots while naked savages danced gleefully around them.

The jokes were to turn out to be less funny, but I did not know that when I arrived in Elizabethville, capital of Katanga and the Congo's second-largest city towards the end of June. Elizabethville was a pleasant surprise, a little bit of Europe in Africa: an agreeable town with tree-lined boulevards, Belgian shops and restaurants, big houses with gardens occupied by the executives of the huge Union Minière mining company, and a pleasant-enough hotel called the Léopold Deux (Léo Deux for short) in memory of the notorious King of the Belgians who had originally acquired the Congo and run it with ferocious, indeed savage paternalism, as if it had been a medieval private estate.

But, on the eve of Independence, those harsh memories

had been put away and Elizabethville presented a smiling face to the world. There was, however, anxiety beneath the smiles and a great deal of political chicanery behind the scenes. The Congo was and is enormously wealthy in terms of minerals and the province of Katanga was the richest of all. There was uranium in the north – indeed the mine at Shinkolobwe had provided the United States with the raw material for the first atom bombs; there was cobalt and platinum, zinc and silver, but above all there were vast deposits of copper which formed the basis of the wealth both of Katanga and of Union Miniére. Many conservative Belgian businessmen, including presumably the majority of the directors of Union Minière, which in turn was owned by the huge financial house, Société Générale, felt that Independence was being conferred over-hastily. They saw their vast investment and profits directly threatened, and listened with growing concern to the angry noises emanating from the lips of Patrice Lumumba, a former post office clerk who looked certain to become the first Prime Minister of an independent Congo. Lumumba was a fiery young nationalist who could not wait to show the Belgians who was the new boss. And he was determined to get his hands on Union Minière and squeeze it dry. Or so the Belgians claimed.

It did not take me long to find out that, well before Independence, the Belgians had started scheming to take Katanga out of the Congo and declare a separate Independence. Their ally in this was the leader of the main local political party, Conakat, a wealthy African called Moïse Tshombe. His father was said to have been the first Congolese millionaire and the young Tshombe had been educated in Belgium where he had learnt European manners and fluent French. On his return he had married the daughter of the Paramount Chief of the Lunda, the main tribe in southern Katanga. It was on this tribal base that he built his political support, which in turn brought him Belgian backing.

I asked to see him and was quickly granted an interview. Journalists, especially non-Belgian ones, were then something of a rarity in Katanga. I explained that I had just arrived. The conversation went as follows.

'Monsieur Tshombe, I'm told that you're going to announce your secession from the rest of the Congo as soon as Independence is declared?'

He stared at me in disbelief, his rubbery face puckered in a frown. 'You already know a lot of things, Mr . . . ?'

'Gall,' I supplied.

He found it difficult to say. 'But who told you all that?'

I could not divulge that the British Consul was one of my sources. Tshombe refused to go into any details, but he was too honest, or naive, to deny the information. I found myself liking him. He was warm and friendly and somehow vulnerable, with his music hall black man's face and manner.

Independence in Elisabethville came and went with bands and marching, Belgian officers leading Katangese troops, and Tshombe taking the salute. Hundreds of Belgians turned out to watch the parade with their wives and children and then strolled off to have their apéritifs in one of the cafés in the centre of the town. We filed our stories, saying that, despite all the threatening noises, Independence, in Katanga at least, had passed off quietly.

Not so in Léopoldville, the capital, where King Baudouin was performing the ceremony. Lumumba, the Prime Minister-elect, had made a violently anti-Belgian speech, confirming all the Belgians' worst fears, and, at the end of the ceremony, as King Baudouin was driving off in his open car, a young African had snatched his sword and, brandishing it above his head, run off into the crowd.

A day or two later, things took a more ominous turn with rumbles of disaffection in the Force Publique, the para-military colonial police force, transformed overnight into the national army, the ANC. The black soldiers were said to be disobeying their white Belgian officers. Early one morning, the 'phone rang in my room at the Léo Deux and Nigel Ryan was on the line from Léopoldville, a considerable feat of communication.

'I wondered if you'd like to come up here for a few days?' he asked, as if he were inviting me to stay for the weekend.

'But I thought you had Serge with you?' Serge Nabokov was the Reuters correspondent from Brussels.

'Well, yes, but Serge is going out shooting crocodiles today and he may have to go back to Brussels tomorrow.' He spoke to someone in the room and I guessed he had Serge with him. 'When can you get here?' Nigel asked.

'Tomorrow,' I said, 'There's nothing much happening here.'

'Let me know what time you're arriving and I'll meet you,' Nigel said and rang off.

I felt very excited. Elisabethville was pleasant enough, but it was a backwater, and things seemed to be moving very fast at the other end of the country. A full-scale mutiny was now reported to be underway in the port of Matadi, in the Bas Congo, the low-lying, intensely hot and humid estuary of the Congo river that lies between Léopoldville and the Atlantic.

Next morning I caught the internal Sabena flight from Elisabethville to Léopoldville. As we came in to land at Njili airport I caught a glimpse of the capital with its shining European centre and sprawling African *cités*, more orderly than most African townships, and beyond the great expanse of the Congo River, about a mile wide at that point.

I knew Nigel Ryan only slightly. We had met briefly in London but, whereas I had done my training in Germany, he had spent several years in Rome under Patrick Cross. He was something of a 'golden boy', tall, good-looking, bright and, as was to be proved in the course of the next few days and weeks, an excellent reporter.

As we drove in from the airport in Nigel's small Volkswagen, passing several lorry-loads of Congolese troops, wearing steel helmets and clutching their rifles, driving at full speed in the opposite direction, Nigel told me what had been happening. Serge, he said, had almost had a nervous break-down and he had had to send him home. That explained the early morning telephone call.

'Did he actually go crocodile shooting?' I asked. After all, this was Africa and people did go on safari.

Nigel cocked an eyebrow at me. 'That was a joke,' he said. 'Serge was standing right next to the telephone. I had to say something.' He went on to explain that Serge had simply ceased to function. At the height of the story, at the end of the Independence Day ceremony, when the African had snatched Baudouin's sword and run off with it, Nigel had had almost to force him physically away from the telex. Insisting that he was the senior correspondent and therefore had the right to file the story. Serge had sat himself down in front of the machine. But, instead of rattling off the first urgent snap, he had dithered about trying to decide on the correct form of words. As every agency journalist knows in a crisis like that, the style does not matter a hoot. All that matters is speed. Nigel said he had almost gone mad trying to force Serge to type out the essential story – that an African had run off with Baudouin's sword. Finally, he had persuaded him to get out of the chair and let Nigel do it. Serge was a distinguished old white Russian with perfect manners and a splendid fund of anecdotes; he was also incidentally, a cousin of the author of *Lolita*, Vladimir Nabokov. But he was not the man for the humid jungle of Léopoldville and he simply cracked up.

'There's simply no time for that sort of thing here,' Nigel said, swinging the Volkswagen viciously round a corner into the broad boulevard which ran, straight as an arrow, towards the middle of the European city. 'Things are happening all over the place,' he went on. 'You can't stay still. You've got to get out and cover news as it happens and then file it to London. And we have to take our turn on the Belga telex.' He avoided a couple of African pedestrians and aimed the car towards the Memling Hotel. 'That's why one person can't manage on his own. There's too much going on.'

We arrived at the entrance of the Memling, where I was to stay. Nigel had a flat round the corner. Even then, a few days after independence, the Memling already had a broken-down, uncared-for appearance. The dank heat of the tropics invaded the lobby, overpowering the air conditioning. The staff were listless and sullen. I dumped my case and five minutes later joined Nigel downstairs. A group of journalists were at the bar and we joined them for a beer: Geoff Thursby and George Gale of the *Daily Express*, a man from the *Telegraph*, a handful of Americans and French. They were all agog with the story of the spreading mutiny in the Bas Congo. What had really started it off was the resentment felt by the Congolese rank and file that, despite Independence, nothing had changed. The officers were still all Belgian; there was not a single black Congolese officer in the Force Publique on July 1, 1960. The Belgians – most of them *Flamands* – continued to give the orders and the Congolese were expected to carry them out. This was in line with Belgian policy generally in the Congo. Nothing had been done by the Administration – and least of all in the Army – to prepare often primitive, uneducated African minds for the sudden transformation. Indeed, just the opposite. Ordinary Congolese, excited by the wilder flights of propaganda from their new political leaders, had been led to expect that all the white men's possessions would be theirs overnight – their cars, jobs, houses and women.

The buzz around the bar that day was that not only were the mutinous ANC soldiers from Matadi and other garrisons hunting down, arresting and beating up their Flemish officers – *Flamands* had a reputation among Africans for being more brutal – but that they had started to rape their women as well.

Everyone was wary of the story. In the atmosphere of mounting panic that was almost palpable in the city, it could be just another rumour among a hundred others. More sensational, certainly, and one that would make splash head-lines round the world. But it was not the sort of story that any reputable journalist would want to write without being absolutely sure of the facts.

Someone said that a convoy of Belgian refugees from the Matadi area was due in Léopoldville that afternoon, and while Nigel went back to the office to monitor the Belga file, I set off to try to find the convoy. I succeeded, in the company of one or two other journalists, late that afternoon. We were directed to a Catholic institute, greeted by the Mother Superior and taken to a room full of women. They were mostly nuns but there was one at least who was not: Madame Rykmans, whose husband was a well-known liberal member of the Belgian Colonial Service, an exception which was said to have cost him promotion despite the fact that his father had been Governor of the Congo. The nuns were in their habits, travel-stained and weary after the long journey from Matadi.

It was the most unpleasant interview I have ever conducted. The Mother Superior said, as she escorted us in, that, yes, they had been raped. But how to begin? We did, somehow. They spoke quietly, haltingly, and gradually their story unfolded. The mutineers had burst into their mission school near Matadi, drunk and waving their rifles about. They had ransacked the place, terrorised the sisters and then started to rape them.

I forced myself to be sceptical. 'That's a very serious allegation. How can you be sure?' I asked.

'Because I saw it,' one sister replied quietly. 'And I was raped myself.'

I found myself stammering in disbelief and embarrassment. 'You were actually raped yourself?'

'Yes,' the sister said, her eyes hard, her voice matter-of-fact. 'I was raped . . . several times. They even raped a seventy-year-old sister, Sister Agatha. She's sitting over there.' She turned and pointed to an elderly nun at the other side of the room, sunk in her own private misery.

Madame Rykmans was also amazingly level-headed and cool. Only her eyes betrayed the inner turmoil. She said the soldiers had forced their way into her house and arrested her husband. (He was later killed.) Then they raped her, several of them, one after another, and finally left. Many questions came to mind, to flesh out the bare tale, but I could not bring myself to ask them. In any case, I was convinced beyond any shadow of doubt that I was hearing the absolute truth.

The atmosphere in the convent was like that of a sick-room, where someone is about to die. We almost tiptoed away, leaving the dry-eyed nuns behind. Then I rushed back to the office to find Nigel. 'Write it,' he said, 'but for God's sake be careful. London will be like a cat on hot bricks over this story.'

I sat down and wrote a plain, unvarnished and strongly

117

verbatim account. As far as I know it was the first detailed eye-witness account of rape to be reported from the Congo. No doubt London agonized over the story, since the implications were extremely ugly and would not be popular with many of our customers. But not for very long. It was too hot to sit on unless there were grave doubts about its authenticity, but I had it all down, chapter and verse, quoting Madame Rykmans and several nuns by name. The rape story made headlines everywhere, creating an image of savagery and chaos that was to persist for a very long time.

In the days that followed the mutiny spread across the Congo like a forest fire. Wave after wave of fleeing Belgians arrived in Léopoldville from other parts of the country, all with the same story: terror, looting and rape. In Luluabourg, several hundred Belgians barricaded themselves in a big block of flats while the local soldiers sniped at them and wreaked havoc in the town. And every day there were fresh stories of Belgian women being raped, often while their husbands were held at gunpoint and forced to watch; so many stories that finally rape became a journalistic commonplace.

Soon after my arrival, I was having a drink in the Stanley just down the street from the Memling, when a group of ANC soldiers burst into the hotel, brandishing their rifles. Immediately, a *frisson* of fear ran through the lobby and conversation stopped. Most of the diplomats and UN people who had been invited to the Independence celebrations were staying there, so the lobby and adjoining bar were full of white faces. A couple of soldiers came striding towards us.

'*Vous, dehors,*' one shouted, pointing his rifle.

'*Journaliste anglais,*' I said, proffering my press card. The words worked like magic.

'*Journaliste? Anglais? Bon, bon, restez,*' the first soldier said, and waved us away. The second had a scrap of paper with a list of names.

'We are looking for *Flamands*' he announced. He read out several names to the receptionist, was given some room numbers and they disappeared upstairs. A few moments later they reappeared with several anxious-looking Belgians in civilian clothes, their short blond hair and military bearing suggesting that they were not the harmless coffee planters they were pretending to be.

Just as they were leaving, a different soldier appeared. His gun pointed. 'You,' he said, 'outside.' I and some other unfortunate who had caught his eye, were shepherded to the door. As army lorry was parked in front of the hotel, tailboard down. I could see a number of Belgians inside.

'Get in,' the soldier said menacingly.

'*Journaliste*,' I said, making one last despairing try. '*Journaliste anglais*.' But to my surprise and relief it worked again.

'*Bon, bon*,' he said. '*Allez.*'

My foot was almost on the tailboard. I backed away thankfully. As I did so, a soldier beside me raised his rifle and fired. I was just in time to see a head being withdrawn hastily from one of the hotel windows: it was the dignified, bespectacled countenance of Dr. Ralph Bunche, deputy Secretary-General of the United Nations and Dag Hammerskjoeld's special representative in the Congo. Luckily, the soldier missed and Bunche escaped with a fright. A moment later they all piled into the lorry and drove away and we went back to the bar to finish our drinks.

In the weeks that followed I was to find my press cards not only invaluable but essential. Moving around Léopoldville constantly, often on foot, we were always being stopped by the army. Most of the time they were hunting down the *Flamands* and production of the press card was usually enough, especially if you were British or American. But you could never be sure. Discipline had virtually collapsed. Nominally, the new ANC had elected their own officers, but in practice they hardly ever obeyed them and each small group of soldiers was a law unto itself.

I seemed to lead a charmed life, always able to talk my way out of trouble. It was essential to display no fear, rather as you might deal with a fierce dog. If you show you are afraid, it will attack you. My self-confidence was almost excessive. One day I drove into the army main camp to try and see the commander. Somehow I got past the main gate and went right on, receiving nothing worse than a few dirty looks. Finally I reached the C.O.'s office. They seemed to be astonished to see me. I was asked my business. I explained that I wanted to check some story with the C.O. One of his aides informed me in chilling tones that it was forbidden for unauthorised persons like me to enter the camp without permission. Did I have permission? No? Then I had better leave immediately. I did, realising I had been extremely rash. I could easily have been arrested and held as a spy.

But, if there was some semblance of order in Léopoldville, there was precious little in the country at large. Reports flooded in daily of Belgians being terrorised, beaten up and occasionally shot, and of groups of them holed up in local strongholds, radioing desperately for help.

The Belgian army, operating from their big base at Kamina, in Katanga, carried out dozens of rescue missions and eventually all these refugees were flown to Léopoldville, where the mass evacuation was being coordinated. Only Katanga, and one or two other places like Kivu, were relatively unaffected. Njili Airport, outside Léopoldville, presented an amazing spectacle. Hundreds and hundreds of frightened Belgians – men, women and children – were crammed together in the terminal building. Every available inch of space was occupied, every office jammed, and people sat and slept on the floor. The mood was one of defeat and despair, and only the fear of not being able to escape acted as a kind of discipline. Sabena did an impressive job, putting almost its entire Boeing 707 fleet on the evacuation and flying non-stop for days until twenty thousand Belgians had been airlifted out of the Congo. Every plane was stripped down to the bare essentials and once a 707 took off with over 300 people on board. The normal load was under 200.

One day a group of Congolese soldiers took over the airport and stopped the evacuation. The Belgian Government, after some shilly-shallying, ordered a detachment of paratroopers from Kamina to drop on Njili Airport and rescue the hysterical refugees. I was in the Belga office around nine one morning when an unconfirmed report came in that the paratroopers had dropped. How could we check? I found the small colonial telephone directory and dialled a number at the airport.

It rang for a long time and, just when I was about to hang up, a gravelly voice came on the line.

'Hello, who's that?'

'It's Reuters here. Who'm I talking to?' I asked.

There was a pause and then a chuckle. 'George Gale here,' the gravelly voice said.

'George! What's going on? Is it true the Belgian paras have landed?'

'Yes.' George's voice sounded muffled. 'But I can't see much because I'm lying on the floor.'

'Any shooting?'

'Yes, but I can't talk any more,' he rasped and rang off.

I was jubilant. I had the confirmation I needed and was able to rattle off a story to London.

I was less jubilant when I heard how George Gale had written the story. He described how he had been at the airport by chance when suddenly the Belgians started dropping. The handful of ANC in the terminal ran outside and started firing, noisily but not effectively. The Belgians landed without casualties and charged towards the airport building. Then George wrote: 'In the middle of the battle, the 'phone rang at a desk near me. No one answered it so I crawled over and picked it up. It was Sandy Gall of Reuters. "Hello, George, what's going on?" he said.

"There's a battle going on," I said.

"Any casualties?" he asked.

"I don't know," I replied. "I can't see much because I'm lying on the floor . . . "'

When George showed me the story a couple of days later, I said angrily, 'You rotten bastard, you make me sound like an absolute idiot.'

'Well,' he said. 'That's what happened. It's true isn't it?'

I had to admit it was.

George Gale and Geoff Thursby made a formidable combination and Nigel and I considered them the best reporting team in Léopoldville, after ourselves of course. Both of them were go-getters in the best Beaverbrook tradition, shrewd, tough and with a sure nose for the action. You had to have energy, luck and friends in about equal proportions. You needed energy, especially in that heat, to keep making the rounds – and it was often in doing so that you came on something exciting: luck because half an hour before or after you would have missed the incident; and friends because, even with all the energy and luck in the world, you were bound to miss something, and you depended on your friends to tell you. Once you had the story, of course, you had to get it out, and in the evening there was only one way, by telex from the Post Office. There was, however, one difficulty: curfew began at seven p.m. and in theory anyone found on the streets after that was liable to be arrested or shot.

Every night, Nigel and I would slip out of his flat, cross the main boulevard and walk through the shadows along a side street to the Post Office. There was always a Congolese soldier on guard at the back entrance, but a couple of cigarettes would persuade him to let us in. Upstairs, in the telex room, there was usually a crisis. The Belgian supervisor, a hatchet-faced, bad-tempered *Flamand*, would be running round the room cursing and swearing, engaged in a tricky operation known as 'changing frequency'. The telex link to Brussels was by radio and, each morning and evening, the transmission frequency had to be changed. Some nights, if there was a lot of solar activity, the frequency change could take hours and, during this time, it was impossible to send any copy. We would stand there, impatiently, George Gale, Geoff Thursby, Nigel and I, not saying much in case we upset the supervisor, waiting anxiously for him to work his magic. Occasionally, very occasionally, when things were going well and he was feeling happy, he would greet us with a smile, take our copy and send it out straightaway. The only other times he smiled were when, with the copy safely gone, the grateful correspondent would press a small wad of notes, preferably in hard currency, into his receptive hand. Nigel eventually bought him up and so ensured a more or less priority treatment for Reuters for months on end. The supervisor, however, was greedy and always liable to double-cross you, so he had to be watched very carefully. I believe he eventually left the Congo a nervous wreck, but a rich man.

One night, after dinner with Nigel in his flat, we noticed a commotion in the square below. The street lighting was poor, but we could see an unusual number of Belgians moving about in the square and also round the Belgian Embassy which was opposite. I told Nigel I would go down and have a look. In the warm half-dark, I walked across the square to the Embassy, passing little groups of Belgians. The Embassy was a large building set back among trees and with a low wall running round it. As my eyes became accustomed to the light, I could just make out the shapes of men in position along the wall and among the trees, and I noticed with a small jolt of fear that they were armed. It looked as if they were expecting an attack.

A lorry full of Congolese troops, the street lights glinting on their helmets and rifles, pulled up at the far side of the square, followed a few minutes later by a second lorry. I could sense the Belgians preparing themselves for action. The Congolese troops in the lorries stayed very still, not speaking, and there was a long pause. I was about halfway between the lorries and the Embassy and there I stayed, I hoped not too conspicuously, as the minutes ticked by. One or two Congolese got out of the cabs of the lorries and stood together talking, looking towards the Embassy, apparently trying to decide what to do. It would only take one false move, I thought, and there would be an ugly scene. I felt as if I were watching two large dogs circling one another, growling, and wondering which one was going to spring first.

Suddenly, into this arena, like a matador entering the bullring, stepped a figure in civilian clothes, a Congolese of about thirty. I watched him walk purposefully towards the first lorry, wondering what effect his intervention would have. After a few minutes of conversation with the men beside the lorry, the new arrival turned and walked across the square to the Embassy. He disappeared inside the gate and was gone for perhaps five minutes. Then he reappeared and made his way, a lonely figure among the shadows of the square, back to the lorries. The soldiers still stood, shoulder to shoulder, motionless, waiting.

There was another, longer conversation and then suddenly movement: the officers were climbing back into the cabs of the lorries, the engines started and they drove slowly away. I almost expected to hear the watching Belgians cheer, but most of them had discreetly drifted away. As the tail-lights of the lorries disappeared into the darkness, I came to my senses. Who was the mysterious man who had saved the situation? I looked across the square but he had already gone. I turned to a couple of Belgians standing near by. 'Who was the Congolese?' I asked.

'Bomboko,' one of them replied emphatically. 'The Foreign Minister, Justin Bomboko.'

'You're sure?'

'*Oui, certainement*,' the man said. 'It was him.'

I walked quickly back to Nigel's flat to file the story. We might be able to get through to London or Brussels by telephone. After an hour or so's delay, we did, to London. It was a good story and it did well. There was only one thing wrong as I discovered later. The man who saved the day was not Bomboko, who did indeed exist and was Foreign Minister. The hero was a complete unknown, one Joseph Mobutu, a former journalist and sergeant in the Force Publique, now an officer in the ANC. Many years later he was to become known to the world as President Mobutu, or to give him his full title, Mobutu Sésé Seko Kuku Ngbendu Wa ZaBanga, President of Zaire.

One day the citizens of Léopoldville were startled to witness the arrival of a British General in full uniform. This was General Alexander, Chief of Staff of the Ghanaian Army. Kwame Nkrumah, the founding father of African nationalism, had been shrewd enough to appoint a neutral Briton as his military commander. He was also eager to aid his newly-independent near-neighbour and when Lumumba, alarmed by the ANC mutiny, appealed to Nkrumah, he got a swift response. Alexander and a battalion of the Ghanaian Army was flown to Léopoldville and made an impressive entry, showing just how disciplined and smart African soldiers could be. Alexander himself was a strong personality and immediately seized the initiative. Whether Lumumba gave the go-ahead or not, a point that was in dispute later, Alexander gave orders for the ANC to be disarmed. They were told to report to the local headquarters and hand in their arms and, such was the vigour of Alexander's approach, that within a day or two the task was almost complete and order was well on the way to being restored.

But such a solution was too simple for the Congo. What happened next was not entirely clear to us on the ground, but Lumumba either changed his mind himself or was encouraged by the UN to change his mind – some said that Ralph Bunche persuaded him to do so. At any rate, Alexander was suddenly told that it was unacceptable for a newly-independent nation to be deprived of its army; so the ANC was rearmed again, the plan to retrain them went by the board and everything was soon back to its original disastrous state of anarchy. Shortly afterwards Alexander and his Ghanaians left. I have always believed that that was a crucial turning-point for the Congo. If Alexander had been allowed to start the retraining of the rabble that the Belgians had left behind, the future of the country might have been very different. Certainly, a lot of the killing that took place over the next few years might have been avoided.

I was at the airport one day, on some routine matter. The evacuation was now a more orderly affair with the airport under the control of Belgian paratroopers. I was just about to drive off when someone told me that Lumumba was also there and was having a row with some Belgian refugees. That was the way you came on a story in the Congo, by word of mouth, and the only way to find out if it were true was to go there in person. We drove alongside the tarmac on the perimeter road until we finally spotted a plane and a small crowd of Belgians near it. The Belgians, all men, had made a loose circle round two Africans. One of them, a tall haughty figure who carried himself with the pride of a warrior, was Lumumba, his glasses and small Leninesque beard making him instantly recognisable. The Belgians were crowding round him and insulting him.

'How would you like your women to be raped?' one man was shouting.

'*Salaud!*' another man cried. 'Is that what Independence means? Raping and looting?'

Lumumba, head high and his lips curling with disdain, turned, and slowly walked towards the plane that was parked on the edge of the tarmac. The Prime Minister was waiting to fly to his home town of Stanleyville, but the Belgian ground staff would not let him go aboard while they were refuelling. That was the excuse, but I suspected they were being bloody-minded and enjoying the indignity Lumumba and his colleague were being subjected to.

As the Prime Minister strode slowly through the crowd, one Belgian, looking extremely agitated, went up to him, his lips working and his mouth clearly full of spittle. It was quite obvious what he wanted to do – spit right in the hated Prime Minister's face. But, at the very last moment, his nerve failed him and, when he was only about a foot or two away, he stopped, as if appalled, by his own temerity; looked round weakly and finally backed away, mumbling inaudible threats.

Lumumba reached the aircraft, turned and stood there at bay, his expression as arrogant as ever, ignoring the Belgians. There must have been a hundred of them, but they were at a loss what to do next. They could not quite bring themselves to offer violence. Perhaps they were deterred by the ring of paratroopers who stood round, although they showed no sign of intervening. Finally, the plane was ready and Lumumba, haughty to the last, climbed aboard. The incident was over and he had won. Although he was a prickly, fanatical character, I could not help admiring his nerve and bearing that afternoon. He certainly made the Belgians look a shoddy bunch of *'petits colons'*.

As we drove away, we passed another car full of journalists heading for the scene. One of them leaned out of his window an asked in an American accent, 'Anything going on over there? Did you see Lumumba?'

Not recognising him and thinking he might be from an opposition agency, AP or UPI, I shook my head and lied cheerfully. 'No, nothing at all. It's all quiet.' And we drove on. The journalist was called Arnaud de Borchgrave of *Newsweek*. He promptly tracked down the Lumumba story and was so furious that I had attempted to mislead him that he would not even speak to me. Eventually, eight years later in Vietnam, we made it up and became good friends.

After three weeks or so I had to desert Nigel. Eleanor was arriving in Cape Town with Fiona, aged one, and Alexander, only six weeks old, and whom I had not yet seen. They arrived in style, as Tony Cole had promised, aboard the *Pendennis Castle*. But, after only a few days of happy relaxation, I was summoned back to the Congo, to Elisabethville this time, leaving Eleanor to take the Blue Train north to Johannesburg.

Elisabethville was virtually unchanged and had almost escaped the upheavals that had convulsed the rest of the Congo. But one incident, when a group of Belgians driving through the town late at night had been ambushed and killed, was enough to cause a panic. Next day, virtually the entire Belgian population got into their cars and drove like lemmings for the Northern Rhodesian border about fifty miles to the south. Even the Belgian officers of the old Force Publique, who had stayed on to serve under Tshombe, took to their heels. There was one big strapping major, the second-in-command, who I remembered from the Independence Day parade. He looked the sort of man who would not run away in a crisis. I asked George Evans, the British Consul in Elisabethville, what had happened to the major. Had he not stopped the rot?

'Him?' George said in his forthright Welsh accent. 'When I went to see him in his office, I found him sitting at his desk with his head in his hands.'

I tried to visualise the spick and span major in such an unmilitary posture.

'So I asked him what he was going to do about the situation,' George said. 'And you know what? He looked at me with a pathetic expression on his face, shrugged his shoulders and said: "What can I do? Nothing".'

'What did you say to that?' I asked.

'I told him what I thought of him in no uncertain terms,' George boomed. 'I said, "Vous êtes un lapin en uniforme".'

George's French accent was very Welsh but unmistakeable. I wondered how the apparently not so gallant major had reacted to an insult like that. Would he get up and punch George on the chin, like a John Buchan hero, or call for pistols at dawn, which would be more in the continental tradition? What did he say?

'Nothing,' George said. 'He took it.' And that just about summed up the courage and resource displayed by the Belgians in the Congo.

After that spasm of rebellion, Katanga reverted to its former calm, while the rest of the Congo seemed to disintegrate more and more each day. Tshombe's alliance with the Union Minière suited both the Belgians and the Lunda tribe who did not seem to be particularly anxious to rape and torture their former masters and were quite happy to go on making a living, sending their children to school and their wives to market.

But while we were still able to buy French perfume and Yves St. Laurent ties and to dine out more safely than in Léopoldville, things to the north, in Kasai Province, were rather more ominous. The new leader there, Albert Kalonji, had tried to imitate Tshombe by also declaring his independence from the central government. In fact he had gone one better and proclaimed himself King, being known as Le Roi Albert Kalonji Premier. But he had neither the muscle nor the money that was behind Tshombe, and the Central Government, understandably alarmed at the prospect of the whole of the Congo breaking up into autonomous mini-states, moved against him. The Russians, even then remarkably quick to get their toe in the door, provided the aircraft to fly several hundred of Lumumba's troops to Bakwanga, capital of Kasai, and very soon a civil war was under way.

Nigel, still coping manfully in the growing anarchy of Léopoldville, wanted to send his new assistant, Vincent Buist, to Kasai, but London suggested that, since I was next door, on the map anyway, it would be a good idea if I went instead. It turned out to be not such a good idea.

The only way to get to Bakwanga was by chartering a plane from the Copperbelt in Northern Rhodesia, and so I looked around for one or two likely companions to share the cost. George Gale, who had recently come down from Léopoldville, showed some interest, and so did Dickie Williams of the BBC, then based in Salisbury.

A couple of days later George was scooped by Peter Younghusband, of the rival *Daily Mail*. Peter, a huge South African, had just flown to some other trouble spot with Ian Colvin of the *Daily Telegraph* and written an exciting story which started off with words which might have come straight from Evelyn Waugh: 'I waded through the crocodile-infested waters of the Lualaba River today . . . ' This purple prose led to some disparaging jokes in the bar, but also to considerable annoyance on the part of his scooped rivals. The *Express* was so angry they sent George an urgent cable saying: 'Mail and Telegraph have exclusive from Bukavu, how come we uncovered?' George replied, truthfully, that the opposition had chartered the only light plane in Katanga and there was no other way to get there. This did not satisfy the Foreign Editor of the *Express*. 'Why you no buy plane?' he cabled back huffily. 'Editor demands explanation.' That was a nasty dig, implying that if George did not pull up his socks he might have to be replaced by someone more aggressive. So, when I again touted the idea of going to Bakwanga, George was enthusiastic. Here was the change to outscoop Younghusband and put himself well in the lead. It was mildly unfortunate for him that Reuters would also get the story, but that was an acceptable minus. As for Dickie Williams, he was just game to go, and had no particular axe to grind.

We found an obliging pilot called Alan Kearns, a large, amiable Rhodesian from the copper-mining town of Kitwe, and we agreed a price. It was something like £400, quite reasonable, considering we were technically in a war zone, and that Bakwanga was a long way north. The day before we left, Dickie and I went round to see the Belgian head of the Katanga Army, a Major Crèvecoeur. He assured us that, after a recent battle, Bakwanga was in 'friendly hands' – meaning Kalonji forces – at least the airport and the town.

I asked if he was sure and he said that he had received radio messages to that effect. Thus partially reassured, we drove to the airport next morning, portable typewriters at the ready, and waited for the arrival of Alan Kearns. He came in on schedule – it was only a twenty-minute flip from the Copperbelt. We climbed in, George and Dickie in the back while I sat in the front beside Alan, his big brown legs looking solidly reliable as he gunned the little Cessna down the runway and up into the bright morning air.

This part of Africa is always known as 'bush country' which is exactly what it is: a vast expanse of flat, almost featureless terrain, about 2,000 feet above sea-level, the light red soil covered with small scrubby trees and bushes. It is also covered with huge red anthills, some twenty or thirty feet high; but from the air all you see is a pale red-brown carpet, patterned with green, stretching to the horizon on all sides and broken only occasionally by a river or a cluster of mud huts. As the tin roofs and gardens of Elisabethville disappeared behind us we settled down for a long dull flight with little to break the monotony of the endless bush.

Alan spread the map on his knee and traced our route with his finger while flying the plane with one hand. He had never been to Bakwanga before but he was an experienced bush pilot and, provided his compass was working properly and he did his sums right, there would be no difficulty.

An hour and a half and 160 miles later, Alan announced that we should be over Bakwanga. I looked down but all I could see was the same sort of bush that we had been flying over all the way up. Alan went back to his map and calculations, and adjusted our course. Five minutes later there was still nothing to be seen, just unbroken bush. Alan, his professional pride at stake, looked worried. We could not go on flying in circles indefinitely. 'I'll give it one more go,' he said, and rechecked our position. Suddenly he pointed and shouted above the din of the engines, 'There it is, right down there!' Sure enough, a small town with two or three rows of neat little European houses, and the less tidy sprawl of an African *cité indigène*, materialised as if by magic out of the bush. The small airport was off to one side and a minute later we were making out approach.

'Control tower doesn't answer,' said Alan, and flew low over the runway to have a look. Everything seemed normal enough so he made a circle and the second time dropped the little plane neatly on to the middle of the runway. We climbed out and stretched our legs, got our typewriters out of the hold, and walked towards the small terminal building. To my surprise, a man approached us, obviously English, and equally obviously a journalist. I was surprised because for no particular reason I thought we would be the only journalists there. The man came closer and he and George recognised each other.

'Hello, George.'

'Hello, Tom,' and to us, 'Do you know Tom Stacey?'

'Where have you come from?' he asked.

'Elisabethville.'

'God, don't tell them that on any account,' Tom said. 'Otherwise they'll arrest you straight away. There was a big battle here a couple of days ago and they're all very jumpy. Say you came from anywhere, but not Elisabethville.'

I looked closer at the troops standing near the terminal and realised with a numbing sense of despair that I was looking at ANC troops from Léopoldville. Our Belgian Army friend had been one hundred percent wrong. These were no 'friendlies', they were the other side.

We had been moving slowly towards the little terminal and now a Congolese soldier dressed in camouflage battledress advanced on us and asked in French, 'Who are you and where have you come from?'

Avoiding the second part of the question and proferring my passport, I said, 'We're British journalists.' Dickie and George did the same while Tom Stacey melted away into the background. To fill the awkard gap, I spoke as politely as possible.

'I'm from Reuters news agency, Mr Williams is from the BBC and Mr Gale from the *Daily Express.*'

The Congolese did not seem to be particularly interested.

He was making a cursory study of the passports. I in turn studied him. He was about six foot, well-built and had the air of an officer – although he wore no insignia of rank. The most noticeable thing about him, apart from his hostile manner, was his ingrowing beard. It covered his chin and throat with small black ringlets which seemed to be embedded in the skin. Perhaps that was what made him so irritable.

He looked up from the passports and asked again, suspiciously: 'Where have you come from now, in your plane?'

I took the plunge. 'From Léopoldville,' I said, which was partly true. George and I at least had both recently been in Léopoldville.

'Léopoldville?' he said disbelievingly. 'Where is your laissez-passer, then?'

'We don't have one,' I said. 'Nobody told us that we needed a laissez-passer.'

This again was true but did not satisfy our interrogator.

'If you came from Léopoldville you must have come through Luluabourg, and you need a permit to enter this area.' (Luluabourg was the capital of Kasai.)

We offered no comment on that, the situation was clearly becoming awkward.

'I don't believe you came from Luluabourg,' he finally said. 'I am going to check with them now. I hope for your sake you are right.'

I did not like the sound of that; but, knowing how inefficient communications were in the Congo, I thought it could take all day or possibly longer to receive an answer. So, if we left that afternoon, we might get away with it. As we stood there rather at a loss for our next move, another soldier, who had been observing the scene, came up and introduced himself: Lieutenant Ali Trabelsi of the Tunisian Army, Commander of United Nations troops in Bakwanga. He wore the blue and white circular UN badge on his shoulder and he was as friendly and helpful as the Congolese had been hostile and suspicious.

The lieutenant offered to drive us round the town and we accepted eagerly, climbing into his white jeep with the UN sign painted prominently on the door. As I got into the front beside him, he unslung his stubby black Stirling sub-machine gun and placed it on the seat between us. Noting my surprised glance, he patted it with his hand and said, *'ça c'est ma bible.'*

'Are things that difficult?' I asked.

'Yes,' he said, 'very difficult indeed.'

Then, as we drove slowly into town, he told us how a week or so before the Russians had flown in a battalion of the ANC in a fleet of Antonovs, and how, after a lot of wild shooting against half-hearted local opposition, they had captured the airport and the town. The Kalonji forces, such as they were, had withdrawn, and the ANC had spent a few days 'mopping up', a euphemism for the usual bout of looting, raping and killing. Some of the Kalonji forces had taken refuge in a mission school on top of a small hill overlooking the town and the ANC had attacked it with every weapon at their disposal – mortars, bazookas, machine-guns and rifles. When some missionaries finally entered the building they found no soldiers but a large group of terrified men, women and children who had taken refuge there. About a dozen were dead, but one old man, who had six gunshot wounds, was still alive lying in an empty bath. A doctor told me later that no Europeans of that age would have survived the shock and the loss of blood. 'Africans,' he said, 'have a much higher threshold of pain.'

Bakwanga had grown up in the middle of the African bush for one reason only – diamonds – and was now the biggest industrial diamond mine in the world. The diamonds were too small to be used as gem stones but were ideal for industrial use. Their discovery had led to the growth of a little European town, a sort of miniature Elisabethville, with neat, white bungalows for the Belgian engineers and staff of the mine, and bigger two-storey houses with well-watered gardens full of frangipani and hibiscus for the managers and senior geologists. As we drove slowly past I realised that the houses were shuttered and empty.

'Where are all the Belgians?' I asked Lieutenant Trabelsi.

'Come and see,' he said and drove towards a large building at the top of a semi-circular avenue of trees.

It was the Belgian Club and inside, sitting and standing

about disconsolately, talking in hushed tones, and glancing up apprehensively every time an ANC soldier swaggered through the main hall, were about two hundred Belgian men and their wives. Several Congolese soldiers were drinking beer and talking noisily in one corner and the Belgians gave them a wide berth. The lieutenant explained to us that the army had rounded up all the Belgians and told them to stay in the Club until further notice. They were under house arrest, in effect, and were camping out as best they could. The mine, meanwhile, was at a standstill.

About an hour later, Lieutenant Trabelsi took us back to the airport where Alan Kearns was waiting for us, an agitated expression on his face.

'What's wrong, Alan?' I asked.

'They won't refuel the plane,' he said. Then he added, 'And I've had a row with your friend, Tom Stacey.'

'What about?'

'He tried to get me to fly him out.'

'Did he, by God?'

'Of course I told him I couldn't do that. You were my clients and I couldn't leave you in the lurch. He tried very hard,' Alan grinned, 'Offered me a lot of money.'

At this moment, the figure of the suspicious Congolese reappeared and made straight for us. We could see at once that he was angry.

'You lied,' he shouted. 'I have checked with Luluabourg and they have no knowledge of your plane. You have no permission to be here. You are under arrest.' He paused and then added the ominous words, 'You are Belgian spies. You will be taken to Luluabourg and you will be shot!' He was very angry, his beard bristling with rage, his eyes flashing.

'No, no,' I protested. 'We are not Belgian spies. We are British journalists. You have seen our passports.'

He cut me short.

'Your plane is from Rhodesia. Your pilot is Rhodesian. You are spies. The penalty for espionage is execution by firing squad.'

He turned to a group of soldiers who had surrounded us.

'Arrest them,' he commanded. 'Take them away.'

134

He waved towards an army Landrover. As we were hustled off, Lieutenant Trabelsi and Tom Stacey came forward and took down our names.

We drove out of the airport and towards the African *cité,* the guards levelling their rifles at us we bumped along the uneven roads. I hoped they had the safety catches on. The beard sat in front, beside the driver.

We drove perhaps a couple of miles and finally turned into the gate of an army camp. It was by now about three in the afternoon. Groups of off-duty ANC soldiers were drifting idly about in the camp, and they stared at the four whites in the back of the jeep with curiosity and hostility. Several of them shouted as we went past and I noticed that a large number of them had bottles of beer in their hands which they drank as they walked about. That worried me, because I knew by now that, after a few large bottles of beer, they would get drunk and hostility could turn to something much worse.

The jeep stopped in front of the orderly room and we were told to get out. Then, with the rifles at our backs, we were marched up the steps and into the room, which was stacked with ammunition boxes. A corporal sat behind a desk at the far end. The beard addressed him in Lingala, the language spoken by the army, obviously explaining who we were. Then he turned to us and spoke in French. He was still angry and his voice rang out.

'I have told this man that you are spies, Belgian spies, and that you will be taken to Luluabourg where you will be shot.'

I was conscious that his voice would carry through the open door, where a small group had gathered. Dickie and I tried once again. George did not speak much French.

'No, that is not true, we are not spies. We are British journalists, British journalists,' we repeated in desperation.

The beard drew himself up angrily.

'No!' he shouted back. 'You are spies and you will be shot.'

He turned on his heel and strode out, and we heard the engine of the jeep die away, to be replaced by the sounds of the camp, shouts in Lingala and bursts of laughter. We started to talk quietly among ourselves. Someone wondered if Lieutenant Trabelsi had really seen our arrest and whether he would or could do anything about it. We were trying to keep our spirits up as we stood in a line at one end of the room facing the corporal at his desk.

Dickie Williams was on the extreme left, then George, then me, and finally Alan Kearns on the right. Dickie was the smallest, five foot five, waspish, intelligent, articulate, with a good rich BBC voice, surprising in one so small, Welsh but not obviously so. George was about five foot ten, quite strongly built, with a mop of unruly ginger hair and a naughty boy's face. When he got going he had a devastating line in repartee, delivered in a harsh voice and often ending with a grating cynical laugh. I was the tallest, well over six feet, reasonably athletic, and my University French was becoming more fluent by the hour. Finally there was Alan Kearns. He looked a stock Rhodesian, with his bulky frame – he was also over six feet, but much more solidly built, with short blond hair, a round brown face and baby blue eyes. He wore a bush shirt, shorts and stockings. Dickie and I wore slacks and sports shirts, George was the only one with a jacket. I had my wallet in one hip pocket and my passport in the other, a scrap of paper and a biro in my top pocket and my rolled gold Rolex, bought in Aden, on my left wrist.

We were still talking, our voices low, when the corporal, who had been silent, busy at his desk, rapped out, 'Stop talking. You are under arrest. Prisoners don't talk.' We stiffened into silence. Until now he had been reasonable, almost friendly. Suddenly he changed. I noticed that more soldiers had congregated outside the orderly room and were watching us through the open door. I was told later some were 'commandos' from Thysville, the first garrison to mutiny after Independence.

The corporal got up, took a bottle of soda water off his desk, and advanced towards us. He shook it up and down hard and released it so that it sprayed over us. I felt it splash over my face and drip on to my shirt.

'No more talking,' he snarled. 'Silence!'

The act, although harmless in itself, was somehow full of

violence. A soldier who had been standing outside stepped through the door, gripping his rifle. Another followed and then a third. The corporal said something and there was a pause. We waited apprehensively, wondering what was coming next. The soldiers who were pressing round the door outside started shouting to the ones inside. Several were carrying big bottles of Simba beer. I began to feel very lonely despite the presence of my two colleagues and Alan Kearns.

Until then things had been happening rather slowly, now they seemed to speed up. More soldiers forced their way into the room and suddenly they all confronted us, menacingly, shouting to one another in Lingala, as if urging one another on. To my surprise, and out of the corner of my eye, I saw the corporal trying to restrain the advancing mob.

'*Non, Non,*' he cried, '*Faut pas entrer ici, ce sont des prisonniers.*'

But they paid him about as much attention as the advancing tide gave to Canute.

The room was hot, crowded and noisy with the din of the soldiers' voices; the air heavy with the threat of violence. I was aware of a row of black faces in front of me and that we almost had our backs to the wall. The corporal, having failed to assert his authority, had retreated to the far end of the room. Suddenly one soldier stepped forward, tugged at my Rolex, which had an expanding strap, and ripped it off. I saw other hands reaching out on either side of me. One soldier reached inside George's jacket and snatched his wallet. We were jostled and pushed back against the wall. Our shoes were torn off. 'On your knees,' they shouted. No, I told myself, stay on your feet, don't fall down or you may never get up again.

On my right, a big brawny soldier wearing a pair of dark glasses – a status symbol among Congolese – his face shining with sweat, stepped forward. He held what looked like a heavy swagger stick in his right hand. Slowly, taking careful aim, he lifted it up high and brought it cracking down on the slightly bald head of Alan Kearns. Alan gave no sound at all. The soldier prepared himself for another blow.

For a moment the scene froze on the retina, like a breaking

wave caught by the camera shutter. During that fraction of a second, while I waited for the all-out attack, the kicking, punching and hitting with the rifle butts, an extraordinary thing happened. Through the open doorway, making a passage for himself, came a venerable figure, a grey-haired ANC officer of the Military Police. He said something in Lingala, the equivalent, I imagine, of 'Hello, hello, hello, what's going on here, then?' Everything stopped. In the long silence that followed, while everyone took stock of the new situation, two young MPs followed him through the door. They were both well over six foot and moved with the almost gentle grace of very big men. Both were extremely black and each wore on his head a red-and-white-striped steel helmet with the letters PM painted on it – *Police Militaire.*

The frozen moment shattered like thin ice on a pond, the soldiers who had been pressing so close to us that we could smell their sweat stepped back and, quietly now, their voices barely audible, started to melt away out of the room. Within ten seconds it was empty except for us, the three MPs and the corporal.

'Are you all right?' the grey-haired captain asked, looking rather bewildered.

'I think you just came in time,' I replied. 'Alan, are you all right?' Alan rubbed his head ruefully and said he was. The soldier had hit him very hard, but the stick was not very heavy. I said that all our watches had been stolen and George and Dickie had lost their wallets as well. The captain shook his head in sympathy and then said: 'I want you to come with me. I'll take you to the UN.'

We went outside, thankful to leave that oppressive room behind, and got into the captain's jeep. As we drove through the camp, the sullen faces glowered at us like animals that had been cheated of their prey. I asked the captain, whom I took to be an old Warrant Officer from the Force Publique, promoted at Independence, how he had known we were there.

'The United Nations reported to us that you had been arrested and asked us to get you back, since you are foreigners.'

Thank God for Lieutenant Trabelsi, I thought to myself. One of the young MPs leaned forward and asked me again what had happened. I told him they had stolen our watches and wallets, and hit Alan over the head, and that I didn't know what would have happened if they had not arrived when they did.

'*C'est terrible*,' he said. 'How can people behave like that?' Then very deliberately, he crossed himself. I found the sight of this simple young giant, making the sign of the cross, his face rapt under the forbidding steel helmet, infinitely moving.

The captain drove us to Lieutenant Trabelsi's headquarters and formally handed us over, explaining that we were technically still under arrest but that he was placing us in UN custody. We shook hands with the captain and thanked him effusively. Trabelsi took over.

'Come and have something to eat,' he said. 'You must be hungry. And then I'll show you where you can sleep.'

Over a supper of tinned meat, bread, butter and bananas, we told the lieutenant our story.

'You were lucky,' he said. 'Extremely lucky.'

We asked him about the man with the beard who had had us arrested.

'He's a nasty bit of work,' the lieutenant said. 'They say he's a cousin of Lumumba's. He certainly comes from the same tribe, the Batatele.'

Afterwards, he took us to an empty Belgian house nearby and told us to make ourselves comfortable. The house was just as the Belgians had left it. We all slept in the sitting-room, and I kept being woken by George coughing and spluttering. He suffered from asthma and did not have his inhaler with him. Each time I woke, I would listen to the dogs howling among the deserted villas at the eerie echo of gunfire. There were no guards about, and anyone could have walked into the unlocked house.

Next day after breakfast, the bearded soldier – he turned out to be a sergeant-major – arrived to see us. The interview took place in Trabelsi's headquarters, another Belgian house, with Trabelsi present. The beard was only slightly less hostile than when we had last seen him; he seemed annoyed that we had escaped from his clutches and was totally unapologetic about what had happened. I told him it was ridiculous to suggest that we were Belgian spies since we all held British passports; and I pointed out that his public announcement that we would all be taken to Luluabourg and shot was an invitation to all the soldiers standing around in the camp to take the law into their own hands. Finally I asked him what he was going to do about getting back our watches and wallets. He promised he would look into it, but we knew perfectly well that we would never see them again. Then he counter-attacked by saying that we were at fault by claiming that we had come from Léopoldville and Luluabourg and that, if we had not lied, we would not have got into trouble in the first place. After he had left, Lieutenant Trabelsi said that he was anxious to get us out of Bakwanga as soon as possible. The situation was deteriorating, he had information that more troops were on their way and that could lead to renewed fighting.

'When do you think we can leave?' I asked.

'Tomorrow, I hope. But you'll have to go to Léopoldville.'

There were cries of dismay.

'We don't want to go to Léopoldville,' we chorused.

'What about my plane?' Alan demanded.

Trabelsi shrugged.

'They won't let you fly out the plane until you've been to Léopoldville and they've decided your case. Anyway, the first step is to get you out of here on the first available flight to Luluabourg where our provincial representative, Monsieur Duran, will look after you. The longer you stay here, the more dangerous it is. I'm worried that they might try and get you back. The sergeant-major would love to get his hands on you again.'

I spent another sleepless night listening to George's asthma, the dogs barking and the ANC shooting at shadows. Then next day, just after lunch, Lieutenant Trabelsi told us that the UN plane was on its way. As we drove down to the airport, we heard the roar of aircraft engines overhead. I

140

looked up. Half a dozen Antonovs were flying low over the town, heading for the airport. Lieutenant Trabelsi, his sub-machine gun on the seat beside him as before, looked unhappy.

'Those are the reinforcements we've been expecting,' he said.

Just as we reached the airport another Antonov came in and was greeted by a long burst of machine-gun fire.

'Jesus, who the hell's shooting?' George asked.

'The ANC,' Trabelsi said. 'They're so stupid they're shooting at their own people. But they're such bad shots they never hit anything.' He was right. The Antonov landed safely and taxied to a stop in front of the terminal. About a hundred Congolese soldiers started to disembark.

'There's your plane over there,' Trabelsi said. 'When we reach it get inside as quickly as you can.'

He drove across the tarmac right up to a white-painted DC3 with the blue UN roundels on the fuselage. We clambered up the steps and waved a quick goodbye. The engines were running and as soon as we were aboard the Swedish pilot started taxi-ing to the take-off point. We just had time to strap ourselves in, and then we were bumping down the runway and lifting off.

We landed at Luluabourg just before dark and were taken straight to UN headquarters. Gustavo Duran was waiting to meet us, an impressive-looking Spaniard with a warm smile and a worldly manner that came from long years in the UN in New York. He had been a Republican commander in the Spanish Civil War and the original, it was said, of the general in Hemingway's *For Whom the Bell Tolls.*

Not having changed our clothes for three days we were all by now extremely dirty and unkempt, so after offering us a drink Duran turned out his wardrobe and presented each of us with a shirt. Mine was a rich plum colour and bore the label of some shop in Martha's Vineyard. Duran made light of our difficultues and of his own – which must have been considerable – and I think he rather enjoyed having someone other than UN officials to talk to. As an example of how suspicious and gullible the Congolese were, he described how, a day or two before, the local ANC commander had come rushing in to his office, saying that a Belgian aeroplane had just landed at the airport with 300 Belgian paratroopers aboard. Duran tried to tell the man there was no such plane at the airport, and in any case no plane then flying could have carried that number of paratroopers with full equipment. But the ANC commander had insisted that Duran drive out to the airport with him. Sure enough, they found nothing but a perfectly innocent DC3, with not a Belgian paratrooper to be seen. The Congolese explanation was that the plane had been there, but must have taken off again.

Next morning we flew aboard another UN plane to Léopoldville, to be met by Nigel Ryan who said he had instructions to take us straight to the British Embassy. We were greeted less than cordially by the Second Secretary, Nigel Gayford, whose first words were: 'So you're the people who've been making such a nuisance of yourselves. You've given the Ambassador a great deal of trouble.'

I was so stung by his Foreign Office attitude, that I snapped back, 'That's what he's here for.'

Gayford did not like that at all, but diplomatic relations were not broken off, thanks to Nigel Ryan, who then departed to check on some story. Apart from telling us how much trouble we were causing everyone, the FO man also informed us that the charges against us – these were never detailed, but presumably still consisted of the bogus spying allegations – would be withdrawn on condition that we left the country immediately. In other words, we would be deported to Brazzaville across the Congo River. This did not worry us one little bit as Brazzaville was then a haven of peace and plenty. Gayford told us to report to the Embassy that afternoon, and he would take us to see the Minister.

We walked back to Nigel's flat through the intense heat and glare of midday. Things in Léopoldville had not changed much since my last visit, except perhaps that they had become even more anarchic and run down. Nigel was out but his talkative servant, Joseph, was in charge and instructed us to look after ourselves. I found a small pot of Danish caviar and a few beers in the fridge and we helped ourselves unashamedly to our first luxury for days. Nigel, looking flustered, arrived half an hour later. He had been down to the port, he said, to see if the ferries, which had been stopped, were running again to Brazzaville. On his way out of the port area he had been stopped by an enormous Congolese sentry. He asked to see Nigel's identity card and, while the latter was fumbling about for it, had suddenly grabbed Nigel by the balls and given them a sharp tug. In pain and confusion, Nigel had managed to beat a retreat before anything worse happened to him.

He had already sent an urgent story to London saying we had been released, which would be in time for the evening papers, and now our London offices were clamouring for the full story. We all settled down in Nigel's sitting room with our portable typewriters and started hammering out the story of our arrest and imprisonment. An hour later we walked to the Post Office. For once the telex was working reasonably efficiently. I was allowed to go first, as the agency man, and my story ticked its way over the machine fairly quickly. Then George's message started off but after a few seconds disaster struck. The line went down and it took hours before George eventually got through.

Later that afternoon, we met Gayford at the Embassy as arranged and went to the Foreign Ministry. After a taciturn Minister had signed our deportation orders, we marched to the port and boarded the ferry for Brazzaville, which beckoned from the other bank of the mile-wide Congo like some shimmering oasis.

The current was so strong that the ferry had to battle a long way upriver through great floating islands of water hyacinth before venturing into midstream, where the brown waves rushed past us with awesome speed. Once in the full grip of the current, we were swept down to the far bank at an angle of forty-five degrees. Far downstream we could see the white line of foaming water that marked the Rapids. If our engine had broken down, we would undoubtedly have been dashed to pieces on the rocks below. But we made landfall safely in Brazzaville, a pretty French colonial town, as friendly and welcoming as Léopoldville had been hostile. The Africans at the landing stage clucked sympathetically when they heard we had been deported. '*Quel pays*,' they sighed. Passports stamped, we drove to the Air France rest house and that night dined off oysters and lobster flown in from France, washed down with a bottle or two of Pouilly Fuissé. Life seemed good again.

CHAPTER V

The Death of Lumumba and the End of the Congo War

I was back in Johannesburg, and it was a different world: the electric light and water worked, there were no roadblocks, and you did not have to produce your press pass every five minutes for a possibly drunken group of soldiers. Eleanor had moved in to a pretty residential hotel called the Balalaika, with thatched roof cottages in the gardens and a swimming pool. The children were happy and she had been befriended by a marvellously kind couple called Tom and Betty Barker. He was the best kind of English South African, a huge jovial man who had once turned up to play golf at Sunningdale in shorts and, to his fury, been asked to leave the bar by the strait-laced secretary.

But, only a couple of weeks later, the first in what was to be a long series of messages from Reuters arrived on my desk in SAPA. Could I get to Elisabethville 'quickest', as the UN was increasing its pressure on Tshombe to give up Katanga's independence. Most of these messages emanated from Doon Campbell, who I could see in my mind's eye bent over his typewriter, hammering away with his good hand like a large, white-crested woodpecker. They were always couched in cablese and felt into three main categories: instructions to move from A to B; congratulations on some success; and occasionally, alas, reproof for failure. Doon was much given to use of the word 'transcendental', and Nigel used to tease me about one cable from Doon which read: 'Your coverage of Katanga fighting superb but costs transcendental.'

One particularly insane cable reached me on a Saturday morning in Johannesburg, just when I was about to clean out my swimming pool. It read: 'Stanleyville rebels threatening to massacre entire population of thousand whites this weekend. How you placed proceed there directly query.' It was signed Doon Campbell and had, I imagined, been dictated from the snug fastness of his home in the Surrey stockbroker belt.

I did not know whether to laugh or cry. I wondered briefly if there were still one thousand whites left in Stanleyville, a handsome town on the banks of the Congo River in the centre-north of the country, and named after the great journalist-explorer. As I ran over the message again, my eye lit on the word 'directly'. A glimmer of hope appeared and grew stronger. It was, I was sure, impossible to fly directly from Johannesburg to anywhere in the Congo except the capital, Léopoldville. I would have to fly there first and then catch a local flight to Stanleyville. I dialled the Sabena office in town to check. Sure enough, there was no direct flight from Johannesburg to Stanleyville, and indeed the next flight to Léopoldville was not until Tuesday. With a sigh of relief I hastily cabled back: 'Regret' – I relished that one – 'no direct flight Stanleyville ex Joburg. Next flight to Léopoldville Tuesday. Please advise.' To which an hour or two later came the reply: 'Your 71015. Thanks forget it Reuter.' I went off to the swimming pool with a song in my heart. During the course of a happy weekend, I occasionally thought about the whites in Stanleyville. As far as I know, the rebels did not carry out their threat and the predicted massacre did not materialise: not until later.

The journey to Elisabethville was a laborious one, first by Viscount to Salisbury, change for Lusaka, where I had to stay overnight, and then on next morning to Ndola, the capital of the Copperbelt, and only a few miles from the Congo border. Flights from the Copperbelt to Elisabethville had been suspended and the only way to get there was by road. That meant hiring a car and that in turn meant Charlie Bloomberg. Charlie was an enterprising gentleman who ran the only hire-car firm in Ndola and, from being in a moderately successful way of business, he suddenly found himself in tremendous demand. Every journalist going to Katanga – and they were flooding in from all parts of the world – wanted to hire a car, or share one, and Charlie had the cars, at a price. A dapper figure in long shorts and bush jacket, sporting a small toothbrush moustache, he watched me carefully while I signed on the dotted line and then waved me off on the fifty-mile trip across the Copperbelt through Kitwe, Chingola and Bancroft to the border. There the tarmac ended and the red murram started, a dirt road running north through the bush, past enormous baobab trees and huge anthills, to Elisabethville. There was very little traffic and very little sign of life, apart from two or three miserably poor villages close to the road.

Eventually, fifty miles later, the road crossed the Lubumbashi River and there, towering above the bush like some extra tall baobab, rose the chimney stack of the Union Minière smelter, trailing a small white cloud of smoke. That plume of smoke was to prove a reliable indicator of political events in Katanga. Only when things were really desperate did the smelter close down and the smoke stop drifting over the countryside. It was the symbol of Katanga's wealth, a fabulously rich vein of copper ore that runs from the south-east to the north-west, from Ndola to Kolwezi, and which had been arbitrarily cut in two by the colonial powers, so that half was in British Northern Rhodesia (now Zambia) and half in the Belgian Congo (now Zaire). As I drove into Elisabethville I saw that the jacaranda trees were just coming into flower, wreathing the town in a wonderful mist of pale blue; and there, too, was the new Katanga flag, green and white, emblazoned with a series of copper crosses.

I pulled up outside the Léo Deux hotel, which was to be a

home from home for me and a hundred other journalists over the next three years, and walked in to find the surly Swiss manager, M. Blatter, behind the reception desk. Grudgingly and after much page-turning and sucking of teeth, he gave me a room. His manner implied that he would have liked to have thrown us all out, but that he was forced to accept us if only because the bar profits were so high. And, indeed, huge amounts of the local Simba beer, whisky, gin and wine were consumed by thirsty correspondents in the extraordinary months that followed. Blatter, the reluctant hotelier, was assisted by an equally obnoxious maître d'hôtel, also Swiss. He had a round pink face, very pale straw-coloured hair and small, darting eyes which led to him being nicknamed the White Rat. He scurried about between the kitchen and the dining-room, getting increasingly bad-tempered and disobliging as conditions worsened, until he too, like Blatter, gave up the unequal struggle. But that was still a long way ahead.

At this stage, things were relatively comfortable. The hotel was clean, the food adequate, and the bar well-stocked. I repaired there immediately to see who else was in town. The answer was almost everybody: George Gale of the *Express*, Paul Johnson of the *New Statesman*, Peter Younghusband of the *Mail*, Donald Wise of the *Mirror*, David Halberstam of the *New York Times*, Ray Moloney of UPI and Adrian Porter from AP. Apart from the regulars there were plenty of visitors who came down from Léopoldville for a few days, like Marcel Niedergang of *France Soir* who told me that his paper, with the biggest daily circulation in Paris, had led with the Congo story for twenty-nine days in a row, which he said was a record; and a dozen other French, German, Belgian, Italian and South African journalists.

There were, too, a dozen photographers: dare-devils like Terry Spencer of *Time-Life* and Philippe Letellier of *Paris-Match*. Television was also represented most memorably in the person of Ernie Christie of UPI, and the great Robin Day himself, who had just left ITN and joined the BBC, made at least one appearance. I have a vivid recollection of seeing him for the first time outside Tshombe's Residence, just as the

UN started to mortar it. About half a dozen shells dropped on or near the road at the back of the building. I was driving along in a car as the first one landed; we braked hard and, as we tumbled out into the ditch, the impressive figure of Robin Day with his sound crew came running nimbly down the road, despite being wired together like Siamese triplets. 'This bloody umbilical cord,' Robin yelled, clutching his microphone as he thundered past, heading for cover.

But at the start of this, my second, visit to Elisabethville, the United Nations had still not arrived. Having watched the subjugation of the luckless 'King' Kalonji farther north, they were now preparing to bring Katanga to heel. This, however, was going to be a much tougher proposition and, as yet, the UN had neither the men nor the authority to carry it out. Unable, because of the logistical problems, to invade Katanga, the UN tried to talk themselves into Elisabethville, but Tshombe was too clever to fall for such an obvious trick. But he feigned cooperation, since he was beginning to realise that he was never going to receive world recognition for his declaration of Independence. So, while his Belgian backers, in the shape of Union Minière, made their plans for a defence of their copper kingdom by recruiting mercenaries and building up a supply of arms, Tshombe sought to placate world opinion by agreeing to meet Dag Hammarskjoeld, the Secretary General of the United Nations.

After much negotiation, Hammarskjoeld flew to Elisabethville. Because of the difficulty of sending messages out by telex, I got a friend to cover the airport arrival – where the Secretary General was given a full guard of honour and took the salute with Tshombe – while I opened a telex line to London. Unfortunately, Hammarskjoeld did not arrive on time and I had to keep the line open for half an hour longer than expected, which at the cost of about a pound a minute produced a bill of horrifying proportions. But, apart from the cost to Reuters, the visit was a success. Tshombe and Hammarskjoeld got on well and Tshombe finally agreed, with certain conditions, to allow a UN presence on Katanga soil. Hammarskjoeld was enough of a realist to accept that Katanga was of much more value to the Congo as a going

149

concern, with its copper mines running and its Belgian technicians at work, so he agreed that the UN at first should send in only white troops – Swedes and Irish, no Ethiopians or other Africans – and that everything would be done to reassure the Europeans. But the arrival of the first Swedish contingent, ultra-white as they undoubtedly were, sent a shiver of apprehension through the Belgian community. Tshombe's recruiters speeded up their efforts, signing up as mercenary leader 'Mad' Mike Hoare together with the nucleus of what was to become his no. 5 Commando. A rival group, no. 4 Commando, consisting mainly of French mercenaries under 'Colonel' Bob Denard were such desperadoes that they were given the nickname of '*Les Affreux*,' the Terrible Ones. In all these mercenary outfits, the number of professional soldiers was small, while the percentage of adventurers and ne'er-do-wells was high.

Mike Hoare, a fair-haired, blue-eyed, middle-class Englishman, who did not seem all that mad, had fought in the British Army in the Second World War, attaining the rank of major. After the war, he had returned briefly to his career of stockbroking, but soon became disenchanted with life in 'civvy street' in austerity-ridden Britain, and emigrated to South Africa. There he had done well for himself but become bored and, when the Congo troubles started, had immediately cast around for a way in which he could become involved. Tshombe was the ideal patron for a mercenary leader: he was rich, pro-white and anti-Communist. Any African politician who favoured Africa for the Africans was automatically considered a 'Communist' by men like Hoare.

Hoare's respectable front was considerably enhanced by his number two, Alistair Wicks, a soft-spoken old Harrovian who, like Hoare himself, might have been a City gent on Safari. But lower down there were some strange characters: men like Luigi, the Italian waiter from Salisbury, and Jock, the swimming-pool attendant from Durban, who wore his kilt on special occasions. Behind them, the money-men from Union Minière were buying arms and equipment in Europe and shipping them in through Mozambique, which was then in Portuguese hands, and the Rhodesias. It was said that the

Cockney landlord of the Elephant and Castle Hotel in Ndola, Len Catchpole, ran one consignment of small arms across the border into Katanga in a lorry load of coffins, with the escorting mercenaries dressed as monks. Len was the local undertaker as well as publican, so it might well have been true. His brother, incidentally, was the Federal hangman. He had a cast in one eye which gave him a sinister appearance as he took your order behind the bar. Len used to introduce him with a wink and jerk of the head. 'Met my bruvver?' he would say. ''E jerks them to Jesus.' Len would laugh, while his brother gave his terrible glass-eyed smile.

With the arms pouring in, it did not take long for the fragile status quo to break down. The mercenaries, especially *'Les Affreux'*, who were more visible in Elisabethville than Hoare's men, were spoiling for a fight, and their discipline was so bad that incidents with the Swedes became frequent, shots were exchanged and before long a small-scale skirmish war, involving snipers and mercenary raiding parties, broke out. The once peaceful streets of Elisabethville became pitted with mortar shell craters, the houses were spattered with bullet holes and the city was divided into rival spheres of influence. Swedish roadblocks surrounded UN headquarters and the Belgian villas they had requisitioned for their top staff, and were scattered around at other strategic points. The Katanga Gendarmerie, expanded from the old Force Publique, demonstrated their new firepower by blazing away at every imaginary target, usually in the middle of the night, which did not help the nerves of the population, black or white.

Incidents happened now almost on a daily basis. One evening I was walking through town when a jeep full of mercenaries screeched to a halt at the side of a small square. Three or four heavily armed men, who looked French, jumped out of the vehicle and started setting up a three-inch mortar. Within a minute they had the thing assembled and opened fire. Because of the speed of the operation, I noticed they did not bother with a base plate, which is fixed in the ground and provides a stable platform. Without it no precise aim is possible. I had no idea what they were shooting at –

probably the UN Swedish Camp – but they were in such a tearing hurry that any hit must have been a fluke. After firing off half a dozen rounds, one after the other, they stopped, dismantled the mortar, piled back into the jeep and raced off – presumably to another spot from which they could loose off another half-dozen rounds. I knew that the Swedes would soon retaliate, if the attack was anywhere near on target, and sure enough, as I hastened away from the scene, the first round in reply came screaming in to explode a couple of hundred yards away, well short. I did not stay to see how accurate the rest were.

A couple of days later, I was woken at dawn by a bang, not very loud, but enough to make me sit up in bed. My room was at the back of the hotel, and looked out on to a quiet street. As I sat there, wondering what the noise had been, I sniffed and caught the acrid smell of smoke. I got out of bed and was moving towards the open window when I heard a high-pitched scream followed by an explosion. It happened so quickly that I did not have time to take cover, and I found myself looking out of the window at a canister lying in the middle of the empty street and sending out a small cloud of smoke which drifted towards me. As I stood there, shivering in the dawn chill, I heard another high-pitched scream and this time I ducked behind an armchair. Again the sharp crack and the puff of smoke, only fifty yards from where I stood. I suddenly thought: marker smoke, they'll be putting down the real thing in a couple of minutes.

I dashed back into the room and started pulling on a shirt and a pair of trousers. I slipped my feet into my desert boots and jerked open the door of my room. Once in the corridor I knew I was safe. I made my way downstairs waiting for the roar of an exploding mortar salvo – they usually came in threes – but nothing happened. The smoke rounds had almost certainly been fired by the UN, but at which target and for what purpose remained a mystery.

In fact neither side knew what they were firing at most of the time. I cannot imagine that the hotel, which was occupied almost exclusively by journalists, was a target for the UN, however much they disliked the Press: and yet, a day or two later, some high explosive rounds fell on the other side this time, between the front door and the Post Office building, shattering a palm tree and knocking a shower of tiles off the verandah roof. That morning the White Rat was late on duty and the breakfast was sub-standard.

But the indiscriminate mortaring did begin to claim lives and a number of houses occupied by Belgian civilians or other Europeans were destroyed. The Swedes hit a hospital near the African city, shattering one ward and injuring and killing several patients. Tshombe went to visit it, tut-tutted for the cameras and told the assembled journalists, who had all been alerted, that this was a 'shameful and cynical' attack by the UN. The Swedes disclaimed all responsibility but it turned out that they had been fired on first and were simply retaliating. They were aiming at some military target, but missed.

It became dangerous to go out at night because, quite apart from the curfew which most of us ignored, the Katangese, who were the worst shots of all, did most of their firing then. Despite this, we would run almost any risk to avoid having to eat Blatter's disgusting dinners. Unfortunately few restaurants remained in business: the difficulty of getting staff and edible raw materials was so great as to deter all but the hardiest and most rapacious of restauranteurs. Of the two or three still open, one luckily was only a few hundred yards from the hotel. One night, about a dozen of us, Peter Young-husband, Donald Wise, George Gale, Ray Moloney, Adrian Porter, Terry Spencer, Ernie Christie, Dave Halberstam and myself, went there for dinner. There had been a lot of shooting during the day and the *patron* was jumpy and disorganised. The menu sounded excellent. Soup to start with, followed by *canard à l'orange.* This proved to be the joke of the week. The duck was so tough that it proved not only uneatable but almost impossible to cut. Suddenly all the lights went out and, under cover of darkness, hostilities broke out in the dining-room: mildly inebriated correspondents seized their inedible portions of duck and hurled them at one another across the room. The *patron*, scurrying backwards and forwards with candles for the tables, also came under fire and took one or two direct hits. Finally we were all thrown

153

out, but only after we had paid over a large amount of money for damages. Then, as we staggered home through the dark streets, the mortars opened up, whether UN or Katangese it was impossible to say. We dived for the gutters where we lay feeling very naked and exposed, until the last crump had died away. They say drunks never come to any harm and so it was in this case. The party returned unscathed and giggling to the Léo Deux, where mercifully the bar was still open.

The first Irish soldiers sent out to the Congo arrived in thick khaki uniforms, quite unsuitable for the tropical heat of Léopoldville: apparently the Irish Ministry of Defence, never having sent troops abroad before, had no stocks of light-weight uniforms. One despondent Irish soldier I met in Léopoldville made me feel his uniform which was almost as thick as a horse blanket. 'It's what we wear at home in the winter,' he sighed. The temperature was about 100 degrees in the shade. I noticed several brown marks on it. 'D'you know how I got those? Well, when they sent us to Katanga,' he said, 'we came right across the country in a wood-burnin' train. It was so damn hot we had all the windows open and, bejesis, before we realised what was happening the sparks from the engine were flying in and setting our suits on fire.'

The Irish had a bad time in Katanga. Not for them the comforts of Elisabethville; they had to make do with the rigours of life in the north of the province, in Baluba country. The Balubas, a warrior tribe whose territory spread across the border into Kasai, were cannibals and haters of all authority, whether Belgian, UN or Tshombe's. Once a week the UN used to run a train from Elisabethville north through Jadotville and Kolwezi, both important mining towns, to the big base at Kamina and then east through the heart of Baluba country to Albertville, on the shores of Lake Tanganyika. The train was attacked regularly by Baluba warriors armed with bows and arrows, and the Irish often had to shoot their way through in the style of the old Wild West. One day the Balubas tore up a section of the track, stopping the train, and then blocked the line behind it. Hundreds of warriors brandishing bows and arrows and spears surrounded the train and launched wave after wave of attacks. The Irish mowed them down as fast as they came, the new recruits amazed at the way these naked savages ran straight at their machine-guns without apparent fear. The more experienced members of the escort knew that the Balubas were 'high' on some drug and had been convinced by their witchdoctor that they were invincible to white men's bullets which would turn to water when they hit their bodies. Visible proof that the white men's bullets were doing no such thing, but on the contrary were taking a terrible toll, did not seem to deter them.

In the end the Irish decided they could hold the train no longer and that their only hope was to break out and try to fight their way to safety. But it was hopeless. They were soon surrounded and, completely outnumbered, were quickly overwhelmed. When the rescue force finally arrived they found all the bodies lying where they had fallen, except for one man, the machine-gunner, who was missing. According to Baluba prisoners, he had been the last to die, fighting bravely, although badly wounded, to the last bullet. When he had finally been overrun and killed, the Balubas, in accordance with tribal tradition, had paid him the supreme compliment, as from one warrior to another. They had eaten him, every last morsel, in the touching belief that his courage and military prowess would pass to them, his victors and consumers. It was the ultimate cannibal accolade.

Patrice Lumumba's meteoric career as first Prime Minister of the Congo came to a sudden end in September 1960 when, after series of crises, President Kasavubu dismissed him. Lumumba appealed to the United Nations for protection and then went into opposition underground. But on December 1 he was caught by troops of Colonel Mobutu, now the army commander, and placed under arrest in an army camp at Matadi, in the Lower Congo, one of the towns where the mutiny against the Belgians had started immediately after Independence. But Lumumba was still a national hero, especially among the soldiers, and after a time Kasavubu began to receive reports that, with his wild personality and silver tongue, Lumumba was winning over some of his gaolers and in danger of talking his way out. In desperation, therefore, Kasavubu arranged to have Lumumba flown to the other end of the country, to Katanga, where Tshombe could be guaranteed to keep him safely under lock and key.

I was one of the few foreign journalists in Elisabethville that day, January 18, 1961, when the amazing news went round that Lumumba was in Katanga. My first reaction was one of utter disbelief. Then I bumped into a Swedish journalist in the hotel who said it was true. He said he would try to find out more details from Swedish UN troops at the airport. The Katanga Government, needless to say, were pretending ignorance, so I rushed over to the Post Office with an urgent message which I sent by telex saying that Lumumba was reported to have been flown secretly to Elisabethville from Léopoldville and was now being held somewhere in Katanga.

An hour later my Swedish friend reappeared. By now he had a graphic eyewitness account of Lumumba's arrival from the Swedes guarding the airport. They quoted the Belgian aircrew as saying that he had been beaten up so savagely with rifle butts during the flight that the captain had had to leave the controls and go back and remonstrate personally, telling the guards that they must stop, otherwise they would damage the plane and endanger everyone's safety. This explained the scene the Swedes witnessed when the DC3 landed and the doors open. They saw a man, his hands roped behind his back, his head on his chest, who could barely stand and who looked as if he had been brutally beaten, being half pushed, half carried down the steps.

'He looked more like an animal than a man,' my friend quoted one of the Swedes as saying. 'They threw him into the back of a jeep like a sack of potatoes and drove off.' The Swedes had also told my friend that the plane had been diverted to Elisabethville in mid-air. Originally, it had been destined for Kasai, the next province to the north, but for some unexplained reason it had been unable to land and Kasavubu had contacted Tshombe at the last minute and asked permission for the plane to land in Elisabethville.

Next day the Katanga Government issued a statement saying Lumumba was being held prisoner at the request of the Central Government, but they refused to say where. We guessed it was somewhere outside Elisabethville but all our efforts to find out failed. I left for Johannesburg shortly afterwards and was in South Africa a month later when, on February 17, the Katangese issued a communiqué saying that Lumumba had been shot dead while trying to escape. They took a party of journalists to the alleged scene: a derelict army camp in the depths of the bush. They showed them the hut in which Lumumba was said to have been imprisoned. One of the walls had a big hole in it and the former Prime Minister was said to have escaped through it. Ray Moloney of UPI and other journalists found the story unconvincing. When they asked to see the grave they were told the location was being kept secret so that it would not become a place of pilgrimage for Lumumba supporters. Even in death his personality still exerted a powerful spell. Apart from his executioners, no one really knows how he died. Years later a former Belgian mercenary claimed that he had been a member of the firing squad which shot Lumumba, shortly after his arrival, under the personal command of the Interior Minister, Godefroid Munongo. Was Tshombe also present? Who knows? What is certain is that Tshombe was blamed for Lumumba's death, becoming reviled throughout Africa and the Third World as his executioner. The real responsibility lay with President Kasavubu and the head of his army – Colonel Mobutu, whose soldiers had originally arrested Lumumba, but the avenging spirit of Lumumba would pursue Tshombe until it brought about his downfall and death, years later, in far-off Algiers.

In 1962 the UN decided the time had come to crush Tshombe once and for all. They therefore brought in some real fighting troops – Indians – who, unlike the Swedes or the Irish, could be used without political repercussions at home. The man behind this move was himself an Irishman, Conor Cruise O'Brien. No doubt he was motivated by the best of intentions, but it was quite clear from an early stage that, in the cause of peace, he was going to make war. Not that Conor Cruise was a man of war himself. One day when I and some other journalists were talking to him outside his headquarters about a mile from Tshombe's residence, a small plane started diving on us from above. It was a Fouga Magister, a jet trainer, which is about as dangerous as a wasp, and equipped with nothing more than a baby machine-gun. But the shrill scream of the plane overhead was unnerving to men unaccustomed to war and Conor Cruise leaped into a foxhole in the garden, closely followed by Lee Griggs of *Time* magazine and myself. Lee, in fact, jumped on top of the UN representative, which irritated him, but he became even more irritated when he realised that the fourth member of the party, Terry Spencer, the *Time-Life* photographer and a former Spitfire pilot, was dancing round quite unconcerned by the Fouga's antics, taking pictures of Conor Cruise in an undignified position at the bottom of the foxhole. The picture duly appeared on the editorial page of *Time*. Conor Cruise was not amused.

The Indians sent some of their best troops to the Congo, Gurkhas and Dogras, under a suave Sandhurst-trained colonel, and they soon fell out with the mercenaries and black Katangese troops. The atmosphere became so tense that one day, when we were paying a visit to the colonel, he told us to keep out of sight of his Gurkha soldiers. 'They are so worked up,' he explained, 'they might do anything and I might not be able to stop them. They think every white man is a mercenary.' We did as we were told, not fancying a *kukri* at our throats.

Shortly afterwards Conor Cruise O'Brien gave the order for the Indians to attack the central Post Office in the middle of Elisabethville. After pouring hundreds of rounds into the building, the Dogras went in, driving the Katangese defenders up the stairs to the roof. There, it was said, they either hurled the last of the defenders bodily over the parapet, or so terrified them with the sight of bare steel that the Katangese jumped of their own accord. The UN of course denied it and there were no survivors to tell a different tale.

The battle for the Post Office was a victory for the UN, but it embittered relations beyond repair and made any faint hope of a compromise unthinkable. Tshombe, and many other people too, believed the UN had used unnecessary force to achieve their ends. The many casualties that day included one member of the Press. Dickie Williams, my BBC friend from Bakwanga, had been running across the square during the battle when he heard a loud crack and felt an intense pain in his heel. He fell to the ground and lay writhing in agony as the battle raged round him. Peter Younghusband heard his cries of distress, ran over at some considerable risk to himself, snatched up the fallen Dickie, who luckily only weighed about nine stone, and carried him as if he had been a baby back to the hotel. There he laid him on a sofa, took off his shoe and sock, and examined the leg: no blood, no sign of a bullet hole.

'You're a bloody fraud,' Peter cried. But the pain was real enough. It turned out that Dickie had snapped his Achilles tendon. 'It sounded just like a pistol shot,' he said, and so he had to be invalided out to Salisbury.

Despatched by an urgent telegram from Doon Campbell, I arrived next day from Johannesburg. It was an uneasy drive from the border, the roads almost deserted except for one or two Belgian cars going fast in the opposite direction. When I reached the outskirts of Elisabethville, I saw approaching me a long line of frightened women, with bundles of belongings on their heads and babies on their backs, walking as fast as they could away from the city.

I drove on, my stomach tightening and my heart thumping, eyes alert for any sign of danger. At the edge of town there was a level crossing. A burnt-out Volkswagen had been abandoned there and an African, possibly the driver, lay beside it, face down, dead. Just beyond the level-crossing was a crossroads. The man in the Volkswagen had obviously been shot as he drove across, so I glanced carefully left and right, took a deep breath and drove on. It was a long, anxious moment but no one opened fire. Then I was past the danger point and heading up the empty road.

I passed one or two more wrecked cars and then spotted a Swedish UN post on a slight rise above the last corner into town. It had gone up since my last visit and was a sign that the UN now controlled much more of Elisabethville than a month ago. The streets were noticeably empty and the whole place had the shattered look that always follows a battle. The Léo Deux was packed with journalists and photographers, and rooms were almost impossible to get. They were short of food, the furniture looked battered, Blatter was hysterical and there were no communications with the outside world. Only one thing really worked: the bar. There, the activity and noise were intense. It was where everyone gathered to find out what was going on, who had arrived and who was leaving and, most important of all, who was working on what story. Most of the old hands tended to belong to one group or another, the membership prompted not so much by friendship as by self-interest. Thus, the main rivals were nearly always found in opposite camps: the *Express* in one, the *Mail* in another, the *Guardian* in one, the *Telegraph* in another, Reuters in one, AP in another.

Journalists, as a species, are rather like fish. Some, the big predators like barracuda and shark, are always on the move, ready for the kill whenever it may present itself; they are usually accompanied by cleaner fish, the scavengers, who glean the pickings from the predator's teeth; and there are always one or two exotic specimens, butterfly or parrot fish, who flaunt their idiosyncracies through the shadowy reefs of the daily news; some, like George MacArthur, in his white suit, did it sartorially; others, like one crop-headed German, did it by being simply mad.

Peter Younghusband, who belonged to the predator class, was the hero of the bar. His rescue of Dickie Williams was admired and toasted even in that cynical community. He was in many ways an impressive person: a huge Afrikaner, very strong but also remarkably gentle, with a true sense of humour which was perhaps the most essential part of the foreign correspondent's equipment in the Congo, second only to a strong stomach. I once asked Peter how he came by the name of Younghusband. His real name, he explained, was van der Westhuizen, a good Afrikaner name, but unsuitable for Fleet Street which has a long tradition of anglicising the foreign names of its stringers abroad for the easier comprehension of its readers in Wigan and Walthamstow. Just about the time Peter started working for the *Daily Mail*, his mother remarried and acquired the name of Younghusband. Peter adopted the name too, and it certainly served him well in the Congo. Apart from sounding frightfully British, it brought back memories of the North-West Frontier and of Sir Francis Younghusband's expedition to Tibet in 1903; the Gurkhas treated him as if he were royalty. Peter enjoyed all this and naturally enough did not go round disabusing all these latter-day admirers of the Raj. His family, however, were less impressed. His grandmother refused to speak to him because he was working for an English newspaper.

Peter brought off another impressive rescue about this time, when he was driving to Elisabethville from the border. There were certain rules we tried to observe about this drive: one was never to travel at night, since the guards on the road-blocks tended to get drunk and therefore dangerous from later afternoon onwards. Another was to have a few packets of cigarettes handy in case you needed to bribe a difficult guard; and it was a good idea to look and behave as if you were the big white *baas*. Yet another very important rule, which applied generally and not just to the Congo, was to avoid having the word Journalist in one's passport: since the Foreign Office does not really mind what you put as long as it is not obscene, I found it much safer to use some bland word like Director, or even Writer.

We regulars on the run from Kasumbalesa on the Katanga-Northern Rhodesian border to Elisabethville knew the checkpoints and how to handle the guards. But new boys often had trouble. At the time of the attack on the Post Office, anti-UN feeling was running high in Katanga. Anyone who might in some way be connected with the UN was therefore highly suspect. Into this highly-charged atmosphere, all unsuspecting, drove two innocents abroad, Lionel Fleming, diplomatic correspondent of the BBC, and an American colleague from the *Chicago Herald Tribune*. He was certainly an innocent abroad, a music critic, en route home from a conference in South Africa when his paper suggested he should have a look at what was going on in the Congo. Lionel was driving him in when they were stopped at a particularly unfriendly checkpoint. They were told to get

161

out of the car and marched into the immigration hut with their passports. One American, the other British. Nothing unusual in that but, for some reason, the guard on duty decided to go through the fine print – he must have been a particularly erudite guard – and discovered the words every British passport carried on the first page: 'United Kingdom of Great Britain and Northern Ireland.' This is repeated in French immediately underneath and the giveaway was the French word: *Irlande*. It did not matter that it added '*du Nord*'.

'*Irlande,*' the guard shouted. '*Vous êtes Irlandais. Vous êtes membres de l'ONU . . .* '

'No, no,' protested Fleming, ironically an Irishman, in his smooth brogue. 'I'm British. That says Northern Ireland . . . ' Fleming spoke French as well as the next man, but the more he explained the deeper he floundered.

The guards, scenting blood, became ugly. They dragged the unfortunate Fleming and the American into another room, hit them with their rifle butts and made them lie down on the floor, hands behind their heads. One of the guards lay down in front of them with his automatic rifle cocked, ready to open fire if they should 'try to escape'. It was in this alarming and uncomfortable position that Younghusband found them when he happened along half an hour or so later. Peter, who was well known at the various checkpoints, could presumbaly have got himself through, despite the truculence of the guards that day, and departed leaving Fleming and the American to their fate. But, being both a brave as well as a generous man, Peter took it upon himself to plead for the prisoners' release: he must have exerted all his powers of persuasion, the urgency of the situation lending his French unaccustomed fluency. In these circumstances, a guard with a gun, however drunk or benighted, is always 'Monsieur' and Peter repeated it many times. Finally, after protesting that the gentlemen on the floor were honourable members of the great journalistic profession, well-known to Peter and indeed respected citizens in their native countries, whose sole reason for travelling to Elisabethville was to be of service to Katanga; after nearly prostrating himself on his knees before

'Monsieur', and risking a blow or two from a rifle butt himself, Peter managed to extricate them. But it was a close thing and, although Peter was very modest about it afterwards, I think they owe their lives to him.

Donald Wise, then of the *Mirror*, was another Katanga regular whose sense of humour saved everyone from what P.C. Wren would have called *'le cafard'*, the madness born of boredom that used to afflict the men of the French Foreign Legion in novels like *Beau Geste*. Donald is as tall as Peter Younghusband, six foot three or four, with a small military moustache and a dashing air that suggest more the Guards and Whites than the *Daily Mirror*. When Don was at Suez, it was said that he was mistaken for the *Times* man and vice-versa.

Donald is also one of the few people I know who actually invents phrases. Of some of our meaner colleagues, who did not like buying a round of drinks, he would say disparagingly, 'He's got a krait (or a green mamba or a puff-adder) in his pocket.' When the Portuguese in Angola were shooting down Africans who had rebelled against them like mad dogs, he started off a story with the words: 'An African nearly fell into my beer today . . . ' Donald had been sitting at a sidewalk café when an African who was being chased by Portuguese soldiers along a roof top was shot and fell to the ground a few yards away. But his longest-running joke came when he joined the *Mirror* and began his feud with the back bench, the subs who edited all copy before it was sent down to the compositors for printing. Once, every so often, somewhere near the end of a story, Donald would insert the phrase: 'A mad bugler on a white horse galloped past . . . ' The first time he showed me one of his stories with the phrase in it, I simply goggled.

'But I didn't see anyone like that,' I said naively. I looked up to find Don grinning at me for having fallen so neatly into the trap. 'It's for those fucking subs,' he said. 'Those miserable bastards who commute up and down from Orpington every day, have never been farther afield than Devon and hack your copy about without the faintest idea of what's going on outside their own pig-fucking backyard. One

163

day I'm going to get the mad bugler on his white horse past them and into the paper and that'll be the day. That's when they'll get their arses kicked all the way to Orpington and back.' He went off into a great shout of laughter.

Once on receipt of a story about Dr. Banda of Nyasaland, now Malawi, the *Mirror* cabled him: 'Urgent, Wise . . . Hotel Blantyre, Nyasaland. How old Banda query.' It was signed with the name of the Foreign Editor. Now, apart from the expense, it would have been much quicker for the *Mirror* Foreign desk to have looked up *Who's Who* or the *Statesman's Year Book* and filled in the Nyasa dictator's age for themselves. But that would have been too easy and would not have conveyed the desired element of reproof. Donald was quite aware of all this, so he neatly denied them their little triumph by cabling back, 'Old Banda fine how you?'

No matter how unpleasant the occasion, how dangerous the assignment, Donald always managed to discover some aspect of the situation that might seem trivial and unimportant to a less perceptive eye, but which he would elevate to a source of wit and laughter. His sense of the ridiculous never failed, indeed the worse the situation, the more humour he seemed to derive from it. His great gift was to turn many a foreign wasteland into a flowering garden of fantasy.

One story his imagination worked on with particular relish was the attack on the Baluba refugee camp in Elisabethville. The Balubas and Lundas, Tshombe's tribe, were old enemies and, during Tshombe's war with the UN, Baluba refugees poured into a camp on the outskirts of Elisabethville. This camp was under UN protection, but everyone else gave it a wide berth – the Balubas were notorious not only for being ferocious, but, as we have seen, for being cannibals as well.

The Katangese Gendarmerie, whether deliberately or by accident, mortared the Baluba camp, causing a number of casualties and great terror among the inhabitants. The Press Corps, hearing the news, set off immediately to find out how much damage had been done. This is how Donald described it to me.

'When we got to the front gate, they were all nicely stirred up, and as soon as we drove in, they came at us like a swarm of hornets. Big buggers, all starkers, with bows and arrows and axes. One of them had somebody's balls in his mouth. He wanted to show George [Gale] the penis he had cut off some poor bloody Lunda . . . George thought they wanted to cut off his penis to add to their collection. He didn't seem to like that idea. At this point we began to realise that we weren't exactly welcome . . . so we gave it full reverse thrust . . . as we drove away, they were coming after us like the mad bugler . . . full gallop . . . holding these balls in their mouths like retrievers . . . ' He gave a demonic shout of laughter, his blue eyes almost disappearing in the brown leather face, his moustache standing up in simulated terror.

On another celebrated occasion, Tshombe, whose forces were being steadily squeezed by the UN, appointed a new commander. His was presumably a political appointment, since it was hard to believe it had been made on merit. Tshombe, still dapper and smiling despite his troubles, introduced the general and then asked if any of us would like to put questions to the new commander. The general spoke neither French nor English, so all questions had to be translated: and, even in his own language, he seemed to be barely articulate. The press conference quickly became a farce and finally the questions stopped. During a long silence Donald's stage whisper was heard to echo across the room: 'Throw him a banana someone . . . ' The assembled Press Corps burst into laughter and the press conference abruptly came to an end. Tshombe was clearly puzzled as to why this new general should cause such mirth.

By now, of course, Tshombe was no longer the innocent that he had been when I first met him. He was very conscious that he received on the whole a favourable press from the large corps of foreign correspondents who reported the Katanga war. This was due partly to the Press's natural inclination to take the side of the underdog – the little man standing up to the big bully of the UN. It was also due to Tshombe's undoubted charm. There was always a certain simplicity and candour about him, which was more than could be said about some of his colleagues, like the sinister

Godefroid Munongo, the Interior Minister. Tshombe was, it seemed to many of us, a more or less honest man. If he had become a crooked politician it was because he had to deal with the crooked politicians of the UN. This was the opinion not only of many of us journalists, but also of men like George Evans, the British Consul, who knew Tshombe well. One night when the UN were mortaring Tshombe's residence, which was next door to George's Consulate, George was disturbed by a knock on the door. Despite the bombardment, George opened up and found to his amazement a dishevelled President Tshombe, wearing only a dressing-gown, standing on the doorstep. George ushered the unexpected visitor into the study and poured him a large Scotch. 'What can I do for you, M. le Président?' he asked.

'Please help me,' the frightened Katangese leader pleaded. 'The UN are mortaring my house. What shall I do?'

George was an immensely experienced and practical man. He had served in the Indian Police for many years and had once had the delicate task of arresting Jawaharlal Nehru, just before Independence, but had remained on good terms with him. A not very accurate mortar attack was really quite a small crisis, so after a couple of Scotches and a bit of fatherly advice George was able to return Tshombe to his Residence the way he had come, over the garden wall that separated their two properties.

In late 1962 and early 1963, the war was approaching its final stage. Tshombe's army was no longer in possession of Elisabethville and the UN were preparing for the final drive that would take them northwards through the Katanga Copperbelt, to Jadotville and beyond. Tshombe's forces, a real ragtag comprising an unhappy blend of Mad Mike Hoare's English-speaking 5th Commando, the French 4th Commando under Bob Denard and all sorts of other adventurers and hangers-on, were trying to make a stand on the main road to Jadotville. To help them, they wheeled out a home-made tank. This extraordinary monster was essentially a bulldozer which had been armour-plated and had a gun mounted on it in the workshops of Union Minière. When it came to the day, of course, the UN infantry simply out-flanked the Magic Dragon and left it high and dry, like a crippled dinosaur, on the side of the road.

Tshombe had been on a secret mission to see Sir Roy Welensky, Prime Minister of the Central African Federation, in an endeavour to drum up support. He was shortly due to return to Katanga for what Reuters guessed might be the last stage of the war. My job was to pick up Tshombe in Ndola, after he had seen Welensky, and to try and go back into Katanga with him. I was in the barber's shop near the Elephant and Castle Hotel when a *Daily Express* man whom I had not met before introduced himself. Arthur Chesworth was a jovial, fresh-faced home desk reporter who had suddenly been translated to the wilds of Africa; or so he thought. He was also bursting with the zeal that marks up-and-coming men on a paper like the *Express*.

Chesworth was full of questions. Where was Tshombe at the moment? What route was he likely to follow? Would we be able to accompany him? Were his security people friendly or would they try and lose us? And so on, ad infinitum. I found myself playing the role of resident expert, the man who has seen it all, and knows all the answers. I must confess I rather enjoyed it.

I had discovered that Tshombe was due to leave at approximately ten that night, so after a simple dinner we parked outside the guesthouse where Tshombe and his party were staying. A little after ten the familiar figure appeared and ducked into a large black American limousine, which shot off into the darkness, closely pursued by two cars full of secretaries and bodyguards, and then by ourselves. In five minutes we were clear of Ndola, and roaring along the main Copperbelt road, virtually empty at this time of night. We crossed the border at a little-used crossing point in the bush. Tshombe was taking no chances of running into an unexpected UN patrol. The dirt road was atrocious and we bumped and lurched our way through the potholes for another hour or so, finally drawing up at a small mining outpost. There were only half a dozen European houses and we were ushered into the largest of these, the manager's, by some waiting Belgians. Inside, a white cloth had been spread and the table laid with an elaborate cold buffet. The small Belgian community were drawn up in their Sunday best in honour of the arrival of 'Monsieur le Président', and as soon as Tshombe appeared, smiling and blinking in the lights, they all broke spontaneously into applause. One large Belgian matron with an ample bosom advanced on Tshombe, threw her arms around him and kissed him heartily on both cheeks. Monsieur le Président beamed with delight and I swear was blushing as he went along the line shaking hands. When he came to me, he looked startled for a moment, not expecting a journalist in this of all places, and then recovered and smiled. '*Ah, c'est vous encore, M. Ga.*' He never could pronounce my name properly.

In the closing stages of the UN war against Tshombe, it was frequently impossible to use the main road to the border. The Swedes controlled it and were liable to shoot up anyone on it, especially if they thought they were mercenaries. The idea that these 'mercenaries' might be journalists going about their lawful business either did not occur to the slow-witted Swedes, or, disenchanted with Africa and its intractable problems, and longing for the snowy fastnesses of their homeland, they did not care.

Shortly before the road became unusable, I drove out of Elisabethville with Peter Younghusband and John Monks of the *Express*, bound for the Copperbelt. As well as carrying everyone's copy, we would collect money – there had been no banking facilities in Elisabethville for a long time – do some shopping and drive back the next day. We had only gone a few hundred yards from the hotel and were rounding the bend that led out of town when a shot cracked beside our heads, very close and loud despite the noise of the Volkswagen engine. Monks shouted: 'Christ, someone's shooting at us.'

Peter put his foot on the accelerator and ducked down so low that he practically put his head underneath the steering wheel, a remarkable feat for one so large in a car so small. The Volkswagen, now travelling quite fast, sweved erratically from side to side. Thinking we were going to leave the road, I shouted at Peter who straightened up just in time to regain control. I was sitting in the back seat and I turned and peered through the rear window, trying to see who had fired at us. There was a Swedish machine-gun post on the bend, looking down on the road, and I guessed the shot had come from there. By now we were out of range and soon forgot about the incident. But, an hour or two later, another car was fired on by the Swedes and its occupants were not so fortunate. The driver, a Swiss, was shot dead. Jim Biddulph, then the Rhodesian Broadcasting Corporation's correspondent, sitting next to him, was badly wounded in the head and the third man, Sanche de Gramont, an American correspondent who was in the back seat, was wounded in the back and legs. They had been hit by a bazooka.

After that it was clearly too risky to use the road, so some of us, Peter Younghusband, Henry Tanner of the *New York Times*, Eric Robins and Terry Spencer of *Time-Life* and a few others, clubbed together to hire an aircraft to fly our copy and film out and supplies in. I could think of no better pilot than Alan Kearns, who had flown us to Bakwanga. I felt I owed him a good turn after what had happened there, the money would be attractive and there would be little danger involved in shuttling between Kipushi, an airstrip near the border, south of Elisabethville and the Copperbelt. I rang up Alan from Ndola and he agreed immediately. Very soon the entire Press Corps was using our shuttle service which worked extremely well. Our only difficulty was getting payment out of some of the less generous users. As Donald Wise would have remarked, a lot of them had puff-adders in their pockets.

On these trips, Alan used to fly a ridiculously small and fragile-looking Tiger Moth. He said it was the only plane that could cope with the Kipushi dirt strip, which was short, bumpy and dotted with anthills. Only some madman like Kearns would have landed on it at all. I flew in with him one day to find Younghusband waiting to go out. As we hailed each other a second small plane circled and came in to land. To our surprise the passenger was Godefroid Munongo, wearing, as always, the dark glasses which gave him the look of a Hollywood gangster. We shook hands and immediately questioned him about the big story of the day, the fate of the Irish Battalion at Jadotville. The Irish, about a thousand of them, had been encircled in their camp by the Katangese; their water had been cut off and they were being called on to surrender. Munongo could hardly conceal his delight at the plight of the hated UN enemy. But he tried to sound statesmanlike.

'We are trying to find a solution,' he said modestly. 'We think it will not be too difficult.' And he was right. Faced with the prospect of fighting their way out, which was not UN style, or of slowly dying of thirst, the Irish had no choice but to surrender. The Katangese made them lay down their arms and walk out of the camp with their hands in the air. The discomfiture of the poor Irish was complete. They never did seem to come out of things well in the Congo. I suspect their heart was not in it.

A month or two after the Irish capitulation, the long-awaited UN offensive against Katanga began. When I caught up with the UN column they were halfway between Jadotville and Kolwezi, advancing slowly up the main road through open bush country. Every few miles we would come to a halt. As Tshombe's army retreated, the mercenaries would blow the bridges and then mortar the crossing point. But resistance was crumbling fast now and it did not take long for the Indian engineers to put up a pontoon bridge. Soon, their armoured cars were rolling across and driving up the road. There was not much more of a fight even when we reached Kolwezi, the most northerly of the copper towns, with its broad streets and neat Belgian gardens full of brilliant poinsettia and bougainvillea, all now deserted. Next day, Tshombe and the Indian UN commander met, apparently cordially, in the town hall and Tshombe signed the surrender document. The Katanga war was over. Or was it?

Soon after surrendering I watched Tshombe bid farewell to his troops. Most of them looked remarkably spick and span in their new camouflage paratrooper uniforms and all were heavily armed, carrying FN automatics and sub-machine guns. Tshombe, standing on a table addressing them, spoke and behaved as if he was the victor instead of the vanquished, joking and waving his arms and apparently saying (he spoke in Lunda) that this was not the end: there would be another day. His troops gave him a resounding cheer as he left – what would be called a standing ovation at a Blackpool or Brighton Party Conference. They certainly did not look like a defeated army to me and I said so in my despatch to Reuters. Most of them went back to their villages, no doubt hiding their automatics in the thatch of their huts, but the hard core retreated west to the Angolan border where they were to remain off and on for the next fifteen years, making sorties on behalf of Tshombe, later, after his death, becoming a lawless band of freebooters, and finally, in 1979, launching their devastating attack on Kolwezi and massacring its white population.

But for the rest of us the road led back to Elisabethville where we packed our bags for the last time, grateful it was over. There were no regrets at leaving the Léo Deux, although there had been an attempt to spruce it up recently. It would also be the last time, I hoped, that I would take the long lonely road to the border, a road that I had come to know too well. As I drove past the Lubumbashi smelter, I recalled one journey that I would not care to make again. It had happened about six months before when Steve Harper of the *Daily Express* and I had gone to Ndola for the night. In the normal way we took down copy and brought back money, each of us picking up funds for about half a dozen colleagues. I was carrying about one thousand pounds in travellers' cheques and cash when we started back the next day after lunch, rather later than planned, in a big Chevrolet belonging to Georges Cailloux, the Blackwood Hodge representative in Elisabethville. Ray Moloney had hired the car from Georges and lent it to me. We reached the border about four, completed the brief formalities without trouble and started off up the road, reckoning we would be in Elisabethville at around six, in nice time for a drink, a shower and dinner. I could feel the bulge made by £1,000 in travellers' cheques in my hip pocket. It was forty-five miles from the border to Elisabethville over bad roads, and difficult to do more than forty miles an hour. The landscape was familiar: giant red anthills and thick bush. We met hardly anyone, only an occasional African on foot who would give us a nervous wave. We had passed a couple of villages and were out in the middle of nowhere, twenty-five miles from home, when the engine suddenly coughed, fired again and then irrevocably died. We both got out, lifted the bonnet and peered inside. I know almost nothing about combustion engines and, after checking the oil and water, both of which were in order, I was at a loss to know how to proceed farther. I got back in behind the wheel and tried again to start the engine. It turned over but did not fire. We checked the petrol: half full. Finally, we sat in the car and considered our not very bright prospects. We were almost certainly stuck for the night. The chances of a car appearing and giving us a lift were by now almost nil. There were, of course, no garages between us and Elisabethville, and no telephones. The choice was simple. Either we sat in the car all night and hoped someone would come along and give us a lift in the morning, or we could walk.

It was Steve who suggested walking. 'We're carrying a lot of money, two thousand quid between us, and that could be very tempting to a lot of people round here.' He meant African villagers. I did not altogether share that view, since Katanga, unlike the rest of the Congo, had remained relatively law-abiding despite the war. But I agreed that it was tempting fate to sit in a broken-down car all night, an easy target if any deserters or tribesmen on the rampage should come along. So around 5.30 with the light beginning to go, we abandoned the Chevrolet on the side of the road and started off in the direction of Elisabethville. At first, the physical movement after so much inactivity was enjoyable. We went at a good pace, like hill walkers setting out on a long trek. Steve in fact had climbed halfway up Everest for the *Daily Express* to cover Hillary and Tensing's conquest of the mountain in 1953, so he considered himself somewhat of an expert. So did I, although I had not done much serious walking since leaving University. I soon discovered, however, that I was at a serious disadvantage. My shoes were too tight. I have long, narrow feet, size eleven, and all my life I have

172

had trouble getting an exact fit. I often buy a pair of shoes which feel comfortable in the shop but, after a while, find they are too small. So with these shoes. They were just all right to stroll around in but I would never have worn them if I had known what was going to happen. As soon as my feet started to expand with the walking, they began to hurt. After a couple of miles, they hurt like hell, but I gritted my teeth and kept on, and – minor miracle – after about five miles my feet became numb. Steve knew nothing of this and, determined to preserve his image of half-conqueror of Everest, kept up a cracking pace. We stopped every hour for a five-minute break but otherwise talked little and just walked. It was now dark, with no moon and only a little starshine, the road a faint grey blur. The main problem, I found, now that my feet had almost lost all feeling, was that it was too dark to see the potholes and I would occasionally stumble into them, which brought back the pain. Surprisingly, we neither saw nor heard any animals.

Around ten or eleven, we saw a pinprick of light in the darkness, shaking and bouncing, and an African on a bicycle came rattling towards us. When he suddenly saw the two white men advancing purposefully up the road, he speeded up and shot past us, not uttering a word! We laughed. He was obviously more frightened of us than we were of him. An hour or so later a more interesting apparition emerged out of the darkness. It had twin lights, shook and rattled more alarmingly than the bicycle, and it was unmistakably a car. Our hopes rose. Could this be the answer to our prayers, despite the fact that it was going the wrong way? Blocking the road, we held up our hands and made the car stop; not that that was very difficult, it was going so slowly. In the faint radiance cast by the weak headlights, I could see it was a very old and fragile-looking Citroën. An African was behind the wheel and there were two or three passengers. '*Bonsoir*,' I said politely. 'Our car has broken down and we are very anxious to reach Elisabethville as soon as possible. Could you possibly give us a lift?' There was a pause and then Steve said, 'We'll pay you well, 200 francs.' We waited anxiously for the answer.

'I'm very sorry,' the African driver said in educated French, 'But I'm only going to my village a few kilometres away.'

'Yes,' we said. 'But we'll pay you a lot of money to take us to Elisabethville. 400 francs.' It was probably more than he would earn in a month. There was a long pause and then the African said apologetically. 'I'm very sorry, but the car is so old that with passengers in it, it will only go downhill. I cannot go to Elisabethville because it is uphill.' This was indeed true. The road rises gradually all the way.

We tried once more, desperately. '*Non, non, Monsieur,*' he said. 'It is not a question of money. I would take you with pleasure if the car would go. But, you see for yourselves, it is too old.'

We had to admit defeat. 'Thank you very much all the same,' I said. '*Bon voyage.*' We watched him rattle off slowly into the darkness, his rear lights trembling like red fire-flies until the darkness swallowed them up. With a sense of redoubled weariness we turned uphill again, both of us so disappointed that we did not speak for another hour.

The rest of the walk became a monotonous slog, and after each break I could feel myself stiffening up, but we were still going a good pace when we arrived on the outskirts of Elisabethville at about half-past five, as dawn was breaking. A Volkswagen bus collecting Sabena workers for the airport offered us a lift, and although Steve was against the idea, seeming to think it was a matter of principle to finish the march on foot, I overruled him, and so we drove the last mile and a half to the hotel. Because of the shortage of accommodation within the Léo Deux, I was sharing a room with Ray Moloney, and when I burst into the room at six o'clock, he sat up in some surprise.

'Good God, what the hell are you doing coming crashing in at this time of the morning?' he said crossly. 'Where the hell have you been anyway?'

'Your bloody car broke down,' I said accusingly. 'Halfway between here and the border. We've just walked all bloody night. That's where we've been.' I sat on my bed, and wearily took off my shoes and threw them to the other end of the

174

room. Then I lay down, exhausted but with a feeling of utter relief, and fell asleep. When I woke, in late afternoon, I was so stiff I could hardly get out of bed. I hobbled down to the bar and ordered a large Scotch. Ray appeared half an hour later, in a bad mood. He had spent the better part of the day recovering the car. When I asked him how he had managed to get it started, he looked at me furiously.

'I don't know what you and Harper thought you were doing,' he shouted, 'I switched on the ignition and it started first go. Nothing at all wrong with the bloody car . . .'

One of the last things I had done in the Congo was to write a letter of resignation to Tony Cole in London, and the reply was waiting for me in Johannesburg. It was a generous letter and I like to think that Tony was a trifle sad at losing me. A week later he was dead, carried off by a heart attack: he had been extremely overweight.

My ten years with Reuters were now officially over. I had joined ITN and was due to start in London in August. Before we left South Africa I had practised addressing a camera and found the experience strangely terrifying. I wondered if I had made the right decision.

CHAPTER VI

A Nervous Start with ITN: then Dallas, the Aswan Dam and Pygmies in the Congo

Although I knew all about being a foreign correspondent, I knew nothing about television. I had hardly been in Britain for ten years, had watched very little television and had even missed the heady days when ITN started on the air. So Geoffrey Cox, the Editor of ITN, a Napoleonic New Zealander, decreed that I should do three months on the Home Desk to learn the business. After a week or two, I was allowed to report a story about a minor shooting. It involved going to a pub in the Home Counties, which had some connection with the crime. There the cameraman, Jon Lane, put me up against the bar, shone the lights on me and, in the kindest possible way, put me through my lines. They were only a sentence or two, in which I said that police were concentrating their inquiries on the area. I was dreadfully nervous and it took me several attempts to get them right. Jon knew this and coached me with great patience.

Another cameraman, Jackie Howard, was an extremely kind man but quite incapable of realising that a reporter might have nerves. We went to report on a Post Office

Exhibition in London and I had to interview the Chief Engineer. The public were also going round the exhibition and, when it came to the time to start the interview, Jackie simply shouted at the top of his voice for quiet. Naturally everyone stopped in mid-stride and looked at me. This was the last thing I wanted and I became so nervous that I gulped and stammered and the man I was interviewing said to me incredulously: 'I think you are more nervous than I am.' He was right. Jackie had no idea of the havoc that he was creating.

At the end of October a shaft in a German coal mine collapsed and eleven miners were trapped underground. The mine was at Lengede, a small town in the middle of the bleak North German plain. For several days I waited for ITN to send a reporter and camera team but nothing happened. I asked the Foreign Desk when we were going to send someone but they simply shrugged and said they were waiting for instructions from the Editor. One morning, BBC radio news reported that the miners' plight was becoming desperate, so I packed a bag and took it with me to the office. As soon as I got there I reported to the Foreign Desk that I was ready to go to Lengede. All morning I waited. Nothing happened. Then, about lunchtime, I saw the Editor, Geoffrey Cox, at the doorway to the newsroom. He advanced into the room sideways, rather like a crab, and without looking at me directly. Finally he stopped, still not looking at me and said: 'I hear you're off to Lengede.'

'Well,' I said, taken aback. 'I think it's time someone went.'

Geoffrey ignored this. 'Any man who packs his bag and brings it into the newsroom deserves to be sent on an assignment.' It was really a little lecture to the rest of the staff. 'Good luck.' He turned on his heel and strutted away down the corridor. I realised then that I had joined an organisation which, when it came to covering foreign news, was a babe in arms compared to Reuters.

I caught the evening flight to Hanover and took a taxi to the hotel near Lengede. The crew were to come on later.

Lengede is surrounded by vast, flat treeless fields where

177

most of Germany's sugar beer crop is grown and, as I drove to the mine, I passed several tractors pulling huge trailers. The beer harvest was in full swing under a cold, leaden sky.

When I went to the local post office to telephone my first report to ITN, I asked the postmaster how long it would take to get through to London. 'Half an hour?' I asked.

'Nein, nein,' he said, offended. *'Zwei Minuten für London.'* And indeed, it took exactly that, with the line as clear as a bell. But, as I remembered, most things do work extremely efficiently in Germany. At the mine itself, everything was planned down to the last detail for the Press, with briefings twice a day and officials constantly on hand to answer questions. They had just sunk a new shaft down to the trapped men and were in communication with them. Eventually they were able to pass down food and drink and even warm clothing. It was a considerable achievement and the morale of the trapped men was now remarkably high.

I was able to telephone reports to ITN, what are known in the profession as 'voice pieces', but no television pictures. The crew had still not arrived. Around the tenth day, the West German Chancellor, Professor Ludwig Erhard, came to see for himself what was happening. He conducted a conversation down the communications shaft with the trapped men which was duly recorded and played back to the Press. It was possible that, in their weakened state, the men did not clearly understand what the jovial Bundeskanzler was saying to them; but there was also a suggestion that, being good Social Democrats, they did not wish to make political propaganda for an opponent – Erhard was a Christian Democrat. At any rate, there seemed to be a distinct frostiness in the exchange and I reported this, quoting their conversation in my evening 'voice piece'.

'Hello, hello, this is the Federal Chancellor speaking. Do you hear me?'

Silence.

'Hello, hello, Bundeskanzler Erhard here. Do you hear me down there?'

Long pause. Then, rather offhandedly: 'Yes, we can hear you . . .'

This was the first report that I did for ITN over which they in any way enthused. I asked Eleanor if she had heard it.

'Yes.'

'How was it, all right?' I was anxious for comment and, if possible, acclaim.

'You were very clear,' she said, and with that I had to be content.

One of the drawbacks for someone like myself starting at ITN without any television experience was that I needed advice and constructive criticism, and no one was either willing or able to give it. When the crew finally did arrive – it was Jackie Howard and his sound man Frank McNally again – ITN said they wanted a ten-minute mini-documentary on the rescue, and I had not the slightest idea how to do it. I had all the facts of course; the eleven miners had been brought to the surface exactly two weeks after being trapped underground and were in remarkably good shape. The whole of Germany was celebrating and I celebrated too with a final voice piece. But then I had to start working out how we would do the film report. We had some film, but not a lot, and much of the story would have to be told by 'graphics' or diagrams. But how did I fit script to pictures? There were no producers or 'fixers' to help the reporter in those days. It was just me, plus Jackie and Frank who were constantly bickering, and whatever advice I could get from London, which was not much. I telephoned Denis Thomas, who was deputy Editor as well as editor of 'Roving Report', and asked for his advice.

'Just speak your script in front of the camera,' he told me airily. 'As much to camera as possible.' That cryptic phrase means that you memorise your script and speak it straight at the camera without looking at your notes. My heart sank, 'But the script is seven or eight pages long,' I protested. 'I couldn't possibly remember all that.'

'Do as much as you can,' he said and rang off. This did not leave me much the wiser, so I consulted Jackie, who had been in the film and television business all his life. Alas, Jackie, fine fellow that he was, proved quite incapable of telling me how we should cope with the problem. The answer, I know

now, was to record separately the bits of commentary which could be covered by the picture, and to speak to camera only one or possibly two short sections: either because we had no picture or because they were so important that they would gain from being spoken by the reporter straight to the camera, and thus to the audience. In my ignorance, however, I stood in front of the camera, with Jackie urging me on, and read out seven pages of script, on camera, but not really to the camera. It worked out in the end, but I shall never know how. The main lesson I learned from Lengede was that television was no different from any other sort of journalism; it was sink or swim and there was no one around to teach you the breast stroke.

The only other thing I recall about Lengede is that I met Freddy Forsyth there for the first time. He was the Reuters correspondent in East Berlin and had been sent down to reinforce the Bonn team. Years later he told me that, after finishing his story of the miner's rescue, he and some friends went out on the town to celebrate. They finished off by beating up the hotel at four in the morning. 'You,' he said scornfully, 'had gone to bed long before.' No wonder, after my agonising struggle with 'Roving Report' and Jackie Howard.

On November 22, I was sitting in the audience in the Village Hall at Groombridge in Kent, watching an amateur performance of *The Gazebo* in which my friend Sheila Bett was playing the maid, when her husband John came to find me urgently. 'President Kennedy has been shot,' he said. 'ITN want you to go to America.'

Leaving Sheila to cope with Act Three on her own, we drove back to John Tudor's farmhouse and, while he poured me a large Scotch, I rang ITN.

President Kennedy had been shot in the head in Dallas, they said. The Editor wanted me to go to New York immediately, but there was no flight until the morning. Money and tickets would be at the airport, the car would pick me up at seven. I'll be ready, I said, and they rang off. They were desperately busy, trying to keep abreast of developments in

180

Texas, five hours behind London, as the grisly story unfolded: Kennedy rushed to hospital, his bleeding head in Jackie's hands, his brain shattered by the bullet from Lee Harvey Oswald's high-powered rifle; Kennedy pronounced dead; Lyndon Johnson sworn in as the new President; the grim flight back to Washington aboard Air Force One; and the stunned reaction of America and the world. What I did not know at the time was that all ITN's top brass, from Geoffrey Cox downwards, were at the Television Ball in the Dorchester Hotel when the news broke. ITN's chief news-caster Andrew Gardner and Geoffrey Cox put down their glasses and rushed back to the studio to put out a series of newsflashes and a special programme. Brian Connell who presented 'This Week' on Thames and was the network's chief commentator, was alerted to fly out too. We met next day in his hotel in Washington, just across from the White House. As we were sitting there, with the television set on, we suddenly saw, unfolding on the screen in front of our eyes, the shooting of Lee Harvey Oswald by Jack Ruby, in the police station at Dallas. Neither of us could quite take it in. But there it was, being repeated in slow motion this time. Oswald, who had been arrested shortly after he had killed Kennedy, was being taken to court to be charged with the murder, when Jack Ruby, a former barman, stepped out of the crowd and shot him at point blank range. Oswald was facing the camera and the agonised expression on his face as the bullets struck home was frozen on the screen as it seemed for ever. A second or two later the telephone rang and ITN were on the line demanding a voice piece. I wrote it on Brian Connell's portable typewriter in the bedroom and telephoned it over to ITN who recorded it five minutes later.

Next day I left for Dallas with a CBS crew to try and recon-struct the events of the Kennedy shooting. The scene of the shooting, as if it had been a Greek tragedy, was a natural amphitheatre. The Kennedy motorcade, with the President and his wife travelling in an open car, had approached from the left, turned right towards the Dallas Book Depository – a sort of warehouse – where Oswald was watching from a top window and then turned diagonally left down a gentle incline towards an underpass. To the right of the incline was a grassy bank with a few small trees, and the crowds were standing all along this section of the route to get a good view of the President and Jackie. As the cars coasted slowly down the slope, Oswald, who had been a marksman in the US Marine Corps, opened fire, getting off three shots in a couple of seconds. One of them hit Kennedy in the back of the head and it was that bullet which caused the fatal damage.

Apart from filming the book store in order to show more or less the view that Oswald had had at the time of the shooting, we went down to the grassy knoll where a number of people had gathered from all over America, to mourn their lost leader. I interviewed a number of them briefly: what are known as 'Vox Pops' in the business. Black and white, they were all vocal in their grief, but one was particularly articulate. He was a man of about fifty, reasonably well-dressed, perhaps a teacher or an engineer. At first he talked with emotion, but in a controlled way, about what the death of Kennedy meant to him, and to America. And then he broke down and cried, but, despite the sobs, he still managed to finish what he wanted to say. He did it with a natural dignity, as if he felt it was his duty to communicate his deep feelings to the outside world. I learned then, for the first time, how much more natural Americans are in front of the camera than anyone else, a product no doubt of their open society. They do not appear to be inhibited by the camera, they speak frankly, without fear or favour.

The interview was used late at night the next night, on a programme called 'Dateline', and Reggie Bosanquet, who was presenting it, was so impressed that he tried to persuade Geoffrey Cox to run it the next day on the main news programme. But the law that says that yesterday's news must never be shown again today was held to be immutable and it was not re-run. Now, we would be more flexible and more imaginative.

So far, apart from the Kennedy assassination, I had been assigned to 'human interest' stories. Now came my second major foreign assignment, the sort of story I really enjoyed reporting. At the beginning of May, Nikita Khrushchev made his first visit to Egypt to open the first stage of the Aswan High Dam. This great engineering project was the ostensible reason for the breakdown in relations between Egypt and the West that led ultimately to Suez. It all began in December 1955 when Britain and the United States offered to finance the building of the High Dam, a visionary scheme that was to transform life for millions of Egyptian peasants by harnessing the Nile and irrigating huge stretches of the desert. Since the time of the Pharaohs, Egypt had depended on the flood waters of the Nile. If the floods failed, the harvest failed and famine followed. The new High Dam would prevent this ever happening again. That was the grandiose scheme but when Nasser, the arch nationalist, became President of Egypt in June 1956, the West got cold feet. And when Nasser decided, against American advice, to accept a large shipment of Communist arms – they were actually Czech but the hand of Moscow was patently obvious – the Americans gave him an ultimatum, wrongly as many people in Britain and Western Europe thought: give up the arms or forfeit the finance for the Aswan Dam. Nasser refused, quite naturally, to capitulate, and John Foster Dulles, the conservative Secretary of State, announced that America was withdrawing its offer. Britain fell into step behind. That was on July 20, 1956. Six days later Nasser announced the nationalisation of the Suez Canal. The Russians were not slow to fill the vacuum. Khrushchev announced that the Soviet Union would finance the Dam.

Now, eight years later, Khrushchev had come to reap his reward, with interest. The Egyptians promised an impressive ceremony and the world's press and television descended on Cairo. For the Westerners, it was a struggle from the start. Egyptian officials, taking their cue from Nasser and his ministers, were extremely suspicious of nearly all Western journalists and correspondingly obstructive. Our first problem was accommodation. The Hilton was full and so was every other hotel. We were finally assigned to cabins on board a Nile paddle steamer, moored near the Hilton, which turned out to be cramped but romantic. To be rocked gently to sleep by the waters of this greatest of all rivers, which rises in the snows of central Africa and disgorges its great brown flood into the ancient Meditteranean, gave me acute pleasure, especially at the end of a frustrating day spent wrestling with Egyptian bureaucrats for accreditation and film passes.

In the evening, we would assemble in the bar of the Hilton to swap stories of unbelievable Egyptian incompetence and red tape. Donald Wise, as jaunty and as immaculate as ever, who referred to the galabiyah-wearing local populace as the nightshirt brigade, had some of the best stories.

In Aswan, we were told, accommodation was going to be even more difficult. The New Cataract Hotel had been reserved exclusively for the Russians, the Old Cataract Hotel for second-class guests, and the Western press, distinctly third-class as far as the Egyptians were concerned, were relegated to the Grand Hotel. Finally about fifty British, American and French journalists, photographers and television crews took the overnight train from Cairo to Aswan, a journey of about 500 miles up the Nile. We each had a separate couchette, a horsehair sofa as hard as a stale bun which pulled out at night to make a sort of bed. The heat was so oppressive that I opened the window wide, but woke in the middle of the night to find the compartment full of choking coal smoke. But there were compensations. Next morning, I looked out of the window and saw the Nile, a sheet of grey and silver, right beside the line. As I peered out, a felucca, that most graceful of all boats, floated into view, its sails mirrored in the smooth water.

A few minutes later we arrived in Aswan and were immediately caught up in the noisy, shouting, scuffling mêlée that is normal at any Egyptian railway station. Porters fought for the privilege of handling our fifteen pieces of luggage, which were then piled on the backs of tiny, long-suffering donkeys, while we were hoisted aboard a rickety-looking gharry and borne off to the Grand Hotel. It stood on the left of the road, looking west across the Nile, and must once have been a rather elegant place. But that was a long time ago, when English aristocrats doing the Grand Tour stopped there to see the Temples of Rameses II at nearby Abu Simbel. But in 1964 the Grand Hotel had clearly gone without a coat of paint for many years, the swing doors creaked on their hinges and the lobby had an air of fly-blown desolation. A pack of Western journalists now converged simultaneously on the reception desk, demanding rooms. The unfortunate Egyptian in charge waved his hands in despair.

'We have no enough rooms,' he screeched. 'You will have to share.'

'No, no,' we shouted back. 'Separate rooms.'

'Not possible,' the man cried. 'You are too much people.'

In the end we had to bow to the inevitable. Grumbling but impotent, Ken Taylor, my giant cameraman, Ronny Hubbard, the soundman and I climbed the stairs and were shown into a barrack of a room in which two Egyptians already lounged in their pyjamas.

'No, no,' I protested. 'We want a room of our own . . . ' I pointed at the three of us. 'For us only, you understand?'

'Wait one minute,' the man darted away and opened another door. This room was slightly better: it had only five beds in it. We gave orders for the fifteen pieces to be brought up and resigned ourselves to the rigours of being a Western traveller in Nasser's Egypt. Later, we set off to tour the Dam which Khrushchev and Nasser would open the next day. There was no question about it: it was enormously impressive. First of all the Nile had been diverted from its course to allow the building of the dam, a huge wall of concrete, in the shape of a horseshoe, which stood in the dry river bed: in it were set a whole row of giant turbines which eventually would provide enough electricity for the whole of Egypt. Workmen were putting the final touches to the preparations and bulldozers were heaving huge boulders into position. To my surprise most of the equipment was British. Our Egyptian press liaison officer, a genial poet who had studied in Britain on a British Council grant, explained that the Russian bulldozers constantly broke down and most of the work had been done by British machines. The Russian equipment was being kept in reserve for tomorrow. The poet, who was called Ahmed, winked.

'All the Eygptians know that Russian equipment is no good. Of course, we can't say so.' He smiled, showing his

185

nicotine-stained teeth. 'But now you know the truth. You can say what you like.'

Ahmed showed us where we would be allowed to position our cameras on the morrow and we returned to the Grand Hotel, dreading the thought that we might have to eat dinner there. Luckily Donald Wise fell in beside us and informed us that he had managed to get a cabin on the same Nile paddle steamer we had occupied in Cairo. Unfortunately, Donald said, there were no free cabins, but we were very welcome to have dinner on board. The food was good and the local red wine, called Omar Khayyam, very drinkable.

Next day, we had to be in our places two hours before the ceremony was due to take place – at noon. Khrushchev and Nasser flew down from Cairo, landed nearby and then drove up the bumpy road to the hilltop where the opening would be performed. The scene had something of a medieval tournament about it. A series of big desert tents had been erected to shield the distinguished foreign visitors from the burning Egyptian sun – the temperature was about a hundred in the shade by now – and the stony ground had been covered by equally extensive carpets. The entire High Dam workforce and every peasant in the area had been rounded up to line the route and the lower slopes of the hill.

Khrushchev waddled in, looking heavier and redder in the face than when I had last seen him in Hungary eight years before. He gave the impression of finding the heat as much of a trial as the Egyptian government. Beside him Nasser looked like a film star, tall, distinguished, his black hair flecked with grey. They took their places on the dais, under the biggest awning and on the thickest carpet.

At precisely twelve noon, Khrushchev and Nasser walked to a kind of lectern and, hands interlocked, together pressed a big red button. The camera was already rolling and Ken Taylor zoomed from the two leaders in the foreground to a distant patch of rocks, about a mile away. There was a dramatic pause of perhaps one or two seconds. Then a puff of smoke rose in the air and at the same time a jet of water shot from the rock, making a silver arch to the floor of the desert. The Nile, diverted for so long to allow the building of the High Dam, was returning to its original course. More explosions followed, the temporary retaining wall collapsed in a cloud of dust and the great river bounded through the widening gap, sweeping all before it. A ragged cheer rose from the watching crowds and Nasser and Khrushchev embraced each other, the short, stocky, cocky Russian and the tall, crafty Egyptian, who had become the symbol of Arab nationalism. As we watched, the water reached the foot of the dam and started to rise. Half an hour later, it had climbed as high as the turbines and was allowed to gush harmlessly down the smooth concrete face of the dam. Khrushchev, mopping his brow furiously, shook hands again with Nasser and prepared to depart. The gesture had been made, the triumph recorded for all the world to see, now he had had enough of this burning desert.

But on his way back he had to pay one more act of homage, stopping off at Luxor, in the Valley of the Kings, and then once more to see the Pyramids and the Sphinx, on the outskirts of Cairo. There, as part of the spectacle, an eccentric Egyptian athlete ran up the Great Pyramid, in the broiling sun, leaping from one great sandstone block to another, to do honour to the distinguished visitor. So much for Khrushchev. We now received a very peculiar request from the Editor, Geoffrey Cox, although it did not come as a complete surprise. He instructed us to head for the Western Desert and its old battlefields where we were to make a film for 'Roving Report'. This, I knew, was an act of nostalgia on his part, but it was one that gave rise to considerable trepidation on mine. As far as I knew there was no 'story' there, in the sense that nothing had happened in the interim and there was no action, except for the sun beating down on the desert stones, the whisper of the wind and the ghosts of the dead. Still, it is difficult to dispute an Editor's whim and, although I doubted the journalistic value of the exercise, as a traveller I looked forward to the trip immensely.

We found a fat and friendly taxi-driver outside the Hilton Hotel, another Ahmed, and hired him to drive us to Alexandria and points west.

We set off early next morning, inching our way over the

Kasr el-Nil Bridge in a snarl of donkey and camel carts, bicycles, scooters, buses and cars all blaring away on their horns, and then took the broad avenue, built for the Empress Eugénie in 1868, towards Giza and the Pyramids. There we turned west on the desert road to Alexandria, 140 miles away. Alexandria, like so much of Egypt, I found disappointing. Years of decline and neglect had given everything a seedy appearance. I looked in vain for Justine or any of the rest of Laurence Durrell's exotic characters. Its colourful and cosmopolitan past seemed to have been submerged by a dismal present that not even the sunshine and the blue of the Mediterranean could dispel.

After lunch at the Cecil Hotel, we pressed on in Ahmed's old Chevrolet, heading west across the stony desert, towards El Alamein, the goal of our pilgrimage. As the edge of the battlefield came into view, we could make out here and there the shape of a knocked-out tank, its rusting gun pointing at the sky, or a dilapidated army lorry, minus wheels and every other removable part: the Beduin, like vultures picking a corpse, had stripped it clean, down to the chassis. Alamein was one of the decisive battles of the Second World War. It destroyed the German dominance of North Africa and ended their threat to Egypt and the Suez Canal. It was also a victory of great psychological significance since it ended a run of British defeats and finally shattered the myth of Rommel's invincibility. It was a battle that hung in the balance for nearly two weeks, until finally Montgomery's Desert Rats, the British Eighth Army, overwhelmed Rommel's élite Afrika Korps. It was a stupendous struggle and the casualties were enormous. Nearly 20,000 British, Australian, New Zealand, Indian, French and Polish soldiers were killed at El Alamein and are commemorated there; and as many Germans and Italians have their own memorials.

The cemetery is the most profoundly moving place in the whole Western Desert, but I did not want to film there immediately. I needed to see all the other battlefields first and come back to Alamein at the very end. So we got back into the car and drove on towards Mersa Matruh, a dusty little place, the colour of the desert but redeemed by a mile-long bay of sparkling white sand. We found ourselves the only guests in the Hotel Lido and, when we changed and went down to the beach for a swim, it was equally empty: the water was deliciously refreshing and crystal clear.

We made Mersa Matruh our base and drove from there towards the Libyan border, to Sidi Barrani and Sollum, always with the desert on our left and the placid peacock-blue of the Mediterranean on our right. But the border was closed and we were not able to visit the biggest battlefield of all after Alamein, Tobruk. The whole desert here is littered with the débris of battle and we found many of the smaller relics of the conflict, petrol tins, water bottles and, the most evocative and personal of all, discarded steel helmets. All along the road, which runs between the sea and the desert, we saw how the Beduin had used the flotsam of the war to enrich their own threadbare lives. But, of all the junk left behind, the jerry can was the most sought-after. Every family had at least one, a prized possession, and at every well you would see the women and the children filling them up and then staggering off under their weight.

As I listened sleepily to the hum of Ahmed's tyres on the hot tarmac, I could imagine the sharper hum that Rommel's command car must have made as it sped along this very road, and the clank and smoke of the German Panzers as they ground their way forward, driving the British before them and threatening, when they were running at full bore, to roll all the way in triumph to Cairo.

We saw hardly anyone on the road. It was as if we had only the ghosts of the forgotten armies to keep us company. Even the sight of an occasional group of Beduin swaying across the desert on their camels seemed to enhance rather than diminish the emptiness. Because of the paucity of anything that could be described as interesting picture, I decided to film local scenes such as Beduin women winnowing wheat by hand, throwing it up into the air so that the chaff was blown away and the grain fell to the ground. This was a scene of Biblical simplicity, an act that had been performed by man since he first started to grow crops, and as such it had for me great beauty. The women were fine-looking, they had no objection

189

to being filmed and behaved completely naturally in front of the camera. I noticed in passing and without thinking twice about it that they were barefoot.

In the hotel that evening, Ahmed came to find me. He pulled a long face. A man from the local tourist office had arrived to see us. Introductions were made, we sat down in the lobby and coffee was brought. Our visitor was small, like a shrimp, with bright eyes behind glasses. He explained that he was not happy with the manner of our filming.

'How so?' I asked. We had permission from the Ministry of Information in Cairo to film the Western Desert and the battlefields.

Yes, he said, the battlefields, but why were we filming things that showed the Egyptians in a bad light? I was amazed. What things?

He sipped his coffee, in irritating silence, and then he came out with it. Donkeys, he said, and bare feet.

Bare feet? I laughed and immediately saw that was a mistake. I tried hastily to explain that there was no intention of belittling the Egyptian way of life. We were simply filming a natural peasant scene. But he remained unconvinced and informed us that we would have to leave the next day. Permission to film further had been withdrawn, he said, looking now like an angry shrimp.

I glanced at Ken Taylor speculatively. There was one shot we particularly wanted to do on the way back: El Alamein station, a desolate, deserted place, with a loose sheet of corrugated iron flapping in the desert wind. During the war, thousands of British and German troops must have passed through it and their ghosts still peopled the platform. Now only one train a day ran between Alexandria and Mersa Matruh, and we wanted to film it. I decided perhaps foolishly to put it to the Shrimp. He listened, lips pursed, and then shook his head. No more filming. We must drive straight back to Alexandria. Ken, all six foot four and sixteen stone of him, towered up in a rage. He had set his heart on that shot and now this pint-sized bureaucrat was refusing to let him do it for no good reason. He looked as if he were about to strangle the Shrimp.

When we left next morning, we were all agreed on one thing. We would have to film the El Alamein Cemetery on the way back, otherwise we would not have a programme at all. Somehow we would have to outmanoeuvre the Shrimp who might follow us and see us off his territory. Luckily there was no sign of him when we reached El Alamein. We left the car and walked towards the cemetery, passing through an imposing triple archway: beyond, stretching to the edge of the battlefield, lay a green oasis, covered not with trees, but with thousands and thousands of identical white crosses, a geometrical forest of remembrance. Seven thousand five hundred soldiers are buried here and on the walls the names of another 12,000 are engraved in stone. In the middle of the vast cemetery stands an altar and on the altar an inscription with the words: 'Their name liveth for evermore.'

As Ken and Ronny began to film, taking close-ups of the individual crosses with the names and ranks of the fallen soldiers, I walked some distance away to find the right words on which to end the programme. As I strolled in the bright afternoon sunshine, among the myriad graves, I became conscious of a great sense of peace; of sadness too, at the loss of so many lives, at the fierce agonies that must have been endured during that terrible battle; but essentially it was a feeling of great peace, embalmed as it were, in the silence and solitude of the desert.

We were still in the desert when Jawaharlal Nehru died at the end of May and, by the time we reached Cairo, his body had been cremated and his ashes scattered in the presence of half a million grieving Indians: Nehru, India's first Prime Minister after Independence, patrician and intellectual but never the darling of the masses in the way that Gandhi, the man he succeeded, was. Despite the delay, Geoffrey Cox still wanted us to fly to Delhi to report on the aftermath and interview the new Prime Minister, Lal Bahadur Shastri. Shastri was certainly the most unimpressive-looking Prime Minister I have ever met. Physically tiny, so soft-spoken as to be almost inaudible and so diffident as to be almost inarticulate, it was a struggle to get anything out of him at all. Shastri was given the job, it was said, because he was a compromise choice among several more positive but more divisive candidates, men like Morarji Desai, a tough, ascetic old bird chiefly known in the West for his habit of drinking his own urine every morning as part of a health régime.

Delhi has its magnificences and its squalors. The New Delhi Government Building designed by Lutyens, including the Viceroy's Palace, which epitomised the splendour of the British Raj, are superb and so in its different way is the Red Fort, the old Palace of the Mogul conquerors, so called because it is built of red sandstone. Between the Red Fort and Government Buildings sprawls the ugly muddle and poverty of modern Delhi; and above them all, wings taut against a pitiless blue sky, wheel the birds that for me symbolise India, the red kites, part scavengers, part predators.

The contrast, a few days later, as I drove from Heathrow across the Thames at Hampton Court to my home in Penshurst in Kent, was startling. But I was not to be allowed to wallow long in the green magic of an English June. In the Congo, where a very different green prevailed, the last UN troops were about to leave after four years. It was the first international police operation ever mounted by the UN and it was worth assessing how it had worked.

Jon Lane, the young cameraman who had coached me so sympathetically on my first story for ITN, Eric Vincent, a smiling, energetic sound recordist, and I flew out of Heathrow for Léopoldville aboard a Sabena jet. It was a night flight and early next day a glimpse of the great river and then Njili Airport was enough to start a chain-reaction of memories and a certain tightening of the stomach. The Memling Hotel was if anything worse than I remembered it, the European city more desolate-looking with grass sprouting in the cracks in the concrete, and the Congolese more sullen. Disaffection weighed on the city like the humid overcast from the Atlantic Ocean, and the heat sapped one's will.

The last UN troops in the capital, the Nigerians, drilled for their farewell parade with commendable panache, showing up the local army for what it was, an undisciplined rabble.

What would happen after they left? There were already

ominous signs of a further breakdown in law and order –
there was said to be increased robbery and violence, and even
diplomats' houses were not safe. More dangerously, rebellion
was in the air and it seemed only a matter of time before the
whole rickety structure began to collapse. We made friends
with a United Nations official, a young American on a six-
month tour, who painted a picture of mind-boggling corruption and inefficiency.

'These UN cats are in it for the money,' Peter explained,
offering us a duty-free Scotch in his flat. 'Even if they are
regular guys and not corrupt themselves, they still can't do
anything about the general corruption. It's the only way you
can operate. The Ministers won't do business unless they get
bribes. They're all the same.'

On Sunday we went for a picnic with Peter and some of his
UN friends, taking a launch up river to an island in midstream. He told us not to swim. A German diplomat, a strong
swimmer, had been rash enough to venture into the river here
recently and had disappeared after a few strokes without
trace, either sucked under by the current, or by a crocodile. I
looked at the heaving brown water and decided nothing
would tempt me to swim in that mill race voluntarily; and I
reflected that there were similarities between river and
country. Both seemed to be heading for the rapids at a
frightening speed.

One night, just as we were finishing the UN story, I had a
drink with the local Reuters man, Derek Blackman. I said I
was looking for an idea for another story before going back
to London. Had he any ideas? 'Yes,' he said, 'why don't you
go and see what has happened to the pygmies?'

'The pygmies? Why? What about them?' I was baffled but
intrigued.

'Well,' Blackman said. 'No one's been there since
Independence and nobody knows what's happened to them.
And Air Congo is advertising a new tourist trip. I think I've
got the leaflet here.' This sounded like a bad joke as there had
not been any tourists in the Congo for over four years. A few
minutes later he came back with a pamphlet in his hand. Next
day I went to the Air Congo office and booked three flights

to Goma. The day after that we paid our bills at the Memling, glad to be rid of its fetid atmosphere, and drove out under a lowering sky to Njili. After the usual delay, we climbed aboard a dilapidated-looking DC3 and took off in the direction of Kindu, 500 miles away across the forest, a desolate little town lost in the depths of the Congo interior. From there we flew on to Goma, in the eastern highlands of the Congo. Here you are more or less in the middle of Africa and it is very different country to the swamp lowlands of Léopoldville. The Belgians called Kivu province, with its lakes and mountains, the African Switzerland, and the description is not entirely far-fetched. It is one of the most beautiful regions of Africa, part of the great north-south lake system, the country high and open, well-forested and well-watered. Goma itself is a pretty little town set on the northern shore of Lake Kivu, once full of Belgians, now semi-deserted. We were met at the airport by our guide, a Swiss called Philippe who was in the travel business and was also the honorary Swiss consul in Kivu. He was a thin-faced rather intense-looking man with a thatch of greying hair and hot blue eyes behind thick glasses. He stowed our cameras and bags in the boot of his Mercedes and we drove off, getting only a glimpse of Goma. We had gone about ten miles when he came to a roadblock manned by a group of ragged tribesmen. One of them came and peered inside the car, asked Philippe a few questions and then, after some debate with his friends, reluctantly raised the pole and let us through. Philippe let the clutch in with a jerk and raced away, swearing in French.

I asked him if the roadblock meant trouble. He shrugged.

'We had a lot of trouble before,' he said. 'But it's been quiet for some time now'. He did not say any more. Presumably he did not want to scare off his new clients. Ahead of us, ten or fifteen miles away, a string of volcanoes ran across the horizon.

After an hour or two we left the plain and started to climb up through the green acres of coffee plantations, once the richest agricultural land in the whole Congo. Here and there we could glimpse a big European farm house, standing back

194

from the road in a clump of trees: even at a distance they looked half-deserted. As we drove past one I noticed several African children playing beside the front door.

'They've all gone,' Philippe said with a nod in the direction of the house. 'Used to be a lot of very rich Belgian coffee planters here. But they all left a long time ago. After the troubles. Now the coffee has all gone to seed and the Africans have moved into the houses. *Tout est foutu.*' He sounded bitter.

We climbed higher: the trees were thick and tall and the air cool; we dropped down the other side of the ridge to flatter country and finally to rolling open bush. Ahead was the Albert National Park, once the pride of the Belgian Parks Department, where we were going to spend the night. The light had almost gone by the time we reached the entrance to the park.

Behind, over our left shoulders, we could see a red glow in the sky from one of the many volcanoes. During the day they had looked extinct, but at night the molten lava at the bottom of the crater glowed like a giant furnace, lighting up the underside of the clouds.

We reached the main camp at about seven, the lights shining a welcome out of the darkness. It was, however, a rather surly African who made us sign the register and showed us to our *cabines*, small circular huts of mud and wattle, with corrugated iron roofs. We were the only guests, although during our frugal dinner a couple of armed soldiers came in and looked at us suspiciously while they drank their beer. Apart from that, there was little excitement to keep us awake and we went to bed early. I fell asleep almost immediately, half hearing the thousand and one sounds of an African night. Then, perhaps two or three hours later, I woke suddenly. I took a moment or two to remember where I was. I lay in the half-dark listening, wondering what had disturbed me. Almost immediately I had my answer: a loud, crunching, ripping noise. Something was just outside my window. Cautiously, trying to make as little sound as possible, I slipped out of bed. There was a faint moon but the play of pale light and equally insubstantial shadow baffled the eye for a moment; and then the biggest shadow, only a few feet from the hut, moved and again I heard the tearing, crunching noise. I froze. The shadow moved closer and the moonlight glinted . . . on what? The eye focuses clumsily in these situations, and then suddenly the picture fell into place; I was looking up at a large cow elephant feeding calmly just outside my door.

I let my breath out very slowly, in relief, but then I tensed again at the thought that if the elephant got wind of me it might attack. As I stood there, stark naked in the night chill, I realised that my hut was very fragile and would offer no protection against an angry elephant. I pondered this dilemma, wondering if I could if necessary make it to the rest house, and then the great beast, reaching up for a more distant branch and chewing noisily, slowly moved away. I tiptoed back to bed.

After breakfast, the following morning, we drove north through the park, reaching a little port called Kamande on the south-west tip of Lake Edward an hour or two later. There was a fish factory on the quayside, and dozens of marabou storks, huge, voracious beasts with bills like spears and ugly red necks like infected wounds, stalked about ready to seize anything edible. They are one of the great scavengers of Africa. Jon wanted pictures of the lake so Philippe commandeered a boat and we set off for a brief sail. We filmed as we went, not at all sure what shape the programme would finally take. We were certain of one thing: no other television crew had been in this part of the Eastern Congo for many years, certainly not since Independence.

The sun was now overhead and it was extremely hot with almost no breeze so we headed back to the quayside and drove away from the lake, heading north-east through the open bush, past herds of giraffe. The noise of the car would make them throw up their heads and then break into a slow-motion, rocking-horse gallop, each stride covering about thirty feet. We climbed the escarpment and bumped our way across flat plains country towards Beni. We had not seen an inch of tarmac since leaving Goma and the dirt roads were pitted with enormous potholes through which we lurched and bounced. I imagine that no one had graded them since the Belgians had left. Philippe was the kind of driver who never seems to anticipate a bump or hole in the road, going full tilt into every one: not surprisingly we had a puncture. Philippe put on the spare and drove on as recklessly as ever, despite our attempts to make him slow down: if we had another puncture we would be stuck. But luck was with us and the protesting rubber held out until Beni. Although it only consisted of one street, Beni possessed the basic amenities: shops, small hotel and garage, run by an obliging Greek. While he repaired the puncture, Jon, Eric and I made for the solitary hostelry. It did not look much from the outside, but the interior resembled a set from a Bunuel film. The reception was on the right as you went in, a bare desk, and behind it sat two young African women with plaited spiky hair, their scalps divided into squares like an ordnance survey map.

We asked if we could get a drink and they replied, as if they were doing us a considerable favour, yes, we could. In there. It turned out to be a large room, presumably once the lounge and almost entirely empty. One or two rickety tables and chairs with broken backs stood about dejectedly, as if they were the survivors of some terrible orgy. One armchair was minus the arms, the stumps sticking up in mute anguish.

At the far end, another girl, her hair also done up in spikes, presided over what had once been the bar. It was a long dirty wooden affair, devoid of any decoration, with a few empty shelves behind and a broken mirror.

'Yes?' she said.

'Have you any beer?' I asked, wondering if they had anything at all in stock apart from broken furniture and flies.

Without replying she reached under the counter and drew out three large dusty bottles of Simba beer, opened them and plonked them down on the top of the bar.

'Any glasses?'

She shook her head. We wiped the tops with our handkerchiefs and drank. The beer was warm and heavy. The woman behind the bar sat and looked at us.

197

'Was this a Belgian hotel before?' I asked.

She nodded. '*Oui, avant.*'

'And the Belgians have gone?'

She nodded again. There seemed to be nothing more to be said. We drank the beer, paid the bill and left. I have never had such an all-pervading sense of the collapse of a society as in that derelict bar.

After Beni we left the open country behind and entered the forest. Huge trees rose like the fluted columns of a Gothic cathedral two or three hundred feet high, spreading at the top to form a canopy so thick that the sun could not penetrate it. The floor of the forest was sunk in a cool, green gloom. Almost nothing grows down there, everything has to reach the light or die. We passed several villages in clearings in the forest, sorry-looking huddles of huts with unsmiling inhabitants who stared at us morosely as we drove past. The light was beginning to go and I was getting a little anxious.

'How much farther?' I asked Philippe.

He gestured vaguely, driving the car ruthlessly on. 'Not too far now.' The forest was thicker than ever, and there seemed to be no habitation in sight, not even an African village. I tried to relax but it was impossible as the car bounded along, the springs protesting each time we crashed into another pot-hole. It was nearly dark when Philippe turned sharply to the right and we started to climb a narrow rutted track through the trees. It was like the drive to a haunted house and it seemed to go on for mile after mile. Each time we rounded a bend I expected to see our destination, but all the headlights revealed was another stretch of overgrown forest track.

Finally we came round a corner, emerged on to a small plateau and, miracle of miracles, there was a house, with lights at the doors and signs of activity. We stopped and got out, easing our cramped legs. A tall white man was coming towards me, hand outstretched.

'Welcome, welcome to Mont Hoyo,' he said in English. And then in French: 'You'll be all right here. Nothing has changed . . . ' He turned and shouted to several Africans to take our luggage. 'Come in and relax,' he said. 'You must be tired after your journey.' There are time when one is exhausted and dispirited after a long journey, and the welcome seems especially warm and heaven-sent. This was one such occasion. As far as we could see in the dark the house was a large wooden bungalow. We went through the entrance hall and then into a big comfortable room beyond with easy chairs and a bookcase. Paraffin lamps gave a soft, yellow light. A large very Belgian-looking lady rose to greet us. There was a third person in the room, a small bird-like man, whom I did not notice at first, he sat by himself so quietly. 'This is Bernard,' our host said. 'He is a butterfly man.'

Madame disappeared majestically from view to supervise dinner and Maurice Tiedemanns busied himself with the drinks.

'Would you like a Scotch?' he asked.

I was amazed. 'Scotch? How on earth do you get it here?' It did seem that we had come to the end of the world.

Tiedemanns chuckled. 'Ah, we have our little secrets. You can get everything you need in Uganda if you have sterling.' I remembered that Philippe had insisted on being paid in sterling.

'How far is the Ugandan border?'

'As the crow flies, not very far. But by road, from here, thirty or forty miles.'

He was eager to talk. I felt that, apart from his wife and Bernard, he had not spoken to another European for months. He told us that he had been in the Eastern Congo for thirty years. Originally he had been a white hunter, running big game safaris. 'I had a lot of British and American clients. There was plenty of game. Elephant, rhino, kudu, everything.' Then like so many big game hunters he had become weary of killing and had turned to conservation and tourism. This is where the pygmies came in. Here at Mont Hoyo, he explained, we were on the edge of the Ituri Forest, the home of the Ituri pygmies, and he had built this house to be near them. We would meet them tomorrow. 'They are wonderful people and we have become good friends. You will see.'

We went to bed early, stumbling through the dark to our wooden bungalows fifty yards from the main house. As we followed the light of our host's torch, a piercing call rent the night air. It sounded like a creature in pain.

'What was that?' we asked, slightly alarmed.

'A rock hyrax,' Tiedemanns replied unconcerned. 'It's very small although it happens to be the nearest relative in the world to an elephant.' We all laughed at such an absurd idea and that such a small creature should make such a disproportionately loud noise.

Next morning, we had a proper look at Mont Hoyo and it was indeed a paradise. It reminded me of Kenya: the smiling servants bringing breakfast, the slight mistiness in the air, the sense of height and space, the stillness, the sunlight dappling the trees. The house was on a ridge at the very edge of the forest and we looked west across a valley to the foothills of the Ruwenzori, the Mountains of the Moon, now as so often shrouded in cloud. It was here, according to Tiedemanns, that Stanley, on his famous west to east expedition in search of Livingstone, finally emerged from the Ituri Forest after a terrible journey which left half his expedition dead or dying. When the African porters saw the sunshine and open country, Stanley records, they threw down their loads and started running and cheering at the tops of their voices.

After breakfast, it was time to meet the people we had come so far to see: the pygmies. We walked down from the house into the forest and there, in a small clearing, a family of about a dozen pygmies was waiting for us. They were indeed amazingly small, the men just over four feet, the women smaller, and not black but a sort of dark apricot colour rather like the Bushmen. The head of the group was a fine-looking fellow of about thirty, with intelligent eyes and a ready smile. Tiedemanns said he was a great elephant hunter.

'They stalk an elephant for days on end then, when the moment is right, they creep up behind it, right underneath, and drive a spear up into its belly. It's a very risky business because, if the wind changes suddenly or they make the slightest mistake, the elephant will kill them.' If they did manage to kill an elephant, the whole family would live off the carcase for weeks. But their customary menu was less ambitious: monkeys and small antelope they shot in the forest with their poison-tipped arrows. We got them to enact a hunt for us, stalking through the trees and finally loosing off an arrow. To test their skill, Jon Lane fixed a cigarette longways on the trunk of a tree and got the men to shoot at it from about twenty paces. They hit it several times. But you expected them to be crack shots. What I did not anticipate was that they would be such good actors, immediately grasping the essential of filming. John was using a silent camera, which confusingly enough makes a very audible buzz. The pygmies were quick to understand that as long as they heard the buzzing noise they should continue to act out the hunt, but as soon as John stopped to change angle or film, they should stop too. They would then pick up the action from precisely the point they had left off.

I remarked on this to Tiedemanns.

'Yes,' he said. 'They are much more intelligent than the Bantu tribes who live on the edge of the forest. They're also very scared of the pygmies' prowess as warriors.' As I watched them moving silently off into the trees, carrying their little bows and poison-tipped arrows, it was easy to see that they would be formidable guerrilla opponents on their own territory. (Years later President Mobutu tried to incorporate them into his army but without much success. I suspect the pygmies were too intelligent for their Congolese officers.)

Next day the pygmies brought in a black and white colobus monkey they had shot and we completed our hunting sequence. We also filmed them making the poison into which they dip the points of their arrows. It is so deadly that after several days it will finally kill an elephant. There was one shot I enjoyed: Jon and Eric lined up all the pygmies, gave them each a piece of our equipment to carry and got them to walk through the forest with me, towering over them like some latter-day Stanley, bringing up the rear. The pygmies took all this in good heart, enjoying the size joke as much as we did. They are very gentle and modest: a few cigarettes made them inordinately happy. As they chatted quietly, at peace with the world, they struck me as being much more intelligent and civilised than many Africans and non-Africans I had met who would no doubt consider themselves superior beings. Finally,

201

Jon took a lot of trouble to get a shot of them all walking off into the forest. The track led past a waterfall and they sang and shouted to one another as they departed in single file. It was an idyllic scene and would, we thought, make an evocative ending to the film. But to our fury it got 'lost' in the 'labs' while being processed.

On our last evening after dinner, we all sat round a log fire crackling agreeably in the fireplace. Up here on the hilltop, you felt apart from and above the cares of the world and almost beyond the reach of the turbulence of the rest of the Congo. I asked Tiedemanns if they had had any troubles. Yes, he said, some. For a time after Independence he had taught in a school in Bunia, farther north, but it became impossible. So the three of them had withdrawn to their hilltop and luckily had been comparatively unmolested. Perhaps they were protected by the presence of the pygmies, those fearsome archers.

Tiedemanns smiled. 'Perhaps. As long as they leave us alone,' he said, 'we will stay. If not . . . ' He let the end of the sentence trail off into the blue smoke that rose from the fire.

Next morning, as we waved goodbye, I knew I was looking at a way of life that had virtually vanished: a colonial past that could only have survived in this remote corner of the forest, high among the trees, like a rare orchid. Philippe descended the forest track to the main road at rally speed and then followed the road towards Beni, the town of the broken-down bar. We turned off to the south-east a few miles short of it and headed for the Ruwenzori, the Mountains of the Moon. The ancient world believed that this is where the Nile rose.

We were heading for a place called Mutwanga, at the foot of the main massif, where we had been told by Tiedemanns there was a hotel run by an eccentric old Belgian. 'I don't know if he's still there, but it's worth having a look. It's a beautiful spot.'

The last few miles were not very encouraging. We left the Albert National Park and traversed an African-settled area for about twenty miles. The road got steadily worse, with huge potholes making progress extremely painful. Worried apart from anything else about the punishment the camera equipment was taking, we urged Philippe to slow down, but he was like a man possessed and ignored all appeals. The last part of the journey was through tall forest with an occasional village emerging in a sprawl of mud huts, naked children and barking dogs. As I had noticed on the way north, the Africans hardly waved and some appeared downright hostile. Perhaps that was why Philippe kept the pace up even in the villages, scattering chickens and children in front of his long-suffering front wheels.

About four in the afternoon, we climbed to a plateau, the trees thinned out and there, at the end of a sandy track, stood a long, low, white-washed house with a thatched roof. After a day of pounding over terrible roads, it was a weary traveller's dream. To one side of the main house were a group of rondavels, small, round huts with thatched roofs used as individual bedrooms. They looked particularly pretty and well cared for and were shaded by wispy, pale green flamboyant trees which in the spring are covered with bright orange-red flowers. The place looked deserted but, as we drew to a halt, the mosquito-netting door at the front opened and a wizened little man came down the steps towards us. He had a gaping smile and a high-pitched, cracked voice.

'Boenens,' he said. 'Gaston Boenens,' and extended a gnarled hand. 'Welcome to the Mountains of the Moon Hotel.'

We shook hands and he gestured us towards the house. A notice in the window beside the entrance said in large letters 'Jam Factory', and a few pots of jam stood rather forlornly beside it.

Boenens saw my glance. 'Yes,' he said with his cracked laugh. 'The hotel is closed. We are a jam factory now. But for you it is different. You are welcome.'

We went inside, signed the register, met Madame Boenens, the smiling *patronne* of the jam factory, and then Boenens showed us to our rondavels, talking non-stop all the way.

'This is where King Baudouin slept when he came here before . . . '

'Before?'

'Before Independence, of course. He stayed for a night. *Très gentil.* Everyone used to come here in the old days. All the big game hunters, American millionaires. English milords, everyone who wanted to see the Ruwenzori. Unfortunately they are in cloud today. Maybe tomorrow you will see them.'

'But the jam factory,' I prompted. 'How did that come about?'

Boenens laid a finger on one side of his nose and looked at me conspiratorially. 'You see, we had to do it. In 1960 when we had Independence, one of those black ministers arrived here one night, with his white girl friend, and wanted to stay in the hotel. I had to take them in. There was nothing I could do. And of course what happens? He doesn't pay the bill. *Sale macaque.* So I say no more. We close the hotel. We call it a jam factory. And, if *macaques* like that come here, I say, sorry, we are not open.' (*Macaque* means monkey and it was used pejoratively for Africans by the Belgians in the Congo.)

The rondavels were pleasant, airy, clean. We turned to walk back through the garden to the hotel. Boenens continued to talk in a rush, like a man who has been silent for too long.

'Look here,' he said, opening his mouth and pointing to his teeth. 'Look what these *macaques* did to me after Independence. They came here one day, the soldiers, demanded this and that and, when I told them to get out, they hit me with their rifle butts.' His teeth were all broken or missing.

He shrugged. 'But this is our home. I am over seventy. My wife is not young either. We will stay as long as we can . . . '

I spent next day writing my script and going over the film sequences with Jon. Eric was busy checking the gear, in case the potholes had done some irreparable damage. He reported that all seemed well but Philippe's driving and increasingly *farouche* behaviour had prompted a new idea. Instead of making the long drive back south to Kivu, we could go east instead. Boenens was eager to drive us to the Uganda border and then to Kampala where he could do some shopping. It was only about twenty miles to the border, although the road was appalling, but after that it was an easy run on a tarmac

204

road all the way to the Ugandan capital. When I broke the news to Philippe he was not at all happy. His pride was hurt but not his pocket. I saw to it that he got his money.

That night, while Madame Boenens cooked us a special dinner of roast guinea fowl, old Boenens descended into his cellar to find something worthy of the occasion. 'I still have some good claret left, from before 1960, and we shall drink it tonight.'

As we sat on the terrace having an apéritif, the gods who live on the Mountains of the Moon suddenly relented. The clouds cleared and the peaks stood out in dazzling array against a deep blue sky. We were so excited that we all got up and Boenens fetched his field glasses. I could see the icefields just below the summit – a gleaming bottle green – and then, just before sunset, the peaks turned blush pink, the colour of a flamingo feather, and for an enchanted moment or two the Ruwenzori showed themselves in all their grandeur. The sight of them filled me with a terrible desire to climb them, but there was no time. We had been out of touch with the office for a week and that is a long time in television. The Government might have fallen or a new war broken out that we knew nothing about. I was sorely tempted, but it was out of the question to spend another three days climbing the Ruwenzori. Early next morning, as if to mock us, they were clear of cloud again, the sun gleaming on the snow and ice; Marguerite, the highest peak of all, towering in frigid splendour, 16,000 feet into the shining air. And then, as so often happens as the sun climbs higher, the clouds closed in and, by the time we left, the Mountains of the Moon had concealed themselves again and when I looked back it was as if they had never existed. Ahead lay twenty-five miles of ferocious potholes to the Uganda border.

In August 1964, Turkish jets bombarded Greek Cypriot targets in the north of Cyprus, killing a number of people, sinking a boat and destroying buildings, and bringing the long-simmering feud between the two mainland governments to the brink of war.

I flew out immediately with Jon Lane, arriving in Nicosia

at about three in the morning. As we made our way wearily out of the terminal with our camera gear clanking behind us, an amazing sight greeted our tired eyes. Savas, doyen of all hotel concierges, honorary Minister of Information of Cyprus, was seated at a desk under the trees with a ledger open in front of him.

'Good morning, Mr Gall,' he said as smoothly as if he had been behind the desk at the Ledra Palace. 'It's a long time since I've had the pleasure of welcoming you to Cyprus. Now, the bus leaves in an hour for the north, how many seats will you need? Three?'

'Good heavens,' I stammered, 'how did you know we were coming?' He did not deign to answer such a stupid question, merely smiled and went on making notes. Savas arranged for us to be taken to the Ledra Palace for a brief rest and wash, and then at six we boarded the bus along with another thirty or forty journalists and were taken on a conducted tour of the battle front. Instead of leaving us to blunder about on our own, the bus drove us straight to the spot where the Turkish jets had done most damage. Once again the incomparable Savas had come up trumps. I do not know why they never made him the Minister of Information.

A day or so later, there was fighting between Turkish and Greek Cypriots in villages in the same area, and the Press Corps, now firmly established at the Ledra Palace, set off up the twisting mountain roads. It was a beautiful drive with the rocky landscape in the thrall of high summer, the olive trees making deep shadows on the flanks of the tawny-red hills and, beyond, the Mediterranean sparkling an intense blue. But the mood was bitter and some of the young Greek Cypriot fighters were trigger happy. An American colleague was driving up the road between the olive groves when a Greek Cypriot machine-gunner in one of the stone villages on the top of the next hill got him in his sights and opened fire. He was badly wounded and had to be flown out next day. It brought all of us up short. We knew that there was an element of risk, but somehow journalists always presume that, even if Turkish and Greek Cypriots are being killed, they are immune. Instead of being a pleasant day's drive, the

journey up the mountain turned into a hazardous undertaking: the landscape that had so entranced the eye with its
beauty now looked sinister and forbidding, a setting for
tragedy, and the blue of the Mediterranean, before so
beguiling, now had something implacable about it.

But even more sinister events were shaping themselves
2,000 miles away in the Congo. In July, the irrepressible
Moïse Tshombe had emerged from his defeat in Katanga to
become Prime Minister of all the Congo. In August a group
of rebels known as the Simbas (Lions), and consisting of
many of the original mutinous Force Publique units from
Independence days, captured Stanleyville, the capital of
Eastern Province and with a population of a quarter of a
million. As the second largest city in the country, it was no
mean prize. In September the Stanleyville rebels proclaimed a
People's Republic of the Congo. This was a direct challenge
to Tshombe's Central Government and in its way was neatly
ironic: the former arch-secessionist now had a secession on
his own hands. Tshombe was not slow to take up the
challenge, sending for his old mercenary captain, 'Mad' Mike
Hoare, now safely retired, or so he thought, in South Africa.
Hoare was eager to answer the call, doubly so since this time
he would be on the side of the angels. Also, there was no
question but that the Simbas were a thoroughly nasty lot: not
only extreme left-wingers but bloodthirsty tyrants into the
bargain. They had rounded up all the white missionaries in
the city, led by an American called Dr. Carlson, and were
holding them hostage: and they were reported to be led by a
particularly unpleasant character known to the popular press
as the Mad Dwarf. It was clear that the Simbas were sharpen-
ing their knives for the unfortunate missionaries and equally
clear that Tshombe was going to launch a major military
operation to recapture Stanleyville. So one day in early
November Jon Lane, Doug Wilkins and I climbed aboard a
Boeing 707 in London and next morning re-emerged in the
clammy heat of Léopoldville.

The mercenaries under Mike Hoare and his old Harrovian
number two, Alastair Wicks, I discovered, were assembling at
Kindu, and we flew there to try and find them and film them.

Kindu has always struck me as one of the most evil places in the Congo, perhaps because it will always be connected in my mind with the murder there of nine Italian airmen from the UN Air Force in 1961.

The first thing we noticed was a big American C130 Hercules transport plane standing to one side of the tarmac. Round it were men who looked suspiciously like white mercenaries. We walked over and very soon spotted Alastair Wicks. He was surprised to see me and a little cagey. They were, he said, assembling there for the push on Stanleyville and the Americans were flying in the equipment. Brand-new jeeps were being unloaded and crates of M16 carbines and ammunition. Mike Hoare's little army was obviously going to be even better equipped than in the old days in Elisabethville.

Kindu is more or less in the middle of the Congo, on the west bank of the Lualaba River which in turn becomes the Congo River. The mercenaries were camped on the outskirts of the town and we drove out to see them. They were the usual curious mixture: a hardened wartime NCO, who had failed to fit into civvy street and was anxious to see some action and pick up a bit of loot before it was too late; drifters who had fallen out with their wives or employers or both; the politically motivated; and the young adventurers. As they sat around preparing their weapons and themselves for the long overland trek to Stanleyville, we set up the camera and did a series of interviews. The one that sticks in my mind best was with the youngest mercenary there. He was in the young adventurer class, about twenty-one, with dark good looks, and was obviously much better educated than the rest of them. I asked him why he had volunteered. Well, he said, he wanted to see Africa and he wanted to do something adventurous. Then at the end of his explanation, after a long pause, when it seemed he had stopped speaking, he suddenly added: 'I suppose it is dangerous and I certainly don't want to die!' Unfortunately, Jon Lane, who thought he had finished speaking switched off the camera at that very moment, and we lost those final words. They turned out to be prophetic. He was killed in an ambush on the way to Stanleyville.

The mercenary column, minus Mike Hoare who was still in

Léopoldville, set off next day. We filmed them driving their American jeeps on to the rickety old wooden ferry (even there, 1,500 miles from its mouth, the Lualaba-Congo was about a quarter of a mile wide). Later that day, we flew back to Léopoldville and shipped our story to London. The question was how should we cover the real climax of the operation: the attack on Stanleyville itself? First of all I consulted an old friend from Katanga days, a South African called George Clay. George had worked for the *Observer* for several years, first as a stringer then as their Africa correspondent based in Nairobi. But recently he had joined ABC, the American Broadcasting Company, starting with radio and then graduating to television. On this occasion he had Ernie Christie as his cameraman. Over lunch at an outdoor restaurant near the Memling, one of the few tolerable places left in Léopoldville, we discussed the coming campaign. George, who had excellent contacts with Mike Hoare, had arranged to go with him in the convoy all the way from Bukavu or Goma (they were taking a very roundabout route), but I was not so sure this was the answer for us. For one thing the mercenaries had limited transport and were neither willing nor able to accommodate a large press party. George and Ernie were very much the exceptions. We had no jeep and it would be difficult if not impossible to hire one in the chaotic economic conditions of the Congo. Finally, even if we did manage to join the convoy, what would happen if we broke down, which was very possible? The mercenaries would certainly be too busy to come to the rescue: we would be on our own, stuck in the middle of nowhere. It was a prospect that did not appeal to me. So I cabled London outlining the possibilities and saying that my inclination was to let the convoy go its own way – and, on past form, there was no guarantee they would ever get there – while we would fly in as soon as the opportunity presented itself.

This, however, did not satisfy the foreign desk at ITN. Back came a cable saying: 'Not happy about your assessment of mercenary convoy possibilities and must insist on firm guarantee that you will do utmost to join convoy. Please acknowledge and confirm.' It was signed by the foreign editor. I read it a second time with growing anger and showed it to Jon and Doug.

'Bloody boy scouts,' I grumbled. 'They haven't the foggiest idea of what Africa is all about.' It irritated me beyond measure that men who were much inferior in experience and neither of whom, as far as I knew, had ever heard a shot fired in anger, should be dictating to me how I should risk my life to no good purpose. Reuters, I thought, would never have sent me such an ignorant cable.

Trying to calm myself, I sat down and typed a reply. 'Received your message but must disagree most strongly. Feel convoy operation extremely chancy even if Hoare agrees to accept us which think most unlikely. Because of distance and transport problems insist we must rule it out and concentrate instead on Stanleyville operation by air.'

They did not like it but there was nothing they could do. George and Ernie departed in great secrecy one morning, flying to Goma to pick up the convoy at the halfway stage. The rest of us waited in Léopoldville. And then we had a bit of bad luck. Doug Wilkins, one of the most devoted and conscientious of men, came to me one morning and said he wanted to go home. He had just heard from his wife that she was not well and he felt he ought to fly back to London. This created a problem. We did not know exactly when the Stanleyville operation would take place – there were rumours that, as well as the mercenary ground attack, the Belgians would launch a simultaneous paratroop drop. It could be a week away or less. On the other hand, Doug was worried and there was no point in holding him against his will. So we sent him off on the next plane and asked London to send a replacement as speedily as possible. We got word eventually that he would arrive on the morning of November 24, the day as it turned out of the attack on Stanleyville.

The Belgians went in from Kamina, their big base in the north of Katanga, landing about a thousand paratroopers at Stanleyville airport. Jon and I, minus sound recordist, spent all day at the airport desperately trying to get aboard a military flight. But the orders were: no Press, and, apart from a Dutch cameraman, Ed van Can, then working for UPI,

210

who locked himself in the lavatory of a DC3 bound for Stanleyville, none of us succeeded.

Next day John and I were back at Njili early and booked on the first flight to Stanleyville. As we taxied out to the runway we passed a Sabena Boeing 707 which had just landed. I turned to John and said: 'I bet you Eric [Doug's replacement] is on that damned plane. Half an hour earlier and he could have come with us.' I was right. Eric was indeed on the plane but it was too late to get him on our flight.

Stanleyville airport was four or five miles from the town, set in a wide green base. Half a dozen Belgian Flying Boxcars and C130s were parked on the tarmac and dozens of tough-looking Belgian paras in camouflage uniforms and red berets were camped out round the terminal. As we walked into a hangar to have our press passes checked, I saw a line of men sitting on the ground, their backs against the wall, obviously under arrest. Halfway down the line, a bearded Indian looked up and said: 'Hallo, Sandy.' I stopped, so surprised that I did not at first know him. Then recognition came. 'Mohinder,' I said. 'What on earth are you doing here?'

'I flew in on a charter from Nairobi,' he said. 'They just arrested us.'

I looked along the rest of the line. They were mainly Asians or Arabs plus a few Africans. 'They are arresting everyone who looks as if they helped the Simbas,' Mohinder said.

'Wait a moment,' I said and went off to find the ranking Belgian officer. He was a colonel, with an eye patch, who looked as if he had seen a lot of service. I promptly promoted him. *'Mon général,'* I began, *'vous avez un ami à moi entre vos prisonniers.'*

'Comment?' he said. *'Entre ces gars-là?'* He was obviously amazed that any friend could possibly be among the riff-raff seated on the floor of the hangar. 'Where is his passport?' he asked. It was on the table with a couple of dozen others, the only British passport there. It did not take long to convince the 'general' that Mohinder was indeed our man in Nairobi.

'Right,' said the colonel, 'he is free, but he must stay at the airport until you fly out.' We left behind a much happier-

211

looking Mohinder and hitched a ride into town with some paratroopers. The road was deserted although we heard a few bursts of automatic fire as we drove in. Stanleyville was once the most modern of all the Belgian towns in the Congo and is built imposingly on the river front. The streets bore the marks of a sharp engagement. A few dead bodies lay at the side of the road, already bloated by the hot sun, one with an arm thrown up grotesquely in rigor mortis. Most of the inhabitants seemed to have fled. Jon and I got out of the jeep and started to film, walking through the centre of the shuttered town, recording the visible signs of recent battle. Outside one building, which looked as if it had been used as an office by the rebels, four or five dead Africans lay sprawled on the grass, their blood staining the rain puddle crimson. They had probably been shot as they tried to escape. Eventually, we came across some of Mike Hoare's mercenaries, and finally Mike Hoare himself. He sat in his jeep looking fit and tanned, his dust goggles around his neck, trying to appear like a latter-day Rommel. He told us that the Belgians had arrived too late; or rather that, as soon as the Simbas saw the planes landing, they had paraded the missionary hostages and massacred them in the street. Then they escaped across the river. We could hear the occasional boom of gunfire echoing in the heavy air. The mercenaries had also arrived late, held up by an action in which George Clay had been killed. They had been ambushed just outside Stanleyville and George, who had been riding in one of the lead jeeps, had been shot by a single bullet right through the middle of his forehead. The mercenaries had lost one other man.

'It was bloody bad luck,' Hoare said. 'A chance bullet. It was in the dark so they weren't shooting at him in particular. He just happened to cop it.' I felt physically sick at the loss of my friend, thinking what a waste of a life. George was such a generous, warm-hearted man, always ready with a smile and a joke. They had buried him there in the middle of the bush: in that heat the body decomposes too rapidly for anything else to be done. We interviewed Hoare sitting behind the wheel of his jeep. He said that by the time they arrived in

Stanleyville the fighting was over, the Simbas had fled. But he was very proud of one thing. On their way into Stanleyville, the column had arrived at a mission station in the bush just as a group of retreating Simba soldiers had been on the point of sacking the place and raping or killing the nuns. They had even set fire to part of the mission and the nuns were screaming in terror when the mercenaries' jeeps drew up.

'We were in the nick of time,' Mike Hoare said. 'A few minutes later and they would all have been killed.' For this act of chivalrous rescue, Hoare told me later, he received the personal thanks of the British Ambassador. The despised soldier of fortune had at last become respectable.

I asked him what his future plans were. He said he had a commission from Tshombe to retake the whole province and 'clean up' the rest of the Simba force. They would begin the next phase in a day or two, after they had rested and refuelled. The Belgians would leave very soon. After that Mike Hoare would be in charge.

One of the mercenary NCOs took over. We would need somewhere to sleep and some food. He had already 'liberated' a flat in a new block which had obviously belonged to a well-to-do Belgian. The NCO, a bull-necked Englishman, opened the doors of the built-in cupboards and pulled out drawers full of shirts and underwear.

'Here,' he said. 'Help yourself.'

'No thanks,' I said. 'I don't need anything.'

But he insisted, pulling a khaki shirt out of a drawer and thrusting it into my hands.

The mercenaries looted as a matter of course. But this was small beer. Later, I was told, they blew up a bank and helped themselves to the contents, although I am not sure that a hundredweight of Congolese francs was of very much use to anyone. But the Simbas were reported to have a much more interesting haul in their possession. At some point in their chequered career, they had also robbed a bank and acquired a large amount of gold. Opinions varied as to how much, but one estimate put it at between a quarter and half a million. Mike Hoare's men never got their hands on it, although in the weeks to come they chased the Simbas north-eastwards, through the bush towns of Paulis and Watsa to the Uganda border. The survivors asked for sanctuary, were granted it and finally reached Kampala with their gold. There the trail went cold. All we knew was that they had been arrested by Obote or Amin, and that their gold had eventually found its way into the pockets of the future dictator of Uganda. (This story so fascinated me that I later wrote a thriller about it called *Gold Scoop*.)

The progress of Hoare's mercenaries across the north-east corner of the country, remote even by Congo standards, aroused a lot of criticism. They were accused of killing Simba prisoners and suspects indiscriminately, shooting them without compunction and dumping their bodies in the river. But, since very few independent witnesses penetrated the area, it was hard to get at the truth. Few mercenaries, however, observe the Geneva Convention.

Jon Lane and I flew back to Léopoldville the next day, taking Mohinder with us. He said he was very glad to say goodbye to Stanleyville and the paras. Every time they looked at him he thought they were going to shoot him. We booked a room for him in the Memling and next day I took him to the airport and saw him through customs and immigration. There was just a chance that some paranoically suspicious immigration man would take against him, and Mohinder, apart from having no visa, spoke no French.

Our film had already gone. It was a minor scoop. Apart from Ed van Can, who did not have a sound camera, we were the first television crew to enter Stanleyville. Ernie Christie, who had been with George Clay, had flown back to Léopoldville ahead of us. Naturally he had stopped filming as soon as George was killed. He came into the telex office just as I was sending the details of our film shipment to London, red-eyed with grief and lack of sleep.

'For God's sake, help me,' he said. 'I can't use a telex.' So, when ABC in New York came through on the line, I had to explain, with Ernie standing at my shoulder, what had happened to George. It took only a few minutes for them to call a senior producer to the machine. I repeated the message and gave him all the information Ernie had. One thing we could not do. He wanted Ernie to arrange for the body to be flown to South Africa. But we had to explain that George had already been buried, near the town named after the greatest of all African explorers. With that, I suspect, he would not have been too unhappy.

CHAPTER VII

Saigon: The Start of the Vietnam War
Borneo: On Patrol with the Ghurkas

In February 1965, President Johnson authorised the first
American bombing raids against North Vietnam and later
that same month the American air force was in action against
the Vietcong in South Vietnam. More and more American
troops were getting ready to go to Vietnam and the Marines
were expected there shortly. I cornered Geoffrey Cox in the
corridor one day and said I thought we ought to be on our
way too. It seemed to me that Vietnam was the most important thing happening in the world at that moment.

Geoffrey gave me that sideways look. 'I'm not convinced,
Sandy,' he intoned in his high-pitched antipodean drawl,
'that this isn't a purely American story. I don't think people
here are particularly interested.' And with that astonishing
utterance he stalked off down the corridor to his office. I
stared after him, rebuffed and frustrated. My next move was
to seek out Nigel Ryan, who had come back to ITN after a
fruitless year with a freelance company called Television
Reporters International. Now he was editing 'Roving
Report'. I told him what Geoffrey had said. 'You'll have to

work on him,' I insisted. 'It's a bloody important story and we damned well ought to be there.'

'I know,' Nigel said. 'I quite agree. But Geoffrey doesn't see it that way. Yet. Leave it to me, though. I'll try and talk him round.'

He did. A week later, I was told to catch the next plane to Vietnam. Once the decision had been taken, you were expected to move like lightning. Visas were easy then, jabs could be got at the airport, but the crew took a few hours to get all their equipment together. We were the first ITN crew ever to report the Vietnam war and so there was a considerable debate about the best gear to take. Rifle microphones, so called because they are shaped like a small rifle barrel and are pointed like a gun at the source of the sound, had just come in. I had used them for the first time in the United States and been enormously impressed at how they could pick up conversations five or ten yards away. But, when I said I wanted to take one to Vietnam, there was immediate opposition. ITN was still using the old-fashioned BBC microphone shaped like a ball on the end of a stick, which you had to hold out flat like an egg and spoon, in a thoroughly awkward manner. Every time the reporter interviewed someone he had to thrust this ungainly and extremely ugly object under the nose of the interviewee. With the rifle mike, on the other hand, the reporter simply approached his victim and started talking to him, with no paraphernalia to worry about, while the sound recordist got on with his job. The rifle mike was revolutionising television news, but ITN did not possess one: and, worse still, did not approve of them. The chief engineer pulled a long face when I said we must have one for Vietnam and muttered something about it not meeting the highest standards for quality. I replied that it could pick up conversations from twenty or even thirty feet away and, more to the point, allowed great flexibility in covering fast-moving events like wars. To hell with the quality if you are getting shot at, I suggested. Very reluctantly he finally agreed to hire one, but he got his own back by imposing a condition, unknown to me at the time, on poor Jon Lane. He could take a rifle mike provided he also took what they call a parabolic microphone, which is shaped like a small radar dish and is about as heavy. The idea of carrying this great lump of metal into battle was obviously absurd. But we won in the end: Jon lost it somewhere between London and Saigon.

So we were going to cover a war, something that ITN had hardly ever done in its history, and something for which it was largely unprepared. There was precious little light-weight equipment about in those days and what there was had still not reached ITN. The worst offender of all was the battery, or vibrator, as it was called, a very heavy rectangular metal object which you had to carry by a shoulder-strap. To run about with it, as you might well have to do if someone started shooting at you, was extremely difficult. However, our sound recordist, Peter McIntyre, was, like Jon Lane, young and strong, and we set off in high hopes.

It was a long flight, via Delhi and Bangkok, and we were all jaded by the time we reached Saigon. But, as we flew in over the emerald green of the rice paddies and saw for the first time the great sweep of the Mekong River, coiling in myriad loops round Saigon before finally unwinding itself into the blue-green haze of the Delta, our tiredness vanished.

As we came in to land, an amazing sight greeted our eyes. Dozens of jet fighter aircraft – mainly Phantoms – each carrying the silver star of the US Air Force, were parked in concrete revetments on the edge of the runway, and, beyond, scores and scores of Bell 'Huey' helicopter gunships were drawn up in ranks on the tarmac, each one bearing the black on green legend – US Army Air. Beyond them again were the fat-bellied C-130s, the great carriers of the Vietnam war. All the time the jets were taking off and landing with ear-splitting howls, their reactors burning orange against the leaden sky; and our ears had their first exposure to the peculiar, flat thud-thud-thud and whine of what Americans called 'heely-copters'.

There was no doubt that there was a war going on. The terminal itself was thick with Vietnamese military police and immigration officials, but we were waved through with the minimum of fuss. Outside, total confusion seemed to reign.

218

For security reasons taxis were not allowed near the terminal and, with our umpteen pieces of camera equipment piled in a heap on the ground, we stood there forlornly, wondering what on earth to do next. Then, quite unexpectedly, the infinitely friendly and reassuring shapes of Donald Wise and George Gale emerged out of the dust and confusion and all our troubles were over. Ensconced in two taxis, we set off for Saigon.

We drove out through the main civilian gate and into a swarm of Vietnamese traffic: cyclists, oxcarts, jeeps, Hondas, lorries, all mixed up in a seemingly inextricable muddle. Emerging from this, we passed some heavily wired and fortified concrete houses, many of which, Donald said, were occupied by the CIA and other American agencies, and then continued more or less straight to the bridge over the Saigon River. The river was low, and the glistening black mud on either bank, exposed to the full glare of the sun, gave off the strong, sickly sweet smell of human excrement. Wooden houses on stilts crowded down to the water's edge and I wondered how the occupants could bear the stench. They seemed to do so, quite unconcernedly. I must have crossed that bridge dozens of times in the next ten years and, each time, the same smell would assail my nostrils. I can still smell it now, overripe and corrupt, the smell of wartime Saigon.

Beyond the bridge the town proper began, and a mile or two further on we turned into the Avenue Pasteur, which runs under huge shady trees, between large French colonial villas, to the centre of the city. There, beside the red-brick Cathedral, we turned right into Tu Do, the most famous street in Saigon, full of shops and flats, finally emerging in the central square. In the middle stood an impressive white building, once the Opera but now the National Assembly, and on either side, facing each other in muted rivalry, the city's two main hotels, the Continental Palace, older, more stylish and patronised by the French, and the Caravelle, brash, modern and frequented by the Americans.

Like most journalists, apart from the French, we were staying at the Caravelle, on the corner nearest the river, nine storeys of concrete and glass, looking rather like one of those multi-layered party cakes. There was a lot of plate glass at street level, and a few polished stone steps led up to a small foyer, furnished in mock-oriental plastic. Donald introduced the manager, Mr. Dang, bespectacled and parchment-faced, who sat behind the desk nursing a long tuft of whiskers which protruded from one cheek. He looked like a dyspeptic mandarin. Mr. Dang shook hands without smiling – he only did that apparently when you paid your bill – and gave us our rooms. They turned out to be furnished in the same mock-oriental style of pale wood and plastic, but they were clean and reasonably comfortable.

We spent the rest of that day and the next being accredited to the Vietnamese and the Americans: the first was largely pro-forma, but accreditation to the Americans was absolutely vital, because only they could issue you with the magic MACV (Military Assistance Command Vietnam) Card which opened all doors. It conferred honorary officer status, which meant the holder could gain access to any American base, use any mess, and travel on any American aircraft from helicopters upwards. Without it you were a complete outsider; with it you were a war correspondent officially attached to the American forces. I was impatient to start filming – one always is; a sort of tension builds up and is only released when the first few feet of film of the first story are 'in the can'. I decided to do a story on helicopters. This was, after all, the first helicopter war and the Americans, it seemed, used them for everything: they were as common as jeeps in World War Two, fetching and carrying and operating a daily shuttle service to the Delta. Their great role, of course, was as gunships, but they were generally used for 'resupply', flying in ammunition and rations to men in the field. Chatting one day to a pilot on resupply, I asked him what he was carrying. 'Ammunition,' he said. 'K Rations. Ice cream.' My mind boggled. 'Ice cream? In combat?' He shrugged. 'It's good for the guys' morale, so we haul it in. What the hell?'

We tried to get permission to fly with the gunships on a combat mission, but the answer was a categorical 'No'. No one, they said, including American television, could do that. Not even the great Larry Burrows, killed, alas, because of his determination to see the Vietnam war through to the bitter end, was allowed to fly on a combat mission. His extraordinary picture story on the helicopter war was filmed from a medivac (medical evacuation) helicopter and took him weeks to complete. So we compromised by persuading the C.O. to let us fly on a training mission. Not that he took much persuading. As I was to learn very quickly, the American forces' attitude to the Press was very different to the British. 'Sure, no sweat' was the answer to most requests for help. Next day, we reported to the helicopter base and were assigned to a rocket-firing Huey.

We flew a few miles from the base, crossed the Mekong and followed the river for a mile or so. It looked like a perfectly normal stretch of river bank but it had been designated a 'free fire zone' by the Americans. This meant that it was considered Vietcong territory and anything seen in it was fair game. The pilot slowed down, went into a hover and pressed a red button on his control stick.

The gunship jumped, there was a crack and, almost too fast for the eye to follow, the rockets streaked downwards to explode with a puff of smoke 300 or 400 yards in front of us. The rockets were carried in two pods on either side of the fuselage, twenty-four rockets to a pod, forty-eight in all. After several passes, the pilot asked if we would like to film from the ground. I nodded, yes. He landed us in one corner of the target area, told us to stay there and not move, and said he would fire his rockets into the far corner. We all hoped he was a good shot.

He took off, climbed in a circle and then came in to the attack, hovering above us for a few seconds. There was a hiss and a bang, a pencil-thin streak of smoke, and then immediately afterwards – although it was at least 150 yards from where we were standing – a noise like a clap of thunder. Even at that distance, it was quite frankly terrifying. The thought of the tender flesh being subjected to that sort of assault was enough to make the courage evaporate and the bones melt in the body. I could just imagine what it must be like for the Vietcong to be under fire from a gunship. If they could not only survive it but fight back, sometimes successfully, they must be pretty tough customers. Of course, the gunship, especially when it is hovering to fire its rockets, is vulnerable, and the Vietcong were already having considerable success hitting them with heavy-calibre machine-guns.

The pilots were outspoken about the heavy ground fire they often ran into. 'We were called out one night to get some Rangers out of trouble, and, boy, it was like the Fourth of July,' one pilot said. 'There was so much shit coming up at us that I don't know how we didn't get zapped.'

When I interviewed the squadron commander, a veteran of eighteen months, he said that the war would have been lost without the helicopter. In 1964 the South Vietnamese forces had been so outclassed and outnumbered by the North Vietnamese regulars and the local Vietcong guerillas that the South had very nearly fallen. It had been touch and go. Only a sudden influx of American troops and the powerful new weapon of the helicopter gunship had prevented collapse and finally swung the battle.

'It was close,' the major said. 'Real close.'

The gunship story would make ten minutes, I hoped, on 'Roving Report' and we shipped it off to London with a considerable sense of achievement. We had only been in Vietnam for three or four days and not only had we completed our first story, but the next story was already beckoning. The U.S. Marines were coming and with their undoubted flair for publicity they were anxious that everyone, including presumably the Vietcong, should know all about it.

Unlike Gaul, South Vietnam was divided into four Military Regions, running from north to south, and the Marines had been assigned to MRI which extended from the 17th parallel, the border between North and South Vietnam, down past Hue, the old Imperial capital, to Da Nang and beyond. Da Nang, a big port, was to be their headquarters, and with their usual efficiency the Marines had already established a Press Centre there. So to Da Nang we all headed, Donald Wise, George Gale, Terry Spencer for *Time*, Larry Burrows for *Life* and a host of other American and British journalists, photographers and television crews, flying up in a C130, which is slow, uncomfortable and extremely noisy, but efficient. Accommodation at the Press Centre was fairly primitive but the bar was well stocked and the steaks, cooked by diminutive Vietnamese ladies, were all-Americans and enormous.

Da Nang itself was once, no doubt, an attractive little fishing port but it was already being swamped by the war, the roads turned into quagmires by the huge American lorries, which seemed to ply non-stop between the harbour and the air base, said to be the busiest airport in the world. It was from here that the Phanton fighter-bombers and the Northrop P4s made their daily strikes against targets in the north. Da Nang gave us our first real taste of the brutalising effect that the war and the American presence were already having on Vietnam: it looked like a huge shanty town that had sprung up overnight.

In this dusty, dirty desert, the Marine Press Centre quickly assumed the appearance of an oasis, and a well-organised one at that. The 'Gunny' Sergeant (senior NCO), in charge of Press facilities, briefed us over the steaks on our first night about the landing of the initial contingent of 3,500 Marines, the spearhead of the Corps' Expeditionary Force to Vietnam. He was a veteran of World War Two and he knew the form. The advance party would be landing with suitable panache the next morning on a beach just south of Danang. We would be ferried there by helicopter and be able to observe, film and photograph to our hearts' content. Then we would be flown back. The only question was: would the landing be opposed? Would the Vietcong be waiting for the Marines and let them have it as they came ashore?

That was the talking point in the bar after dinner and, although the consensus was that the 'gooks' would be too smart to meet such a display of force head-on, an element of doubt remained. So, next morning, we were ready and expectant when the buses came. The air base was operating at full blast, the humid air loud with the roar of jets taking off and heavy with the stench of vaporised kerosene. As they burned off into the sunlight, the Phantom F4s left a thick trail of exhaust fumes hanging in the sky.

Our helicopters took off in line ahead, climbed above the base and the town and then headed south. A helicopter gives you an unrivalled view and for short distances is the perfect way to travel. You see the country as a bird sees it, its shape and texture, and unlike passengers on larger, faster aircraft you remain in touch with the landscape. Through the plexi-glass windows, I could see just how narrow the coastal strip of Vietnam is. On our left the beaches ran south for golden mile after mile, totally deserted, and beyond the white line of surf the South China Sea stretched grey-blue to the horizon. Below us, the rice paddies made a neat chessboard of emerald green, and then, only a few miles inland, the mountains began, gentle foothills at first, but thickly wooded, and rising in long ridges to two or three thousand feet and the cloud base. It was from the hills, we knew, that the North Vietnamese divisions would come. The natural cover of the jungle, blanketing practically the whole of Vietnam right up to the border with Laos, was their best ally. It was something the Americans would have to learn to master or lose control of the war, and by the very nature of things they would never be able to do that.

All that lay in the future, of course, but to a prescient soldier it must have looked pretty intimidating terrain. About twenty miles south of Da Nang, near a village called Chu Lai, the helicopters wheeled and headed down towards a long flat beach. We landed in the dunes and assembled to hear the Gunny's words of wisdom. 'This is Omaha Beach,' he said, 'and the first Marines will be coming . . . ' he consulted his watch ' . . . in about half an hour from out there.' He pointed at the sullen expanse of the South China Sea. Indeed, about two miles offshore, we could make out the shapes of a dozen or more landing craft and a destroyer or two as well.

We stood on the low dunes, with the scrubby bush behind us, rather like punters at an early morning gallop, hoping to spot the favourite's form from a hidden vantage point.

'This would be a good time for the Vietcong to zap us,' someone joked. I looked round rather nervously. Apart from a handful of Marines and the small reception party which had flown in with us, there was precious little security on the beach. We waited, a trifle uneasily now that someone had planted the seed of doubt, wishing the Marines would hurry up. Donald, with that gift for discovering a vein of humour where apparently none exists, made us laugh for the intervening ten or fifteen minutes until suddenly someone said, 'Hey, they're really coming.'

The landing craft were travelling at full speed, hulls low in the water, bow waves angry white. With the cameras firmly in mind, they came in tight formation, in two lines, straight for the flattest part of the beach, right below us. About fifty yards offshore they dropped their ramps and the tanks came heaving forward into the surf, wallowing for a minute or two in the waves like overweight ducks, and then with a roar and a surge emerged on to the beach, water pouring off their hulls as if they were prehistoric monsters. They stormed up the beach towards us, as Jon filmed away dementedly. One tank, obligingly, came right at us, churning up the sand with its tracks, the commander peering out rather bewilderedly through his goggles. Having spotted the Press and not quite knowing what to do next, he lurched to a faltering stop at the edge of the bush. More tanks followed, and then several hundred 'Grunts', as ordinary Marines are called, dripping wet from the surf, stumbled over the sand under the weight of their equipment. A few minutes later the beach was officially declared secure. The Vietcong, after all, had not fired a shot. But none of us had any doubt that they were watching, with interest, from somewhere up in the hills.

In these early days, there was an amazing sense of euphoria. The Marines, with their great record lending them an understandable arrogance, thought that Vietnam, if not exactly a pushover, could not be more than a minor campaign among many more illustrious campaigns. Compared to the Pacific war, how could it be anything more than a two-bit affair? Most GIs and even some officers talked about being home for Christmas. But then soldiers always do. One or two more thoughtful officers did remember that Korea had proved an unhappy experience. But that was because China, with her cannon-fodder millions, had entered the battle despite General MacArthur's assurances to the contrary. So

Korea was different. And then more recently there was the French experience in Indo-China, culminating in the disaster at Dien Bien Phu, when some of France's best troops, including the famous Foreign Legion, had been ground to pieces by the despised *'petits hommes – verts'* – the French equivalent of 'gooks'. But few American generals seemed to have bothered to study the French campaigns, claiming that they were not relevant and that anyway they could not possibly make the same mistakes. After all, who had won World War Two?

The American attitude was very understandable but perhaps not very wise. Never underrate the enemy is a prime maxim of military philosophy. But then, in all its 200-year history, the United States had never lost a war, and they simply could not comprehend how a lousy little country like Vietnam, with relatively little and unsophisticated weaponry, could do more than cock a snook at the giant that was America. And when I watched the jets streaking down the runway at Da Nang, hoisting their dreadful payload of high explosive and napalm into the morning sky, I too could not imagine how such a pathetically inferior David could hold out for very long against such a technologically superior Goliath. Already in 1965, the arsenal of weapons the Americans had shipped to Vietnam was enormously impressive. And among the most impressive was the Phantom F4.

Jon Lane wanted to fly in a Phantom on a strike, but, since that was prohibited, just as it was with the gunships, we found a friendly radar operator and gave him a camera. He was something of a cine enthusiast himself, and after a little coaching he said he was sure he could get some pictures. He also explained that he would have one big advantage over someone who was a more experienced cameraman but not a trained Phantom pilot. The G forces were so intense, he said, that unless you were used to them you would probably be unable to hold the camera steady.

He did so brilliantly and brought us back impressive footage of a napalm strike on Vietcong targets, inside South Vietnam, the napalm making an angry ball of fire and oily smoke as it rolled over the forest. He also took some superb air to air shots of the squadron as it flew towards the mission. Fleshed out with our own footage of pilots being briefed and Phantoms being armed with bombs and Sidewinder missiles before a mission, it made a good third story – the build-up of the Marine expeditionary force in Vietnam.

We came back to the Press Centre late one afternoon to find a message waiting from the Roving Report Editor, Nigel Ryan. He had telephoned from London and left a message to call him back urgently. All sorts of dire thoughts went through my mind. Was someone dead? Had all the film been lost? Was it no good? With some anxiety I called the local Marine operator and asked for Saigon. It would take at least an hour, he said, because they had to go through Vietnamese channels, and as everyone knew the Vietnamese telephone system was on its last legs. They were watching some American movie on the big open-air screen in the Press Centre and I kept half an eye on it as I hung on the line. The Marine was right. It took about an hour to get Saigon. As instructed, I then asked for the offshore operator and after a good deal of argument got through to this elusive character.

From there the call went via Guam in the Pacific to San Francisco, and then to New York, where I had to give the London number. 'I'll give you Ruislip [the American base near London],' the operator said, and finally, after much shouting, I heard, very faintly, the voice of the ITN operator.

'It's Sandy here!' I roared, almost drowning the sound track of the film. 'Put me through to Nigel Ryan.' I could just hear the girl acknowledge and then, after a minute or so, Nigel's voice came on the line. It had now taken something like an hour and a half and most of my voice to get through to the 'Roving Report' office.

'Hallo, Nigel,' I shouted with what was left of it. 'Sandy here, anything wrong?' There was a long pause and what sounded like the distant roar of the sea. 'No, I just wanted to see if you were all right.' Nigel's voice came faintly over the line, via New York, San Francisco, Guam and Saigon, rising and falling sometimes inaudibly. Being an old hand at long-distance calls, however, he repeated everything twice.

227

'Yes, yes, we're okay,' I shouted. 'Got some good film which we'll be shipping from Saigon tomorrow or the day after. Including a Phantom strike.'

'Good, good. Fine, fine. Well, look after yourselves . . . ' Nigel's voice trailed off into the static. I put down the receiver, feeling stunned with exhaustion, and walked into the bar where Jon and Peter were waiting with expectant faces.

'Nothing,' I said, sitting down weakly. 'He just wanted to know if we were all right.'

We flew back to Saigon the next day to ship our film. This was an operation in itself, necessitating countless documents, stamps and customs clearances and a long and time-consuming trip to the airport. When it was finally consigned aboard Pan Am or Air France we felt relieved but not entirely sure that it would ultimately reach its destination – ITN in Kingsway, London. That done, we took a day or two off in Saigon and it was agreeable after the rigours of the Da Nang Press Centre to go out to lunch at the Royale or one of the other French restaurants where you could eat and drink better than you would in most London restaurants and at half the price. The Royale, run by an opium-wizened old Frenchman, was much patronised by the staff of the Associated Press, notably the photographer Horst Fass. As his name implies, Horst was a German, large and loud-spoken, and already making a name for himself as a risk-all war photographer. Festooned with cameras and extra rolls of film, Horst could be seen wherever the action was, charging along like a Wagnerian hero, hurling himself down flat as the bullets started to zing past and then blazing away with his cameras, almost as if they were weapons. He used them so effectively that he eventually won a Pulitzer prize. Donald Wise, with his mordant tongue, used to say that to see Horst going into action was to be reminded of the devastating onrush of German Panzers in World War Two.

Horst was such a good trooper, in the sense of being battle-wise, that he knew exactly where to go, what risks to take and when to go no farther – always the mark of a good war correspondent or photo-journalist, though of course you

228

need luck as well, because inevitably, and especially to get good pictures, you have to take risks. In Vietnam, photographers like Horst and Larry Burrows took a lot of risks. Both were finally so vastly experienced that they seemed to develop a sixth sense for danger, and to become invulnerable. But, in the end, you need luck. Horst survived. Larry was killed when the Vietnamese helicopter in which he was travelling was shot down over the Iron Triangle – the corner where the Vietnamese, Laotian and Cambodian borders meet – in 1971. Larry was totally different to Horst and I knew him a good deal better. He was English, and whereas most senior *Life* photographers were too busy with their tripods and subtle lighting to risk the hurly-burly of the Vietnam war, Larry became intensely involved, finally moving to Hong Kong so that he could be on the spot to cover it. He was a tall, bespectacled, quiet-spoken, almost diffident man, looking, I always thought, rather like a professor even in the heat of battle, and he approached all his assignments with a great deal of care. Other journalists would consult him whenever possible and I always found his advice extremely thoughtful and generous. Many people in Vietnam were so busy planning and executing their own coverage that they had no time for a less well-informed or experienced colleague, especially one fresh out from London. Larry always had time for everyone, which was a tribute to his character and also to his own pre-eminence. Someone like that, at the peak of his career and powers, knowing that he is one of the best photographers in the world, should be sufficiently detached to take an Olympian view.

He had, at that time, just finished his long essay on the helicopter war, 'Yankee Papa 13'. I asked him how he had managed to get the fantastic shots, taken from outside the helicopter, of the door-gunners blazing away.

'I got the chopper people to fix a bracket on the outside of the fuselage and I mounted a camera on it.' With this remote-controlled camera, and the others round his neck, Larry photographed Yankee Papa near Da Nang in early 1965. The Marines were airlifting South Vietnamese troops into an area believed to be a Vietcong staging point and, as they came in

229

the first time, they ran into a murderous cross-fire. For once, Larry stayed in the helicopter, photographing from the door. They lifted off and went back for another load. But, as they came in the second time, they saw another Marine helicopter stranded on the ground with the crew still on board. The young crew chief of Yankee Papa 13, James Farley, jumped out, and, followed by Larry, ran to the downed helicopter. While a Vietcong machine-gun seventy yards away began to blast holes in the fuselage right beside them, Farley tried, and failed, to pull the pilot out of the cockpit. He was dead. Two other crewmen, although wounded, managed to scramble back to Yankee Papa. As they took off, Farley's big 30-calibre machine-gun jammed and Larry's camera caught him as he shouted to the other door-gunner, 'Cover your side. I'll help these guys.' They were the two wounded crewmen, their uniforms splattered with blood, sprawled out on the floor of the helicopter. Larry noticed three bullet holes right beside the open doorway. 'Had I stayed there in my usual position feeling that was the safe spot,' he said afterwards, 'then I could easily have been killed. It is all a matter of fate.'

Larry's pictures of Yankee Papa made the cover of *Life* and stand as one of the great photographic essays of the Vietnam War, and indeed of any other war.

Every afternoon, MACV gave a press briefing known irreverently as the Saigon Follies, in a big white building, formerly the Rex Cinema. The briefing was usually a bureaucratic litany of operations carried out, casualties inflicted on the enemy, and allied casualties – American and South Vietnamese – sustained. Because of arguments about South Vietnamese claims, the Americans insisted on 'body counts' of the enemy dead. Despite the precaution, the numbers of enemy dead or KIAs (Killed in Action), as the jargon had it, often seemed extremely high. The Follies were part of a huge propaganda exercise but the Americans did pass out a great deal of information that few other countries, if any, would have divulged. This American openness is of course based on their Constitution which specifically lays down the right to Press freedom. Any attempt to withhold information is therefore contrary to the Constitution and any American President or government official who attempts a cover-up, does so at his peril.

The Follies were saved from tedium by one man, Joe Fried, the diminutive and acid-tongued correspondent of the *New York Daily Post*. He would sit up near the front and, as the briefer, usually a major or a colonel, ploughed on through the day's ration of statistics, the nasal Bronx accent of Joe Fried would suddenly cut through the waffle like a sharp knife.

'You said yesterday that the VC were wiped out near Dak To [in the Delta] and yet today we have a major attack on the South Vietnamese position right beside the town. How do you explain that, Colonel? Were they airlifted overnight?' This would be greeted by laughter from the assembled pressmen.

The colonel, reddening, would do his best. Nervous briefers would stammer and stutter. Then, if he floundered about, Joe would be on to him like a flash, a hawk diving on a mouse. He had the inquisitorial manner to perfection. I have never heard it wielded so skilfully and so devastatingly, not even by Robin Day. Joe Fried kept the brass on their toes and they must have loathed him. But at a more mundane level they were extremely helpful. You could go anywhere, at any time, to cover almost any story. If there was a battle being fought in any part of Vietnam, involving American troops or South Vietnamese, or both, the Press could go there simply by climbing aboard a helicopter or fixed-wing aircraft. No pass or permission was needed, apart from the MACV card.

When we made our first trip to the Delta, a day or two later, the sergeant on the desk said, 'You wanna go to the Delta tomorrow? Okay. There's a heely-copter going out of Tan Son Nhut every hour on the hour, from six on. You wanna come back in the afternoon? Okay. The last heely-copter leaves Can Tho at six. Be sure you don't miss it. Otherwise you'll have to spend the night down there. Much better service in the Caravelle.' We all laughed dutifully.

Then, just as I was turning to go, he called: 'You got

wheels?' For a moment I was non-plussed, and then I understood. Did we have transport? 'We'll get a taxi,' I said.

'No,' the sergeant said. 'They won't allow taxis in the gate. You can catch a ride with us. We'll pick you up at the Caravelle at seven. Okay?'

American frankness, at this level, was so remarkable that on some occasions we British journalists thought it went too far. For example, MACV would announce details of strikes against the North as they were actually in progress. The agencies, AP, UPI and Reuters, would flash the start of a bombing raid and such was the speed of their teleprinter system that the news would be in Hanoi before the planes were overhead. This led to the charge that the agency reports, by alerting the enemy, were actually endangering the lives of the aircrews and may have led to some of them being shot down.

When, therefore, MACV announced that it would no longer release details of air strikes against the North until each operation was over, there was a howl of protest from some members of the American Press Corps. They were, naturally, intensely jealous of any restrictions of their freedom. Interestingly, few of their British colleagues agreed with them. Most of us thought it criminal folly to divulge military secrets in this way and even to risk the possibility of an agency flash leading to the death or capture of a pilot. This urge to be up to the minute seemed to me to push the principle of freedom of information to insane lengths.

It was commonly said that the Vietnam War was really about the Mekong River Delta. This was an exaggeration, but there was a lot of truth in it. Vietnam is shaped like a lop-sided hour-glass. At the top, the north, you have the wide delta made by the Red River, which flows past Hanoi, then the country narrows to a waist which the Americans called the Panhandle, and in the south, round Saigon, it swells out again to form the Mekong River Delta. This is one of the world's most productive ricegrowing areas, and was known in *Time Magazine* English as the 'rice bowl'.

We took off early in the morning. There was a slight haze,

the light was translucent, washed. I think I fell in love with the Delta at first sight. The pilot and co-pilot, in their large plastic flying helmets, looked as if they were fresh out of college. The pilot pressed the start button. There was a loud whine and the rotor started to turn until it was a blur above our heads. When pitch and speed were right, we lifted up, very delicately, until we were about five feet above the ground, and then, with a slight dip of the nose, taxied smoothly down between the ranks of parked Hueys, turned out on to the runway, hovered for a moment and finally, cleared by the tower for take-off, applied full power. It was like leaving your stomach behind on a roller-coaster. We rose straight up, fast, and then, dipping the nose, went into a forward climb at an angle of forty-five degrees. The sensation of sheer power lifting you into the sky was exhilarating.

Saigon receded behind its smoke haze and I looked towards the Delta. The Huey has a plexiglass nose which give almost all-round vision and in Vietnam they always flew with the doors off. A door-gunner sat on either side of us, leaning unconcernedly on his heavy machine-gun. With any luck, we would not need them today.

We were now at about 1,000 feet and I could see what looked like a whole series of circular ponds in the flat green expanse of the rice paddies.

I gestured to the crew chief. What are those? He put his mouth right up to my ear. 'Craters,' he shouted. 'Bomb and shell craters.' We were only a few miles from Saigon, but every field had at least one crater in it. We could see the loops of the Saigon River, uncoiling like a silver snake until it met the Mekong, a giant of a river, split here into several arms, each half a mile wide, sweeping towards the distant South China Sea. As we flew over, tiny sampans like water insects crawled below us and wooden villages clung to its banks. The engine beat changed and we started to float down towards our first stop, My Tho, a busy provincial town, on the northern edge of the Delta. We stopped only long enough to drop the other television team and were off again, flying over the heart of the Delta now, a mysterious green, bare land, water-borne, tidal, but, despite its apparent emptiness, heavily populated with many villages hidden among the trees along the river. Can Tho is the capital of the Delta, a busy market town built on the main arm of the Mekong, here in its final, majestic phase, a great sombre brown flood heavy with silt. Who would guess, looking at it here, that the Mekong rises 2,500 miles away in the snows of Tibet, flows south through China, between its ice brothers, the Yangtse Kiang, which finishes up at Shanghai, and the Salween which enters the sea at Rangoon, and, longer than either, goes on to skirt the Golden Triangle, washes the temples of Luang Prabang and Vientiane, makes the border between Laos and Thailand, carves its way through Cambodia, past the capital Phnom Penh, until it finally reaches Vietnam and Can Tho at the end of its monumental journey?

We walked through the market which despite the war seemed to be operating at full blast. The tough old Vietnamese peasant women squatted on their haunches haggling over the round wicker baskets full of live fish, tiny softshell crabs, rice, fat, juicy vegetables, and hundreds of trussed chickens and ducks, lying patiently on their sides awaiting their purchaser and eventual executioner.

Out in the paddies on the outskirts of town, we came across an artillery unit. The captain in charge, young and self-confident, explained that his job was to fire H and I. What was that, I asked.

'Harassment and Interdiction,' he explained. 'If we get the word that the VC are out there in the paddies we let them have it.' He paused to give orders to some of his men unloading the shiny great rounds for the big guns from their packing cases, brought in on the resupply helicopters.

'We got thirty last night,' he continued. 'They were sitting out in a field. We didn't know they were there but we were putting down H and I around evening time. They found 'em next morning.'

'How did you know that they were Vietcong?' I asked.

'Sure they were VC,' the captain said emphatically. 'Who else would be sitting out in the middle of a paddy at that time of day? They were all in their black pyjamas, anyway.'

It seemed a pretty hit and miss business, H and I. I

wondered how many innocent Vietnamese got 'zapped' along with the VC. It was a worrying thought.

For me, Saigon will always be the city of Graham Greene. I cannot remember when I first read *The Quiet American* but it was before I ever went to Vietnam. His grasp of the political situation that evolved at the end of French rule and with the arrival of the first over-confident Americans was uncanny.

His literary ability belongs to another category entirely, but as a journalist I had to admire his reporter's skill. He is, if you like, the journalist's novelist *par excellence*. In Saigon, Graham Greene stayed at the Continental Palace Hotel, to give its rather too imposing title, and walked the same streets that I now was inspecting for the first time. The Continental terrace was the place where everyone went for a drink in the evening: journalists, Vietnamese politicians, American contractors, thick-necked and with their Vietnamese mistresses in tow, pimps and prostitutes, and hanging around the fringes, chased away by the waiters but darting back like scavenging minnows as soon as the coast was clear, a horde of infant peddlers, shoeshine boys and beggars, many of them cripples, most of them selling American cigarettes or chewing gum, all of them on the look-out for a few piastres or, if luck was with them, a dollar, a greenback, already the only currency that mattered, and the only one that still matters, nearly twenty years later, in today's Communist Vietnam.

I liked to stroll down Tu Do (in Greene's day it was the Rue Catinat) when I had time, when the war was quiescent or we were between stories, especially the part that ran from the Caravelle Hotel to the river. It was full of tailors' shops, including the establishment of Mr Minh, an extremely polite, unsmiling refugee from Hanoi who made the most elegant safari suits in Saigon; there were also jewellery and antique shops and cafés but above all there were the bars. Even in 1965, in the early days of the war, the girlie bars were sprouting like weeds. In their dark, noisy depths flitted scores of heavily made-up, tightly-sweatered bar girls, some as

235

pretty as dolls, but most looking what they were, peasant girls who had come to the big city to cash in on the GI boom. As soon as you walked in the girls would rise and twitter like a pack of starlings, eyeing the customer as to the size of his wallet rather than ogling him in the more overtly sexual Western way. Even before you sat down, one would grab your arm and whisper invitingly, 'I your friend, you buy me a drink?' If you failed to respond the girl would snuggle up closer and repeat the question until her sheer persistence if not her feminine charms eventually prevailed.

On being offered a drink the girl would flash a mechanical smile and order a Saigon Tea, a brightly-coloured, non-alcoholic concoction that tasted of nothing but cost a lot. The girls got commission on the drinks they and their 'friends' consumed, but of course the real profit went to the shady characters who ran the bars. They in turn had to bribe all the right people in government and the police who controlled the concessions. So the spiral of corruption worked its way from the bar parlours of Tu Do right to the very top. But, despite this sleazy traffic, Tu Do still had a certain elegance about it. The French had planted trees on both sides of the road and, even when the sun was beating down at midday, it was like a leafy tunnel, along which cycled pretty Vietnamese girls in their semi-transparent *ao dais*, the traditional dress with a high collar and tight-fitting bodice and long skirt slit to the knee. For everyday wear, Vietnamese women had white *ao dais* but on special occasions they would choose more exotic colours: deep purple, pale apple green, orange and electric blue. They floated along rather than trod the ground, managing to look ethereal and untouched by the horrors of the war. These middle-class girls of good family would not talk to any American, so, if a GI wanted female company there was really no alternative to the bar girls.

At the bottom of Tu Do there was a narrow side street which contained the 'Bank of India', as the press called it. Here, in a couple of back rooms up a rickety stairs, a group of Indian money-changers operated a discreet, efficient and no doubt very lucrative black market. Even then, in the early days of the war, the unofficial rate of the Vietnam piastre to the dollar was double the official rate. Later it was to climb to four to one and even higher.

Just beyond, on the corner, stood the Majestic Hotel, a large and imposing establishment with a handsome view over the river. For some reason it was never patronised by the Press, presumably because the Caravelle and the Continental were more central. But the Majestic had one attractive feature. You could sit at a table underneath an awning, a beer in your hand, and watch the busy life of the docks go by in front of you. Naval Headquarters were upstream to the left, and opposite, beyond a dusty little garden, the passenger ferries from Gia Dinh, on the far side of the river, unloaded peasants coming to market in the early morning and took them home in the afternoon. A few hundred yards downstream from the Majestic, just before the commercial docks began, a couple of floating restaurants were moored close to the bank. One, the My Canh, had good seafood and was popular with the Press. One noon, when the war was having a slack day, Donald Wise, George Gale and a couple of other friends and myself decided to have lunch there. It was blisteringly hot as we walked down Tu Do, past the Majestic, along the quay, and up the gangway to be met by the scurrying welcome that only film stars or cabinet ministers command at home, but which any almost white foreigner, especially an American, automatically received in Saigon. All you needed was to be the possessor of that universally desirable commodity, a pocketful of green. We sat on deck enjoying the breeze off the river, eating freshly-caught, grilled prawns and drinking French white *vin ordinaire*. Both were delicious. We talked about the war and the prospects for either side. The American commitment was already impressive and growing by the day. But so too was the opposition, both the Vietcong, as the home-based guerrillas were called, and, more importantly, the regular divisions of the North Vietnamese Army which were infiltrating down the Ho Chi Minh Trail.

Their predecessors had seen off the French, who were probably better soldiers than the Americans, man for man. We all agreed the French Government lost its will to prosecute the war. That, rather than the defeat at Dien Bien

Phu, had put paid to French colonial rule in Indo-China. But, as far as the Americans were concerned, the will to win in 1965 was indisputable, and with their apparently overwhelming advantage in equipment and technology, their helicopter gunships and Phantom F4s, eventual victory seemed to be a foregone conclusion. That is what the others thought and I agreed with them.

After lunch, as we walked down the gangway, Donald stopped in mid-stride. He would not be surprised, he said, if any day now the Vietcong were to float a mine down the river and blow the My Canh and its customers sky high. Flown with wine and food, we laughed at his joke. Three or four days later, around eight in the evening, Jon Lane and I were sitting in the bar of the Caravelle before dinner when we heard the howl of police sirens racing down Tu Do. We rushed downstairs to be told that there had been a big explosion at the docks. Someone said the My Canh restaurant had been blown up. We snatched up the camera and sound gear, piled into a taxi and were on the scene within minutes. Opposite the My Canh, police cars and ambulances were parked, their blue lights flashing blindingly. Blood spattered the ground and on the pavement several bodies lay under sheets. Other victims, wounded but alive, were being loaded into the ambulances. What had happened? An American said that a bomb had gone off aboard the My Canh, and as the terrified diners had rushed down the gangway to get off the boat another more powerful bomb, planted on the quayside, had caught them head on. It had been an American Claymore mine, which hurls hundreds of small metal balls, like ball-bearings, in a flat, scything trajectory, specifically designed to catch someone on foot. It was typical of the resourcefulness of the Vietcong that they should either capture, steal or copy an American weapon and turn it back against its makers, although, in this instance, the victims were almost entirely Vietnamese families who had been dining out.

Later that evening, I was summoned to the telephone. London was on the line, a call from Nigel Ryan.

'Are you all right, Sandy?' His voice was a little louder than it had been in Da Nang.

'Yes, fine, Nigel, why shouldn't we be?'

'I've just heard that the Vietcong have blown up the best restaurant in Saigon and I thought you were bound to be in it.'

'Well, I did have lunch there a few days ago but it's not the best restaurant in town. Anyway, we've just filmed the carnage and it will be on its way to you tomorrow.'

'Okay, ole boy' – he couldn't resist copying Tony Cole – 'Just as long as you and the crew are all right. That's all that I wanted to know . . .'

At the beginning of July we flew from Saigon to Singapore with instructions to report another smaller war – 'confrontation', as it was pompously called – between Malaysia and Indonesia. Both countries had been colonies until the end of the Second World War, Malaysia being British and Indonesia Dutch, and both had recently become independent. Indonesia's first President was an overweening playboy called Sukarno, more noticed for his amorous than for his military exploits. But he judged, not entirely wrongly, that the Malaysians would be a pushover and so he launched across the Straits of Malacca a series of commando raids which soon had the Malaysians badly rattled. They turned automatically to their old colonial protectors and the British responded by sending several thousand troops, mainly to Borneo, a huge island bigger than Malaya itself. Two thirds of Borneo belonged to Indonesia, but the northern third, comprising the Sultanates of Sarawak and Brunei, was part of the Malaysian Federation. Sukarno was particularly interested in Brunei, a tiny enclave of jungle and mangrove swamp, because it had oil, making it *per capita* one of the richest places in the world.

On the advice of Donald Wise, who was then based in Singapore, we booked in at the Cockpit Hotel. This was a modest enough establishment but with a friendly atmosphere and the great advantage of being built round a swimming pool. My first priority was to meet the British Army's local press officer and arrange for our onward flight to Borneo. The second was to visit Raffles, the most famous hotel in Singapore, named after the founder of Singapore, Sir

Stamford Raffles, a nineteenth-century adventurer in the grand tradition. My father had always stayed at Raffles on his way to and from 'Home' and I suppose I expected it to be virtually unchanged. The reality was sadly disappointing. It had been all tarted up in garish colours and, although the skeleton was the same, the spirit was not. My nostalgia evaporated before I finished the first drink. Our meeting with the army PRO to arrange accreditation for Borneo was equally disappointing. Five minutes with the major were enough to convince me that, when it came to dealing with the Press, the British Army had learnt nothing since Suez.

In Vietnam, although we were not Americans, the MACV card had opened all doors. In Singapore, I felt, they really did not want to be bothered with us. The first problem, the major explained, was actually getting there. Well, we said, weren't there aeroplanes? He looked pained. Yes, of course, but not many, and we might have to wait several days to get seats. After the abundance of helicopters and every other sort of aircraft in Vietnam the paucity of the British war effort was striking. That was understandable; we were a small country and this was a small war. What I found harder to accept was the standoffish attitude of the Army to us, ITN, with our enormous audience and tremendous influence. And it was not as if we were hostile. On the contrary, we were extremely sympathetic to the whole British endeavour. Here was no repressive colonial war, no adventure, for example like Suez, which was dividing the country and causing Ministers to resign. Britain and the Army were on the side of the angels. Indonesia was without any shadow of doubt the aggressor, we were there purely on the invitation of the Malaysians, to help to defend their territory and their independence. God knows Britain, in the last days of Empire, had had to bear enough criticism and opprobrium. But this was a heaven-sent opportunity for any publicist. I could just imagine an American PR man's response: 'Get them over here, wheel them in to see the general, ask them what they want to do, lay it on for them, see they have the best facilities, briefings, transport, anything they want . . .'

Well, of course, it did not quite work out like that. The

major, when we finally tracked him down in his shabby office, was rather like a prep school master meeting the parents of an awkward boy. He was decidedly unenthusiastic. After a preliminary skirmish, he asked us rather reluctantly where we wanted to go.

I said to the Kuching area where the Indonesians had just attacked across the border and inflicted several casualties on the British. The major pulled a long face. Everyone wanted to go to Kuching, he complained, and although there had been an incident there, it was all quiet at the moment.

Yes, I argued, but that was one of the most sensitive areas, was it not, and that was where we wanted to go.

The major looked even more embarrassed. Well, he said, the colonel in command had just had an unfortunate row with the *Daily Mirror* correspondent, who had preferred to write stories of what was wrong with the men's living conditions rather than record the progress of the war. As a result, the colonel had banned all pressmen from the area. A hunted look came into the major's eye. If we insisted on going there we would get no cooperation and quite honestly he would not advise it. Far better to go somewhere else where at least the soldiers, if not the natives, were friendly.

Very reluctantly, I agreed. We finally settled on two places. One was a forward base at Bario, where the Gurkhas were stationed, and the second was at Tawau, in the north-east, where the Gordon Highlanders were patrolling the mangrove swamps only a few hundred yards from the Indonesians. There was an additional advantage in going to Tawau: the major commanding the Gordons, John Simpson, was a friend from far-off Kent. He, at least, should be more forthcoming than the irate colonel at Kuching. From Singapore we flew due east across the South China Sea to Kuching on the western tip of Borneo, which was British headquarters, and then over what appeared to be endless jungle, broken only occasionally by a great brown river, to Brunei. Down there, we knew, were the headhunter tribes like the Dyaks which had terrorised the early British colonisers but had long since been brought under control; or more or less. It was common knowledge that, during the war against the

241

Japanese, who occupied the whole of Borneo after the fall of Singapore, the headhunters had been allowed to revive their old habits, on the strict understanding that only Japanese heads were removed, shrunk and later hung up for display in the long houses, rather as we would hang a treasured painting.

After a brief stop at Brunei, the airport giving little sign of the place's great wealth, we embarked for the final leg of the journey, flying right across the north-east tip of Borneo to Tawau. Tawau was the end of the line, a nondescript little town at the mouth of another huge, muddy brown river. The whole estuary was covered in mangrove trees, their roots half-sunk in the tidal mud and matted together like a witch's tresses. Over the mud scuttled countless crabs, plopping into the water as you went past in a boat.

The Gordon Highlanders were based here and although their home terrain is totally different – the glens and straths of north-east Scotland – they had taken to their new aquatic role with remarkable versatility. They had formed a couple of boat squadrons and raced up and down the mangrove swamps in a fleet of rubber dinghies with powerful outboard engines. John was not there to meet us. He told me later he had been up all night, had just gone to bed and was fast asleep when he was woken by an importunate signaller who thrust a piece of paper into his hand. It said: 'Sandy Gall and ITN camera team arriving on morning flight from Brunei. Grateful you look after them if duties permit.' The commanding officer offered a few curses and went back to sleep.

In his temporary absence we were met and taken to the Gordons' camp by the sergeant-major. It was strange to hear the homely accents of 'Buchan', as that part of Aberdeenshire is known, out here in the remote spaces of Borneo. The men looked just like the 'fairm loons' that I had known as a boy: fresh-faced, rather slow moving, but with a solid inner strength. And the army had speeded them up, toughened them. John arrived in a swirl of dust and screech of brakes a couple of hours later, and came storming in to see us. He was larger than life, all six foot four of him, bursting with energy,

242

looking peculiarly Highland Brigade, so much so that I half expected him to be wearing the kilt instead of his tropical khaki, and despite his lack of sleep he was jovial and hospitable. Since he had very little fighting on his hands, he went to great lengths to meet our requirements. He was a natural and gifted publicist. Within half an hour we had our programme planned and were put in a boat and sent off with a couple of Jocks for what the Army calls a 'familiarisation trip'.

The Jocks spoke broad Scots to one another, thinking none of us would understand, and it gave me a quite extraordinary thrill to be able to eavesdrop on their conversation with complete comprehension.

Next day, John took us to see his pride and joy, an observation post in the middle of the estuary, only half a mile from the Indonesian positions on the other side. It was in fact an old river steamer, anchored in the middle of the stream, and, because of its exposed position, christened by the Jocks, 'Proper Charlie'.

We skimmed out to it in a fast rubber assault boat and clambered over the side.

'Don't show yourselves more than is necessary,' John said. 'You never quite know what the ruddy Indonesians are going to do. They've already had a couple of goes at "Proper Charlie" but we've seen 'em off both times.'

There was always one Jock on board, equipped with a pair of binoculars and a notebook, and his job was to keep an eye on the Indonesians opposite and log their movements.

'We can keep a check on everything they're doing,' John explained, indicating the binoculars which were fixed to a tripod. 'Have a look through these and you'll see what I mean.'

I put my eye to the lens and with startling clarity the Indonesian headquarters on the far side of the inlet came into view. There were several large huts beside a landing stage and I was just in time to see a group of men entering one building.

'That's the officers' mess,' John said. 'They'll just be going into lunch. Make a note of that,' he said to Jock, who wrote it down in his notebook.

'Had any activity?' he asked the soldier.

'Verra quiet,' the young Jock said calmly. 'A coupla boats going out on patrol, that's all.'

'Once they had a real go,' said John. 'Came right up close with guns blazing. That was just after we first moved "Proper Charlie" into position. They didn't like us watching everything they did. But we let 'em have it back. We've got quite a useful gun on board,' he pointed to a machine-gun half concealed in the cabin. 'And they buzzed off. Haven't bothered us much since then. Got all the film you need?'

But Jon, who was a painstaking craftsman, was not ready. After the hectic rush of agency journalism I was learning that filming was a rather slower business, although news cameramen can work with amazing speed.

'What about an into camera piece?' Jon asked. 'It'll look good.'

'Good idea,' I said. This meant that I had to think up a few pertinent phrases and say them to the camera, as if I were speaking directly to the audience. They would then be fitted into the film, so you had to think carefully about the context. I still found these on camera remarks difficult to do, at least in a natural, relaxed manner, and I had to make several attempts. Jon and Peter were always extremely patient and in the end I got an acceptable one. It was indeed a good location, 'Proper Charlie' rising and falling gently on the current, the Indonesian positions, which you could see clearly through our long lens behind me, and the Jock peering obligingly through his binoculars for us. The rather Ruritanian character of the war was beautifully caught by the nickname of 'Proper Charlie'. Only the British would think of something like that, turning the joke against themselves. I am sure it was lost on the Indonesians.

A few days later, we flew on over the jungle to Bario. When the famous Tom Harrisson parachuted into Bario under the noses of the Japanese during the war, the whole community had lived in one huge 'long house'. It was still much the same when we arrived twenty years later; the long house was still the centre of the Kelabit village, said to be the highest inhabited village in Borneo. On our first evening, we were taken along to pay our respects. Europeans have been brought up, because of the climate and the accidents of history, to seclude themselves in their own little houses. The Kelabits and other Borneo tribesmen live on the open plan system, with the chief in the middle and the other members of the clan in descending order on either side of him. This particular 'long house' – what Tom Harrisson calls a 'complete village and (even more) a nearly complete living unit within one roof' – was about a hundred yards long and stood on a little knoll above a small stream. Round it the rice fields glowed like emeralds, but beyond this small cultivated patch the jungle and the mountains climbed to the sky. We walked to the long house with a young Gurkha officer, Vyvyan Robertson, who was to be our friend, guide and mentor for the next week. In the evening light, the place looked almost enchanted, the smoke from the cooking fires curling up into the air, the cries of children mingling with the squeals of the piglets and the squawking of chickens.

We climbed the steps and followed Vyvyan inside. In front of us, curved like the deck of an old sailing ship, the hundred-yard-long wooden floor disappeared into the gloom. We trod carefully past smiling Kelabits until we came to the centre of the long house and, after more smiles and handshakes from lesser members of the family, were finally introduced to the paramount chief, a gap-toothed, wizened old boy wearing all manner of strange beads and an army greatcoat over his sarong. We were bidden to sit down, cross-legged on the wooden floor, and some strange and powerful drink was brought. Vyvyan warned us that it was very potent but that courtesy demanded we drink it all and look as if we were enjoying it. I took a sip. It was both fiery and foul, but I made an effort to smile. While the Kelabits harangued Vyvyan and our interpreter in their incomprehensible language, I examined our hosts. They were pleased to see us, there was no doubt about that. Of course, from the beginning, they had been not so much subjects as allies, who had fought for the King across the water with blowpipe and poison dart first against the Japanese and now, on a smaller scale, against the Indonesians. Officially they were used to gather intelligence, but no one minded if they engaged in a little head-hunting, provided the heads were Indonesian, Vyvyan discreetly pointed some out to us. They were dark and discoloured, about the size of a large cooking apple, with a wisp of hair at the top and the features compressed into a rubbery leer. Obviously proud of them, the Kelabits giggled slyly as they watched us examining their macabre little trophies.

'All Japanese,' Vyvyan said with a wave of the hand in the direction of the little collection. The old chief nodded assent vigorously, smiling his widest gap-toothed smile.

We walked home rather merrily in the soft dusk; the dreadful long house cocktail had done its work.

'Would you like to go on a patrol?' Vyvyan asked as we neared our camp. 'We can go out in a few days' time, in any case. I can bring it forward, and arrange for you to come with us.'

'We'd love to go,' I said, 'and possibly see some action?'

'If you do,' Vyvyan said, 'it'll all be over so fast that you'll be bloody lucky to get anything on film. The jungle's so thick that you can't see more than about twenty or thirty yards in any direction.'

'We'd be happy to give it a try. How long will it take?'

'Well,' Vyvyan said. 'We usually walk in, which takes a day, we patrol for two or three days, and it takes another day to get back.' He looked at me sideways. 'But, since you probably haven't got all that time, we'll chopper you in and out and spend a couple of days on the border.' I said that would be perfect; we were getting used to going everywhere by helicopter. Next day Vyvyan sent off his Gurkhas and the day after that the helicopters came in under the clouds from Brunei and lifted us out across the jungle canopy to just below the border ridge.

Our patrol, who were waiting for us, had chopped down a few trees to make a landing pad, and the pilot dropped down into the little clearing with the precision of a lift in its shaft.

'Get out smartly,' Vyvyan shouted into my ear. 'These chaps don't like hanging about.' I could understand why. If any Indonesians had been on the ridge above us, the hovering Wessex would have made an easy target. We scrambled out and ran into the trees where the Gurkhas had taken up covering positions.

We started the patrol in the late morning and worked our way along the ridge all afternoon, stopping at five, as the light began to fade. Vyvyan's batman immediately started to brew 'chai' (tea). The rest of the patrol scattered itself in well-rehearsed order along the ridge, just off the track, setting up ambush positions at each end.

'The Indonesians never move at night,' Vyvyan explained. 'Certainly not if they know that the Gurkhas are around. But we do it as a matter of course.'

The grinning batman brought the tea, deliciously thirst-quenching after what was for us at any rate a hard day's march. We discussed the chances of seeing any Indonesians.

'Not very great,' Vyvyan said. 'What the Gurkhas hope for of course is to be ambushed themselves.'

This seemed to me to be such a piece of masochism that I thought I had misheard. 'You can't be serious,' I remonstrated.

'Absolutely,' Vyvyan insisted. 'They'll tell you it's the easiest way to find the enemy. And they're so much better fighters than the Indonesians that they'll always come out on top.'

I reflected on this. All afternoon I had been walking along, hoping that we would not run into an Indonesian ambush, surrounded by Gurkhas who had been fervently hoping just the opposite.

The batman and a friend were busy chopping down a few saplings with their kukris, shiny, ferociously-sharp knives which the Gurkhas use for every sort of task, but principally for slicing their enemies' heads off in battle. Ground sheets were spread on top of the twigs and our beds for the night were ready. A few minutes later, with miraculous efficiency, hot curry appeared and each of us was handed a strong tot of rum. Like the Royal Navy of old, the Gurkhas get a daily rum ration. It was very potent, making the curry taste delicious, and when I rolled into bed about nine, after a long chat with Vyvyan, my twiggy mattress felt as soft as a feather-bed. It was an uneventful night, apart from a few mosquitoes who braved the rum fumes, and morning 'chai' appeared soon after dawn. Breakfast followed in no time at all, and soon after that we were on the march again.

As we plodded along in the hot, green gloom of the jungle, with Indonesian territory only spitting distance away, I marvelled at the tough little men who carried heavy machine-guns and mortars with such apparent ease. I had seen the Gurkhas in the Congo but never been with them on active service. Now, after talking to Vyvyan and spending a night and a day with them, I was a complete convert. First of all, they were clearly the most consummate professionals and yet they had the modesty and charm of amateurs. They made it all look so easy and such fun. They were always smiling, always cheerful. And yet they had this fearsome reputation as the best jungle troops in the business, and the most ferocious hand-to-hand fighters. That was when they used their kukris with such lethal effect. Being small and brown they blend with the jungle like chameleons and make Europeans and Americans look like blundering incompetents. It was interesting to compare their patrolling technique with that of the American Marines we had seen in Vietnam. The Americans smoked and talked on patrol and moved with the noise of a wagon train. The Gurkhas never smoked on patrol and talking was kept strictly for orders. They made no sound and they seemed to be aware of natural signs and noises that escaped the senses of a Westerner. But the most fascinating thing was how such cheerful friendly people could be transformed into such deadly warriors before you could say kukri. That to me was the paradox of the Gurkha personality.

Vyvyan had told us that his men were desperately keen to go down the far slope and get to grips with the Indonesian marines who had a camp a few miles down the valley. But the British Government was adamant that there was to be no cross-border raiding. The only exceptions to this rule were the four-man SAS teams who were allowed to operate behind Indonesian lines, gathering intelligence and carrying out sabotage missions. Recently a team had run into an ambush and one SAS man had been killed. The others had managed to disengage and, although separated, had found their way back to safety. As I looked down the steep slope into Indonesian Borneo, I thought what risky work it must be, and how easy to get lost in the jungle. We stopped for a rest at lunchtime. Vyvyan looked us over quizzically and said to Jon, 'That camera must he heavy. If you're tired, we'll get one of the Gurkhas to carry it for you.' Jon shook his head. 'No trouble, you know,' Vyvyan said. 'If you get really tired, they'll carry you as well.'

We reached our rendezvous at about three without having to accept the offer, and sat in the sunshine while Vyvyan called in the helicopters by radio. Half an hour later the Wessex came in with pinpoint precision and hoisted us out of the jungle, lifting straight up between the enormously tall trees. But, despite all the information and some excellent pictures Jon had got of the Gurkhas on patrol, we were still short of film. So, when we got back to Vyvyan's camp, which was high up the mountain above Bario, we looked around for something that would amplify the footage already shot. As we walked round the hilltop position, something caught my eye: a big, black, vicious-looking Browning machine-gun.

'If the Indonesians were ever stupid enough to attack this place, we'd give them a nasty surprise,' Vyvyan said, patting the muzzle affectionately.

'A pity we couldn't get some shots of it in action,' I said hopefully.

'You wouldn't see anything,' Jon objected. 'Unless . . . '

'Unless what?'

'Unless we filmed it in the dark . . . '

There was a pause and then Vyvyan said, 'We could load up some tracer for you. You'd see that all right.' We all grinned. So did the Gurkha machine-gunners when Vyvyan explained. Obviously there was nothing they liked better than letting rip with their pet Browning.

I had one slight qualm. 'What are we going to shoot at? We don't want to hurt anybody.'

Vyvyan waved in the direction of the jungle-clad slopes that rose to the horizon.

'No one there, except possibly a few Indonesians,' he said. 'And it would serve them bloody well right.'

After supper, the inevitable curry washed down with rum, we moved back outside to the machine-gun post. All was ready, the gunners in position, the ammunition belts waiting to be fed into the breech. The mood was light-hearted, almost as if we were going to watch a cabaret turn, with jokes and laughter. Jon and Peter set up the sound camera, asked what pattern the firing would take and pronounced themselves ready. Vyvyan gave the order to fire.

The darkness was lit up by a great spurt of flame from the muzzle of the machine-gun and at the same time a deafening din hammered our ears. The tracer, a steady stream of red light, carved a parabola across the night sky. Jon was crouched in concentration over the camera, Peter half turned away as he struggled to keep the roar of the Browning within recording limits. Recording gunfire is extremely difficult on news equipment; even the loudest bangs tend to reproduce with about the same ferocity as a champagne cork popping.

The firing stopped for a few minutes and we all rejoiced in the sudden stillness. Jon explained that he would like to film it again, from a slightly different angle. Vyvyan told the Gurkha machine-gunners who grinned and altered their aim. A few seconds later the same harsh roar exploded in our ears and the tracer went whizzing off into the darkness and disappeared into the jungle a mile or two away. When the firing finally stopped, the echoes rolled round the hills for several seconds before finally dying away. The silence that followed was startling in its intensity. Then someone lit a cigarette, the Gurkhas started chatting among themselves, and the sounds of the night returned to normal.

We returned to the mess for a nightcap and went to bed happy with our day's work. Next morning, Vyvyan sent us back to the base camp in a Landrover and we arranged to meet later.

It was around six that a rather subdued Vyvyan put his head round the door of the officers' mess – a little house on stilts – came in and sat down.

'What's wrong?' I asked, seeing he was not his usual jaunty self.

'Just been to see the Colonel,' he said. 'He was not amused by our little shooting practice last night.'

'Why, what was wrong?'

'They thought it was a full-scale Indonesian attack. Got everyone out of bed and stood the whole place on full alert.' Vyvyan paused, took a sip of whisky. I had to prevent myself from laughing. I could just imagine the stir in the camp as the shooting echoed round the hills. It must have seemed like the real thing. Vyvyan continued.

'Colonel wasn't amused when he found out that it was merely an exercise – for your cameras. Not at all amused. In fact he called me down specially to tell me exactly what he thought of me.'

'God, I'm sorry, Vyvyan. All because of us. It never occurred to me . . . Do you want me to go and see the Colonel and say it was entirely our fault . . . ?'

He shook his head. 'It's very kind, but I think not. He's said his bit and that's that. Better not to reopen the subject.' He managed one of his old smiles. 'I'll be going on patrol again in a day or two and it'll soon blow over.'

We had to spend another couple of days in Bario waiting for the weather to lift so that a helicopter could get in. We saw the Colonel fleetingly a couple of times. He was polite but distant and I imagined the next Press party might have problems if they wanted to go on patrol with the Gurkhas.

On our last night, as we were sitting chatting to a couple of young officers in the mess after dinner, the door was thrown open below us and two wet and dirty figures in jungle green came stumping up the stairs. The one in front strode into the middle of the room, while we goggled from our chairs at this strange apparition, and threw his wet pack into the corner.

'Christ, what a relief!' he said. 'We've just walked twenty miles, come right through your sentries without being challenged and we could both do with a bloody big drink. Steward . . . ' The bellow brought a servant running. The second man was dark and serious-looking and obviously junior. The first man downed half of his whisky in one go and looked round with a gasp of pleasure. 'Sorry, bloody rude. Ought to introduce ourselves. I'm John Slim, and this is Dr. . . . We've

251

just been on a little exercise. Dropped in last night but the jungle was so damn thick we had to walk in the river for most of the way.' Slim paused and gave a grin. 'The doctor here nearly drowned. He was carrying the radio set and it weighs a ton.'

While he was talking he had rolled up his wet trousers to reveal half a dozen or so big black leeches stuck to his legs. He now proceeded to pick them off casually and, with every sign of satisfaction, crush them under his heel on the mess floor.

'Bastard,' he pronounced as a particularly juicy one was ground into extinction.

John Slim was the son of Field Marshal Bill Slim. He was then second-in-command of the SAS and later went on to command it. I liked his cavalier way with the leeches.

CHAPTER VIII

Hong Kong, Macao, Taiwan and Vietnam

In January 1967, I went to Hong Kong. The waves created by Chairman Mao's Cultural Revolution were only now beginning to lap the shores of the outside world. Western reporters had been unable to enter Communist China since 1949 so Hong Kong had always been the great listening post, where the China-watchers practised their arcane art. Some of it was crystal-ball gazing, but there was also a lot of skilled listening in, scanning of provincial papers and de-briefing of defectors.

The Americans, who had reacted almost hysterically to the victory of the Communist Mao Tse-tung over the pro-Western Chiang Kai-shek, were the biggest China-watchers of all. Their Consulate-General on the hill about the harbour was enormous – bigger than most of their embassies, and staffed by hundreds of experts who listened to every radio message transmitted in the People's Republic and perused every printed word they could lay their hands on. After the monitoring and translating came the detailed analysis, when the information that a farmer in remote Szechuan had been sent to prison for refusing to sell his quota of wheat to the state was logged and compared with happenings in other villages the length and breadth of China. Out of these tiny pieces an overall picture of Chinese food shortages, or whatever it might be, was painstakingly built, like a mosaic. Inevitably this was an incomplete picture, with lots of gaps, and often the most important information came from the rare high-level defector (there were, it seems, extremely few) or from the interception of secret radio messages. But, even then, the experts seemed to have only the vaguest idea of why the Cultural Revolution had been started by Mao in the first place, and what effects it was having. Individual cases, like that of Anthony Grey, the Reuters correspondent who was kept under house arrest in one room of his flat in Peking for eighteen months, shed much light on, say, the Red Guards' attitude to foreigners. But what was happening in the vast hinterland, where foreigners had not been allowed to penetrate for twenty years or more; or in places where they had never actually seen a foreigner? No one really knew.

While making this programme I arranged to interview one of the most famous China-watchers of all, Richard Hughes of the *Sunday Times*. Dick, as everyone called him, was part of the folklore of Hong Kong, a magnificent Australian with a wonderfully innocent pair of blue eyes which had seen every kind of wickedness and human folly and yet reflected his own splendidly optimistic nature. Dick was a big, powerful man with almost episcopally rubicund features and a tonsure of white hair. But there was nothing ecclesiastical about the flow of language when he was annoyed. He has, as far as I know, the unique distinction of providing the original for major characters in two of the century's best thrillers. In Ian Fleming's *For Your Eyes Only* he appears as the tough Australian intelligence chief Dicko Henderson. (Fleming had been the Foreign Manager of the *Sunday Times* and Dick Hughes was his man and mentor in the Far East. When I once called him Dicko he said: 'Sandy, you musn't call me that, that's what Ian Fleming used to call me.') The other book is John Le Carré's *The Honourable Schoolboy*, in which Dick appears as Old Craw, the British SIS man in Hong Kong whose cover is that of a resident journalist. I hardly dare mention in the same breath that, at my own much humbler level, I too have cast the great man, as the hugely knowledgeable and experienced foreign correspondent, Dick Rutherstone, in my thriller about Hong Kong called *Chasing the Dragon*.

I had met Dick through Donald Wise in 1965 when I was on my way from Borneo to Saigon, and now he immediately agreed to give me an interview, bidding me to lunch with him first in the Grill Room of the Hilton Hotel where he was a well-known and much-esteemed customer. We lunched extremely well, eating Sydney oysters and quaffing considerable quantities of Loire wine. Dick's talk was as good as his hospitality and we had a marvellous time. He has a trick of addressing anyone who even temporarily wins the accolade of his approval as 'Your Grace'. This was heady stuff for a mere television reporter like myself. 'Your Grace,' Dick would intone in his rich Australian brogue, 'there is nothing that would give the Holy See and its miserable incumbent in this God-forsaken, materialist hell-hole more honest-to-God pleasure than to see your most excellent and revered self ingest another dozen of those miserably inadequate oysters from an altogether unworthy city. My birthplace, incidentally. If Your Grace would forgive the inadequacy of the offering it would give your humble servant great satisfaction and send him on his way rejoicing. And another bottle of the Sancerre, Patrick.'

The sharp blue eyes scrutinised me sharply to see if I were indeed worthy of this genial outpouring of hospitality, wit and learning that ranged from the best brothels in Shanghai in the Thirties to the intricacies of the Samurai system in Ancient Japan. In between mouthfuls, he let fall the odd jewel garnered from his long experience of China-watching, and then, drawing himself up erect, spat out a rancorous remark about 'those Commy dogs' and how they would trick you and cheat you and were not to be trusted at any price.

We filmed the interview the next day, and although a little nervous to start with Dick was finally majestic and pithy at the same time, his agile and unusual turn of phrase making him almost as much of a pleasure to listen to on film as he was in the flesh. Robert Louis Stevenson once said that Books were a mighty poor substitute for Life, which is just as true of television, perhaps more so, since television is so insidious that it is easy to believe that it is the real thing. However, for anyone who did not have the good fortune to meet him in person, then at least the television screen gave some impression of the richness of the man.

From Hong Kong it is an easy trip by hydrofoil to Macao, the old Portuguese territory forty miles to the west, at the mouth of the Pearl River. Fifty miles up river lies the great Chinese city of Canton which has given the world, through its export of innumerable cooks and restaurateurs, one of its most popular cuisines. The Cantonese coast is impregnated with history, none of it very flattering to the West. It was here that the opium trade first flourished and it was from their toehold in Hong Kong that the British peddled the product of the poppy that has caused so much misery, fighting, turmoil and death. And all for money. It was pure greed that drove the East India Company to sell its opium to the Chinese, which in turn gave rise to the Opium Wars.

Macao has been Portuguese longer than Hong Kong has been British, and in 1967 the small bars and cafés along the front were to a British eye still delightfully Continental. Hong Kong is vibrant and exciting, but what charm it had has long been submerged by tons of steel and concrete. Macao has never really changed, the Portuguese influence sitting comfortably on the essential Chinese character of the place like a cherry on a cake. But the Cultural Revolution had sent shock waves even as far as Macao and the small Portuguese community, sitting sipping their white port in the Posada Hotel, were worried. The Governor, a youngish army officer, was running scared and the small Portuguese army garrison, numbering only 200 or 300 were confined to barracks. The local Red Guards had virtually taken the place over, as they had tried to do in Hong Kong. But whereas the Hong Kong police, with the British Army on call if necessary, put down the riots firmly, in Macao the Portuguese had backed down. When the local Communist Party boss, it was said, called to see the Governor, the Chinese put his feet on

the table and harangued him into submission. The wretched
Governor knew he was on his own and that there was no help
coming from faraway Portugal. He turned down our request
to see him but we did see the Red Guard bosses. They had an
exhibition in the middle of the town in which they were
displaying photographs of Portuguese atrocities; committed,
they said, when the Portuguese army had opened fire on
demonstrators, killing half a dozen people. The Portuguese
were obviously powerless to stop the exhibition of what was
pure propaganda. After filming for half an hour or so we left
and set up the camera in the street outside. Within five
minutes one of the Red Guard commissars appeared at my
elbow and said, 'No more filming. Not allowed.'

'What, in the street?' I asked. 'Anyway, we have permission to film from the Portuguese.'

This was not strictly true but he was not to know that.
However, his answer was revealing.

'Portuguese give no permission,' he said. 'Chinese people
give permission and Chinese people say no.'

His face was tense with anger and a crowd of watchful
Chinese was gathering round. I gave in.

'All right,' I said to the Red Guard. 'We've got all we
want. Thank you.' And then to Alan Downes I added,
'Come on, we'll go somewhere else. One street in Macao
looks much like another.'

We stayed a couple of nights at the Bela Vista, an old
Portuguese hotel overlooking the shallow bay where the boats
went fishing at night for prawns. They carried lanterns at
their prows to attract the prawns and the water was so still
and the reflection so true that it looked as if each boat had a
double light. In the half-dark they seemed to float between
pearly sea and pearly sky, as in a misty Chinese painting. On
the other side of Macao, beyond the junk harbour, other
lights would tremble into life as the darkness descended.
These were the lights of Communist China, mainland China
as the locals called it, only a mile or so away but infinitely
remote.

The Bela Vista was next door to a big house with a high
wall round it. This belonged to a Chinese millionaire who

owned among other things a shipping company and a bank. Nothing strange in that, admittedly. What was unusual was that he was also Macao's most prominent Communist, with high connections on the mainland. Like Hong Kong, although on a much smaller scale, Macao's value to China is as an earner of foreign currency. So Mr Big was tolerated by both sides because he brought in the hard currency that China so badly needed.

Macao used to have another fascinating sideline. One day every week a Catalina flying boat landed in the bay and offloaded a consignment of gold bullion. The gold arrived legally in Macao, but then disappeared. That is to say, officially, it remained in the vaults of the bank. But, unofficially, it was shipped out on junks to the far corners of the South China Sea and the Indian Ocean, and sold for a handsome profit. Much of it found its way to India, where traditionally the richer citizens keep their wealth in easily transportable form and where the import of gold is heavily taxed. I tried to discover if the trade still flourished but was told that it had greatly diminished. Instead, the Chinese entrepreneurs had moved into gambling. A number of casino junks were moored in the harbour and did a roaring business twenty-four hours a day. With their usual censoriousness the British have banned gambling in Hong Kong, except on the race course, and so any Chinese who wants to play fan tan or any of a dozen other strange Chinese gambling games would catch the hydrofoil from Hong Kong and an hour later be happily throwing his money away in Macao. The Chinese passion for gambling is comparable to that of the Irish for horse racing, the English for cricket, the Welsh for rugby football and the Scots for soccer; except that it is stronger and more compelling than any of them.

Apart from the handsome eighteenth-century Portuguese Town Hall, the yellow ochre Governor's Palace and one or two big houses, on the bluff beyond the Bela Vista, Macao is a completely Chinese town, with narrow streets and small, dark, fascinatingly smelly shops selling all sorts of roots, herbs and powders. Someone had recommended a restaurant where they specialised in roast pigeon and we found it in one of those narrow, shop-packed streets. Next door to the restaurant was a snake shop, with examples of the stock displayed prominently in glass cages in the windows. As I came out of the restaurant a well-to-do Chinese woman walked into the shop. I watched through the window as she presumably asked for a particular kind of snake. The salesman produced a wicker cage and after some consultation a long, healthy-looking snake, which may or may not have been poisonous, was selected and withdrawn from the container. The salesman held it up for the customer to make a closer inspection. It was about four feet long and hung there limply. The woman nodded approval. 'I'll take that one,' she obviously said in Cantonese. The salesman dropped the snake to the floor, put one foot on its neck and with a deft stroke of his knife severed the nervous system behind the head. Then he proceeded to skin it alive, peeling the wretched and still wriggling reptile as if it were a banana. The gory remains were deftly wrapped and the woman came out of the shop looking pleased with her purchase. I asked a friend later what snake tasted like and he said, 'Like chicken.' The Chinese say it heats the blood and they like to eat it in winter.

Next day, we filmed a sequence at the border between Macao and mainland China. We were allowed only as far as the Portuguese post. Two hundred yards farther down the road, beneath the ornate archway which marked the entrance to the People's Republic, we could see the olive-green uniforms and white gloves of the border guards. Above them waved the blood-red, gold-starred flag of Communist China.

As we were filming, a procession of Chinese appeared, and walked towards the archway. They were carrying half a dozen plain oblong boxes, which on closer inspection turned out to be coffins, and chanting a monotonous dirge. Wailing music and a couple of dozen more mourners followed and, when they all reached the border, the white-gloved guards waved them through without delay. I enquired what they were doing and was told that they were poor Chinese from Macao going to bury their dead in mainland China. In Macao they had to pay for a burial plot but, in China, the land was free. So, with their atavistic and pecuniary instincts happily coinciding, the humbler citizens of Macao were able to satisfy both conscience and pocket.

After considerable difficulty I managed to meet a Chinese defector in Macao. He was a well-educated young man, a musician who had fled China a few months before, at the height of the Cultural Revolution, and he was waiting rather desperately to emigrate to a Western country. He spoke reasonable English but he was far too frightened to give me an interview on camera. Indeed, with the upsurge in Red Guard power in Macao, he was nervous about talking to me at all. His message was quite simple. Personal freedom was impossible in China, he said. He had not wished to spend the rest of his life conforming, so he had escaped, leaving behind family and friends. It must have been a brave and lonely decision.

After a couple of days in Hong Kong, during which I shipped off our Macao film, we flew to Taiwan, the headquarters of the rival China of Chiang Kai-shek. When Mao and his Communist armies won control of China in 1949, Chiang and his followers escaped to Taiwan, a big, mountainous and beautiful island off the east coast of China. They took with them as much of the old Imperial treasure as they could lay their hands on: the Museum in Taipeh is full of Ming and other priceless things. The defeated Nationalists simply took over Taiwan, relegating the local Taiwanese to a subservient status and running the island as the personal fief of Chiang Kai-shek. The old warlord was now in his eighties and not much more than a figurehead. His remarkable wife, who had been such a brilliant ambassador for her husband's cause in the United States during the war and immediately after, was more active. But the real power was wielded by their son, Chiang Kuo, who paid lip service to Western democratic ideals but in reality ran Taiwan as a police state.

We were met at the airport by our local stringer, a spry-looking Chinese of about sixty with a sharp, intelligent face and the unlikely name of 'Newsreel' Wong. He even had it on his card: H.S. 'Newsreel' Wong. I asked him how he had come by such a remarkable name. 'Well,' he said, 'during the Civil War, when I was covering the fighting between the warlords, I stayed for a long time in a big hotel in Shanghai. I was working then for Hearst Metrotone News, of Chicago, and they used to send me cables addressed to Wong. There were lots of Wongs in the hotel, it's like Smith or Jones in England or the States, so the manager used to shout out "Wong of the Newsreels – telegram for you". So I told the people in Chicago to identify me as the "Newsreel" Wong.'

'Newsreel' had covered the Japanese invasion of Manchuria and he got his most famous scoop in 1937 when the Japanese air force bombed Shanghai, China's biggest city with a population of more than ten million. The railway station was one of the worst hit areas and, when 'Newsreel' got there, it was ablaze.

'I had to fight my way in because the people were desperate to get out. The building was on fire, the roof was collapsing and hundreds of bodies were lying round all over the place. Finally, when I had just about run out of film, I came on a baby lying screaming on the platform but apparently unhurt. The mother had been hit and was dying. The rest of the family were all dead. The baby was the only one left alive. I checked my camera. I had only ten feet of film left. I used it all to film the baby, lying on its back as the station burned all round us, screaming its little head off.'

When the film ran out, 'Newsreel' scooped the baby under his arm and ran for the exit, dodging pieces of falling masonry. They got out safely and he handed the baby over to the first first aid team he met. Then he rushed back to the hotel to unload the film and send it out to America as fast as he could. When it finally arrived it created a sensation. Hearst Metrotone printed a still frame of the screaming baby and it made the headlines everywhere. Roosevelt, then running for his second term as President, saw it and used it on television, holding the picture up and exclaiming, 'This is what the Japanese are doing to China.' It became one of the most famous images of its day.

Later, when he was in America, 'Newsreel' happened to be

the only cameraman in the office when a plane crashed on top of the Empire State Building. When he got to the building, he discovered that the power had failed and none of the lifts was working. 'So I started climbing and I climbed the whole goddam way up, right to the top of the Empire State, the highest building in the world. But I got the picture of the plane hanging there right on the top of the building. It was a world scoop.'

With 'Newsreel' at our elbow, we filmed in Taipeh, where the small children marched to school in well-disciplined crocodiles, and the guards marched American-style outside Chiang Kai-shek's palace. We also interviewed a professor about what was really happening on the mainland. He reproduced the official Nationalist line which was that the Chinese were tired of Mao and Communism and that a new revolution was imminent. He was not actually prepared to say that the Nationalists, who had a big standing army, would invade. But it was clear that Chiang fervently hoped and possibly believed that the Communist system would collapse of its own accord and he would be invited back into power. To hurry the process along the Nationalists bombarded the air waves with continuous propaganda. But they also bombarded Red China in a more literal sense. Every day, the Nationalists fired rockets stuffed with propaganda leaflets from the offshore islands of Quemoy and Matsu at the mainland, only three miles away. The Communists reciprocated, directing their propaganda at the Nationalist garrison.

This rather noisy but harmless battle, with all these heavily armed Nationalist troops sitting just off the mainland of Communist China, was the real object of our visit to Taiwan, and was intended to be the main feature of our fifteen-minute report. We had made our application to visit Quemoy and Matsu as soon as we arrived, and eventually clearance came through from the military who controlled all access to the islands. We were to go next day. 'Newsreel' was not coming with us, but he had briefed us fully on what we could expect to see.

Next morning we were at the airport by seven. We checked

in and sat down to wait. At 7.30 the flight was called. I got up and was just about to walk to the departure door when an airline official came up to me and said: 'You are not going on the flight.'

'Why not?' I asked. 'Is the flight cancelled?'

The man looked uncomfortable. 'No, flight not cancelled. But we just been instructed, you not to go on flight.'

'Who says so?' I asked, feeling my temper slipping out of control. Alan Downes was also beginning to bristle with annoyance.

'Yes, who the bloody hell says so?' he asked angrily. I could see the rest of the passengers disappearing towards the plane. The official's face was a mask of impassivity.

'Ministry of Information just called,' he said. 'They give instructions that you not to board flight to Quemoy and Matsu.'

'Right,' I said. 'I want to talk to the Ministry. Can I use your telephone?'

'Certainly, sir,' he said. 'Please come this way.' He led me through to an office and got the number for me.

I asked for the official we had been dealing with.

'What's going on?' I asked. 'We got our passes from you yesterday and we were all ready to board the plane this morning when we were told we could not go. What the hell's going on?'

'I am very sorry, Mr Gall, but those are the instructions we received.'

'From whom?' I snapped.

'From General Chu,' he said. The general was head of the Ministry of Information.

'Put me through to the general, would you please? I'd like to talk to him.'

'Hold on a minute,' the official said. There was a long pause and then he came back. 'I'm sorry, the general is not available at the moment.'

I fulminated inwardly.

'What is the reason our visit has been cancelled?'

The official coughed.

'I do not know, Mr Gall. I was simply given instructions by

General Chu to inform you that unfortunately your trip had to be cancelled.'

'Please inform the general that I am very angry and that I demand a full explanation,' I said.

'I will pass on your message,' the official said without emotion.

I put the 'phone down and swore.

'The flight's leaving,' Alan Downes said. We watched the old DC3 trundle down the runway and take off into the blue morning sky.

I swore again. There was nothing for it but to go back to the hotel and see if we could get on the next flight. We drove back in silence. It was not just that we had been excited by the prospect of visiting the offshore islands and filming a very unusual scene – the two Chinas hurling insults at each other across a narrow strip of water; this was a key sequence in our film and without it the programme would fall as flat as a pancake. That was my real concern. It was imperative, I told myself desperately, that the situation should somehow be retrieved.

As soon as we reached the hotel, I telephoned 'Newsreel'. He was as surprised as we had been, and said he would try and find out what had gone wrong.

He rang me back an hour later. 'They won't tell me the reason,' he said. 'It's obviously security, but I don't know exactly what.'

'Is it something they have against us?' I asked.

'No, no, it's nothing to do with you personally. It's security. Maybe they are moving troops and they did not want you to see them. Or something else may be happening on the islands that they don't want you to know about. Or maybe Chiang Kuo himself is paying a visit.' 'Newsreel' was clearly as upset as we were.

All that day and the next we worried over the problem, trying to find an explanation. But at the end of it we were none the wiser, and I never did succeed in seeing the general. Finally, it became absolutely clear that the veto on our trip was not going to be lifted. 'Newsreel' was deeply puzzled because, as he explained, normally the Taiwan Government was only too keen to show Western journalists and television teams how they were standing up to the Communists in Quemoy and Matsu. This made our failure to get there all the more maddening. To overcome their disappointment Alan and Mick went off to visit a famed bathhouse in the hills. I, for some inexplicable reason, decided not to go but instead busied myself cabling London explaining our misfortune and suggesting we move on to Vietnam where the Americans now had well over a quarter of a million troops in the country and were sending in more every day. London cabled back agreeing.

Sadly, we said farewell to 'Newsreel'. He felt the débâcle over the offshore islands as a personal failure. But finally, with Oriental acceptance, he shrugged and said, 'You know, this isn't America or England. This is a goddam police state. If they don't want you to see something, there isn't a goddam thing you can do about it.' With those philosophical words, he waved us up the steps of the plane on our way to Hong Kong, and then Vietnam.

In Saigon, I decided this time to stay in the Continental Hotel, rather than the Americanised Caravelle. This was partly an attempt to divorce myself from the American view of the war, but mainly because the Continental was more civilised. It was certainly more spacious, with huge dark bedrooms and a pleasant open-air bar at the back. All the staff spoke French and the service was more personal than in the glass and concrete palace across the square. It was never easy to get a room at the Continental but in February 1967 the war was grinding along in a relatively unspectacular way and the Press Corps was smaller than in 1965. After a couple of days in Saigon for reaccreditation I decided to head north to Da Nang. At the big air base activity was intense. Helicopter gunships fluttered up and down like autumn leaves at one end of the field, C130 transports plodded off between the giant C5A Galaxies on re-supply missions, and the sharp teeth of the US Air Force, the Phantom F4s and the A5s, whistled down the runway and howled up into the sky carrying their lethal loads of high explosive and napalm.

They were bombing the North round the clock, day in, day out, knocking out bridges and anti-aircraft batteries, blasting sections of the Ho Chi Minh trail. In the South they flew close support for American and South Vietnamese ground troops in countless minor battles with the Vietcong. Watching such a display of supersonic firepower taking to the skies with such regularity, I concluded, along with many others, that it was only a matter of time before the might of the American war machine overwhelmingly crushed the opposition, however brave and however determined. But there was another aspect to the war in 1967 which was being much talked about: pacification. While the Phantom teams emerged from their air-conditioned, muzak-filled messes to blast the often invisible enemy with a couple of tons of 'ordnance', the 'grunts' on the ground were trying to win over the 'hearts and minds' of the Vietnamese villagers with various schemes.

I was told that a Marine unit near Da Nang under a certain Colonel Corson was deeply involved in pacification and I decided to go and see him. Corson was an intelligent, articulate man who talked extremely convincingly about his task. He was certain that, if his men could meet the Vietnamese on equal or near-equal terms and understand enough about their customs and characters to make friends with them, it would be relatively simple to wean them away from the Vietcong and thus deny the Communists the food and intelligence they got from the villagers. To this end Corson had learned some Vietnamese and made a point of playing Vietnamese chess, Bao-Dai, with the villagers whenever he had a spare moment, while his Marine 'medics' bandaged wounds and passed out antibiotics. Corson had even started a fish-farming scheme for the benefit of some villagers who had been uprooted and lost their livelihood because of the war.

The fatal flaw, it seems to me now, was that the Americans were trying to achieve 'pacification' without the help of, indeed, despite, the South Vietnamese army and officials, who had the reputation for being both corrupt and careless.

One began to hear repeatedly how village headmen used their positions to enrich themselves and how when a South Vietnamese army unit moved through even a friendly village the soldiers would help themselves to whatever was going: chickens, ducks and rice. This sort of automatic levy had probably been the practice of all Vietnamese armies since time immemorial, but the difference now was that the Communists promised to end it. Their soldiers were by all accounts scrupulously well-disciplined and never looted. They would come into the village at night, drag the headman out of his hut and assassinate him in front of the rest of the village, *pour encourager les autres*. Whether he was corrupt or not was immaterial. What mattered was that he represented the Government. Like the Vietminh before them, the Vietcong had a clear-cut policy of fairness on the one hand, and exemplary terror on the other. The combination was probably too strong for Colonel Corson's brand of 'hearts and minds' especially since the Americans were frequently let down by their South Vietnamese allies. But American commanders, less concerned than Corson, also sabotaged 'pacification' by burning down villages because they thought that a handful of Vietcong might be in them.

One famous case occurred just after we were in Da Nang. A CBS reporter, Morley Safer, and his camera team went with a Marine unit on a search and destroy mission. They came to a village where a Vietcong force was believed to be hiding. Some shots were fired and the Marine commander, a lieutenant, pulled out his Zippo lighter and set fire to the thatch of a hut. His men followed suit and before long the whole village was in flames. Safer filmed the whole scene and his film caused an outcry when it was shown on the television evening news throughout America. It prompted Americans to ask if this was the way to defend democracy in South Vietnam.

To see Colonel Corson's ideas in action, we spent a day with one of his platoons in the foothills behind Da Nang. The Marines had rebuilt the school and were running a free and efficient medical service to the farmers and villagers in the area. But every so often, on patrol, a Marine would step on a dagger-sharp, fire-hardened 'punji' stick embedded in the ground, his own weight driving it through his combat boot and deep into his foot. Or, worse still, a patrolman would stumble on a small anti-personnel mine and blow his foot off. It was that sort of low-key, hit-and-run war, but all the time the American cualties were mounting.

Other casualties were also mounting. On February 21, Bernard Fall, who perhaps knew more about Vietnam than any other American, was killed by a mine not far from Da Nang. He had been on a day's visit to a section of the 'Street without Joy', the old French name for the north-south highway that runs along the coast. Accompanied by a handful of staff from the Marine Press Centre, he had been walking along perfectly peacefully when one of the party set off the mine. Fall was killed instantly. The 'Gunny' sergeant who ran the Press Centre heard that we were flying back to Saigon next day and he asked me if I would take Bernard Fall's effects, for forwarding to his wife in the United States. It was a pathetically small bundle of clothes, papers and a tape recorder. As I flew back carrying Bernard Fall's little bag, I thought about his death. If he had been reporting a battle, it would have been understandable. But to be killed like that, so pointlessly, suggested to me that life and death were truly haphazard affairs. It made me conscious, perhaps for the first time in my life, that I too was engaged in the same chancy enterprise and that a stray bullet or rocket could just as easily put an end to my fragile existence. For the first time, I think I was a little afraid of what might be waiting for me, round the next corner.

As the frantic traffic of Saigon enveloped us once more, my thoughts turned to more mundane matters: where we should have lunch; and, after that, what our next story should be.

I went to bed early that night, in my high-ceilinged bedroom facing the square. Early next morning I was woken by a faint but persistent rattling of the glass in my windows. Each *tremblement* lasted for about twenty or thirty seconds. There would be a pause, and then it would start again. This went on for about half an hour, between 5.30 and 6.00, just as it was beginning to get light. At six there was a tap on the door and the room boy arrived with a pot of tea, his bare feet squeaking gently on the polished wooden floor. As I drank my tea, a chance remark of the day before gave me a clue to the strange rattling noise. The Americans had started bombing with B52s only ten or fifteen miles from Saigon. That was what I was listening to – the distant rumble, like an earthquake, of a B52 strike. The eight-engined B52 flies at 40,000 feet and releases its bombs on the unsuspecting target far below. I tried to imagine how devastating the effect must be, what an Armageddon of fire and blast must accompany a B52 strike if, ten miles away, it made the glass in my windows rattle loud enough to wake me. The other surprising and sobering consideration was that the enemy were so close to Saigon, the capital, and so well dug in, apparently, that the big bombers had to be brought into play to dislodge them.

One of the most fearsome things about the B52 is that it lays down a 'carpet' of bombs, completely destroying a given area half a mile long by a quarter of a mile wide. It seemed incredible that anything could survive such an onslaught but, although the B52 undoubtedly wreaked terrible damage, the Vietcong and the North Vietnamese did somehow survive them by digging tunnels and bunkers deep underground. The B52s were never stationed in Vietnam. They flew from their bases in Guam, in the Pacific, high above the clouds, dropped their bombs without ever seeing the target and flew back again. In the seven years from 1965 to 1972 the B52 dropped thousands of tons of bombs on Vietnam.

Despite the closeness of 'mainforce' Communist units to Saigon, the security situation in 1967 was considerably better than it had been two years before. The test was how safely you could travel through the countryside by car. In 1965 we went to the Delta by helicopter. Now we could go by car. This was less exciting but gave a better impression of what was really going on. I found an unusually well-educated driver called Chih, with an unusually good car, a Peugeot, who was prepared to take us down to the Delta for about £50 a day. He spoke excellent French, in fact he had a French wife and had until recently been living in France. Chih was a good driver and very polite, but extremely lugubrious. I tried hard to make him laugh or even smile, but it proved almost impossible. He lectured me earnestly about the dangers of travelling by road. Each time we set off he would describe the latest disaster: a bus blown up here, a car there. The pattern was fairly consistent and was remarkably similar to what it had been in the days of the French. The Vietcong guerrillas, operating in small groups, would set up ambushes and plant mines in the roads at night. The first vehicles to use the road in the morning always ran the risk of being blown up, and frequently were. By day, control of the roads reverted to the South Vietnamese army. Then at nightfall, when the South Vietnamese withdrew to their camps and outposts, the Vietcong came stealing back into possession again.

As we drove through the rice fields towards My Tho and Can Tho, the main Delta towns, I found myself watching the road for any holes in the tarmac covered over with earth. These might be potholes left by mortar shells, or they might be holes dug by the Vietcong to plant mines. It paid to be careful and I noticed that Chih gave such holes a wide berth, especially in the morning. He never liked to start too early, for obvious reasons. Coming back in the afternoon, he was more relaxed, reckoning that the day's traffic would have detonated any mines planted the night before. But towards dusk he again became more nervous. There was always the possibility that the Vietcong would suddenly appear out of the rice paddies and stop us. They were bold enough to do that, sometimes even just outside Saigon. Occasionally we would pass a bus lying on its side at the edge of the road and Chih would explain gloomily, in his excellent French, that it had been blown up by a Vietcong mine a couple of days ago and that half a dozen peasants had been killed.

In pursuit of the elusive pacification story, we were invited to accompany another American colonel to Rach Vieng province, about fifty miles south of Saigon, deep in the Delta. Rach Vieng had been a Vietcong stronghold for years, its inhabitants abandoned by the Vietnamese Government. Now the Americans had persuaded them it was in their interest to try and win over this recalcitrant population. The South

Vietnamese army and their American advisers had gone in to 'secure' the town a day or two before.

The Colonel and his staff, a party of Vietnamese officials, half a dozen other journalists and ourselves left Saigon early and helicoptered across the Delta. Within half an hour we were losing height and putting down in what seemed to be the middle of nowhere. The rice fields here had been harvested and the helicopters landed delicately, like so many steel butterflies, on the short, crunchy stubble. As the rotors stopped turning I looked round the flat empty land and was struck once again by the silence of the Delta, and its secretiveness. You had to look carefully to discover the outlines of the village – the houses were so well hidden among the trees. With the colonel leading we set off to walk the mile or so to the middle of the village. As we approached I saw that it was almost a ghost town, with only a handful of ragged children and a few suspicious-looking adults waiting to see what we brought. The market square, which is always the heart of a Delta village and at this time of day normally bustling with activity and full of produce, was empty and desolate. It looked as if there had been no market in Rach Vieng for a long time.

The colonel held an impromptu press conference – in the middle of the square. 'Take a good look round,' he ordered. 'This is what two years of Communist rule have done to Rach Vieng. They closed the schools; these kids haven't had any education at all. They even closed down the market. The people are almost starving. And this right in the middle of the Delta, the richest rice-growing area in the whole of South-East Asia.'

The colonel's team had brought in sacks of rice and tins of dried milk and these were now distributed.

An hour or so later, as we trudged back through the intense heat of noon, I wondered how much of the rice and dried milk would remain with the villagers of Rach Vieng, and how much would be appropriated by the South Vietnamese army. Perhaps the presence of their American advisers would deter them. But, as someone pointed out to me, it was unfair to put the blame entirely on the Vietnamese soldier. Very often the

271

soldiers would not have been paid and their families might be short of food. It was the system that was so rotten.

As I lay in bed the following day, listening to the B52s rattling my windows, I began to feel that we were concentrating too much on the purely American and military aspects of the war. What about the Vietnamese themselves, the civilians? How badly were they being affected as the war spread and grew almost daily? We heard that a small British team of nurses from the Save the Children Fund were running a hospital for badly wounded and crippled Vietnamese children in the provincial capital of Qui Nhon, on the coast about half way between Saigon and Da Nang. After making enquiries we were told that they would welcome our visit.

We flew by slow, desperately noisy but extremely reliable C130 to Qui Nhon, a dusty town on the edge of the South China Sea. Miles and miles of empty white beaches lay beyond the barbed wire that encircled the Save the Children hospital and kept away the unwelcome attentions of the Vietcong. It was run by three British women, an administrator and two nurses. The hospital itself was small and simple and should have been a place of despair. Thirty or forty young Vietnamese, all of them minus a leg or an arm or otherwise seriously handicapped, were being taught to manipulate their shattered bodies and new artificial limbs. One little girl had lost both legs in an explosion – no one seemed to be quite sure whether it was a Vietcong mine or an American shell – and she was learning how to walk again. The Save the Children Fund had flown her to England, sent her to Stoke Mandeville hospital where she had been fitted with artificial legs and then, after an initial period of rehabilitation, she had returned to Qui Nhon to complete her training. As well as being a cripple, she was also an orphan, but instead of being depressed and bitter this little girl was all sweetness and smiles as she laboured clumsily to master her artificial legs, so skilfully made and lovingly fitted, but so unwieldy and primitive compared with her own limbs, which had been destroyed so brutally by just one of the millions of mines, shells and bombs that were being daily unleashed on the once lovely and now wretched land of Vietnam.

I came away from Qui Nhon feeling – as I was to feel so many times in the next few years – just how pointlessly cruel and wasteful war is, and how, whatever else it may achieve, it inevitably maims and destoys the very people on whose behalf it is allegedly waged. And I thought of the countless hundreds, no, thousands of bright-eyed, dark-haired children of the Vietnam War. But I shall never forget that girl in Qui Nhon and I shall see her always as a symbol of triumph over pain and adversity.

CHAPTER IX

The Six-Day War:
The Israelis as the New Romans;
and Biafra, the War of the Roadblocks

Cairo in May was sweltering, both climatically and politically. There was a feverish mood in the city. On May 19 Nasser had demanded the withdrawal of the United Nations peace-keeping force from the Egyptian-Israeli border in Sinai, and on the 22nd he had closed the Straits of Tiran to Israeli shipping. This meant that Israel lost the use of Eilat, her only Red Sea port; and, since the Suez Canal was also closed to her, all Israeli cargoes including oil had to go round the Cape, which was much slower and more expensive. If not a full-scale economic blockade it was the next best thing. It put the Israelis with their backs to the wall, a position they did not enjoy being in.

Nasser's propaganda machine, led by Saut el Arab, the Voice of the Arabs, broadcast continual threats at the Israelis, whipping up the local population into a state of war hysteria. Everyone wanted to interview Nasser on the central issue of war or peace, but he played extremely hard to get. ITN was one aspirant, although I knew from the rudeness of the Ministry of Information officials that we had little chance. In the Nile Hilton there were several other candidates for this privilege: Robin Day of the BBC, Christopher Mayhew, the Labour M.P. and future Minister, on a temporary mission from BBC 'Panorama', and Antony Nutting, who had resigned from the Tory Government over Suez in 1956 and who was in Cairo for one of the other ITV companies. Robin Day, Christopher Mayhew and I shared a taxi to the Egyptian National Assembly to hear Nasser speak on May 30. It was hard to decide which was the more interesting, the ride in the taxi or Nasser's speech in Parliament.

Labour had been in power for three years, and as we crawled and hooted through the dreadful Cairo traffic, Robin asked Mayhew about Harold Wilson. What sort of a man was he?

'Well,' Mayhew replied. 'Let me tell you a little story. I first came across the name of Harold Wilson in my first year at Oxford when I put myself down for the Newdigate History Prize. "Do you know who you're up against?" a friend asked. "No," I said. "Who?" "Harold Wilson," the friend said, "and if you don't know what that means you'll soon find out." ' Sure enough Harold Wilson won the prize, but, Mayhew said with satisfaction, he won it the following year. As our taxi weaved and darted between the buses and the camels, Mayhew continued.

'The point about Harold Wilson is not that he is extremely clever. There's no question about that. But that he has absolutely no idea of what to do with his cleverness. His ambition was always to get to Number 10 but, now he's there, he has absolutely no idea of what to do with it.'

When Robin Day and I expressed astonishment, Christopher Mayhew insisted: 'He is extremely clever intellectually, but he has no profound principles at all. Getting there is all he cares about. He will be a disaster. You mark my words.' Robin said he was amazed to hear this and that he doubted Mayhew's evaluation. But there was no doubt it was spoken out of a deep conviction.

We paid off the taxi and walked into the large and crowded National Assembly building. As we were escorted to our seats, I noticed that Jon Lane, who had gone on ahead, was installed at the front with the camera. A few minutes later, to tumultuous applause, Nasser strode on stage. Physically he was an impressive man, tall for an Egyptian, well-built, handsome and with a film-star quality which turned heads and made him the centre of attention. But his most noticeable feature was his smile. It came on like an electric light, the shiny white teeth flashing on and off. Now, after a brief illumination of the hall, he got down to business. And it was in sombre mood that he addressed his audience and, beyond them, the world at large. Arabic is said to be given to hyperbole, but to my ears it sounded very much as if Nasser was declaring war on Israel.

Sir Humphrey Trevelyan, then our Ambassador in Cairo, says in his book, *The Middle East in Revolution*, that Nasser was a born conspirator and intriguer, but that afternoon he seemed to have abandoned all caution. I wondered afterwards if he had already taken the fateful decision to make war on Israel. That, after all, was what most Arabs wanted: the destruction of the hated enemy who had humiliated and driven the Palestinians out of their homes in 1948, when Israel was founded. Nasser was the unchallenged leader of the Arab world and this would be the apotheosis of his remarkable career.

But there was one other fascinating question. What sort of role did the Russians have in all this? They had trained his army and equipped it with some of their best and latest weaponry. But more than that. Nasser had had to mortgage the Egyptian cotton crop to pay for his weapons, so their influence, for or against war, must have been considerable.

Did the Russians encourage Nasser to take the plunge? After all, they had little to lose. If the Eygptians were defeated, there would always be another time, or another ally. They were not risking a single Russian life and there were always more arms to be supplied – at a price. And the prize – spreading Russian influence even farther throughout the Middle East – was a tempting one. From what we have seen of Russian strategy since, in the Middle East, Czechoslovakia, Angola and Afghanistan, it is not hard to believe that they urged Nasser to have a go. The Israelis certainly believed they did.

We already had a crew in Israel, so it was decided that we should fly to Jordan where King Hussein was due to give a Press Conference on June 7. We arrived in the evening and, by the time all the camera equipment had been checked and stowed away, it was late. I wanted to go on to Jerusalem next day, an easy drive over the Allenby Bridge. An American crew, making a 'special' on the Middle East, was leaving early. But, because we had arrived late and the crew were tired, we arranged to leave at ten. Just as we were departing someone in the lobby of the Intercontinental said, 'The war's started.'

I thought he was either an alarmist or given to making bad jokes, so we got into our taxi and set off. But we had only gone a mile or two when we came to a road block. Jordanian Military Police were waving everyone to a halt. 'We not allowed to go on,' our driver said.

A young MP, looking harassed, came towards the car.

I took out my Press card and told the driver to say we were Press and we had to get to Jerusalem.

But the MP was adamant. 'He says the road closed. No one allowed to go on. We have to go back Amman.'

I tried again, but the young MP was getting angry. The driver started to turn the car. 'We must go back,' he said. 'They are fighting in Jerusalem.'

Now, whereas a sane person would turn round with alacrity and feel thankful that he had been warned of the danger ahead, the reaction of a journalist is exactly the opposite. I was furious and at the same time bitterly disappointed. There they were fighting at the gates of Jerusalem only fifty miles away and we had absolutely no way of getting there. If we had made an early start, as I had wanted, we would be there now, I thought angrily. If we had arrived one day earlier . . . I checked my thoughts. There was no point in torturing myself with recriminations. Always think positively, I told myself. Was there any way round it? Could we get special permission from the Ministry of Information? Could we get accreditation to the Jordanian Army? I knew the answers even as I formulated the questions. The Arabs had still not learned that, if they wanted a sympathetic Press, they would have to take the Press into their confidence. That sort of sophistication was still a long way off. At the moment they were much too suspicious and much too frantic to have any thought apart from their own survival.

Events were moving fast. We had only just got back to the hotel and taken the camera and sound equipment upstairs when we heard the high-pitched scream of jet aircraft. I rushed to the window, searching the sky for the source of the noise. After a few seconds, I found them: two jet fighters, high in the cloudless blue, far above the city. As I watched, I saw them begin to dive, down, down, down, and suddenly realised what was about to happen.

'Christ,' I said. 'They must be Israelis, and they're going to attack Amman.'

Jon was working furiously to set up the camera and tripod near the open window. A second or two later there was a heavy rolling explosion and the two French-built Mirage fighters screamed towards us. For one moment I thought they were going to attack the Intercontinental which stands invitingly up on one of the highest points in the city. But they swept right overhead in a steep climb and then vanished out of sight. Behind them, a thick column of smoke was rising from the vicinity of the airport. By this time John had the camera ready and was filming. We were also recording sound so we all kept silent. We could hear a thin crackle of anti-aircraft fire and above it the sound of the jet engines.

Just then there was a commotion in the corridor outside. Someone was going from room to room, banging on the doors and shouting. It sounded as if people were being told to leave their rooms. A second later there was a loud hammering on our door. I put my finger to my lips and we all stayed absolutely silent. Someone tried the door, rattling the handle, but it was locked. He shouted something in Arabic and then moved away. We grinned at one another. Then we heard the sound of the jets again, coming in for another attack. Jon bent over the camera and started to film. They came swooping down again, two small black specks in tight forma-tion hurtling down in a steep dive, flattening out over the airport and then climbing straight at us. They were lower this time and I half ducked as they roared overhead. Again there were two heavy, reverberating explosions, and another thick column of smoke rose into the still air. The anti-aircraft fire was noisier now, but quite ineffectual. The Mirages made three bombing runs and then lifted into the sky and disappeared. The column of black smoke – it looked as if they had hit fuel tanks – started to drift across part of the city.

Downstairs, we found the lobby was full of plain clothes security police. When the air raid started they had rounded everyone up and made them go down to the night club in the cellar, which became a temporary air raid shelter. That was the cause of the banging and shouting in the corridor. They looked at us suspiciously and muttered among themselves and I realised that they were wondering where we had been. If they knew we had been filming they would certainly have tried to confiscate the film. Jon had already unloaded the camera and hidden the tin away among the undeveloped film, so for the moment we were safe. When we switched on the twelve o'clock BBC World Service to hear the news, we realised why all the Jordanians in the hotel, security men and staff, were so depressed. The Israelis had launched a full-scale armoured attack against the Egyptians in the Sinai and the Syrians in Golan, and heavy fighting was in progress. They had also launched a devastating pre-emptive strike against the Eygptian and Syrian air forces, catching the bulk of their planes on the ground and destroying large numbers.

Our little air raid did not get a mention but it was obviously in the same pattern. In fact most of the small Jordanian air force, consisting mainly of British Hawker Hunters, was at Mafraq, the old RAF base in the north near the Syrian border. The Israelis destroyed most of it on the ground, too. Fierce fighting was also reported around Jerusalem and we heard later that the producer of the American crew which left early had been shot and killed while filming. An Israeli machine-gun had raked the front of the Jerusalem Intercontinental where they had set up the camera.

Originally, the Israelis had not intended to attack Jordan, hoping that its well-trained, tough Beduin Army would remain neutral. But, as King Hussein was to reveal later, he had had a fateful telephone call from Nasser a few days before, in which the Eygptian dictator called on Hussein to join the 'Jehad' against the Israelis. Hussein must have felt a certain wry irony in the situation because for many years Nasser had done his best to have Hussein assassinated: not once, but many times. Now, here was Nasser appealing to his old enemy for help. Hussein stalled, saying that his air force was weak and no match for the Israelis. Don't worry, Nasser replied, we will give you all the air cover you need. And on that basis Hussein had reluctantly agreed. And, being a man of honour, he had sent in the Jordanian tanks in support of his ally. The result, as I discovered over the next three days, was catastrophic. The Eygptian air force had already been destroyed on the ground and, when the Jordanian tanks rumbled into action across the bare hills round Jerusalem, the Israeli pilots picked them off with ease, their high-explosive rockets ripping the Centurions apart like tin cans and leaving the flower of Hussein's Beduin tank corps dead on the hillsides.

In the late afternoon of that first day, and twice every day afterwards, I walked the 200 yards from the hotel to the British Embassy where the Ambassador, Philip Adams, obligingly briefed me on what he had heard. I telephoned ITN in London at five and gave them a short report on the fighting from the Jordanian side. Philip Adams, a charming and helpful man, was close to the King and better informed than any other ambassador in Amman. With his help I was at least able to contribute to the verbal reportage of the war. But our main concern was how to get the film of the air raid out of Jordan, and to London. Jon and I spent hours trying to work out a possible exit route, but it was quite hopeless. The Israelis had complete control of the skies, and the few Jordanian aircraft that could still fly were firmly grounded. Apart from my visits to the Embassy and the Jordanian Ministry of Information opposite, we were more or less under house arrest in the Intercontinental. The town itself was out of bounds. This was for our own safety, we were told. As the news of the devastating defeat of the Egyptian, Syrian and Jordanian armies filtered through to the souks, the local population turned sharply against the Americans and British, blaming them as allies of the 'Jews' for the disaster that had overtaken them. Anyone who looked American or British would be set on by the mob in the streets, we were told. It was a neat way of isolating us and there might have been some truth in it.

Our only source of news of what was happening on the battlefields was the BBC World Service, and we listened religiously to almost every news broadcast. By the third day the rout seemed to be complete. The Israelis had smashed their way across Sinai, catching the retreating Egyptian Army in the Mitla Pass and inflicting crippling damage. Now they were close to the Canal. On the Golan Heights, after fierce fighting, the Israelis had captured the positions from which the Syrians had been shelling their kibbutzes for so many years and driven them headlong towards Damascus only twenty miles away.

The Jordanians had suffered as heavily as their more powerful allies. The Army, which relied on discipline and bravery rather than on sophisticated equipment, had been brought to its knees.

On the Thursday, King Hussein called a press conference in the Basman Palace on top of one of Amman's seven hills. The entire Press Corps, thankful at last to be able to do something, crowded into the big conference room, hung with chandeliers. Hussein walked in, dressed in combat fatigues, and a keffiyeh, the red and white chequered headscarf worn originally by the Arab Legion under Glubb Pasha and now standard wear for the Jordanian Army. But the most noticeable thing about him was his eyes. They were red, both red-rimmed and bloodshot.

Looking at us with those red eyes, Hussein attempted a joke. 'You may wonder why my eyes are so red,' he said. 'Well, you may think I have been weeping but that is not the truth. My eyes are red because I have not been to bed since this business started. I have been in my headquarters in command of the armed forces.'

Then he came to the heart of his simple message.

'The Jordanian Army has suffered heavy casualties. Our troops have fought with tremendous courage and honour, to the limit of their endurance and beyond . . . ' his voice broke. 'But they can fight no more. I have ordered them to stop fighting and I have accepted the ceasefire proposed by the United Nations.'

There was a pause. Then: 'President Nasser promised to provide us with air cover and he has given us no air cover at all. Our forces were exposed without any protection from the air to repeated and savage attacks by the Israeli air force and suffered terrible casualties.' (The British Embassy estimated that the Jordanians had lost two-thirds of their armour, and nearly the whole of their air force.)

Hussein seemed to be close to tears as he ended his brief statement. It was bad enough to have lost the bulk of his army. But the disaster did not stop there. The whole of the West Bank from the River Jordan right up to and including East Jerusalem had fallen to the Israelis. All those ancient Biblical towns, Nazareth, Bethlehem, Ramallah, Jericho, Nabatiyeh and Hebron, were now occupied territory. Hussein had lost half his country, and the richer half, both in financial and cultural terms.

It was easy to say that he should not have joined Nasser and the Syrians. No doubt his native caution told him it was a risky undertaking. But he really had no option. If he had stayed out, he would have been called a traitor to the Arab cause and his position inside his own country might have become untenable. It was a brutal defeat and one that almost certainly made him decide never to commit his army again, unless attacked first.

At the end of the press conference the King announced that, because of the anti-Western feeling stirred up in Jordan by the Arab defeat, he was arranging for us to be flown out of the country as soon as possible. Then he stood and shook hands with all of us as we filed out. It was the first time I had met Hussein and I was impressed by his courage and dignity.

A day or two later we took off from the ruins of Amman airport. The United States Air Force airlifted nearly a thousand people, virtually the entire Western population of Jordan, leaving behind only the diplomats and a few key technicians. The runway was still pitted with bomb craters, and a few burnt-out Hunters stood where the Israeli jets had caught them. The C130 needs only a fraction of the runway a normal passenger jet requires and the American pilots were able to land and take off between craters. I asked a crew member where we were going.

'I cain't tell you,' he replied laconically. 'Somewheres, I guess.'

It turned out to be Teheran. As soon as we landed we made straight for the air freight office to arrange shipment of our film to London. A long wrangle ensued, the Iranians trying to enforce some absurd rule that no foreign television crew could ship film within forty-eight hours of arrival. We finally got round it by a mixture of threats and bribes. Then we took a taxi into the city. I thought Teheran was one of the least attractive cities I had ever seen. The centre is a wilderness of ugly concrete buildings, constructed apparently without any thought for the visual consequences. The traffic was equally murderous, and to cap it all the hotels were full. We finally got in at the brand new Intercontinental, which had a fine view of the distant mountains. They at least appeared to suggest something of the fabled beauty of what was once more prettily called Persia. The next thing I did was to put in a telephone call to London, and amazingly it came within an hour or so. I was able to tell them that the film, both the still unseen footage of the Israeli raid on Amman Airport and King Hussein's press conference, was finally on its way to London. That done, it was time for dinner.

After only a fortnight we were in the air again for the Middle East, heading this time for Israel. Tel Aviv was as complete a contrast to Amman as it was possible to conceive. Known to the Romans as Philadelphia, Amman is an ancient town, built of honey-coloured stone on a series of small hills. Beyond those dry, stony hills, which support little life apart from herds of sheep and goats, lies the semi-desert: great empty spaces, uncultivated and uncultivatable, where only the Beduin and their camels can survive.

Tel Aviv, on the other hand, built on the sea, is a modern European city – central European – transplanted to the

Middle East: ugly, vital, prosperous and brash; above all, brash. We booked in at the Dan Hotel, the oldest of the sea front hotels, once patronised by all the roving correspondents, but now superseded in favour of the plusher Hiltons and Sheratons. We hired a taxi from one of the garrulous, friendly and exorbitantly expensive drivers who wait outside and set off for the Sinai Desert and the Suez Canal.

It did not take long to reach the old border and then we were on Egyptian territory, the route taking us past El Arish to Gaza, a scruffy town which had been full of Palestinian refugees since 1948, and then on, leaving the date palms behind and with only the desert stretching away in front of us. There was a good tarmac road and we sped along it as the sun climbed higher and the air heated up. We stopped at a fly-blown desert outpost for a cup of coffee, served by a couple of ragged Arab boys. A dozen or so Israeli soldiers were there also, their uniforms combat-stained, towels round their necks to wipe away the sand and dust. Every so often we passed a wrecked lorry or car, and occasionally a destroyed Egyptian tank, although most of them had already been towed away. But halfway to the Suez Canal, we came on a huge depot where the Israelis had assembled hundreds of pieces of Egyptian war booty – tanks, tank transporters, field guns, armoured personnel carriers and fleets of lorries. It was a windfall worth millions of pounds and most of it would later be put into service with the Israeli Army.

We reached the Canal at about one, a seven-hour drive. The waterway is surprisingly narrow, only about a hundred yards across, the sides ruler-straight. It was like a millpond, the water an opaque green. Nasser had sunk several block ships at each end of the Canal in the early hours of the war, stopping all traffic and trapping a number of cargo ships in the Great Bitter Lakes below Ismailia. We stopped at an Israeli Army command post and gazed across the water. There was practically no sign of life on the Eygptian side. In their defeat they had pulled well back from the Canal, leaving the Israelis in sole, cocky possession. The victors had dug themselves in and now sat sunning themselves, their blue and white flags fluttering above them, lazily watching the far bank just in case the Eygptians should be foolish enough to try something. As we drove down the Canal, the sun delivered hammer blows to the tops of our heads, and when I asked Stan, the cameraman, to climb a dune for an elevated shot he almost had apoplexy.

The Israelis were relaxed and self-confident, letting us film whatever we wanted, the taxi-driver acting as an unofficial conducting officer. We drove far enough south to see the outline of Ismailia, once the headquarters of the British Canal Zone, shimmering in the heat of the far side of the canal. Then it was time to start the long journey back, bumping for miles over dirt roads before we reached the tarmac again. To the south, but unfortunately out of reach, was the Mitla Pass, a narrow defile through the mountains, where the Egyptian Army had been caught by the Israeli Air Force nose to tail and shot to ribbons. I had seen aerial photographs of it; it looked like the pile-up to end all pile-ups, a huge scrapyard of Soviet-made transport and weaponry, much of it brand new.

But we had to hustle back to Tel Aviv. Our film must be shipped first thing in the morning, for the next day, July 7, 1967, was the inauguration of 'News at Ten'. Geoffrey Cox, the Editor of ITN, had been negotiating anxiously for weeks with the network to start Britain's first half-hour news. To get it he had to sacrifice our half-hour weekly news documentary programme, currently called 'Reporting '67' – a price that many of us regretted. Now, after a last-minute frenzy of rehearsal, the show was about to go on the air. A dozen reporters and camera teams had been sent to the far corners of the globe to bring the news back to ITN and show that we were not only the newest but the best. We raced back across the desert, reaching Tel Aviv at about eight, exhausted but triumphant. I had a shower and some dinner and sat down to write my script. We recorded it late at night in the hotel bedroom and drove to Lod airport south of Tel Aviv next morning. The film was duly air freighted, arriving in London that afternoon, in good time, I told myself, for 'News at Ten'. Unfortunately, there was so much on offer that first night that our worthy but rather dull piece from the Suez Canal was crowded out. However, we were not to discover that until later and, in the meantime, we drove towards Jerusalem to shoot our second planned story: the Israeli occupation of the West Bank.

The road climbed gently at first up from the coast, through the dark green of the citrus groves, past the old monastery of Latroun. Until the Six-Day War this had been Jordanian territory, bringing the border to within a few miles of the sea. It is only when you see how narrow a strip of land the state of Israel is, that you understand their preoccupation with secure borders. After Latroun, the road rose steeply through pine forests and bony, rocky hills. At one bend we came on an abandoned Jordanian armoured car and, farther on, several trucks lying in the ditch. We climbed to a plateau and there, before us, serene in the morning sunshine, Jerusalem came into view. We drove past the blocks of flats which even then formed a ring round the Israeli half of Jerusalem, still climbing, until suddenly the great battlemented city dating from the time of the Crusaders rose up magnificently before us. We got out of the car and walked towards King David's Gate, a massive stone portico which leads to the souk and the old city. Israeli soldiers carrying their short-barrelled Uzi sub-machine-guns with the nonchalance of a shopping basket strolled towards us down the narrow street, past Arabs in galabiyeh and keffiyeh who walked on as if we weren't there. Old men in red fezzes sat in open-fronted cafés sucking on their hubble-bubbles, watching the passing scene through eyes that betrayed no emotion. Maybe they were still too stunned to comprehend fully what the loss of East Jerusalem and the West Bank would mean to their lives. Maybe Jerusalem has been fought over so many times that, in its long perspective, this was just another occupation.

We climbed up on the battlements and looked towards the Garden of Gethsemane with its symmetrically-sculpted cypresses. The roofs of the city lay spread out before us, hundreds of white washed domes, gilded by the sunlight, sharp against the clear blue of the Palestinian sky.

We walked on, the streets becoming narrower, until we emerged in a recently-cleared space. There, in front of us, its massive stones rising in a majestic pile, stood the Wailing

Wall, the only remaining vestige of the Second Temple, and Holy of Holies for all Jews. A dozen or more were standing at the foot of it now, in their black suits, beards and small black caps. As they prayed, they pressed their hands, face and lips against the ancient stones. Under Jordanian rule, the Wall had been partly hidden by buildings, some of them actually leaning against it. These the Israelis had promptly torn down, clearing and roping off an area in front. Another coachload arrived as we watched and twenty or thirty people rushed towards the Wall, crying and sobbing aloud in paroxysms of joy. But it was more than just religious fervour, powerful as that was. The Wailing Wall represents for Jews a unique link with the past, a past in which David and Solomon walked and worshipped in the golden age of their ancestors before the Diaspora.

We drove on down the winding road that leads to the bottom of the Jordan Valley, past the dusty city of Jericho, the temperature rising remorselessly the lower we dropped, until we finally came to the river. I felt more and more excited. Here I was, about to catch my first glimpse of the river whose name I had known from childhood, in whose waters, as every schoolboy knows, Jesus had been baptised. Here, finally, the word, would, so to speak, be made flesh. As the car drew up and I gazed out of the window, however, I was aware of a strong feeling of disappointment. The river itself was only about twenty or thirty yards wide and its waters, instead of being sparkling and pure, were muddy and sluggish. Was this the river immortalised by John the Baptist? The Allenby Bridge had been damaged in the fighting and its middle section lay, in a despairing sag, under water. Israeli engineers had put up a temporary bailey bridge and a stream of Arab refugees were crossing it, the women carrying bundles on their heads. They were mostly West Bankers who had fled at the start of the fighting and were now going home. A knot of Israeli soldiers at the end of the bridge suggested something unusual was going on and we elbowed our way forwards. A baldish man in the middle of the little group turned his head and I saw the black eye-patch of General Moshe Dayan, the Israeli Defence Minister and hero of the

Six-Day War. He was speaking in Arabic to a group of refugees. As we came up, an Israeli I had known in the Congo, Moshe Perelman, who had been Ben Gurion's special envoy in Léopoldville, recognised me and waved to us to come closer. Dayan turned and Perelman introduced me. I held out the microphone.

'What were you saying to those refugees?' I asked.

'I was asking them where they were going. They said they were going home. They had heard that things were peaceful now, but they wanted to know if there was any water. I told them there was.'

'Aren't you surprised that they were willing to talk to you at all?'

Dayan's good eye flashed dissent. 'No, why shouldn't they? Arabs and Jews have lived side by side for a very long time. I grew up with Arabs and I've spoken Arabic since I was a boy.' He broke off to say something to another Arab family. They stopped and answered and I wondered if they knew who he was. One or two Israeli soldiers lounged nearby, their sub-machine-guns slung over their shoulders, listening to what was going on. If they were impressed by the presence of Dayan they did not show it. There did not seem to be any special security. Dayan was dressed in an open-necked shirt and baggy slacks. His figure was less than soldierly, but it was in the set of the head and in the intelligence and force of the one good eye that you got the feeling that here was an exceptional man. Dayan, at this time, was a national hero, *the* national hero, and the black eye-patch was the symbol of his military dash and skill. He had lost that eye as a young man, on patrol with the British during the days of the Palestine Mandate. They had gone out at night and been ambushed by a group of Arabs. In the skirmish that followed Dayan was wounded in the eye. But he seemed to bear no grudge against the Arabs. He was no hater, no extremist.

'A lot of people think the Arabs and the Jews are born enemies. It's just not true. The ordinary people have always got on together. It's crazy that just because of the stupidity and arrogance of some politicians these people should suffer like this.' He waved his hand at the long line of refugees. The

288

Israeli soldiers, young, tough, tanned, searched them all, methodically, dispassionately. The Arabs submitted passively. There was nothing else they could do.

The Israeli Army was different to any other army I have ever seen before, a fascinating mixture of efficiency and slovenliness. Most armies equate excellence with spit and polish. The Israelis seem to do the opposite. Being essentially a reservist army, called up at short notice whenever there is an emergency, shiny boots and immaculately-pressed trousers do not count for very much. More important is that the soldiers should be able to climb straight into their tanks or jet fighters and know exactly what to do. And that is the Israelis' strong point. The vast majority are technologically centuries ahead of their Arab opponents, and it is largely their technical superiority that has kept the Israelis undefeated in four wars.

Perhaps because they were so intelligent, the privates being just as well-educated as the officers, the Israelis were more argumentative than any other soldiers I had seen. Privates would argue the toss with their officers, forcefully and articulately. Even in the American army in Vietnam, with its easy camaraderie and lack of the social divide that separates officers from men in the British Army, I had never seen anything like this. And yet, as they had just proved, when it came to battle, they were superb. It was the combination of extreme individualism on the one hand and an overwhelming sense of the threat to the nation's survival on the other that made the Israeli army such a formidable fighting force.

In those heady days immediately after the Six-Day War there was more to Israel than just military success. Discussing it with Winston Burdett, a vastly experienced and wise CBS correspondent, we came to the conclusion that the early Romans must have been like this: dynamic, intelligent, well-organised and militarily superior. There was one other quality, hard to define. The Israelis' courage, their small numbers, their determination never again to be the lamb led meekly to the slaughter gave them, we believed, a moral superiority. Their struggle for survival had something noble about it.

*   *   *

In those early days of 'News at Ten', we tended to move rapidly from one story to another, and, only ten days after flying home from Tel Aviv, I was on my way to Africa to cover a very different war: Biafra.

A rich Sandhurst-trained officer in the Nigerian Army called Colonel Ojukwu had set himself up as the leader of the Ibo people and declared their new state of Biafra independent. The Ibos were sometimes known as the Jews of Africa because of their intelligence and commercial skill. They were the administrators and businessmen *par excellence* and had carved out a strong niche for themselves all over the country and especially in the Muslim north. This inevitably led to jealousy and finally to an explosion of hatred. Twenty thousand Ibos were slaughtered in the north, in a savage series of reprisals, and fearing a pogrom on a national scale their fellow-tribesmen fled from all over Nigeria back to their homeland in the south-east. Secession followed. It was Katanga all over again.

There it had been copper and uranium. Here in Biafra it was oil. Seventy percent of Nigeria's oil lies offshore in the Port Harcourt area and that was now firmly under the control of Colonel Ojukwu.

Some wars are easier to cover than others. In Biafra, nothing was easy, neither getting in, nor reporting the war. Obviously we could not go via Lagos, the Nigerian capital, and there were no flights to Biafra itself. Instead we had to fly from Paris to Douala, an ex-French Colonial port on the old Slave Coast of the Cameroons. We arrived on a Saturday and immediately started trying to organise our onward journey. I discovered that it was a five-hour drive over terrible roads to Mamfe, the main Cameroons town near the Biafran border. Much better, I was advised, to fly to Mamfe and drive from there.

Next morning I managed to hire a twin-engined Piper Aztec to fly the 150 miles to Mamfe. It was one hour in the air, instead of five or six by road. Tantalisingly, it would have taken only another hour to fly on to our destination, Enugu, the Biafran capital. But because of the fighting the Cameroons had banned all flights to Biafra. So, reluctantly, we climbed out and gave the pilot a rather optimistic rendez-vous for exactly one week ahead.

While the police at Mamfe were inspecting our thirteen pieces of camera equipment, the first of many searches that would follow, a Landrover drove up and two men got out, the driver in a dirty, tattered vest, accompanied by a crafty-looking individual who did the talking.

'Master, you go border?'

'Yes, perhaps, why?'

'You like good car, very good car, master?'

I looked at the Landrover. It seemed pretty dilapidated to me. 'How much?'

'21,000 francs, sah.'

I made a rapid calculation. 'Why, that's far too much, that's £30.'

'21,000 francs, master.'

'No, no, no, that's ridiculous. Why, how far's the border.'

'Forty-five miles, master. Very bad road, you need take good car, this good car.'

I took another look and discovered that the foam rubber cushions from the back seats were missing. 'No, what about 15,000 francs?'

'Sorry, master.' He looked away.

I thought, God, what a bloody journey! I gave in.

'All right, dammit, let's go.'

'Yes, master, we load quickly, master.' The driver and Crafty immediately started loading the thirteen pieces. The luggage, Crafty and Mick Doyle, our soundman, got in the back, while Cyril Page, the cameraman, and I squeezed into the front seat. I was on the outside and, after we had gone twenty yards, the door flew open. Crafty made encouraging noises, urging me to slam the door. I did. Fifty yards farther on, it burst open again. Slam. Open. Slam. Open. Very big slam. Stays shut.

We had only gone about a mile when the engine coughed and we lurched to a stop. Crafty jumped out and announced we were out of petrol.

'Out of petrol? That's ridiculous, we've only just started.'

Not a bit put out, Crafty simply grinned and demanded money to go and buy petrol. I knew from past experience that African drivers have a habit of putting in only a teacupful of petrol and then asking for an advance when you hire them. I hovered on the brink of losing my temper but finally forked out instead. Crafty had already commandeered a bicycle and now pedalled off down the road, petrol tin in hand. Luckily there was a small African bar beside the road and we went in and ordered three large Carlsbergs. Since reaching Mamfe, we had come one mile in an hour. Only the solace of the beer and a small cigar made the next 300 miles seem at all possible.

Crafty returned in ten minutes and we set off again, bumping along painfully until we reached a Cameroon police checkpoint just before the border. An insolently-lounging sergeant in a red beret and with a pistol on his hip inspected our baggage. An officer arrived and said in French, presuming we did not understand, 'Find out what they want, make sure they don't have any arms, and ask them if they've been invited by the Biafrans.'

The sergeant passed on the questions.

'We've been invited by the Biafran Government and they're expecting us in Enugu today.'

The sergeant translated and the fat officer eyed me slyly.

'Have they got a letter of invitation?'

'No, I'm afraid not. But a representative of the Biafran Government in London gave us a personal invitation from Colonel Ojukwu.'

There was a pause for consultation and then we were waved on.

At the border I peeled off a huge wad of notes for Crafty. The driver then approached and asked for a tip. £30 for the fare *and* a tip. That was too much, I thought. You could take a taxi from the middle of London to Heathrow for £3.10 then. I dismissed them angrily.

Then we had an enormous stroke of luck. We came out of the customs post to find a green Peugeot estate car, which had Nigerian plates and looked in good condition, setting down a load of passengers. The driver agreed to take us to

Enugu for less money than Crafty had charged, although it was four times as far.

The Biafran customs post was very British and the police post farther down the road even more so. A strong sense of bobbydom prevailed. Here we picked up a passenger who had sat next to me on the flight from Paris to Douala. His name was Okoli and he was a senior official in the Ministry of Works at Enugu. He had been in Europe on Government business when the war started on July 6, and was now on his way home. Okoli was to prove an invaluable companion over the next twelve hours. Indeed, without him, I doubt if we would ever have got through.

We left the Nigerian police border post at Ikang at two, the dirt road snaking away in front of us through the huge stands of secondary jungle. Occasionally a butterfly like a dark jewel swerved past the windscreen. We passed mud and thatch huts with the odd stone house which almost certainly belonged to an Ibo. Although the Ibo are the main tribe in the east there are others, and we were at that moment in non-Ibo territory.

At three we reached Ikom, a fair-sized provincial town on the main road to Enugu and asked for the Divisional Officer. Only he could authorise our journey to the capital, according to Mr Okoli. Unfortunately he was out so we decided to have lunch at the Progress Hotel, still referred to by its old colonial title of Catering Rest House, which overlooks the vast, misty mirrors of the Cross River. Tiny figures in dugout canoes, looking like insects on the surface of a lake, inched their way laboriously across to the far horizon. While the cook prepared sausage, eggs and yam chips (what could have been more British?) we drank cold tinned beer and gazed at the river, the far bank a green blur of mangrove trees, while the ghosts of dead, departed British DO's hovered at our backs.

Finally, the Divisional Officer, a young Ibo with glasses, appeared and signed a laissez-passer. But, by then, the sun was beginning to set beyond the Cross River in a blaze of orange. We were going to have to travel in the dark, never advisable in Africa when there is a crisis, and sure enough we had only gone fifty yards when we ran into trouble. An excited young man with a weapon flagged us down. His eyes grew wild as they roamed the car and discovered three white faces in the back. As we discovered later, every Biafran was on the look-out for 'white mercenaries'.

'Come down,' he shouted. 'Come down.'

I noticed a firefly glowing green on the bonnet. Mr Okoli began to explain our mission. A second youth appeared.

'Who are all these people?' He also carried some sort of gun.

Okoli, patiently. 'They are journalists, from British Television.'

'You, who are you?' another demanding young face was thrust aggressively through the window at Okoli.

'I have just been explaining to your . . . colleagues over here that I am a senior official in the Ministry of Works. I have been abroad on Government business and am now on my way back . . . '

More youths arrived, wearing armbands and looking fierce, walking with exaggerated springy steps. Most carried dummy wooden guns but one or two had 12-bore shotguns. It was almost dark now, no moon, only the flicker of street lamps.

'If you are an official you must have a paper, a document.'

'But we do have a paper.'

'Show it, please.'

The DO's letter, held to catch the poor light, was perused by several youths craning to read it together.

A new man arrived. He seemed in some indefinable way to be superior. He shouted at no one in particular.

'Who are these people? Come down at once all of you. Come down. You, come down. I want to search the car. Driver, you come down immediately. Open the boot. Search them.'

Wearily, cursing under our breaths, we scrambled out and stood by the roadside. Mr Okoli continued to explain patiently and calmly. Finally, he got through.

'Enough,' the man who had been examining the pass called. 'The letter is in order. You may go.'

As we drove off, more youths were arriving, attracted by the commotion. The firefly, glowing on and off like a morse signal lamp, was whisked away by the rush of air. The crowds in the main street fell back and the headlights reached out and caught the shapes of the forest again.

We had only gone a few miles when we had to stop again, for another roadblock, and then another, and yet another. Progress became desperately slow and tedious. Cyril, who has a short fuse, became more and more tetchy. Despite eloquent pleading by Mr Okoli, all the camera equipment was repeatedly strewn across the road and searched.

'What the bloody hell do you think we've got here, chum, the Crown Jewels?' Cyril snapped at a puzzled black youth. Luckily his Cockney was too fast for them.

'All right, then, have a bloody look,' Cyril threw open the lid of a box. 'Satisfied? Right, that's your lot.' He snapped the case shut again. Although they were presumably looking for arms, strangely enough none of the searchers showed any surprise at the sight of the rifle microphone, a long thin tube with a trigger grip and a bulbous rubber windshield that made it look like a weapon. In fact, we had earnestly debated whether it was safe to bring it. But, at roadblock after roadblock, when told it was a microphone the young Biafran home guards simply nodded their heads sagely and passed on.

About midnight, with my legs beginning to get cramp and other parts of my body having lost all sense of feeling, I saw a big steel bridge swing into our headlights. I looked anxiously for any sign of a roadblock or a sentry because I was worried that we might drive past one in the dark, not hear his challenge and get shot for our pains. The bridge was deserted but tied to each of the main supports was enough TNT to blow it and us to smithereens. A few yards the other side of the bridge, a sentry jumped out of the darkness into the beam of our headlights, like a dog out of kennel. We were ordered out of the car once again, but the soldiers were much more efficient and polite than the home guards. The unmistakable accents of Sandhurst floated reassuringly through the warm night air, giving us clearance and sending us off on the last lap. But, on the outskirts of Enugu, we ran into the last and worst roadblock of all. For half an hour we argued, explained, cursed and staggered about wearily among the camera cases until finally even the home guards tired of the game and allowed us to pass. I calculated we had been stopped and searched at twenty road blocks. We reached the Hotel Presidential at two and were in bed fifteen minutes later. A pretentious mausoleum built by the Israelis at the cost of a million pounds, it seemed then to be the very last word in luxury.

Next morning, thinking all our troubles were over, we took a decrepit old Morris Minor taxi to the Ministry of Information to announce our arrival and obtain Press passes. We were shown into a small office jammed with five or six people, including a police constable, and stumbled over legs, chairs and tables to shake the hand of Mr Agbasi, the Press and Information officer. Apologetically, he explained that the Director was 'indisposed' and so the Press passes could not be signed. We would have to come back for them. The Director's indisposition was to prove a costly one for us. On the way back to the hotel we had to negotiate a road block every hundred yards and did so successfully until an officious teenager sporting a brand-new wooden rifle dragged me off to a home guard post installed in a nearby medical dispensary. Luckily I was able to get Mr Agbasi on the telephone and I was free with apologies. As we drove back to the hotel, I suddenly took in the significance of the posters that were plastered up all over Enugu. A soldier wearing a tin helmet and clutching a rifle glared balefully at us. 'Be Vigilant. Report any strangers to the police.'

I was still pondering the implications of this message when we were stopped at yet another road block, this time at the entrance to the Presidential Hotel which stands about fifty yards back from the road.

First home guard: 'You can't go in.'
S. Gall: 'But I'm a guest here.'
First home guard: 'Oh, he's a guest.'
Second home guard: 'Where's your documents?'
S. Gall: 'They're at the Ministry of Information.'

First home guard: 'Without documents, you cannot enter, sah.'

Second home guard: 'You stay in the hotel?'

'S. Gall: 'Yes, I do and I want to go and have my lunch.'

Second home guard: 'Oh, you want to go and have your lunch, is that it?'

S. Gall: 'Yes, that's right.'

Ferociously suspicious glances are directed into the taxi. Then to the driver.

'Come down, you, driver, come down at once. Open up the boot, man.'

After a quick inspection: 'Okay, you may go on.'

After lunch, emboldened by my skill at getting through road blocks without a pass, I set off to visit an old friend, Bob St Leger. We had both been at Aberdeen University and had made many expeditions together. Bob, who had joined the Colonial Service and was now chief adviser to the Ministry of Works, was married to a Nigerian girl, Priscilla, the daughter of a chief from near Ikom.

I ran into a road block not far from Bob's house, and I was ordered out of the taxi. They were extremely officious.

'Search him.' Fingers like sticky black bananas ran up and down my body.'

'Papers.'

I explained that, alas, I had no papers yet. They were at the Ministry of Information waiting to be signed. Suspicion flooded the eyes of the home guards. No papers. They muttered and then I was ordered to drive to Military Police headquarters. There I was taken into the orderly room and made to stand while another body search was carried out. Then I was made to sit while, rather apologetically, the black fingers searched in my hair. Then shoes and socks had to come off, and stooping down the indefatigable gentleman diligently looked between each of my toes. Heaven knows what he thought he might find there. My supply of micro dots, or a miniaturised radio transmitter? At least he had the grace to look embarrassed afterwards.

A lance corporal then called a young private with an automatic sub-machine-gun to stand guard over me.

'If he tries to run away, shoot him,' he said unnecessarily loudly. I tried to look nonchalant.

Someone else came in and asked me if I had any friends in Enugu.

'Yes,' I said, 'my friends are in the Presidential Hotel.' Immediately the words were out of my mouth, I cursed myself. I knew what would happen. Sure enough, half an hour later the door opened and Cyril Page and Mick Doyle were marched in. I tried to make a joke but it fell rather flat.

Half an hour passed and then two officers arrived. 'Ah,' I thought, 'we'll get some sense at last.' But they were both so drunk they could hardly stand upright. They staggered out and we were left for another half hour or so, as the afternoon dawdled to its conclusion. Suddenly, the door opened and we were told we were being taken to CID headquarters. There we were ushered into the presence of a very smooth police officer. Another telephone call to Mr Abasi, and then, regretfully, I thought, the policeman said there seemed to be no reason to hold us. We were free to go. This time we had an escort to the hotel. By now, it was almost sundown and I was fed up with the Biafrans and their paranoic suspicions. I rang Bob St Leger and explained what had happened. He said he would come down and collect me in his car. With his official pass, we had no trouble and I spent a couple of hours in his house, drinking whisky and talking. Priscilla's father came from a small non-Ibo tribe and she had little sympathy with the Biafran cause. Neither had Bob. He said the Ibos had largely engineered their own downfall by being too greedy and self-assertive. His sympathies were firmly on the side of the Federal Government. This was a new point of view for me and most of my colleagues. Indeed, emotionally, the British Press were almost solidly on Ojukwu's side.

Day 2: Lagos Radio announced that our hotel had been bombed. This came as a surprise as we had heard nothing. I did wish, though, that someone would put a bomb under the hotel switchboard. It took them about an hour to handle one outgoing call. We were finally issued with our Press passes. The Biafrans asked if we would like to film the Biafran civil defence force in training? Since there was nothing else on offer, I said yes. We were taken to a big, open space on the outskirts of Enugu, and there, drawn up in ragged formations, were about 10,000 men in T-shirts and trousers, mostly barefoot and armed solely with wooden guns. Some were carved and shaped to look like the real thing. Others were very approximate. After we had filmed them marching and counter-marching, sloping arms and about-turning, we got into our car and started to make our way through the throng to the exit. Halfway there we were besieged by a mob of several hundred young men. They surrounded the car, pressing so close that the driver had to keep stopping, banged on the roof and shouted at us. It was quite frightening and I began to wonder if they were going to turn the car over. But our driver said they were not hostile, they were simply demanding money and food. They were volunteers who had come in from the country districts to join up and they had not eaten all day.

Day 3: We finished filming the civil defence force and were driving back to Enugu when we were stopped at a road block by a very angry young man. His wrath fell on our escort, a senior Biafran civil servant, who was understandably curt with this wild underling. The young man's voice rose. 'Next time you stop when I tell you or you will be in big trouble.' His face was contorted with anger. 'If you don't' . . . there was a tense pause ' . . . I'll have to shoot you.'

I looked through the window and saw that the young vigilante was tightly gripping a very flimsy, home-made wooden gun. His finger was curled round where the trigger would have been.

That afternoon Mr Agbasi arrived at the hotel in a cold fury and confiscated our Press passes. Bitter complaints all round. Apparently two people from *Life* magazine had gone to the front-line town of Nsukka, without getting permission from the Ministry of Information. So we were all in disgrace. Mr Agbasi, his pockets full of our Press passes, went off still spitting. We looked at one another.

'Without Press passes we can't do a bloody thing,' Cyril said. 'We'll get picked up at the first road block. What a fucking dog's breakfast . . . ' We all agreed and went off to the bar to have a drink. I was especially angry because we had planned to drive to Nsukka ourselves next morning. A university town, it was said to be the intellectual centre of the Biafran rebellion and it was more or less in the front line. Also, it was only forty miles away, up a good tarmac road. But now we were effectively prisoners in Enugu.

That evening, the Press Corps held a council of war in the almost empty hotel. Round the table were Lloyd Garrison, of the *New York Times,* George de Carvalhao, of *Life* magazine, his photographer, Priya Ramrhaka, from Nairobi, later killed in Biafra, Freddy Bayat, a Visnews cameraman, Freddy Forsyth, then of the BBC and later of *Day of the Jackal* fame, Arnold Amber, of Reuters, Cyril Page, Mick Doyle and myself. The last time I had seen George he had been sporting a white suit. That was during the Six-Day War. Now, more soberly attired, he circulated the text of a strongly-worded letter addressed to Colonel Ojukwu, complaining about the attitude of the Ministry of Information officials and asking for his help in getting us to the front to witness the fighting. George and Priya were particularly upset because they had been told that they would receive no more help from the Information people. While the draft was being debated round the table, Mike Ekensi, Ojukwu's Press Secretary, arrived and sat down. He was a pleasant-looking, well-spoken Ibo of about thirty, educated at Princeton and presumably aware of what we wanted. But at the end of half an hour it was quite clear that he was not the man to open the doors to Ojukwu. At this point, a broad-shouldered, smiling American came up to our table and, addressing no one in particular, asked:

'What's your prallum, gennelmen?'

'You ought to know, you've been eavesdropping for long enough,' someone said.

The smile on the American's face did not flicker.

'Well, I couldn't help overhearing what you were saying and I thought mebbe I could help. I know His Excellency pretty well.'

With those magic words, a place was immediately made at

the table for the genial American, who said his name was Jim Most and that he was a contractor building a road from Calabar in the south to Ikom in the east. He consulted his watch and said it was not too late in his opinion to ring His Excellency, who was up all night, anyway, running the war. While he was out of the room telephoning, various opinions about Mr Most were put forward. The general view was that he was either drunk or an imposter, or both, although I must confess he seemed sober enough to me. He came back in a few minutes and sat down.

'Well, boys, His Excellency will see you tomorrow. He almost decided to see you tonight' – it was past eleven – 'but he said he had a couple of things he ought to do and he prefers to make it tomorrow.'

Everyone started to talk at once.

'Oh, don't thank me. I happen to be on pretty intimate terms with His Excellency, we just happen to get along pretty well together, and if there's anything I can do to help His Excellency and you boys do your job, why, I'm very pleased to be of service.'

It turned out that Mr Most would not have been in the Hotel Presidential at all that night if he had not fallen foul of a particularly awkward road block twenty miles out on the Calabar Road and been forced to return to Enugu.

Day 5: It promised more hope than its predecessors although the sky continued to be a grey overcast. After breakfast we brought our camera gear down to the lobby. Everyone sat waiting for the call but nothing happened. The only stranger there was a German-American who said he had been flying in a plane-load of arms for Ojukwu but had crashed into the river at Douala. Plane and arms had been promptly seized by the Cameroonians.

The morning ticked away. Finally, disgruntled and disappointed by yet another delay, we had just sat down to lunch when Ojukwu's press man, Mike Ekensi, arrived out of breath and told us to get ready for an immediate departure to 'the front'. Afterwards we would have the honour of being received by His Excellency, the Head of State, at State House.

301

Our little convoy consisted of a Landrover and three cars, plus our hired Cortina.

From Enugu the road rises steeply to the top of the escarpment and then switchbacks for miles through dense forest and plantations. A mile or two from Nsukka, where the road climbs out of the trees up to rolling grassland, we met the first wave of refugees. As we drove slowly along for a couple of miles, they loped past us at a swift walk, mostly women, their possessions on their heads, moving silently and with pathetic grace, their children running wide-eyed with fear in front of them. As we breasted one slope, a line of Biafran soldiers with yellow 'rising sun' shoulder flashes ran across the road in front of us and moved cautiously into the long grass. They kept looking across the valley apprehensively as if they had just been shot at. We stopped and got out, Cyril hoisting the sound camera on to his shoulder while Mick plugged in the rifle mike. A Foreign Ministry official from one of the other cars came running towards us.

'We have to go back now, please, for the interview with His Excellency. Into the cars, please,' he shouted.

'We've only just arrived,' we shouted back, fanning out past him and starting to film. Ahead of us, at the top of a rise, a group of fifteen or twenty Biafran soldiers were milling about, silhouetted against the green hills, the blue sky and the white clouds. They started to move towards us carrying one man who appeared to be wounded. There was a feeling of expectancy, as if they were waiting for the shooting to start again, and the refugees were still running past us down the road, away from Nsukka, absolutely silently.

We were filming all the time, while the man from the Foreign Ministry became increasingly agitated. Some of the other cars were beginning to move off. The soldiers were close now, led by a sergeant holding a small pistol almost delicately in his hand.

'Stop taking snaps,' he shouted as he came towards us. We continued to film. He advanced menacingly.

'Stop, no more pictures.' He waved his little gun.

The convoy was already moving. Cyril let the camera run for as long as he could and then, when I thought the little sergeant might start shooting, we jumped into our car, and moved off. We had come 5,000 miles and had spent five minutes at the 'front'.

The convoy drove back to Enugu at breakneck speed and went straight to State House, the old Provincial Governor's residence. Then, of course, we had to wait for His Excellency, Colonel Ojukwu, President of Biafra, to appear. We waited half an hour. Finally he stalked in, dressed in a leopard-spotted battledress, his black beard as big and bushy as W.G. Grace's, and sat down in front of a Biafran flag depicting a huge rising sun against a black and green background. Ojukwu of Biafra was more sophisticated than Tshombe of Katanga. Like Tshombe, he was the son of a millionaire businessman. Tshombe had gone to school in Belgium, but not to university, whereas Ojukwu had been to both Oxford and Sandhurst. He spoke slowly and in a rather monotonous voice, but he undoubtedly had presence. He exuded optimism, saying that he was quite sure his army would be able to hold off the Federal troops. I was not so sure. Having just seen the nervous retreat of some of his men at Nsukka, I would not have thought the Biafrans were great fighters. The Federal army was mainly drawn from the warlike Muslim tribes in the north, and in theory were better trained and equipped. On the other hand, the Ibos were fighting for their lives and it was clearly Ojukwu's policy to encourage the belief that defeat would mean the destruction of the tribe.

The interview over, Ojukwu stalked out. He looked like a man beset by many problems, but I could not help wondering why someone who obviously depended for his survival on the sympathy of the outside world did not take more advantage of our presence. Despite his fluent English he was not a particularly persuasive spokesman. Perhaps he was too British to trust the Press. But I thought that, with the *New York Times* and *Life* magazine there for America, with the BBC and ourselves for Britain, and with Reuters there for the rest of the world, Ojukwu had a remarkable opportunity to spread his message far and wide. But, in my opinion, he muffed it.

On our way back to the hotel, we all agreed that we had as

much material as we were likely to get and that there was no point in hanging on in Enugu. Also, the only way we could be sure of getting our film back to London was by taking it ourselves.

We would leave next morning if I could persuade the Ministry of Information to lend us a Landrover with a driver and police escort to get us through the road blocks. As an inducement I offered to take all the dispatches and film from the other correspondents to London as well. The Ministry agreed but explained that we would have to go the long way round, via Calabar, since the road we had come in by had been cut by fighting. The situation had deteriorated that much in five days.

That evening I had a drink with Freddy Forsyth in the hotel. He said he had been sacked by the BBC for sending 'biased' reports of the fighting. (Much later Freddy told me that the BBC had tried to suppress his first-hand accounts of the battle for Biafra, which at the time had quite truthfully depicted a string of successes for Ojukwu.) Because of his interest in the story he had decided to stay on and report the war as a freelance. That must have become more and more difficult as the tide of war turned against the Ibos. In the months that followed he became very close to Ojukwu and indeed was about the only means Ojukwu had of getting his views over to the rest of the world.

Freddy made several trips to London during the Biafran war and I interviewed him two or three times at ITN. He looked tense and rather anaemic particularly towards the end, but I admired his devotion to what was obviously a lost cause. I had no idea, then, that he was engaged in writing *The Day of the Jackal*.

Day 6: We left after breakfast, carrying all our colleagues' film and copy, and with our affable young police escort, Gilbert, making passage through the road blocks child's play. We drove through lush, thickly populated country, full of small villages surrounded by plots of bananas, maize and sweet potatoes. There was no sign of the war. The most frightening thing was the stream of gaily-painted lorries, festooned with slogans and quotations, which thundered along the roads, so heavily laden that they listed alarmingly. Some of these mottoes were very funny. Look out, here come de Lord' was one . . .

After we had been travelling for an hour or two we had a puncture and, as we were standing by the side of the road while the driver changed the wheel, an African came up carrying a crocodile in a basket on his head.

He stopped, placed the crocodile on the ground beside the Landrover and entered into conversation with Gilbert.

'What's he want?'

'He wants to sell you his crocodile.' I noticed that the beast, which was about six feet long, had been killed by a spear or knife thrust just behind the eye.

'How much does he want?' I asked out of idle curiosity and not with any intention of buying the crocodile.

A short conversation ensued and then Gilbert said.

'He wants £4.'

'Christ,' Cyril said. '£4 for that ugly bleeder?'

'I'm very sorry,' I told Gilbert, having difficulty keeping a straight face, 'it's a very nice crocodile but I'm afraid we don't have any room for it.'

Gilbert relayed this sad news and, looking suitably disappointed, the African picked up his crocodile and started off again along the road.

At three, we reached the Cross River again but this time considerably farther south at Oron. The great coffee-coloured flood swept by at a smooth gallop between banks a mile apart. We lunched off a couple of tins of bully beef, bought from an African woman stall-keeper whose knife we borrowed. We also purchased several big bottles of cold Star beer. As we tackled this simple repast, a dugout canoe with six young Africans went gliding past us down river. One youth stood in the stern, steering with a long paddle. The others rested on their paddles, watching the activity on the landing-stage below us. Then, in perfect unison, they all lifted their paddles and drove them into the water with a stabbing motion. The canoe shot across the smooth water, the paddles rising and falling in time, the shiny black backs curving with the effort, the sharp prow of the dugout cutting through the water like the beak of a predatory bird. On the far side of the Landrover, a queue of Africans had formed at the inevitable check-point for the ferry. The soldiers opened every bag and basket, their hands carelessly searching through the handful of possessions. No one seemed to mind very much and there were even a few jokes before the women hoisted the baskets on their heads and walked away, hips swaying, to the landing stage. Some of the men carried coloured golf umbrellas although there cannot have been a golf course for a hundred miles. A half-finished six-storey concrete building towered above the ramshackle huts on the other side of the road, weeds sprouting from its balconies and fungus staining the walls. It looked abandoned and derelict and lent the whole place a feeling of desolation. A thin rain began to fall.

At four the ferry arrived and we went on board. A plaque on the rusty superstructure proclaimed that it had been built in Liverpool and was operated by the Elder Dempster Line.

To my surprise there was a first class section on the after-deck. Our travelling companions were a Biafran Prisons Office and a Divisional Officer – the post-colonial equivalent of the old British DO. A steward brought tea and biscuits, British Railways-type, and we leafed through old copies of *Britain Today* as the ferry chugged down river past mangrove swamps. The river widened steadily until it was like a sea. In the distance, dugout canoes moved infinitely slowly across the vast expanse. Calabar came into sight at about six, just as the light was failing, a handful of white chips against the green baize of the jungle. In the west the sunset was red and gold, the air still and misty and there was a great sense of calm. We drove to the Catering Rest House, standing by itself among several giant trees, overlooking the vast estuary of the Cross River. After dinner of chicken and yam chips we went to bed early. We all knew tomorrow would be the worst part of the journey. Despite the heat and humidity I slept well.

Day 7: We set off early, after a breakfast of fried eggs and yes, yam chips. Calabar, from where, in the eighteenth and nineteenth centuries, thousands of slaves were shipped to the New World in conditions of terrible privation, has a sort of deep sadness about it, as if its past lay as heavily upon it as the humidity of the Bight of Biafra.

From Calabar our route ran east to the border, less than fifty miles away, but over roads that were almost impassable in places. Only a vehicle with four-wheel drive could have got through. The gallant Landrover pitched up and down like a ship in a storm, crashing into potholes with spine-jarring force, and then hauling itself out again with the engine labouring. It was one of the worst journeys I have ever made. We reached Mamfe at 4 p.m. To my utter amazement, our charter aircraft was just making a pass over the airstrip. I think the pilot was equally astonished to see us climb stiffly out of a Landrover, dead on time. We had given him a rendezvous for four and there we were. We said a fond farewell to the excellent Gilbert and our long-suffering driver, and ten minutes later we were airborne and on our way back to Douala. The assignment had taken exactly one week.

CHAPTER X

I Nearly Miss the Tet Offensive;
The Rockets Just Miss Me

Right at the beginning of 1968, it became clear that the war in Vietnam was moving into a new phase. On January 3 the North Vietnamese attacked Da Nang air base, damaging or destroying a number of American planes. On the same day the Vietcong struck at Ban Me Thuot, farther south, putting fifteen American helicopters out of action; similarly at An Khe, where the American 1st Air Cavalry were based. On January 10, the Vietcong attacked an American infantry command post twenty-four miles north-west of Saigon. More importantly, on January 21, an estimated 16,000 to 20,000 regular North Vietnamese troops laid siege to the isolated American base of Khe Sanh, astride one of the main infiltration routes from neighbouring Laos. The Americans flew in 1,000 men to reinforce the Marine garrison, but low cloud and bad visibility hampered subsequent air activity. The North Vietnamese moved up their big guns and started to shell the base and its airstrip. By January 26 all flights in

South Vietnam had been cancelled except those carrying reinforcements to the northern provinces. In all 15,000 men were airlifted, including two brigades of the Air Cavalry, to meet what the American Commander, General Westmoreland, called a 'sizeable invasion' from North Vietnam. Ominous parallels began to be drawn between Khe Sanh and Dien Bien Phu, where the French had been so devastatingly defeated in 1954. You did not have to be a Henry Kissinger to see that, in January 1968, the war in Vietnam was moving towards some sort of climax.

Reading the reports in London and hearing from friends like Donald Wise and Ernie Christie, now working for 'Panorama', that they were off to Saigon, I urged that we should go too. Geoffrey Cox, however, ever mindful of his budget, was a difficult man to persuade. Finally I spotted him in the corridor and found what I thought was an unanswerable question. 'Is there any reason,' I asked, 'why we should not be in Vietnam?' 'Let's think about it over the weekend and decide on Monday,' was all he would say. I did not see why the weekend should bring particular enlightenment, but there was nothing I could do except, reluctantly, accept his decision. Nigel Ryan, then the senior producer on 'News at Ten', was confident that on Monday we would get the go-ahead. The crew had been alerted – it was to be Alan Downes who had been with me in Vietnam the year before and a keen new sound man, Mike Williams. We had got our visas and had our jabs for cholera and smallpox brought up to date and, to save time, I even packed over the weekend, which was unusual for me. I was very conscious of important things happening on the other side of the world and of us being stuck in England, missing out on a 'big story'. I knew my friends and rivals were there and that made me all the more impatient.

On Monday 29, 5,000 miles to the east and six hours ahead of London, long before ITN made its decision, the South Vietnamese government cancelled the ceasefire already announced for Tet, the lunar New Year holiday, in the five northern provinces. At the same time, the Americans announced that four North Vietnamese divisions had been spotted south of the Demilitarised Zone, or DMZ, which formed the border between North and South Vietnam.

About lunch time I got the news that the Editor had finally decided we should go to Vietnam as soon as possible. A furious flurry of activity now ensued. Money had to be organised, flights booked and the crew had to sort out and pack all the camera and sound equipment we would need to film a war on the other side of the world, an assignment that might last for a month or two. The next flight turned out to be the following day, from Paris via Delhi and Bangkok to Saigon. We would have to leave London early to make the connection. On the 30th, the Vietcong launched a whole series of attacks in the northern and central provinces. But in our first class cabin (thanks to the cameramen's union) we were blissfully unaware. Delhi came and went, Wednesday the 31st dawned and we landed at Bangkok. Airborne again and with Saigon only a couple of hours away, I was just settling down for a short snooze, when the French captain emerged from the flight deck and stopped by my seat.

'Bad news, I'm afraid,' he said without preamble. 'Saigon is closed. They're fighting at the airport so we'll have to overfly. I can either put you down at Phnom Penh' – he looked at his watch – 'we'll be there in about an hour, or you can carry on with us to Djakarta.' He looked at me inquiringly.

'Djakarta?' I said with disbelief. 'But that's Indonesia.'

'That's right,' the French captain agreed. 'I'm afraid it's one or the other.'

I groaned. 'There's no point in going to Djakarta. We'll have to get off at Phnom Penh. Damn!'

Alan and Mike, sitting nearby, had heard the conversation and were equally appalled. We did not know it yet, but that very morning, at 3 a.m. local time, the Vietcong had launched their Tet offensive, attacking American and South Vietnamese targets all over the country. The heaviest blows fell on Saigon, the capital, Hue, the old imperial capital, and the Mekong Delta. Thousands of VC, as the Americans called them, had infiltrated Saigon in the days before the Tet holiday and then carried out pre-planned attacks on key points in the city. The main targets were the Presidential Palace, where they blew in the gates, but failed to get into the Palace itself, the radio station which they held for twenty-four hours, and, most important of all, the American Embassy where a suicide squad of twenty guerrillas blasted a hole in the outer wall and tried to force their way into the main building with mortars and grenades. The Marine guards just managed to shut the heavy metal Embassy doors which were operated electronically; otherwise it is hard to see how the VC could have failed to take the whole building, which would have been for them a sensational victory. As it was the Vietcong held out in the Embassy compound for six hours until airborne troops were helicoptered in and recaptured the grounds, killing nineteen of the intruders. American losses were four military policemen and one Marine killed, plus one Vietnamese civilian.

Of all this we were, of course, completely ignorant. We simply cursed our luck and made ready to disembark at Phnom Penh, the capital of Cambodia. It was the last place I wanted to be. Although Phnom Penh was only an hour's flight from Saigon, there were no diplomatic relations between the two countries, and so no air service. We would be on the doorstep but we might as well be in England. All this was going through my mind, but uppermost was the thought that, if we had only left London one day earlier, if ITN had made the decision before the weekend and not after it, we would be in Saigon now, in the thick of the action. As it was, the opposition would be scooping us unmercifully. It was only later that day, when we listened to the BBC World Service, that I realised just how big a scoop they were getting.

Phnom Penh was laid out by the French and had then a certain elegance and charm. We booked in to the Monorom Hotel, a simple French establishment on the main boulevard. My first act was to cable the bad news to London. Then I rang our air attaché at the Embassy, Group Captain Palmer, who asked us to dinner. There we listened to the BBC and heard just how extensive the fighting was. The Vietcong had occupied considerable areas of Saigon and its twin Chinese city, Cholon, where they had set up headquarters in the An Quang Pagoda. The airport and the nearby South Vietnamese army headquarters had come under heavy fire. President Thieu had declared martial law and imposed a twenty-four-hour curfew. In Hue, the intellectual and cultural centre of the country, the Vietcong, supported by regular North Vietnamese troops, had entered the city at the same time, 3 a.m. on the 31st, occupying nearly the whole of it and freeing 3,000 prisoners from the jails. In particular, they had established themselves in the Citadel, a massively-fortified enclave built by the French for the then Emperor in 1810 and which contained the Imperial City.

The Palmers explained that we would either have to fly to Hong Kong or Bangkok and that there was one flight a week to each place. Next morning Thursday, February 1, I made my way to the local airline office to discover there was no flight out until the following Tuesday and that was to Hong Kong. Flights to Bangkok, they said, had been cancelled. On Friday, I suddenly found out that either the information had been wrong or that the Bangkok flight had been reinstated; but as I made this discovery only half an hour before the departure time, we had no chance of getting all the equipment assembled, into a taxi and to the airport in time. There was a lot of cursing and swearing and I began to have a terrible premonition that this was going to be a disastrous trip. I went back to the airline office and checked and re-checked the timetable. There really was nothing until Tuesday's flight to Hong Kong. The Palmers took pity on us and asked us to dinner again. I could hardly bear to listen to the World Service which continued to lead with the battles for Saigon and Hue. I also had no inclination to explore the beauties of Phnom Penh. But, at the Palmers' suggestion, I decided there was no point in sitting in our hotel moping over the weekend. We could hire a taxi for a few pounds and drive north to see one of the architectural sights of the world, the ancient and ruined city of Angkor. Alan and Mike, who felt just as frustrated and unhappy as I did, readily agreed. Anything to get away from the nagging feeling that we had in some way failed.

312

On Saturday morning I hired a Peugeot taxi from the stand in front of the Monorom to take us to Angkor and back for £30. We travelled through a radiant countryside consisting of endless rice paddies, kingfisher-green in the sunlight, intersected by abundant rivers. Abundance might have been the motto of Cambodia then. The people seemed happy, the villages clean and prosperous, the oxen pulling the peasants' carts sleek and well-fed. I realised that this is what Vietnam must have looked like before the war had come to tear up the paddy fields, shatter the trees and raze the villages: a green and pleasant land, full of smiling people. Like their neighbours, the Thais, the Cambodians are famous for their smile of welcome.

The last part of the journey took us parallel to the northern shore of the Tonle Sap, the great lake that fills the centre of Cambodia like a huge fishpond. The nearest town to Angkor is Siem Reap, at the top of the lake, and the ruined city lies a few miles to the north, on the edge of the jungle.

That evening there was to be a performance by the Royal Ballet in the open-air in front of the main temple, Angkor Wat. The approach was extremely impressive, consisting of a magnificent long causeway decorated with carved stone dragons. On either side there was a shallow moat and at the far end, rising in three-towered, floodlit splendour, the huge shape of Angkor Wat. In front of the temple, a wooden stage had been erected and rows of wooden seats set out.

The reedy tones of a Cambodian orchestra floated upwards as the bats, hunting for insects, swooped over our heads. A troupe of dancers, led by a gorgeous creature in jewelled headdress and golden robes, appeared on the stage. One of the daughters of Prince Sihanouk, the God-King who had cleverly transformed himself into Prime Minister, was the principal dancer of the Royal Ballet and this may have been her. Cambodian dancing is slow and subtle, with delicate and highly erotic movements of the hands, in which the long-nailed fingers curl right back with what to a Western eye seems an impossible suppleness. The feet are bare, highly arched and the toes also turn back. There is little body movement and the whole effect is one of a stylised courtly routine. Although we had no idea of what the hand movements meant, we were all bewitched by the beauty of the dancers whose dark eyes and sinuous beauty we were to see next day reproduced in the sandstone carvings of the temple.

We visited Angkor Wat first, climbing up the great staircase that leads to the topmost tower and the holiest shrine, in which a large Buddha held court, staring out impassively over the smiling countryside. Above his head hundreds of bats clustered, squeaking in protest at the sound of our voices and threatening to descend like a dark cloud on our heads. Angkor Wat was built in the twelfth century when the Khmer Empire was at its height, but the city was abandoned in the fifteenth and remained lost in the jungle until the nineteenth century, when a Frenchman called Groslier re-discovered it. The Grosliers, father and son, spent most of their lives exploring and restoring the ruins, which cover a huge area. Apart from Angkor Wat we had time to see only the two other main temples of Angkor Thom and Bayon. Angkor Thom had the finest approach of all, a paved road with a balustrade on either side, surmounted by superb stone carvings of elephants, tigers, gods and devils. Alas for Cambodia, the Vietnam war was to engulf it shortly afterwards and Angkor was lost to the world for the second time. Although I did manage to pay a brief visit there twelve years later, it was deserted, falling fast into decay and some of the finest carvings had been looted. The dancers were long gone.

On Tuesday we caught the plane to Hong Kong, booked in at the Hilton and I started to ring round my friends. How did one get to Saigon? There was only one way, they said. Ring up the American Consulate tomorrow and get your name on the Press list. They'll tell you to fly to Bangkok, contact the Americans there and book yourself on to a military C130.

I did as suggested and was told that the American Air Force would be happy to take us to Saigon on Friday, the Vietcong and the military situation permitting. Then a strange thing happened. The phone in my hotel room rang and a familiar voice came on the line: Don McCullin, a photographer for the *Sunday Times.*

'I need your help,' he said. 'How do I get to Saigon?' I told him what I had just done but then suggested he should ring Richard Hughes, who after all was the *Sunday Times* correspondent in Hong Kong.

'I've tried,' Don said. 'But he won't talk to me. He's one of those journalists who don't talk to photographers.'

I said I was sure Don was making a mistake. Richard was a splendid friend and colleague. Perhaps he was not well. 'Anyway,' I added, 'Ring the American Consulate and they'll fix you up.'

We all caught the same plane to Bangkok on the Thursday and were on the same C130 to Saigon on Friday. We landed at the familiar airport more steeply than usual and were accompanied by the crackle of gunfire across the tarmac. I noticed the marks of mortar or rocket fire on the terminal building, and a few burnt-out helicopters lay off to one side. Inside, the place was like an armed camp, with Vietnamese soldiers everywhere in apparent confusion. Somehow we managed to hitch a lift and piled our thirteen pieces of equipment into the back of an American truck. 'The Caravelle Hotel,' I told the driver. I hoped they still had our bookings. We were only nine days late.

Next day, February 10, eleven days after the Vietcong attack on Saigon, there was still sporadic fighting in various parts of the capital. I decided to drive to the west of the city, to Phu To racecourse, which a Vietcong battalion had occupied until the previous day when American troops were flown to recapture it. By the time we got there the fighting was over and the Americans, who until then had been kept out of the city for political reasons, were busy digging themselves in. Whole areas of Saigon had been flattened in the fighting, some by the South Vietnamese Air Force, and in many of the poorer parts of the city pockets of Vietcong were still holding out. Just how dangerous it had been at the beginning of the fighting was borne in on me by the story of four journalists. They were in a jeep touring the city on the look-out for action when they heard shooting and moved towards it. Vietnamese running away from the battle warned them the Vietcong were up ahead, but like any enterprising journalist they drove on, finally running into a Vietcong road block. One of them was killed outright, the others ordered out of the jeep and shot by the side of the road. In the chaos of battle the Vietcong had presumably taken them for American servicemen although none of them was carrying arms.

Next day I decided we should take a look at Cholon, the Chinese quarter. On the way we stopped the car in a fairly quiet street so that I could record my commentary for the previous day's story. We had just finished when there was a burst of gunfire a few streets away. Then another burst. 'Let's go and have a look,' I said. Alan swung the camera on his shoulder, Mike got his amplifier round his neck and his rifle mike, like a long-barrelled pistol, in his hand, and, telling the driver to wait, we set off on foot towards the sound of the firing.

Leaving behind the big French colonial houses on the main street, we plunged into a kind of shanty town of small, wooden, tin-roofed shacks, crammed together in dense squares intersected by the geometrical pattern of narrow streets. Suddenly we came on a South Vietnamese at a crossroads, an automatic rifle at his shoulder, firing short bursts into the huddle of houses opposite. The sharp staccato of the gunfire bounced back noisily off the tin shacks.

I asked a Vietnamese photographer what was going on. 'VC in there.' He pointed among the houses. We now came to another wider street, running parallel to the one in which we had left the car. Here there was more activity and a few American soldiers as well. I repeated my question. One of the Americans said, 'there's a bunch of VC in there. We're going to get 'em out. We're jes' waiting for some more firepower.'

A few minutes later a jeep roared up with four hefty Americans in it and a contraption at the back which looked like a rocket tube. It was a recoil-less rifle. A very big GI, in T-shirt and flak jacket, was in charge. He made the jeep turn and back until he had it in the right position and then loosed off a couple of rounds. They made a tremendous bang and, although we could not see, I imagine the damage must have been equally impressive. They moved the jeep a few yards and let go another salvo. More American troops arrived and were ordered into the maze of shacks. They were going to try and winkle out the Vietcong one by one. They had only gone a few yards when the Vietnamese started pointing and shouting. Smoke was rising above the houses. Within a few minutes a fire was roaring through the matchwood houses, flames leaping high in the air. We moved forward to film. Someone said the Vietcong had started the fire in order to escape in the resulting confusion, but it seemed to me it might just as easily have been started by the recoil-less rifle. When the fire had gutted almost the entire block of shanty houses, there was a commotion about a hundred yards away. We sprinted down the road to find South Vietnamese soldiers herding three Vietcong suspects at bayonet point, blindfolded and their hands tied tightly behind their backs. A bare-headed South Vietnamese police officer, wearing a flak jacket and with a pistol at his belt, appeared to be in charge. This was General Loan, the Saigon Chief of Police, who had come down personally to supervise operations. A few minutes later, General Loan and the prisoners moved off and we heard later that he had shot one prisoner in the head with his pistol in the middle of the street. NBC News filmed it. A couple of still photographers also got pictures. We cannot have been more than a couple of hundred yards away but we saw nothing. The NBC film made an enormous impact and did the South Vietnamese – and the Americans – great harm, making them look like brutal executioners. Nobody bothered to ask how many civilians had died in that shanty town because of the Vietcong action. The fire was finally brought under control and we drove back to our hotel. It was quite clear that the capital of South Vietnam was still heavily infiltrated. In fact the fighting lasted until the end of the month.

Our first story appeared on 'News at Ten' the following day, Monday, and the second one, the battle in the shanty town, on Tuesday. For our third story, we took the desperate plight of thousands of homeless in Saigon. One area, called the Jasmine quarter, was particularly bad. It had been heavily damaged by South Vietnamese efforts to dislodge the Vietcong, and now the refugees were living almost in the open air: in lean-tos made of packing cases, in huge drainage pipes lying about on waste ground, in the backs of lorries, anywhere they could lay their heads. The Government, overwhelmed by the disaster that had struck so unexpectedly, was able to do little or nothing. But, with their amazing resilience, the Vietnamese were somehow surviving, suspending their hammocks amid the ruins of their homes and retrieving their few miserable possessions from the rubble.

But, if Saigon was slowly being brought under control, the situation at Hue, in the north, was much more serious. A number of North Vietnamese troops, supported by local Vietcong, were still in possession of the Citadel, resisting every effort to dislodge them.

We flew to Da Nang on Thursday, the 15th, the day our third report appeared in London. It was a long tedious flight in a C130. In Da Nang, unlike the south, the weather was cold and rainy. Next day, we hitched a ride on a Marine lorry that was going to Hue, sixty miles up the coast. It was a miserable day and it did not make us any more cheerful when the Marines told us that previous convoys had come under rocket and mortar fire.

The road was crowded with big American lorries carrying ammunition and stores to Hue, but there was no mortaring. As the trucks splashed through the villages, Vietnamese children lined the roadside and waved at us. A young 'grunt' in our truck threw packets of sweets at the children as we swept past. Cheering shrilly, the children fought one another in the mud for the shiny packets.

But there was no waving in Hue, which was three-quarters destroyed, and half-empty. The main bridge across the Perfume River, linking the two parts of the city, lay brokenly in the water, affording a shaky crossing point for refugees. The air was loud with the noise of battle and smoke hung in a pall across the city.

We had arrived at a critical moment. The Americans were about to make a major attempt to recapture the Citadel. A Marine battalion was boarding a couple of barges, intending

318

to sail up the Perfume River and launch their assault from the rear. A French television team and ourselves joined the first barge, which was also carrying a large quantity of ammunition. The French reporter was a woman. It was the first time I had ever seen a woman television war correspondent; she was very professional and I concluded she had probably seen more action than I had. The Marines and ourselves were all wearing steel helmets and flak jackets. As soon as we set off up river a terrific din broke out.

The Americans appeared to open up with every weapon they possessed, blasting away at the Citadel side of the river. There was so much noise aboard the barge that we could not make out whether we were being shot at too. We presumed we were and tried to make ourselves as small as possible, although Alan kept filming throughout. Half an hour or so later we landed in comparative calm at the rear of the Citadel and watched the Americans form up. At the local Command Post, a major explained the plan. There would be a battalion-size assault by the Marines. Bravo Company would go first. We asked if we could accompany Bravo Company and permission was granted. Nobody seemed to care if we went along or not. We were not particularly welcome but nor were we made to feel specially unwelcome. You can tag along, but don't expect any special treatment, they seemed to imply. Everyone was tensed up before going into action.

Bravo Company, under the command of a negro major, 'moved out' at around two. We picked our way forward through the rubble-strewn streets. Most of the houses were badly damaged and looked empty. It did not take long for me to realise that we were extremely ill-equipped for our task. In order to film, the camera had to be connected up with its power unit. This was a large battery in a metal case with a shoulder strap, weighing at a guess twenty pounds. To carry both needed considerable strength and to try to duck and run with them from one vantage point to another, as the Marines were doing, was downright impossible. Since I was carrying nothing except pen and paper, I volunteered to carry the battery. It was not designed for combat, as I quickly discovered, and it kept slipping off my shoulder. We came on one dead body, a Vietnamese, lying at the side of the road, and stopped to film, plugging the power in and then unplugging to move forward again. We crossed a wide deserted street and caught up with the rear of Bravo Company. As we picked our way through a house with only the walls standing, a group of Vietnamese suddenly appeared and advanced towards us silently, plainly terrified and with their hands in the air. The American gunny sergeant (warrant office), the senior NCO in Bravo Company, waved them past and said a few kind words. The old man leading the small group managed a silent toothless smile in which gratitude only just triumphed over terror.

We moved on slowly, the Marines in front having to probe each building and assess the risk of moving into the open to cross a street. There were Communist snipers in the tangle of ruins ahead. We could hear frequent bursts of gunfire. It was amazing how quickly you got used to it and took it for granted. At one point we came on a little group huddled round a wounded Marine. He was groaning in pain, the blood soaking through the field dressing. A bespectacled 'corpsman' was bending over him, administering a pain killer. The gunny sergeant pulled a face. 'That's the third man that bastard's got in the last hour.' The sniper had a field of fire over a road that the advancing Marines had to cross.

'We'll have to get that sonofabitch before we lose anyone else,' the gunny said. He gave order and half a dozen Marines fanned out to try and get behind the sniper. Ten minutes later there was the sound of grenades exploding and word came back that the 'gook' sniper had been 'taken care of'.

The gunny was certainly a veteran of the Korean War and possibly of the Second World War as well. He seemed to be the only man in Bravo Company with any real experience of house-to-house fighting and the only man with any force of personality. He was the best kind of NCO, tough, resourceful, popular with his men. At one stop he shook his head confidingly. 'These boys ain't been taught street fighting,' he said. 'They got plenty of guts but they're green as hell. It's a goddamn shame.' There was no doubting the

320

Marines' courage. But they were all young conscripts, aged about twenty, with little or no experience of combat. They were learning the hard way. In the days that followed, Bravo Company lost about half its fighting strength, most of them wounded by snipers.

The North Vietnamese regulars, the shadowy enemy we hardly ever saw, were skilful and determined opponents. They retreated slowly, making the Marines fight for every yard. By late afternoon, we had only advanced 200 to 300 yards. It was beginning to get dark and the gunny said we had better spend the night in the Company CP. This turned out to be one of the less-damaged houses in the Citadel. It must have belonged to a fairly well-to-do family, since it was large and solidly built. But the war had swept the inside bare, like a tide scouring the beach. Pressure lamps were lit and in the kitchen the Marines started brewing up tea. We had two badly wounded men in the house, one white, one black. The black major tried to comfort them. 'Cheer up,' he said to the black Marine. 'You know you're a lucky bastard. Yessir. You're going back to the United States tomorrow. To the U S of A. No more war for you. You're a lucky Marine. Yessir.' The wounded man lay on his makeshift bed, groaning and sweating with pain. He barely acknowledged the major's words. He probably did not hear them, too busy with his own private torment to care.

The major's own morale, despite his show of encouragement, seemed to be low. The company had had a number of casualties that afternoon and there was the prospect of a lot more house-to-house fighting. Everyone was conscious of the two wounded men, one of whom, the white Marine, looked as if he might die. Into this gloomy atmosphere suddenly stepped a small, waif-like figure, hair cropped like a boy's, neatly turned out in combat fatigues and with a couple of cameras round her neck. This was Cathy Leroy, a French war photographer who had already made a name for herself in Vietnam. There was no assignment too dangerous, no battle too fierce for Cathy. And she was a brilliant photographer. The American GIs were said to have cheered when she arrived on Hill 881 where a particularly bloody battle was in progress. That night in Hue, she appeared as a ministering angel. The Marine major had heard of her and said he was proud to have her 'aboard'. The Marines always speak as if they are at sea. The morale of the young 'grunts' perked up when they saw they had a woman in their midst. Cathy radiated confidence and self-sufficiency. She opened her little side-pack in which she carried spare film and cigarettes, and produced some hoarded 'C' rations. Marching into the kitchen she quickly boiled some water and made two cups of cocoa, its aroma filling the dank 'hooch'. One she gave to the major who brightened visibly. Then she went over to the wounded and comforted them in small ways. By the end of the evening she had raised the morale of that CP by at least one hundred percent. It was an impressive performance, all the more so because it was done so unassumingly.

We had supper – 'C' rations and tea – and afterwards, since there was not much else to do, I decided to go to bed. 'Bed' was the top of a table in a small room off the main part of the house. I made myself as comfortable as I could with a haversack for a pillow and, being very tired, soon fell asleep. I was woken two or three hours later by the most tremendous banging and thumping. It sounded as if an artillery barrage was being loosed off right next door. Or was an artillery barrage coming our way? I could not tell but thought it wiser to get off the top of the table and take refuge underneath. Alan and Mike were also awake and most of the Marines as well. Every ten or twenty seconds there would be a terrific thump from close at hand and a Marine would say 'outgoing' or, less frequently 'incoming'. That was more serious because it meant that someone was shooting at us. I listened carefully, trying to distinguish between 'incoming' and 'outgoing'. I decided that 'outgoing' made a crisper sound, a bang, whereas 'incoming' made a duller noise, a thump. Sometimes the bangs would be all strung together, only a few seconds apart, and I imagined this was a salvo of mortar 'outgoing' from a Marine fire team nearby. In between the thumps and bangs loud music suddenly started next door. I could hardly believe my ears. It was the Beatles singing 'Love, love, love . . . all you need is love'. Every ten seconds or so it would be obliterated by a bang and then it would start triumphantly up again. We looked at one another in the half-dark in amazement and then burst out laughing. I have never been able to hear the song since without being vividly reminded of that night in the Citadel at Hue.

Morning when it came, was more peaceful, in fact eerily quiet. The Marines drank tea and ate C rations and then under the authoritative eye of the gunny sergeant, made ready to move out. We left the 'hooch' in a single line and walked through the ruined houses for about fifty yards until we came to a street running from left to right. In the middle of the street was a dead body. After a brief discussion whether there was a sniper ahead, the Marines began to cross, singly, running across the exposed width of the street to take cover on the far side. One Marine, carrying a length of wire, edged forward to inspect the body.

'Don't move it,' the gunny barked. 'It may be booby-trapped. Jes attach the wire and get back here.'

The Marine came running back and they began to haul on the wire, dragging the body across the dusty street like a piece of wood. When it was close, I could see the red tabs on the tunic, which meant North Vietnamese regular army. As we were filming the scene, another group of Marines arrived and with them a photographer. It was Don McCullin. Like Cathy he carried only a couple of cameras round his neck and a small haversack. He was in American combat fatigues and, like us, looked unshaven. We greeted each other briefly and then the gunny shouted: 'Okay, you guys, move it out. Right, move . . . move . . . move . . . ' Like a despatcher on a parachute drop, he sent them running across the empty road one at a time, just in case there was a sniper. It would be our turn in a minute. Alan stopped filming and turned to me: 'We're just about out of film and power. There's no point in going on.'

I was taken aback. It never occurred to me that we would have run out so quickly. Alan pointed to the rucksack with our film. 'We've shot a hell of a lot,' he said. 'We're at the end of the last roll now. There's maybe twenty feet left.'

'Keep it,' I said, 'just in case.'

'The battery's flat in any case,' Mike said, 'even if we had more film.'

'I'm sorry,' I said to the gunny. 'We're out of film and power, we'll have to go back.'

'No sweat,' he said. 'Good luck.'

We watched them disappear among the houses opposite, moving forward carefully, Cathy and Don with them. I felt a stab of envy that they could carry all they needed so easily, a couple of cameras and a small bag of film. The Americans would give them C rations and cigarettes and they would sleep in their clothes. I looked at our equipment: the heavy, cumbersome television camera, the equally heavy and now useless battery, Mike's unwieldy recording equipment, our big rucksack of film, spare leads, camera tape and all the other odds and ends.

'Fuck it,' I said. 'Let's get to hell out of here.'

We trudged back through the ruins, retracing our steps of yesterday and passing only a few Marines bringing up supplies and ammunition. We could hear the sounds of battle behind us, but paid no more attention than if they had been traffic noises. It took us less than an hour to cover the same distance which had taken us four hours the day before. As we neared the river we came on a cart loaded with American wounded. They were all Marines, their young faces racked with pain and exhaustion. A medical 'corpsman' was doing what he could for them and a chaplain walked behind the cart, praying. It was a classic vignette of the Vietnam war.

'We must get a shot of that,' I said to Alan.

'I know, Sandy,' he said, the exasperation breaking through his voice. 'I'll try, but we have no power left and bloody little film.' He put the camera on his shoulder. 'I'll have to handcrank it,' he said, meaning that he would try to turn the roll of film inside the camera manually. He handcranked until we ran out of film, but the picture never materialised.

So it was in a sombre mood, because of the carnage as well as our own frustrations, that we set off back to Da Nang. I was very conscious of the advantages that still photographers

324

like Cathy and Don had over a television crew like ourselves. That was in the nature of the beast. But what made me deeply angry was the fact that so little thought had gone into refining our equipment and making it at least half-way portable under combat conditions. (I was still so angry when I got back to ITN weeks later that I gate-crashed the Editor's morning meeting, carrying the unwieldy battery with me. 'This,' I said, holding it up for all to see, 'is the battery I had to carry in Hue when they were shooting at us. As you can see, I can hardly lift it with one hand, let alone run with the damn thing. It's time that something was done about lighter equipment.')

We got back to Da Nang late that afternoon and sent off our film to Saigon aboard a C130. Then we had to make a difficult decision. Should we go back next day to Hue and carry on where we had left off? Or should we divert our attention to another story that was now very much in the headlines: the siege of Khe Sanh? Since we had been in Hue the situation had become critical and the base was almost completely cut off. The North Vietnamese mortar and rocket teams were so close they were able to shell the airstrip with pinpoint accuracy. The Americans had lost so many fixed-wing aircraft that only helicopters were now being used to ferry in much-needed reinforcements and supplies. In trying to make the right decision I calculated that the battle in Hue would last for several more days and I argued that, if we made a two-day trip to Khe Sanh, we could be back in Hue in time for the final act there. The others agreed and we decided to leave next morning.

North of Da Nang, running east and west, just below the Demilitarised Zone, the Americans had built a string of 'fire bases' to try and stop the infiltration of North Vietnamese troops. Khe Sanh, the most westerly, was supposed to block off the approach routes from Laos. On our way west we stopped at one fire base, perched on top of a high stony outcrop, called Rockpile. From the top of Rockpile the Americans could monitor a vast area while being immune from attack themselves. Or so we thought. We were standing out in the open on top of the rock, talking to Colonel Dick, the American officer in charge, when we heard a 'whoosh' and a loud bang very close, followed by five or six more in rapid succession.

For a moment we all stood there as if petrified and then the colonel shouted, 'Quick, take cover', and led the way at full pelt towards his underground CP. Another hail of rockets came over as we ran the fifty yards or so to the entrance and hurled ourselves inside.

'Those sonsabitches seem to have our range all worked out,' the colonel grinned.

'What were they?' I gasped.

'Chinese 122 millimetre rockets,' the colonel said. 'Range about five miles and not always as accurate as that.'

Mike Williams let out a cry. 'The sound recorder's outside. If we lose that we'll have to pack up and go home.'

'Christ!' I said. 'Where did you leave it?'

'On the ground, just where we were standing.'

I moved to leave the bunker. 'Wait a minute,' the colonel said. 'I'll get it. You stay right there.' He ran crouching through the doorway and out of sight. We waited, holding our breath, in case there was another round of 122s. But he was back again within a minute, triumphantly clutching the recorder, which was undamaged. Without it, we would have been incapable of shooting sound and it would have taken at least a week to have another sent out from London.

We flew on to Camp Carroll from where we hoped to hitch a ride on a helicopter to Khe Sanh. We reported to movement control and were told that bad weather had delayed several flights. There was a big backlog of Marine reinforcements waiting to go in and we would have to take our turn. Perhaps we would be able to get a flight that evening.

We squatted down beside the runway, near a group of about a hundred Marines, wearing full battle kit, who were also waiting for a helicopter. Away to the west, the jungle-covered hills rose in a series of ridges, one after another, like waves. Somewhere over there, in the mist, was Khe Sanh. The cloud lifted for a while and then came down again. Two big Chinooks, the latest thing in helicopters, lifted off full of Marines but were back again an hour later. They had been unable to land because of the cloud. We managed to obtain three beers and ate some C rations. Then we sat down to wait again. Everyone was tense, including the Marines in their battle kit. At three I began to wonder if we had made the right decision. Then we were told that two Chinooks would be going out at four for Khe Sanh and we would be able to get on board. We cheered up, delighted at the prospect of action at last. At 4.30 the Marines struggled into their packs and picked up their M16 Armalite rifles with the perforated black stock. We followed them towards the Chinooks and walked up the tail ramp. Inside, the Marines stood jammed together, holding on to tapes suspended from the roof, like commuters in a rush-hour tube train. We squeezed in beside them. No one said very much or looked at anyone else. The jet engines came to life with a high-pitched whine and the big twin rotors started to swish round above our heads. I tried to smile, pretending I was pleased we would soon be airborne for Khe Sanh. A despatcher came aboard, counting. Finally he stopped beside us.

'You guys,' he said. 'Where ya' from?'

'British television,' I said. (It was no good saying ITN, they had never heard of it.)

'Sorry about that,' he said. 'We'll have to ask you to step aside.'

'But we've been waiting all day for a flight,' I complained, reaching for my MACV Press card.

He waved it away. 'I know,' he said. 'But we need to put some more men aboard and reinforcements have to take priority.'

I knew we could not argue with that. Khe Sanh was expecting a major North Vietnamese attack at any moment and was desperate for reinforcements. Even the Press had to give way.

We walked down the tailboard and three more heavily-loaded Marines climbed aboard. I felt a twinge of relief that we did not have to run the rocket gauntlet at Khe Sanh, where on landing everyone had to jump out and run for cover while the crew threw the supplies out on to the runway. The helicopters never stopped moving and, as soon as the last man and the last box of ammunition were out, they took off again as fast as possible. Even so, they kept getting hit.

We stayed the night at Camp Carroll, hoping the weather would improve. But next morning the mist was still hanging heavily over those forbidding dark green hills and, as the Americans say, we decided to abort the mission. There was nothing for it but to fly back to Da Nang and head towards Hue. There, things were moving more quickly than I had anticipated and the Marines were on the point of capturing the Citadel. As we crossed the Perfume River for the second time, I tried to imagine what it must have been like in peacetime. The banks were lined with willow trees beneath which the young lovers of Hue would have strolled and perhaps gone boating on the placid waters. Now the only fragrance was the stink of decomposing corpses. We made our way through the shattered houses near the Citadel and finally penetrated to the Imperial City, a miniature copy of the Forbidden City in Peking. The Americans had tried to avoid direct damage and had largely succeeded. The main building, a huge open-sided audience room with the elaborately carved thrones of the Emperor and Empress at one end, was more or less unharmed, although one or two of the magnificent ornamental blue vases on the terrace in front had been smashed.

Hue fell to the Americans and the South Vietnamese on February 24, but the last North Vietnamese and Vietcong troops had managed to withdraw from the Citadel and slip away before that. Shortly afterwards mass graves were found on the outskirts containing more than a thousand bodies, many of them senior officials and known anti-communists: most of them had been shot with their hands still tied behind their backs. They had been rounded up from a 'death list' when the Communists entered Hue and marched to their deaths.

About half of the city had been destroyed. The battle to retake it had lasted three weeks and caused an enormous number of casualties. Of the population of about 150,000 at least half had fled. As we left, the refugees were still crossing the big bridge over the Perfume River, edging their way over the broken spans, pathetically clutching a few possessions, their faces still frozen in impassivity with the shock of the catastrophe. That was the last picture in our final report from Hue, and the last image I have of that tortured city.

The battle for Hue had caused so much dislocation even of the highly efficient American transport system that we had difficulty getting out. We had to spend the night at a helicopter pad, on the southern outskirts. There were no beds but we dossed down on a huge rubber petrol storage tank. It was like sleeping on a trampoline. Next morning, we hitched a lift aboard a helicopter to Da Nang. They told us that Walter Cronkite, the famous CBS newscaster, who was on a reporting mission to Vietnam, had also been in Hue. He not only came in his own helicopter, he had two back-up helicopters with him as well and an escort of generals. In Saigon he stayed with the American Ambassador but conducted a series of interviews with leading Vietnamese politicians on the roof of the Caravelle Hotel. We would see them being wheeled in front of the camera every morning as we were having our breakfast.

Cronkite was one of America's most influential journalists and the Ambassador, Elsworth Bunker, and the generals must have done everything they could to impress him favourably. At the time, General Westmoreland, the Supreme Commander in Vietnam, was preaching that the Tet offensive had really been a defeat for the Vietcong and had bled them dry. All he needed to clinch the victory was another 200,000 American troops. With half a million already there and opposition to the war mounting at home, even President Johnson balked. When Cronkite returned to New York, he summed up his assignment in Vietnam by saying that, from the American point of view, the war did not seem to be winnable. This caused a furore, not least in the White House. President Johnson is reported to have said that, if Walter Cronkite did not believe America could win the war, the Government would never persuade the American people otherwise. Certainly Tet was a watershed. In the Delta, away from the heat of the action, I heard American officers express doubt for the first time that victory was possible. If Tet could

329

take place despite the presence of half a million American troops and a million South Vietnamese, plus all the equipment and the firepower the Americans had lavished on the South, something must be seriously wrong, they said. Official predictions were too optimistic, the South Vietnamese were just not capable of shouldering their share of the war. Like Cronkite, they now believed the war could not be won.

About a week after leaving Hue, we arranged to fly on a C130 supply drop over Khe Sanh, which was still under siege although the threat of an all-out attack had apparently receded. The only other journalist in the party was Clare Hollingworth of the *Daily Telegraph*, a remarkable lady past the first flush of youth, but as spry and tough as they came. She had first heard the bullets go zinging over her head as a young reporter in the Western Desert. One night, she told me, out with an army patrol, they had camped in a hollow between the dunes. Next morning, they heard voices and the sound of activity very close by. Peering over the top of a dune they observed a large party of Germans who had also camped out overnight. Being heavily outnumbered the British hoped the Germans would depart without discovering them. They did, although Clare remembers lying in the sand too frightened to move and hardly daring to breathe.

While we waited for our C130 to load up at Da Nang, we talked about the hazards of our job. Clare, fixing me with one piercing blue eye while the other hid behind a drooping lid, announced: 'I never worry about it. It's always the other fellow who gets shot.'

I objected that this was not very logical.

'You have to believe that,' she said firmly, 'otherwise it's no good. It's always the other chap who gets it.'

I looked over to where Alan Downes was sitting, his camera by his side, happily smoking a cigarette. As my eye ran idly over the cargo they would be loading shortly, I noticed with horror that he was actually sitting on a petrol drum.

'Hey,' I shouted, 'you're sitting on top of a load of petrol. For God's sake put out that cigarette.'

330

The weather over Khe Sanh was still overcast as we came in low, making a wide circle over the jungle. The rear door of the C130 started to open wide, like a whale's mouth, and the wind whipped at our clothes. Alan, always athletic, had clumbed up in the fuselage above the open door so that he could film from above as the despatcher made the drop.

We levelled out for the dropping run and I wondered if the North Vietnamese were shooting at us. I presumed they were since they shot at everything over Khe Sanh. But the noise from the engines and the rush of the wind made it impossible to tell.

The dropping light in the hold started to flash. Each load of supplies was strapped to a pallet which ran down a twin line of rollers in the floor of the hold. As it went over the edge into the void, a parachute blossomed and the load floated away rapidly towards the ground. The Air Force sergeant jerked his release lever and the crates of petrol, ammunition and C rations slid down the rollers and toppled over the tailgate into thin air. Between the parachutes we could see the huddle of huts and bunkers that was Khe Sanh and the runway, scarred with shell craters. The wrecks of several American aircraft lay beside it, reminders of the North Vietnamese gunners' accuracy.

The last load went out with a rumble, the door whined shut and we turned for home. From the air it was hard to see why Khe Sanh was so important.

A few days later I was asked to have lunch with President Thieu. This was in place of the interview I had asked for and which he declined to give. There were about eight of us, all journalists, and I was the only non-American. Flora Lewis, then of *Newsday*, with the fierce blue feline eyes, sat on the President's right, the rest of us were seated in a circle round him. The President's English was better than I expected and he was particularly outspoken about Khe Sanh. 'The Americans are making a big mistake,' he assured us. 'The same mistake as the French made at Dien Bien Phu. As you know, they let themselves be surrounded and destroyed. Why does General Westmoreland make the same mistake? I have told him this. You should retain mobility, I told him. Not allow yourself to get boxed in like that. It's a big mistake.' He looked round the table, his dark eyes bright with conviction. I thought his argument convincing. The French had built Dien Bien Phu for the same reason: to bar infiltration from Laos. Dien Bien Phu is in the north and Khe Sanh in the south, but both are near the Laos border, in hilly jungle, and both turned out to be inviting targets for the North Vietnamese artillery. The difference in the two sieges was air power. Bad weather, in both, delayed reinforcements and the limited striking power of the French Air Force led to the surrender at Dien Bien Phu, one of France's greatest defeats. But, despite, bad weather, the American Air Force was able to keep pounding the North Vietnamese besiegers of Khe Sanh. The B52s flew above the weather, dropping their tons of high explosive round the clock. In the end the North Vietnamese decided the cost of trying to turn Khe Sanh into another Dien Bien Phu was too heavy. But they gave the Americans a nasty fright. That day, with the worst of Tet over and no doubt believing his own and the American propaganda that the Communists had suffered a major defeat, President Thieu was in an optimistic mood. He was confident that the South Vietnamese army, about which one kept hearing discouraging reports, would eventually be able to hold its own against the North Vietnamese. I do not think that anyone around the table really believed him. They had all seen too much of the ineffiency and corruption that permeated South Vietnamese society in general and the government and the army in particular to believe that the South could ever stand up to the almost fanatical determination of the North Vietnamese. But I do not imagine anyone there could have foreseen just how totally, once the Americans had gone, President Thieu's ramshackle régime would collapse, seven years later, in the spring of 1975.

There was one comical postscript to that Vietnam assignment. In the excitement of the battles in the north, I had forgotten to cable for more money and I was almost broke. So I sent a telegram to ITN asking urgently for £300 to pay my hotel bill. Unfortunately, although I was not aware of it at the time, the Saigon Post Office added an unintentional nought to the cabled figure, which arrived in London reading £3000. This produced a nasty shock at ITN and an urgent reply from the Editor, Nigel Ryan, which said: 'Your request for more funds. You supposed to be reporting Vietnam not buying it . . . '

CHAPTER XI

Black September and King Hussein's Old Harrovian Slang

During the late Sixties, I made several visits to Jordan where the uneasy alliance between King Hussein and the Palestinian guerrillas was deteriorating into barely-veiled hostility. Jordan, which has a long common border with Israel, had always taken the brunt of the Palestine refugee problem. After each war – in 1948, 1956 and above all in 1967 – thousands of refugees poured across the border, first to the West Bank, and then later into Jordan itself. After the Six-Day War in 1967, refugee camps mushroomed all over the country. Many, like Beka'a, which housed around 40,000 people, were set down on the open plain miles from the nearest town. I first visited Beka'a in the winter of 1970 and it was a miserable place. The lucky ones were living in corrugated iron lean-tos supplied by UNRRA (The United Nations Relief and Rehabilitation Agency), the unlucky ones were still in tents. The ground between them was a sea of mud and we squelched our way from tent to tent and hut to hut. Remarkably, few of the refugees complained to us. Perhaps they were past complaining. Relief workers were much more vocal. They were alarmed at the number of babies that were dying because of the cold and inadequate facilities. But what was almost equally disturbing was the alienation that the conditions were breeding. The hundreds of young Palestinians in Beka'a and other camps were natural recruits to the guerrilla groups that were springing up almost daily. I was given the names of fifteen different organisations on one visit. In Beka'a most of the refugee boys were in El Fatah's 'Lion Cubs'. We watched them, tough little customers of ten or twelve, learning how to throw a grenade and fire an automatic rifle. They were also being indoctrinated in the legends of Palestinian oppression and loss of the homeland and it was only too obvious that here were being moulded the terrorists of the future. Naturally the Jews were enemy number one, but the Americans and by association the British were not far behind. Nobody pointed out to them that virtually all the money which poured into Jordan to keep the refugees' bodies and souls together came via the United Nations from the West, mainly from America but with Britain paying her share.

Up in the hills above Beka'a one day I watched young Palestinians of about twenty training with live ammunition. Their camp was set in wonderful country, thick groves of fir trees, green as a linnet's wing against the brilliant blue of the sky. We watched the guerrillas, dressed in full battle kit, being put over an assault course. At one point, they had to crawl under barbed wire while instructors fired live ammunition right beside them. We could see the bullets kicking up the soil as they crawled forward. One young recruit panicked and got stuck in the wire. An instructor fired a burst too close to him and hit him. The young man cried out and lay jerking on the ground. The exercise stopped in confusion, with everyone shouting at one another. He was dragged out from beneath the wire bleeding profusely, his face ashen, and was carried off. He died shortly afterwards. I was sad and disgusted, I suppose partly because I felt we were in some way responsible – the instructor had been showing off in front of the camera. I remarked to the Palestinian guerrilla in charge that I was deeply sorry about what had happened and he replied, 'It is of no consequence. He gave his life for the Palestinian cause. They are ready for this.' I felt like saying that it had been a pointless death, due to the ineptitude of the instructors, but I thought better of it. It would not bring the young man back to life.

Throughout the summer of 1970, the influence of the Palestinian guerrilla groups grew apace. Whole areas of Amman, originally refugee quarters, had become armed camps, and Palestinian guerrillas in their black and white check kaffiyehs controlled traffic in and out. Stories about the growing power and, some said, arrogance of the guerrilla groups multiplied. Many concerned the mounting anger inside Hussein's largely Beduin army. Soldiers who lived in Palestinian areas used to go home in civilian clothes so as not to draw attention to themselves. Those who went home in uniform were disarmed and insulted. The guerrillas started coming into the Intercontinental, the main hotel used by foreigners, rattling their money-boxes under the noses of customers. They were to be seen all over town, strutting along the pavements in twos and threes, their Kalashnikovs over their shoulders. They were more in evidence than the Jordanian Army itself and the police were obviously scared to tangle with them. The British military attaché told me that, when he took his wife to the hairdressers in Amman, he was nervous of sitting waiting for her in his car in uniform. In short, the Palestinian guerrilla movement had become a state within a state. Their public statements about the King and his government grew daily more disparaging, more dictatorial, more threatening. It sounded very much as if they were challenging Hussein for the leadership of Jordan and they seemed to be winning by default. Hussein, deservedly, had a great reputation for being a survivor. He was an adroit politician, instinctive rather than logical. He had always displayed a combination of flair and luck. Now, both seemed to be deserting him. The army waited, impatiently, for a signal, but none came. Rumours flew of senior officers warning the King that, if he did not act soon against the Palestinians, they could not answer for the consequences. In

336

other words, there was a risk of an army coup against the King, something that was almost unthinkable.

The most extravagant story of all was that King Hussein had been forced to lie down in the middle of the road to stop his Army's tanks taking the law into their own hands. I did not believe the story but it certainly reflected the mood in the capital that autumn.

What I do believe is that his army commanders, convinced that it was 'them or us', finally talked the King into giving the order to attack.

The battle began on September 17 and it was a bloody one, Jordanian army tanks against Palestinian guerrilla fighters using first-class Soviet weaponry: rocket-launchers, which could knock out a tank, heavy machine-guns, Kalashnikov assault rifles and apparently unlimited ammunition. Since the guerrillas fought in and from their positions in the refugee camps, civilian casualties were high, although not as high as the Palestinians themselves made out. The figure of 40,000 which was quoted by Yasser Arafat, the PLO leader, was a huge exaggeration.

I missed the fighting in Amman, but the large international press corps already there did not see much of it either. They were kept prisoner in the Intercontinental Hotel except for one or two favoured colleagues like Geneviève Chauvel, a handsome blonde photographer who was staying at the Palace and her husband, 'Pussy', who was ferried from the town to the Palace in an armoured car. When it was all over the Intercontinental Press Corps were flown out, rather as we had been in 1967 at the end of the Six-Day War, on the pretext that their safety could not be guaranteed.

I had been on holiday when the fighting started but now ITN were desperate to send me in to replace Michael Nicholson who was being evacuated with the rest of the Press Corps. The Jordanians, however, were barring all journalists, so how were we going to get in? Nobody had any idea. On my first day back at work, I had lunch in Manzis' just off Leicester Square, with two old friends, Ed Hughes and Terry Spencer, both of whom had worked for *Time/Life* of

America. We were discussing the problem when Ed suddenly said, 'Why don't you fly to Damascus, have a look at the fighting on the border and then drive down to Amman later?'

I looked at him in disbelief. 'Syria? It's impossible to get in there, isn't it? Especially if they're fighting.'

'You never know,' Ed said. 'There's just a chance. They've been having a trade fair in Damascus and, if you play your cards right, you could walk straight in.'

I sat and considered this for a moment. 'They'd never let us in with all the camera gear,' I said finally. 'We'd have to hide it and go in as tourists, or businessmen.'

'It's certainly worth a try,' Terry said. 'All you lose is the airfare.'

'Why don't you give Syrian Airlines a ring?' Ed said. He fixed me with his bright, inquisitive, jackdaw's eye. 'They're in the book under Syrian Arab Airlines.'

I walked up the stairs to the first floor where they have the telephones, looked up the number and dialled. An Arab voice asked if she could help me.

'Yes,' I said. 'I want three seats on your next flight to Damascus. First class. Anything today?'

'We don't have a flight today,' the voice said, 'but we do have a flight tomorrow. You want three first class.' There was a pause and then she said. 'That'll be all right. What's your name please?'

I went downstairs in high spirits. 'I've booked on the flight tomorrow. No problem.'

'Great,' said Ed. 'What did I tell you?'

But, when I got back to the office, the girl on the Foreign Desk was waiting for me. 'Syrian Airlines have been on the phone asking if you're a journalist.'

'Christ,' I said. 'What did you tell them?'

'I said you were out but I would get you to ring them.'

I dialled the number. 'Oh yes, Mr. Gall,' the same voice said. 'I wanted to be sure that you are not journalists, because we have to get special permission for them.'

'No, no,' I said, lying brazenly.

'You're not journalists?' She did not seem convinced.

'No,' I said. 'Of course not. We're businessmen.'

338

'All right,' she said. 'Your seats are confirmed.'

The next thing I had to do, apart from getting the approval of the Editor, which was a formality, was to consult my crew, Chris Faulds and Mick Doyle. We decided to take a light-weight Beaulieu 16mm camera and a small tape recorder. The disadvantage of this 'double system' equipment was that we would not be able to record sound on film, but the advantage was that it was much lighter and could pass as amateur equipment. Chris and Mike were going to pack it in their suitcases so that we would at least look like businessmen or tourists. We did not need visas in advance. We would get them on arrival.

The flight left next afternoon and went by way of East Berlin, arriving in Damascus after midnight. We were a trifle nervous as we got off the plane and walked towards immigration and customs. There were a few other Westerners on the flight, but not many.

As we shuffled into the arrival hall, I caught sight of a poster advertising the Damascus Trade Fair. My heart sank. It had ended the day before. I felt like a secret agent who has just had his cover blown. Nervously I handed my passport to the man behind the desk. With hardly a glance he flipped it open, stamped it and handed it back. Chris and Mick got the same treatment. But we still had customs to overcome. If they searched our bags and found the camera equipment and tape recorder and suspected we were a television team they would put us on the next flight out. But the customs man was even more obliging. He did not want to inspect anything. He made his chalk mark with a flourish and a smile.

'Have a good stay,' he called and waved us through.

We could hardly believe our ears. After that it was a simple matter to hail a taxi and drive to the hotel. It had been built by the French and had seen better days, but was perfectly comfortable.

Next morning I took a taxi to the Foreign Ministry, but luckily, it being a public holiday, they were closed.

'Let's drive to the border,' Chris and Mick said. 'To hell with the Foreign Ministry. They'll only tell us we can't go there.'

'I agree,' I said. 'We've tried anyway.' The taxi driver was a white-haired man of about sixty-five who spoke some French.

'We want to go to Dera'a,' I said. 'How long will it take?'

'Two hours, approximately.'

It was ten o'clock. We should be there round noon.

We cut through the Damascus traffic and drove almost due south across a flat agricultural plain that gave way to stonier, hillier country – the edge of the great Syrian Desert. The road was good, the traffic light, and we reached Dera'a, a small, dusty market town about two miles from the Jordanian border, before noon. (It was in Dera'a, in the First World War, that Lawrence of Arabia was caught by the Turks, flogged and possibly sexually assaulted – depending on which version you believe – by a sadistic Turkish officer.) We had seen anti-aircraft gun positions on the outskirts and now in the town itself there was a lot of military activity. Chris had rolled down his window in the back and was taking shots with the Beaulieu. We drove straight through Dera'a and headed for the border. The road swooped up and down several steep ridges and then at the bottom of the last hill we saw the border post. Beside it stood a huge tank transporter with a Russian-built T54 tank on top of it. There were burn marks on the hull and it looked badly damaged.

'Quick,' I said unnecessarily to Chris. 'Get a shot of that tank.' He was already filming as discreetly as possible out of the window. A frontier guard came out of the control post and started waving at us angrily. Playing for time, I got out of the car and walked towards him. 'We want to cross the border to Jordan,' I told him in French.

'Fermé, fermé,' he shouted making vigorous sweeping movements with his arm. His meaning was unmistakable. I got back in the taxi and we made a slow circle. As we did so another transporter with a second badly damaged T54 on top of it came grinding noisily through the checkpoint and started up the hill towards Dera'a. We followed it and got a close-up shot of the tank and transporter as they laboured up the slope.

We had heard that Yasser Arafat was in Dera'a and we

tried to find him, but got short shrift from the PLO office. They were visibly upset about something and I guessed it was their lack of success against the Jordanians. Officially, the tanks that had crossed the border into Jordan, apparently intending to drive on to Amman to help the guerrillas in their battle against Hussein, were PLO tanks. But the two we had seen were quite clearly Syrian Army tanks with a hasty PLO sign quickly painted on the front. On the road out of Dera'a we saw more transporters with more knocked-out T54s. It looked as if the Syrians had really got a pasting.

We stopped by the roadside for twenty minutes while I wrote and recorded my commentary. Then we filmed what the Americans call a 'stand-upper', in which the reporter delivers his remarks straight to the camera and thus to the audience. I said that, from all the evidence we had seen, the military action against Jordan was almost entirely Syrian. Any Palestinian involvement was purely cosmetic. Then we got back in the taxi and drove to Damascus as fast as the old car could go. Two things surprised me. First that, despite all the Syrian military activity in Dera'a and near the border, no one had stopped us filming. (I think the fact we were in a taxi was a big help.) Second, that the taxi-driver, who obviously knew exactly what we were up to, did not try to stop us or report us to the police. Both would have been natural in a police state such as Syria.

We arrived at the hotel at about five and, while the crew went to pack up the film, I enquired about taxis to Beirut, a hundred miles away over the mountains. (It was the only route out for the film. If we had tried to fly it out of Damascus, it would almost certainly have been confiscated.) The hall porter said there was no difficulty. There were taxis going to Beirut all the time. He took me outside and introduced me to a driver sitting in his car by the front door.

'I want to send a package to Beirut,' I said cautiously.

He nodded. 'Pictures?' he said affably.

'Umm, yes,' I said, looking round.

'Okay,' the taxi driver said easily. 'Forty Lebanese pounds [about ten sterling]. You ready go now?'

'I'll just get the package.' Ten minutes later he was on his way, the address of our office in Beirut clearly printed on the envelope. I thought there was a very good chance that it would never get there, but later that night, after dinner, the 'phone rang and our man in Beirut said the film would be on the midnight plane to London. It arrived next day and was the lead item on 'News at Ten' that night. It was the first film of the fighting between Syria and Jordan.

Damascus was full of surprises. That night, studying the not very impressive wine list over a not very impressive dinner, I spotted some Veuve Cliquot champagne. I beckoned the head waiter.

'Have you still got some of this champagne?'

'Oh yes, M'sieu,' he said. 'We have had it for a long time. Since the French used to come here.' He looked round the dining-room at the shabbily-suited Czechs and East Germans and curled his lip. 'The customers nowadays don't drink champagne! They have no money.'

'We'll drink it,' I said. 'Put a couple of bottles on ice and we'll have it before lunch tomorrow.'

Next day we left the hotel early, drove to the border, completed our story, and were back in time for the champagne and lunch. Despite the fact that it had been in the cellars for years, it was still in excellent condition.

When we finally made contact with the Foreign Ministry, they had no idea that we had already been to the border and filmed their tanks being withdrawn from Jordan.

'Syria was not involved,' the spokesman said. 'Only the PLO. We'll take you there tomorrow to see for yourselves.' Next day, accompanied by a group of French journalists, we were escorted to the border by the Syrians. Without the slightest hesitation they drove five miles down the road to Ramtha, the first Jordanian town. There were signs of fighting everywhere: several wrecked tanks and lorries and gaping shell holes in the houses. All the soldiers we saw including those occupying the town were Palestinian guerrillas. They took us to their Command Post and pointed to a low ridge about two miles away. 'Jordanian tanks,' they said. I could just see the muzzles of their guns poking over the top of the ridge.

It was only later that I heard the full story of the fighting. The Syrians had attacked with a large tank force and a handful of PLO hangers-on, at the height of the battle in Amman. Their intention was to drive straight down the road to the Jordanian capital and overthrow Hussein's government. The Syrian President ordered his air force commander, Colonel later President Assad, to provide close support. But Assad, who was a political rival, refused. This was the key to the ensuing battle. Hussein's small air force now proved decisive, but it was a near thing. Of his dozen or so Hawker Hunters, eight or nine were being converted and only two or three were operational when the Syrians invaded. Luckily for them, the Jordanian pilots found the skies empty and the Syrian tanks sitting ducks. They rocketed and machine-gunned them until they ran out of ammunition. Then the Jordanian tanks moved in and mopped up the demoralised remnants.

As we tramped round the battlefield, I wondered why there were not more signs of the Syrian defeat. The answer was that, having seen them off, the Jordanians had sensibly allowed the Syrians to save some face by letting them drag their damaged tanks away. We had arrived at the border just in time to see the last of the evidence being removed.

A few days later, when the border reopened, I decided to see if we could drive to Amman, only sixty miles away. After a long discussion at the Jordanian army's forward position on the Ramtha road, they agreed to let us through. On either side of the road, we could see their tanks dug in, hull down, right across the desert, just in case the Syrians made a second attempt. The road south was first-class and it was easy to see that, if the Syrian air force had supported the armoured push, nothing could have stopped the Syrians motoring all the way to Amman: Hussein's tanks were too busy in the capital. It was wonderful wild country, the road running through the narrow green valleys and emerging to climb across the bare, bone-dry fringes of the desert, inhabited only by the Beduin and their flocks of goats.

We drove straight to the Intercontinental to find it crowded with rich Jordanian refugees and expatriates and their families getting ready to leave the country. All they could offer us was the Royal Suite, a penthouse on top of the hotel. This had taken a peppering during the fighting and the sitting-room floor was littered with broken glass from the shattered picture windows. I found an unexploded Kalashnikov high velocity bullet lying nakedly in the bath. It had come through both the outer concrete wall and the thin inner wall, punching a hole the size of a small plate in the plaster before finally coming to rest.

Next day we toured Amman. In the refugee areas, whole rows of houses had been demolished by shellfire, and in many parts of the city, including the diplomatic quarter round the Intercontinental, nearly every building was pitted with bullet marks. Even the Royal Palace had not escaped. The guerrillas had fired long bursts of machine-gun fire across the valley, forcing the evacuation of one wing which included the King's office. Thousands were homeless, picking their way in a kind of stupor through the shattered remains of what had been their homes. One felt once again that fate and the extremist folly of their leaders had served the Palestinians ill.

The guerrillas themselves, disarmed and despondent, were under orders to leave the capital and move to camps in the hills to the north. Having lost the battle they had no choice. But you could sense the hostility and the hatred that would later give rise to even more extreme groups, including one that called itself, commemoratively, Black September.

A day or two later, the irrepressible Ed Hughes arrived from Beirut. I told him gratefully how successful his idea of flying to Damascus had been. He rubbed his hands gleefully when I described how we had filmed the Syrian tanks limping back across the border.

'There's a Pakistani brigadier here you should meet,' Ed said. 'He's very well informed. He's adviser to the Jordanian Army on tank warfare.' Shortly afterwards, we all happened to be in the Intercontinental Hotel and Ed introduced me to Zia. He was a good-looking, friendly Punjabi with very white teeth and very black hair. 'Come and have curry at the house,' he said. 'How about tomorrow?'

Zia had been a young subaltern in the Corps of Guides, the

famous Indian Army cavalry regiment, at the end of the Second World War, serving in Burma and Malaysia. He was very British in manner, but very Muslim in his private life. His wife appeared briefly, to serve dinner, but the rest of the time she and the other women remained out of sight. Zia, Ed and I ate an excellent curry together. We drank beer but I cannot remember whether Zia did. During dinner I criticised the incompetence of the Jordanian Government's press department.

'They complain about the PLO getting all the publicity,' I said, 'but it's impossible to get any cooperation from them.'

'What exactly do you want to do?' Zia asked.

'Well, being in television, we need pictures. What I would really like is to spend some time with the King. We've done several stories on the Palestinians and it's time we did the other side. But, although I keep saying this to the Ministry of Information, nothing ever happens. I've asked to see the King, but I don't think he ever gets the request.'

Zia, who had listened attentively, said, 'I think you are right. They should give you their side of the story. Let me see what I can do to help. I'll talk to someone tomorrow.'

I did not really expect anything to happen so I was pleasantly surprised next day when I got a 'phone call from a man; obviously a Jordanian, who did not say who he was, only that he wanted to come and see me.

It was about six, the light fading from the tawny hills of Amman, the street lamps beginning to pinprick the evening haze. Through the repaired plate-glass windows of the Royal Suite, I had a panoramic view of the nine hills on which the city is built. The 'phone rang and the porter at the desk said a gentleman was on his way up to see me. I went out of the suite and waited by the lifts in the half-dark: they had still not repaired the lights. The lift door opened and a man stepped out. I ushered him into the suite and offered him a drink which he declined. He was very dark, almost sinister-looking, and wearing dark glasses.

'I can't stay long,' he said. 'I understand you feel you are not getting the cooperation you would like.'

I repeated what I had told Zia and he said, 'All right. Please stand by tomorrow. We hope we can take you somewhere and show you something that will interest you. I will send a car for you.'

'What time?' I asked.

'Early,' he said. 'Be ready.'

He held out his hand. 'Until tomorrow.' I had no idea who he was, nor what we would see the next day, but the authority of his manner led me to hope it would be interesting.

Next morning, a little after eight, a big black car with an army driver in uniform arrived outside the hotel. It had a crown on the number plate, so I knew it came from the Palace. We had no language in common so we had no idea where he was taking us. It turned out to be the air force base, next to Amman airport. We were waved through the main gate and taken to the officers' mess. Two Alouette jet helicopters were parked on the tarmac outside. After half an hour or so, the engines started to warm up and five minutes later we lifted off and started to climb, heading north over the stony desert plateau. Beneath us I could see the miniature black figures of Beduin children, their upturned faces white blobs as they looked up at us. We flew for perhaps half an hour north, towards the Syrian border, the black ribbon of the road threading together a string of small white towns. The hills were brown and empty. Then we were losing height, aiming towards a small green valley. We touched down in the middle of a group of tough-looking soldiers in British-style battledress and green berets. There were Hussein's special bodyguards, all Beduin.

A few minutes later we heard the rotor beat of a third helicopter. It came swooping down towards us and as it landed I saw that King Hussein was at the controls. The bodyguards made a protective ring round the helicopter. The King jumped out with a grin and went forward to greet his local commanders who were drawn up in a line, shaking hands with and embracing each one in turn. It was curiously touching, emphasising a bond that was deeper than mere military discipline. Then he was led off to an underground bunker for

346

a briefing. Someone gestured to us to follow and I knew then that we were on the inside track.

After the briefing we all got back into the helicopters and flew for about ten minutes, the three helicopters in line ahead, skimming over the hillsides. Ahead, in a shallow depression, I could see 300 or 400 soldiers waiting in a big group. The King's helicopter put down first in a cloud of dust and by the time we had got out Hussein was in the middle of a shouting, pushing, gesticulating mass of soldiers. We struggled to get close enough to film but it was almost impossible. The bodyguards round Hussein fought to make a path for him, one officer laying about him with a cane. Finally the King, who is quite short, got on a table and started to speak, his slow, deep voice carrying clearly through the desert air. Every so often the soldiers would cheer and then silence would fall again. Athletic as ever, Alan Downes hoisted himself up on top of a signals van. It turned out to be a brilliant move. Hussein finished speaking and started to walk towards us. The soldiers went wild, fighting to get near enough to the King to touch him, even kiss him. The bodyguards tried in vain to clear a space round him. In the crush, his hat was knocked off and for a moment he vanished in the mêlée, suddenly reappearing, being carried shoulder high in triumph. It was an amazing demonstration of loyalty and affection. But then Hussein is not only a King and a Beduin chief and of course commander-in-chief. He also claims descent from the Prophet Mohammed and thus is a spiritual leader as well.

We flew to another forward base and the reception was equally ecstatic. Some soldiers were so carried away that they would stand up and sing what seemed to be impromptu verses in Hussein's honour. It was the first time the King had visited his front line troops since the war and, watching the almost hysterical devotion, it was hard to believe that the army had been as critical of the King over the Palestinians as had been said. But these were Beduin soldiers and their personal loyalty to Hussein has never been doubted.

Just before we boarded the Alouettes to fly back to Amman, I asked an aide if the King would give us an informal interview. He came forward at once, relaxed and friendly. I asked him if these were the troops who had fought the Syrians.

'Yes,' he said. 'They gave a very good account of themselves.' I asked him about the number of Palestinian casualties. The PLO claimed 40,000.

'Quite untrue,' he said. 'We are still checking the exact figure but it was hundreds rather than thousands.'

We sent the film off that night to London and it was the first item on 'News at Ten' the following night. It ran for seven minutes, filling a quarter of the half-hour programme. Pictorially it was superb and it was the first time King Hussein had been seen in action since the end of the war. Alan Downes later won a deserved award for his camera work.

I was so impressed by Hussein's career and also by his star quality, that I asked if I could make a full-length documentary on his life, which had never been done before. The request went through the man in dark glasses who had come to the Royal Suite in the Intercontinental that first night. He turned out to be Moraiwid Tel, the King's private secretary and brother of Wasfi Tel, the Prime Minister, who was later assassinated in Cairo by Palestinian gunmen in revenge for Black September. I got my answer almost immediately. The King would be very happy to take part in the film. Apparently, after my report on 'News at Ten', I could do no wrong.

In the spring of 1971 I took three weeks off from ITN and flew to Jordan with a $20,000 contract in my pocket from NBC of America which I hoped would cover the cost of making the film. I had Eleanor and my son, Alexander, with me as well as the camera crew and, as we drove into Amman from the airport, we could hear the sound of gunfire echoing among the hills. But the almond trees were in flower and, when we went to Aqaba next day, the stark outline of the desert was softened by a delicate wash of green, splashed with the reds and pinks of the spring flowers.

Aqaba is a rather disappointing huddle of houses on the flat northern shore of the Red Sea, although the mountains

348

which tower up above it, sharp-crested through the purplish desert haze, are magnificent. Aqaba's ordinariness was, however, transmuted for me by the knowledge that in 1917, at the end of the First World War, Hussein's grandfather, King Abdullah, and Lawrence of Arabia led the Arab army to a great victory there against the Turks. The Turkish guns had all pointed out to sea and, when Lawrence and his friends came storming down the *wadi* from the landward side, they caught the Turks with their baggy trousers down, and a great slaughter ensued. All that remains today is a line of palm trees beside the shore, romanticised by Lawrence in *The Seven Pillars*, and the mountains.

Right on the beach, and only a mile or so from the Israeli town of Eilat, which shares the top of the gulf, King Hussein had built himself a house, and there, next day, we were bidden to appear. The royal beach house was as delightful as the rest of Aqaba was dreary: a long, main bungalow, with smaller villas alongside, the whole thing only fifty yards from the sea, set among trees and flowering shrubs. It also had its own helicopter pad and a speedboat marina. Hussein was in residence with his second wife, Muna, a blond, buxom English girl, whom he had met and married in 1961. They had two sons, Feisal and Abdullah, and enchanting twin daughters, Zein and Ayesha. The house was full of English friends and their children, all having lunch when we arrived. Hussein was in his bathing trunks, sunning himself on a reclining chair, while Muna did the honours. The twins – each a fascinating miniature of one parent, Zein dark-haired and dark-eyed like her father. Ayesha blonde and blue-eyed like her mother – were busy climbing over their reclining father while he tried to teach them a nursery rhyme.

'Humpty Dumpty sat on a wall . . . ' Neither Hussein nor the twins seemed to know the words and they had several shots at it. The whole atmosphere was wonderfully relaxed and we moved about freely, filming as discreetly as possible until Hussein's air force ADC and helicopter pilot, Badr Zaza, a thin-faced Circassian with a Clark Gable moustache, thought we had intruded enough. Interposing himself between Hussein and the camera, he said to me it was time to leave. If Moraiwid Tel, the King's secretary, had been there I would have appealed to him. But we had made a good start and the last thing I wanted to do was to have a row. So we retired as gracefully as possible to our modest hotel farther down the beach.

That evening I worked hard on Badr who came to the hotel for dinner. He was an extremely vain man and, when I suggested that we would give him a special credit on the film if he would allow us to use the helicopter for aerial shots, he soon became more helpful. He was an invaluable ally and would have been a bad enemy. (He was killed with Queen Alia, Hussein's third wife, when their helicopter crashed in a storm in 1977.)

Hussein tends to get up late so it was not until about noon that he was ready to go water-skiing. As he walked along the beach, Hussein came on my son Alexander.

'How are you finding things in Jordan?' the King asked.

'A bit boring,' Alexander replied, not knowing who he was. Hussein laughed and walked into the water to don his mono-ski. Geoff Mulligan, the cameraman and Badr took off with a roar of rotor blades and the rest of us climbed into two speedboats.

The first speedboat shot away and, with an ease I envied, Hussein rose out of the water and proceeded to give an expert exhibition of water-skiing. The speedboat made a circle of the shallow bay and returned parallel to the beach. There were hardly any swimmers and Hussein was able to come close inshore, at one point so close that he just missed a rock, swerving at the last moment. My heart missed a beat, although I think he did it deliberately. It was his own private game of 'chicken'.

Afterwards, he and Muna skied together and then Hussein demonstrated his own special brand of surfing behind the speedboat. The shot of him riding up out of the water, slowly getting to his feet and balancing on the surf board, a determined expression on his face, was so striking that I used it as the title shot of the film. Later, I had a go at water-skiing myself – unlike Hussein I needed two skis – and fell once, swallowing a mouthful of very salty seawater. But, when I did manage to complete my run, subsiding neatly near the royal speedboat, Hussein stood and applauded. 'Bravo,' he said, apparently without sarcasm. I was immensely pleased with myself.

A couple of days later we left for Amman, expecting Hussein to follow. But, as we drove north along the Desert Highway, we ran into a cloudburst. The whole desert was awash and water was pouring across the road so violently that I began to doubt that we would get through. We did, but in Amman houses were swept away in the flash floods and several people were drowned. Hussein decided to stay on in the sunshine of Aqaba, not returning to cold and rainy Amman for five days. I did not know this at the time and I pestered Moraiwid for the reason for the delay. He, poor man, was as much in the dark as we were, and as I fretted impotently, watching the days and the budget slipping away, I began to realise how difficult it is to pin down someone like Hussein. His unpredictability is part of his character. But it had been reinforced, in my view, by the constant threat of assassination. To cope with it, he has deliberately evolved a way of life that is without a pattern. Thus, the official diary is kept to a minimum and known to a minimum of people. Hussein will get up in the morning and decide whether he is going to pay a visit to an army unit, inspect an irrigation scheme in the country, or hold a cabinet meeting. His officials genuinely did not seem to know what he was going to do next. We had been told, for example, that he was planning a visit to Irbid, Jordan's second largest city and previously a stronghold of the *fedayeen*. But it was impossible to find out exactly when. The reason, I believe, was that there was no date. There may have been various tentative dates but no final date until Hussein took the decision himself. 'We'll go to Irbid today,' he would announce, and the wheels would start to turn.

This undoubtedly kept everyone on their toes. It must also have made life as difficult for his staff as it did for us. But, if none of his Ministers and advisers knew his movements in advance, what chance would an assassin have? And, if there should be a spy or a traitor in high places, then Hussein's unpredictability would make his task that much more difficult.

Despite this deliberate policy of living from moment to moment, Hussein was nearly killed twice during the Black September period. Zeid Rifai, an old friend of Hussein's and then Jordanian Ambassador in London, told me about one of these occasions. It was the eve of the war against the Palestine guerrillas and the King was driving from his palace at Hummar, ten miles from Amman. Near the village of Suweileh, they ran into a *fedayeen* ambush. The gunfire was so heavy that the King's convoy was pinned down. Eventually, Zeid, who was with the King in the back of the car, managed to open the door.

'There was a hell of a lot of shooting,' Zeid recalled. 'The bullets were hitting the road like rain all around us. To protect His Majesty I pushed him into the ditch at the side of the road and then jumped on top of him, to shield him with my body.' (Zeid is a heavy man.)

'HM hurt his back and when I went to see him in bed afterwards he said: ''Never do that again. You're more bloody dangerous than the *fedayeen*.'' He said it with a grin but he meant it.'

Hussein himself described both incidents when I interviewed him on camera in the palace.

'Last year, we had at least two road ambushes and, in the one, we were fired upon from a dominating position while the vehicles were stationary. [They had stopped at the crossroads in Suweileh.] I was coming into Amman to see what was happening – in fact firing had broken out in the capital – and to try and put an end to it. We lost a sergeant of my guard and four were wounded and it was in fact the first time I fired back at anyone in anger.

'The second one was on my way to the airport to meet my daughter and again, just by good fortune, I believe one of the ambushers opened fire just a couple of seconds too early and whilst we were still a little bit out of range, and we exchanged fire with them for about twenty minutes and managed again to extricate ourselves from the roadside.'

In fact Hussein is so modest that it was not easy to get him to talk about the numerous assassination attempts that have been made on his life in the thirty-odd years he has been on the throne of Jordan.

His first brush with death, as it happens, occurred when he was fifteen and ADC to his grandfather, King Abdullah. Abdullah, Lawrence's old comrade-in-arms, had apparently singled out the young Hussein even then, as his successor. This is how Hussein described to me his grandfather's assassination.

'He was to me more than a father really. I had spent the last few months of his life with him almost entirely. I left him at night, I was with him in the early morning. He supervised my studies. I went with him, whatever he did. We went to Jerusalem on a visit that morning. We went also to visit Nablus and then the people in Nablus attempted to keep him for the day. There was talk of danger in Jerusalem but he refused. We returned to Jerusalem and left for the Al Aqsa Mosque and, just as he was entering the main gate, maybe three or four paces and to his right, an individual appeared from behind the door, gun in hand and fired. I was completely stunned for a second or two. Everything seemed to stop. My grandfather was hit in the head and he began to fall. I rushed immediately for the assassin and he turned and continued firing. One of his bullets glanced off the medal I was wearing, another tore lightly, slightly into my ear' – Hussein brushed the lobe of his right ear – 'and then he was shot down. So I went back to my grandfather and it was obvious he had died in fact. We carried him out, the doctor came and tried to see what he could do and then we carried him to hospital which was rather close by. Unfortunately nothing could be done.'

Hussein's father, Talal, succeeded to the throne, but he was a schizophrenic, manifestly unfit to rule, and in 1953 he abdicated and made way for his son, who was still a schoolboy at Harrow.

After Hussein had been proclaimed King, he went back to England, to the Royal Military Academy at Sandhurst, where he had to suffer the same indignities on the parade ground as every other officer cadet, including being shouted at by the redoubtable Regimental Sergeant-Major Lord, who is said to have addressed him in time-honoured fashion, as 'you 'orrible little King, you'.

When Hussein became King of Jordan at seventeen, President Nasser of Egypt was the most powerful figure in the Arab world, and immediately started plotting the young king's downfall. As part of his dream of an Arab nation stretching from the Persian Gulf to the Atlantic, Nasser had just engineered the union of Egypt with Syria. And so, although Hussein's next brush with death occurred when he was flying over Syria, there was no doubt in his mind that Nasser had a hand in it.

'One day I was leaving Jordan for Europe in a small twin-engined Dove of the Royal Jordanian Air Force, my own personal aircraft, and while overflying Syria, we were told we must land there. Relations weren't extremely friendly at that time between us and the régime, it was at the time of the Union of the United Arab Republic both in Syria and in Egypt, and when we asked if we should return to Jordan, we were told that we were not permitted and that we must land in Damascus – we were very close to it. So I dove down and flew very low to the ground trying to reach the nearest point in Jordan when two MiG 17s crossed us from the direction of Jordan going into Syria and then later caught us up. That time was really one of the many times that I felt it was extremely close and my own reaction – I was flying the aircraft myself – was to try to ram the first aircraft as it turned in for an attack on us. But fortunately I had with me a man who taught me how to fly in the first place and who had a great deal more experience and who said he would take control. As a result of knowing that our aircraft was much slower and could manoeuvre much better than the faster jets, he did manage to evade the first attack and eventually we were able to cross into Jordan by turning inside their circle every time they came in. We didn't continue our trip but one year later almost to the day we overflew Syria under better conditions and, although I had a bit of a stiff neck looking around for any possible aircraft that might come to meet us, it was a pleasant journey after all.'

Hussein has a dry sense of humour and a good turn of phrase. Zeid Rifai told me another story from the Black September days which showed that Hussein could make a joke even when things were looking particularly grim.

'I think it was the day after the fighting started. We had been up all night in Army headquarters and Hussein was being given a briefing by one of the commanders. This chap went through all the events of the past twenty-four hours and things were looking pretty bad and, when he came to the end of his report – he was speaking in English so that other people in the room wouldn't understand – he said: 'And that, Your Majesty, is the situation.'

The King was silent for a moment, then he said: 'That's not a situation, that's a shit-uation.' He had not been to Harrow for nothing.

Some of the other assassination attempts Hussein described were so bizarre that I would have had difficulty believing them if I had not heard them from his own lips. Like the story of the nose drops. Nasser's campaign against Hussein, whom he saw as a stooge of the Imperialist British, was then at its height and the Egyptian secret service were busy concocting one assassination attempt after another. Here is the macabre little tale as Hussein told it.

'I have suffered a great deal from sinus, partly as a result of my flying activities, and I use nose drops. I used them at that particular moment of time and I had had an attack and had decided that I would use these drops. The bottle looked rather old and so I poured it down the sink and started using another one and, as I did so, the metal began to change colour and it began to, sort of, boil. Somebody made a test and it turned out to be acid and – it was rather shocking in a way.' One did not need much imagination to guess what that same acid would have done to the inside of Hussein's nose and throat. It would undoubtedly have destroyed his vocal chords if it had not killed him.

Then there was the case of the cats. Again, it was so unlikely a story that I would have put it down to bazaar gossip if he had not vouched for it personally. Hussein then lived in the Basman Palace, which is in the middle of Amman and which, like everywhere else in the city, has its full complement of cats. One day one of the gardeners found a dead cat, the next day another, the following day yet another and so on. The head gardener alerted the palace guards and, after an investigation, the poisoning was traced to the cook, a relatively new recruit. He had apparently been planted there to poison the King but, not being an expert, he had experimented first on the palace cats. Too successfully, as it turned out.

Much more ambitious was the attempted coup, in April 1957, by the Chief of Staff, General Ali abu Nuwar, a strong supporter of President Nasser. He was later accused of being in the pay of the Egyptians. There was then a left-wing, pro-Egyptian government in Jordan, led by Suleiman Nabulsi, as Prime Minister.

On April 10, Hussein dismissed Nabulsi and three days later fighting broke out at the big army base at Zerka, near Amman, between troops loyal to Hussein and other units which supported General Ali. At midnight on April 13, Hussein decided to drive to Zerka, taking an unwilling General Ali with him. The situation was extremely confused but apparently a loyal Beduin regiment had surrounded the camp and was determined to prevent another unit, under the command of General Ali's cousin, Colonel Ma'an abu Nuwar, from marching on Amman to overthrow the King. Hussein must have known that he was walking into the lion's den. But he did not hesitate.

'Zerka itself was quite a sight really, quite an experience. Firing from every direction, people in a great state of tension, agitation, and it took me several hours, moving from one position to another, stopping here and stopping there and telling them to control themselves and telling them that everything was all right and that we lived and died for Jordan anyway and trying to prevent the confusion because the artillery had been told that the infantry was moving against me and that was how they had got them to take that position and start firing on the infantry and the infantry had the same feeling. Shooting was very, very heavy. It turned out that we had also passed over a bridge that had been mined the day before. The person who was to detonate it on my arrival

356

got hit by a stray bullet and was wounded and was unable to do so. In any event after several hours of trying and meeting the type of feeling and the type of emotion that I've never seen – soldiers some of them with their faces half shaved, with soap still on, carrying sticks or carrying rifles, civilians joining them – we managed to restore order and control there. And that was a turning point in terms of Jordan.'

It was typical of Hussein, as I was to discover, that he allowed the treacherous General Ali abu Nuwar to escape to Syria. That in itself was a fairly tolerant gesture. Later, after Ali abu Nuwar had spent several years in exile in Egypt, Hussein pardoned him and let him return to Jordan. And his generosity did not stop there. A now reformed Ali abu Nuwar was eventually appointed Ambassador to Paris. When I asked Hussein why he was so forgiving to his enemies, he gave a typical answer. All Jordanians are members of the same family, he said, and they all had something to contribute to the common cause. The only other possible explanation is that Jordan is so short of talented people that a man like Ali abu Nuwar, whose career in Britain, say, would have ended in total disgrace, was able in Jordan to rehabilitate himself and return to high office.

If Zerka was a turning point in the fortunes of Hussein and Jordan, the Six-Day War and Black September were to prove equally serious challenges. Hussein has grown in stature with each crisis, becoming a skilful politician and a wise statesman, while never forgetting the grassroots from which he draws his support: the more tribally-minded section of the population, the Beduin. And it is from the Beduin in turn that the bulk of the Army is recruited. The Army, as far as one can tell, in 1971 as today, is totally loyal to Hussein. As long as it remains so, he will survive, unless felled by an assassin's bullet.

But there was a lighter side to our stay in Amman. We were allowed to film Hussein working his 'ham' radio. He was a real addict, probably the world's only royal 'ham' and of course everyone wanted to talk to him when he came on the air. Having tuned his powerful set, a birthday present from Muna, he started sending out his call sign.

'The handle is Hussein. Hotel, Uniform, Sierra, Sierra, Echo, Independence, November, calling from Amman, Jordan . . . '

When the mood took him, he would spend hours on the air. He found it relaxing and of course politics are banned by the 'ham' radio code. During Black September, however, Hussein's set was for a time the only link Jordan had with the outside world and, although he refused to give any details about the war to other anxious hams, he was able to pass on messages to his family that he was alive and well.

Finally I wanted to know whether the thought of danger and death was constantly on his mind. If it was, he would not admit it. 'There have been so many dangers I've faced for so many reasons, from so many quarters, some accidental, some otherwise . . . I never think of that, I never try to keep them in my mind. Maybe as I go on, one becomes a little bit more cautious here and there . . . There is so much danger that one would be completely unable to cope or keep going if one were to think of danger all the time and what it meant. I live my life as if I am going to live for ever.'

Brave words, but Hussein is a brave man. Even his enemies – and he still has plenty – cannot deny him that.

CHAPTER XII

Over The Khyber Pass in a Taxi and the First ITN Man to Visit China

On December 3, 1971, after a prolonged series of border squabbles, India and Pakistan went to war for the second time since Partition in 1947. Most of the fighting took place in East Pakistan, now Bangladesh, where Indian troops invaded in support of the local Bengali population. Pakistan never really had a chance. In the first place, India had a superiority of about three to one, and secondly, it is impossible to conduct a war efficiently when one half of the country is separated from the other by a thousand miles of enemy territory. The Bengalis had always resented domination by the West Pakistanis and, led by Sheikh Mujibar Rahman, they started a breakaway movement, encouraged by India. When the West Pakistanis tried to stop this seccession by force, war broke out.

We already had a crew in Bangladesh and so I was asked to head for West Pakistan in case the Indians should launch a full-scale invasion there. We were immediately confronted by one major problem. Pakistan had closed its airspace to all civilian flights, so the only way to get there was to fly to

Kabul in neighbouring Afghanistan and then cross the border by road.

Kabul is what I have always imagined the end of the world to be like: a sprawling, ramshackle town with broken roads and teeming gutters, populated by some of the most villainous-looking individuals I have ever seen and surrounded by high, snow-covered mountains. They at least are beautiful. But we had little time to explore Kabul.

The first essential was to make sure that all our camera equipment had arrived safely and the second was to find a taxi to take us in the direction of Pakistan. Both were accomplished within half an hour, although the taxi driver said he would only get us as far as the border. It was a stupendous drive, through country of a savagery that must have daunted the British soldiers who tried to defeat the Afghans three times in the last two centuries and which must equally daunt the Russians in their turn. We had not gone very far when the sound recordist, a big Dutchman called Piet, asked if we could stop for a moment. He got out of the taxi and went towards a group of Afghans who were doing business by the roadside.

When, wearing a big grin, he got back into the car, I asked him what he had been buying.

'Hash,' he said, and then in case I did not catch his meaning. 'Cannabis. Grass. Dey have de best hash in de world here in Afghanistan.'

I looked at the cameraman, Ed van Can, who was also Dutch, with an interrogatory eyebrow. He simply shrugged, but later he told me that he had had to find a soundman in a hurry and he picked up Piet, whom he hardly knew, in the bar of the Press Club in Amsterdam. In fact Piet did not turn out to be as disastrous as I first feared, provided we kept him off the 'hash' when he was working.

The road swooped up and down among the mountains, the country steadily becoming wilder, until we entered the Khyber Pass. The road snaked its way in breathtaking fashion along the side of the mountain, on one side the rocks falling away steeply to some rushing torrent below, while above, as I craned my head out of the window, I could see the jagged crests where the Afghan riflemen must have hidden to take pot shots at the British. The rocks were brown, streaked with rust and purple, sharp as the edge of a saw against the light blue sky – beautiful but savage.

At the border, the driver indicated that was as far as he was prepared to go and pointed to a waiting Pakistani taxi. The new driver said he would take us to Peshawar, fifty miles down the road, so we transferred the camera gear and ourselves and set off. The Pakistani side of the Khyber is rich in nostalgic relics of the Raj. Beau Geste forts with crenellated parapets and loopholes for the old Lee-Enfields sit on commanding positions along the Pass. On them I could read plaques bearing names like the Khyber Rifles and North-West Frontier Force. It must have looked just like this in Kipling's day.

We hurried down the valley and, with the dusk advancing, saw the lights of Peshawar in front of us. Peshawar is another old British garrison town, capital of the North-West Frontier Province and the old headquarters of the British in the wars against the Afghans.

We drove straight to Dean's Hotel, another ramshackle reminder of British India. The main building was wrapped in sepulchral gloom, only partly caused by the black-out, and in the dining-room, where we supped off Brown Windsor soup and stringy roast chicken, the turbaned waiters on silent bare feet padded to and fro between the sparse tables. There were few other guests, only one or two ancient British memsahibs in carefully permed hair – or were they wigs? – and 1940s dresses, who presumably had stayed on, preferring Peshawar to Pimlico.

Afterwards we were escorted to our rooms, stumbling through the darkness behind a bearer with a paraffin lamp. Each of us had a separate suite and, although mine was furnished with spartan simplicity, the wood fire burning cheerfully in the grate in the sitting-room gave the place a sense of old-fashioned comfort that I found delightful. I had three obedient bearers to attend to my wants, but when I pulled back the curtain to see the stars they became frantic, explaining that I was breaking the black-out regulations, and one even went outside to make sure that no chink of light was escaping. Needless to say, Peshawar was not the least bit likely to be the target for an air raid, but the Pakistanis, like the Indians, are nothing if not sticklers for the small print. If a blackout was ordered, however unnecessary, then a blackout there must be. Cars and lorries had to paint their lights blue and, as a result, every night scores of lorries ran into one another or finished up in the ditch. Casualties caused by the black-out were higher, I imagine, than any losses caused by the Indians in West Pakistan.

Next day we crossed the mighty Indus, beneath the frowning gaze of the great fort at Attock, and then headed southeast across the plain to Rawalpindi, the goal of our journey of just under 300 miles. Rawalpindi is a scruffy, dusty town with the old British cantonment giving it what little distinction it has. The town itself is devoid of all character or charm. There was then but one modern hotel in Rawalpindi, the Intercontinental, and we went straight there to find, as I expected, a large group of mainly British and American journalists and television crews hanging about and complaining at the ineptitude of Pakistani military bureaucracy.

The first step was to register our arrival with the military and get our Press passes. Being the last of the major companies to arrive, we found that a lot of the spade work had already been done. By dint of bullying, protesting and complaining, our colleagues had finally persuaded the Pakistani Army to organise some sort of expedition to the front. There was to be a briefing that afternoon. Meanwhile our names were added to the list.

The briefing was given in a dusty garden outside the Army Press Office by a distinguished-looking Pakistani major with a large grey cavalry moustache. Addressing us in the tones of the Indian Army, he explained that we would all be transported next day towards the front at Chamb, in the foothills of Kashmir, where we would be able to see advance Pakistani units defending the soil of the fatherland.

He started to read off the list of people who were going and their organisations. When he came to ITN, the BBC cameraman, a large figure in ill-fitting fatigues, put up his hand in protest.

'I object,' he shouted, 'ITN have just arrived. We've been asking for this facility for days. It's not right that ITN should be allowed to gatecrash our facility.' There was a murmur of surprise and dissent among the assembled colleagues.

I felt some sort of intervention was necessary. 'It's true we've just arrived,' I said. 'But, if the facility is a general Press facility and not exclusively for the BBC, then we have as much right to go as anybody.'

There were more murmurs, of approval, I thought, and then the moustachioed major announced, 'There's only way way to settle this. We'll have to take a vote. Everyone who thinks that ITN should *not* be allowed to go on tomorrow's facility, put up their hands.'

The BBC team raised their hands but, as far as I could see, no one else did.

'Now, everyone who thinks ITN *should* go on the facility, raise their hands.'

Almost every hand in the group went up in the air and I felt a keen sense of triumph. The BBC correspondent came over to me and apologised, saying that it was his cameraman's idea and he had nothing to do with it. I accepted his apology although I felt that he should have overruled the cameraman. Journalism is as competitive as anything else and people will try by all sorts of methods to gain an advantage, often by paying out money. But I have never seen anyone try and prevent the opposition from getting to the scene of a major event by such boorish and clumsy means.

We set off the next day in a convoy of cars, under the command of the major, from Rawalpindi down to the great flat plain of the northern Punjab, where villages made up of primitive mud huts straggled into the distance, one after the other, to the horizon. By mid-afternoon we had progressed as far as the small town of Mirpur, where we were given beer and sandwiches at the District Commissioner's house. Accomodation, the major informed us, was a problem. The District Commissioner could put up a few – the people sitting at the front grabbed those places – and the rest of us would have to take our pick between schools, a rest house and the railway station. Somehow Ed, Piet and I drew the first-class waiting-room at the railway station. Any illusions we may have had about first-class waiting-rooms in a provincial Pakistani railway station were soon dispelled. First we had to force our way through a huge crowd of people jamming every inch of platform space. The station master shouted and shoved, with us hard on his heels, and, after a struggle, unlocked the waiting-room door. We were ushered in, the door was locked against the surging crowd and, since it was getting dark, a paraffin lamp was lit and hung up in the middle of the room. The sight that greeted our weary eyes was not very encouraging. The room was bare of any furniture except for three charpoys, which serve as beds in the Indian sub-continent and are wickerwork mats stretched over a wooden frame. There were no blankets or pillows, although it was getting chilly. There was also one dilapidated chair and a lavatory in the corner.

Given the limited recreational facilities, we soon prepared for bed, which meant lying down on the charpoy, more or less clothed, and trying to make ourselves somehow comfortable. I could hear the others swearing in Dutch, as they wriggled about on their hard beds and then, as silence descended, someone started hammering on the door very loudly and very determinedly. Perhaps he was also a first class passenger? But we refused to open the door, indeed, we were unable to, as the station master had gone off with the key. Instead we shouted, 'Quiet,' and finally, 'Bugger off.' We could hear the crowd scrabbling and moaning outside and I could sense that they were pressed close to the doorway, dozens of them, their eyes glued to every crack, attracted like moths to the light.

We turned down the lamp and fell into uneasy sleep, only to be woken in the early hours by a noise which reminded me of a huge flock of starlings. Hundreds of them seemed to be chattering to one another in a mood of mounting excitement. Soon the chattering was explained and drowned by a louder, more emphatic noise, the rhythmic pant of a steam engine and then the steady clank of a passing train. It was a long train and it did not stop. Then I noticed something else: something was biting me. I began to scratch and the more I scratched the more unbearable it became until I had to get off the charpoy. Too late I realised that the charpoy was infested with bed bugs which had sallied out in the night and dined off me while I slept. Groans and curses from the other charpoys told me that I was not alone in my misfortune.

An efficient correspondent would have had his insect repellent in his overnight case, but we were woefully ill-prepared. There was nothing for it but to twist and turn, scratching and cursing as the ammunition trains clanked through, never stopping, and the multitude outside on the platform whistled and chattered until dawn.

I have never been as pleased to see a railway official as I was to see the station master of Mirpur when he arrived with his keys at dawn. Then, forcing our way once more through the crowd, who had been standing up all night – they were so closely packed that most of them had no room to sit – we went off to find the rest of the party. The majority seemed to have spent a rather more comfortable night, so perhaps the BBC had got their revenge after all.

Breakfast and a cup of tea restored our spirits and we set off refreshed for the still-elusive front. About mid-morning, with the sun gilding the plain and burnishing the dust of our convoy, we followed the dirt road across the border into disputed Kashmir, passing a few Pakistani tanks, a dead Indian soldier, a few dead animals and the wreckage of a downed Indian MIG 21, until finally we reached the village of Chamb, which showed plenty of signs of having been fought over. Shellfire had ripped roofs off houses, torn gaping holes in their walls and driven the population out in terror. A Pakistani officer who had joined our party said the Indians shelled the place fairly regularly. But they had had a few rounds that morning already so he did not expect any more for the time being.

We drove on, arriving half an hour or so later at the most forward Pakistani position, an artillery battery. Their American 105s were dug in and hidden under camouflage nets and the gunners dozed in the afternoon sunshine. We were made welcome and offered tea. Chatting to the young captain in charge, I asked him if they had seen much action. It all looked so peaceful.

'Now and again,' he said. 'We fire a few rounds morning and evening and they sometimes shoot back. But they're not very good. They haven't hit us yet.' He grinned.

'Are you going to fire more rounds soon?' I asked hopefully. He looked at his watch. 'Usually in about an hour from now,' he said.

'You don't think,' I said, in my most persuasive voice, 'you could advance that a little, do you? So that we could get a picture of your guns firing? I hate to ask, but I know the major here wants to start back for Rawalpindi as soon as possible.'

The gunner captain grinned. 'I don't see why not,' he said affably. 'Let me see what I can do.' He started shouting orders in Urdu and the reclining gunners leaped to their feet.

The BBC cameraman came shambling up and asked: 'What's going on then?'

'They're going to fire a few rounds,' I said grudgingly.

'Oh, great,' he said and hustled away to get his camera.

Within a few minutes, the Pakistani gunners had laid their guns, adjusted range and elevation, and were ready to fire.

'Number one gun, fire,' the young captain shouted. There was an earsplitting crack, a belch of smoke and a 105 shell went whistling away across the dusty landscape to its invisible target four or five miles away. Number two gun followed, then number three and the rest of the battery. They fired for about five minutes, the spent shell cases making a hollow sound as they bounced on the hard ground and the lethal projectiles hurtling away into the sky with an awesome echoing swish.

After they had shot off their standard number of rounds, they stopped firing, we stopped filming and, after much shaking of hands and saying of thank-yous, we moved off.

Years later, I was describing the incident to Ray Moloney, also of ITN but who had then been with ABC of America.

'Wait a minute,' he said. 'You were at Chamb with the Pakistani artillery when they opened fire on the Indian positions? It must have been the first or second week of December.'

'Yes,' I said, 'about the 10th or 11th.'

'You bastard,' Moloney exploded. 'I was on the other side when the goddam shells started raining down on top of us.'

I laughed, not really believing him.

'Why are you laughing?' he demanded angrily. 'It's true. We were bloody nearly killed. We had to dive for cover. The goddam shells were falling all round us. As soon as there was a lull we got to hell out of there. And now I know you were the bastard on the other side who nearly got us blown to bits.' He gave me a withering glance, turned on his heel and stalked off.

Going back to Rawalpindi, we seemed to make better time and, to our infinite relief, we did not have to spend another night in the railway station at Mirpur. The bone-hard charpoys and their ravenous inhabitants would have been unbearable two nights running. I would rather have slept in the open, anywhere. We arrived late at the Intercontinental, which as always on these occasions now seemed the very height of luxury. The last fifty miles or so had been painfully slow. We had been forced to go at a snail's pace, in case some blacked-out lorry with almost invisible blue lights should come hurtling out of the darkness and knock us into the ditch. We passed dozens of lorries which had similarly come to grief. But shooting the film and bringing it back to Rawalpindi was only half the battle. We still had to get it to ITN which meant sending it all the way over the Khyber Pass to Kabul and then putting it on a plane to London. Luckily we found a photographer and his girl friend who were delighted to make the trip for a fee. Since they carried the film and pictures for a number of people, we were able to pay them a fraction of what it would have cost to send Piet; and, with his penchant for 'hash', it was doubtful if I would ever have got him back again.

A day or two after the Chamb expedition, I bumped into my friend Zia from Jordan. He had been recalled from Amman and promoted to Major-General. He looked depressed and tired and did not want to discuss the war. I could understand why. The news was bad for Pakistan. The army in the East was close to defeat and, a thousand miles away in West Pakistan, there was nothing they could do to help them.

The end came a few days later on December 17; Pakistan surrendered. Next day President Yahya Khan, the general who had been in power for ten years and whose stupidity had largely brought about the catastrophe, was deposed and the ebullient Foreign Minister, Zulfikar Ali Bhutto, was recalled from the United States to take his place. He flew in to Rawalpindi in a white suit, to the plaudits of his supporters and the universal hope among Pakistanis that out of the débâcle he could at least salvage something. He did, although less than six years later he was to be deposed in turn by General Zia. But that is another story.

One evening in June 1972 John Mahoney, ITN's Foreign Editor at that time, came across to where I was sitting at the 'News at Ten' desk. 'Sandy, how would you like to go to China?' he asked.

'When?'

'Tomorrow or the day after.'

'I'd love to.'

'Great,' he said. 'Anthony Royle is taking a Foreign Office delegation there. It's the first official British visit since the Communists came to power in 1949. We have to give the names to the F.O. I'll come back to you as soon as I've got the details.'

It took longer than either of us expected. For some reason, Nigel Ryan, the Editor, did not want us to go – either because ITN was short of funds (a perennial problem) or because he did not think it was justified in story terms. After a long wrangle between him and John, in which I took no part, and an intervention from Royle, then Under-Secretary of State and number two to Lord Home, it was finally agreed that we would go.

I was enormously excited. The long freeze between China and the West was just beginning to thaw. Henry Kissinger had made several secret visits to Peking the previous year and, in February 1972, Nixon had made his historic visit to China, which changed the face of East-West relations. We would be the first major British television team to visit China for as long as could be remembered. ITN had certainly never been there before. We flew to Hong Kong by BOAC and spent a luxuriously comfortable night in the Mandarin Hotel. Next day we joined the RAF VC10 which was flying Anthony Royle and his glamorous wife Shirley from London to Peking.

It was a small Press party: a shy intellectual from the *Financial Times* called Smith, my old friend Clare Hollingworth from the *Telegraph*, and from ITN Jon Lane and Hugh Thomson, veterans of many joint assignments and myself. The Foreign Office team were civilised and friendly and in Peking we met Michael Richardson, a brilliant young Sinologist who acted as interpreter, and his pretty wife Celia. They lived in the foreigners' compound along with all the other diplomats in accordance with the Chinese policy of segregating the Western imperialists as far as possible. The thaw was beginning but there were still a lot of icy patches.

As we drove into Pekin, I was struck by two things: there were very few cars, all of them official, so nearly everyone rode a bicycle; and everyone looked the same, men and women. Rush hour Peking did not mean traffic jams and petrol fumes. It consisted of thousands and thousands of men and women in blue boiler suits, with high Mao collars, peddling along in near silence.

Our hotel, the International, then the only one used for Westerners, was a square, unattractive, dirty beige stone building near Tien An-min, the Square of Heavenly Peace, and the centre of Peking. In the foyer, touched-up pictures of Mao looked down at us with phoney benevolence and the place had that fusty, down-at-heel look that seems inseparable from Communism. There was remarkably little joy about for a so-called worker's paradise. But the view from my room on the fourth floor was much more encouraging. I looked out over the Forbidden City and at virtually the same skyline as China's Emperors had gazed upon – with the exception of a radio tower and of course the International Hotel which I fortunately could not see.

The Forbidden City is in fact the old Imperial enclave, separated from Tien An-min and the rest of the city by a high wall, and so vast as to make Buckingham Palace look like a gardener's cottage. On the south side of Tien An-min a massive gate led into the Forbidden City and above it hung a giant portrait of Mao himself. It was from this point, in 1949, after his victory in the Civil War against Chiang Kai-shek and the Nationalists, that Mao proclaimed the birth of the People's Republic.

To pass through that gate is to make a leap back in time, a century or more, and to find oneself, in the imagination at any rate, in the formal and extremely beautiful world of the Chinese Emperors, a world in which dragons glare from the eaves of the palaces and pagodas and stone lions grimace at the foot of a great flight of steps. One courtyard leads into another, so the visitor works his way towards the heart of the Forbidden City, where the Emperor, the Son of Heaven, sat on his throne in a splendid isolation that no lesser mortal was allowed to sully. The British Ambassador, for example, considered by the Chinese as a minor being from an inferior civilisation, was kept well away from the sacred presence and at a lower level. The Emperor, quite literally, looked down on all other beings. China was known as the Middle Kingdom and the Chinese believed it was the centre of the world.

All this went through my mind as the official party climbed the stairs and was led through the intricate maze of magnificent rooms full of elaborately carved furniture and exquisite paintings of mountains and rivers, lakes and plains shimmering in a pearly mist. There were also more stirring scenes – battles, hunts and celebrations – and in one room a solid block of jade, ten feet high, had been carved into a replica of some famous mountain. Every detail was perfect down to the tiny leaves on the trees. Other rooms held suits of armour and others still some of the most elaborate jewellery I have ever seen, exotic birds glittering with semi-precious stones and one small pair of gold and enamel leopards with ruby eyes that I immediately coveted for myself.

We then came to the high point of the tour. Anthony Royle was asked to inspect the latest find of the archaeologists, carefully sealed in a perspex case. It was the Flying Horse of Kwangsi, a magnificent bronze statuette of a horse at full gallop. To emphasise the prodigious speed of the beast, the artist has allowed only one foot to touch the earth, and that rests on a swallow, pinned to the ground by the flying hoof. It was the first time the Flying Horse had been shown to Westerners – it was later to be the centre-piece of the Chinese Exhibition when it came to London, Paris and New York the following year. I wanted to film it, but Jon insisted that we would have to take it out of its case. A long, polite argument ensued, with Anthony Royle doing his best to persuade the Chinese that this would be in everyone's best interest, but to no avail. The excuse was that the key could not be found. But I suspect that no one wanted to take the responsibility of opening the case.

The Forbidden City was once inhabited by 20,000 people, from the Emperor's family, the courtiers, the mandarins and the Imperial Guard down to the army of servants. Now it is a museum, a relic of China's past grandeur, except for one corner where I noticed a couple of white-gloved sentries stood on guard day and night. When I asked my interpreter who lived there, he shook his head, pretending ignorance. Either the Reuters man, Jim Pringle, or one of the diplomats enlightened me about the 'compound'. This was where Mao and the other top members of the Communist Government had their private houses. Here, the myth of one society ended and privilege reared its ugly head.

The Chinese present such a disciplined and apparently contented face to the outside world that it takes a little time for the visitor to realise that he is looking at a society in which practically every move is pre-ordained from above. Our translator, who was assigned to us for the entire visit, revealed just how strict life in China was. Driving back to the hotel in the car, I asked him how he had come to join the Press Section of the Foreign Ministry.

'I was assigned by the State,' he said.

'But did you apply to join the Foreign Ministry, did you want to become a diplomat?' I persisted.

He giggled in embarrassment. 'No. In China the State

decides what each person is best fitted for and how they can best serve the country. It instructs everyone what to do.'

'But, if you wanted to leave the Foreign Ministry, would you be able to?'

He giggled again and shook his head. 'No, that would be impossible.' I asked him where he lived and whether he owned his house. He smiled at my simple ignorance. 'No one owns a house or flat in China,' he explained. 'The State allocates each worker and his family a flat. I live in a flat allocated to me as a worker in the Foreign Ministry.'

Chinese diplomats, when they are posted abroad, nearly always have to leave their children behind and they are only allowed to take their wives if they too are diplomats or have some other official role to play. Otherwise they stay at home. It suddenly dawned on me that no one in China does what he pleases. He does as he is told. Even when it comes to the number of children. Two is the officially prescribed number. Anyone going above that is reprimanded and penalised. With such a vast population to feed, nearing 1,000 million now, it is understandable that the Chinese Government should take such a strict line. But authoritarianism ran through the whole system. No one dared to express views that were at variance with the official party line.

We were standing one day in Tien An-min, with Mao's portrait gazing at us from the Gate of Heavenly Peace.

'Every Chinese,' the interpreter said, 'wants to come to Tien An-min at least once in his life to see Chairman Mao.'

'Why?'

'Because he is the father of the nation. Every Chinese loves Chairman Mao!'

'What would happen if someone disagreed with one of Chairman Mao's beliefs of policies?'

The interpreter giggled. 'They would persuade him to change his mind.'

'But supposing he refused to change his mind? Supposing he continued to hold an opposing view?'

The smile disappeared and the interpreter looked severe. 'He would be very unwise to do that.'

'But suppose he did.'

372

'Then he would be punished.'

'How?'

But he was not going to answer that and his expression said very plainly that the subject was closed.

I asked if we could interview someone in Tien An-min and find out why he had come there.

The interpreter looked baffled. 'We could try, I suppose, but no one has ever done it before.'

A man was walking across the square in our direction. 'This man coming. Ask him if he'll speak to us.'

The interpreter stepped forward, a bit diffidently, I thought, and accosted the man. He turned out to be a railway worker from the provinces, a cheerful self-confident fellow of about thirty-five, and he was quite willing to talk to us.

'Why have you come?' I asked.

'To see Chairman Mao.' He turned and gazed in unfeigned respect towards the huge portrait.

'Why have you come to see Chairman Mao?'

'Because Chairman Mao is the father of China.' I tried to decide whether the interpreter was doing an honest translation or dressing the answers up for our benefit.

'What does he do?'

'He's a railway worker from . . . that's a small town about a hundred miles from Peking.'

'How much money does he get paid? Would he mind telling us?'

Finally after some discussion: '150 yuan a month.'

'That's about £15,' I calculated. 'Is he happy with that or would he like more money?'

The railwayman responded volubly, gesticulating animatedly. No, no, he's very happy with his present wage. He does not want more money.'

'In Britain,' I said, 'the railwaymen often go on strike for more money. Does he not want to do that too?'

The interpreter answered, almost too quickly, I thought: 'No, no, he's very happy. He does not want to go on strike.'

We shook hands and the happy railwayman strode off across the square to pay his respects to Chairman Mao at close range. He was a simple soul, no doubt, but he was also, like all Chinese, well aware of what Chairman Mao expected of him. It would never do to reveal to a foreigner, certainly not in front of a government official, that everything was not for the best in the best of all possible worlds. That would have been like putting his head in a noose. And, simple soul though he may have been, he was, I am sure, by no means a fool.

One day the Foreign Ministry invited the delegation to lunch at the Peking Duck, perhaps the most famous restaurant in China. It dates back to imperial days but, whereas its patrons used to include the rich and the high-born, now it is used almost exclusively for official banquets. Not unexpectedly, we had Peking Duck, but it is not as simple as it sounds. Being an economical people, the Chinese eat practically every portion of an animal or bird. Thus we started with the crisply-fried webbed feet, chewy but tasty, followed by its gizzard, its liver and its heart. Like a symphony, the meal consisted of three parts: that was the first and was followed by a soup. Soup is always served in the middle of a meal in China. Now came the *pièce de résistance*. There was a stir of excitement and everyone turned to watch two chefs walk into the middle of the room bearing aloft huge silver salvers on which, glowing golden in the sunlight, rested half a dozen whole ducks. The applause rang out, the birds were lowered to the table and the chefs proceeded to carve them into very thin slices. Platefuls of thin wheat pancakes now appeared and my Chinese neighbour leaned over with his chopsticks and showed me how to proceed. First he laid a pancake on my plate, smeared it with dark red plum sauce, chose one or two succulent morsels of duck, added a touch of spring onion and deftly rolled the whole thing into a cylinder about the size of a large Havana cigar. I lifted it with my chopsticks and nibbled it. It melted in the mouth, the duck so succulent, with just a sliver of crisp skin, the pancake as light as lace, and the slight sweetness of the plum jam leaving a delicious after-taste and making you want to eat more. We did. We ate and ate until the plates were bare.

That was the second movement. Then came the third and it had me baffled. For some reason, perhaps to demonstrate that anti-climax must follow climax as night follows day, we were now served roast chicken. It too was delicious but by now I was almost full. Green tea and speeches followed and then, merciful release, we were allowed to rise from the table and make our way back to the hotel across Tien An-min. But so skilful and light is Chinese cooking that I did not feel at all bloated. We had several other splendid meals, notably a final banquet in Shanghai, but the Peking Duck is the one that sticks in my mind.

Next day we set off for the Great Wall of China, now almost a tourist cliché, but then something that few Westerners had seen. We drove north of Peking for a couple of hours, the country becoming more and more rugged, until suddenly, in front of us on the skyline, we were confronted by the Wall, a spectacular sight as it switchbacked along the crest of the hills.

After Tien An-min and the portrait of Chairman Mao, it is the most famous sight in China and hundreds of Chinese were clambering off buses and milling about the entrance. We climbed steeply up for a hundred yards or so and emerged on the main section of the wall. For as far as the eye could see in either direction, the wall rose steeply, fell away, curved left and right, following the crest of the hills, plunging into valleys and climbing again until it disappeared into the distance. It runs like this for nearly 4,000 miles right across the northern provinces of China; small wonder that it was the only man-made structure the astronauts were able to identify from space. But it was more than just a wall. It was also a roadway, protected by a rampart and wide enough for a chariot to be driven along at full gallop. In this way, the Chinese were able to patrol their long northern border and bring up reinforcements rapidly if needed against the Mongol hordes.

A day or two later we were shown another aspect of China's ancient civilisation: acupuncture. We were invited to watch operations being performed in one of the big Peking hospitals, in which acupuncture was being used to anaesthetise the patient. We were able to watch three operations, one a hernia, one an eye operation and, the third, the removal of a large tumour from a woman's stomach. This sounded the most interesting and, suitably smocked and masked, we followed the surgeon into the operating theatre.

A woman of between thirty and forty lay on the table, a screen across her chest so that she could not see what was happening lower down. The acupuncturist, a woman, now approached and planted six needles in the woman's face and neck; one on each temple, one beside each nostril, and the other two in the neck behind the ears. The needles were then connected to a machine which made them vibrate. Each needle was precisely placed to hit a nerve and the vibration eventually produced the anaesthetic effect. The surgeon hovered beside the patient, talking to her reassuringly while a nurse gave her sips of tea from the spout of a teapot. The woman was completely conscious and looked calm.

After about ten minutes, when he was satisfied that the needles had done their work, the surgeon began, making a big incision in the woman's stomach and cutting out a tumour as big – and as green – as a large avocado pear. It was all over in five minutes. The woman lay quietly throughout, while the nurse talked to her and continued giving her sips of tea. The strain showed on the woman's face but she never moved. As the surgeon finished the stitching and the scalpels and swabs were removed, he leaned over and spoke to her.

I knew he had been trained in the United States and spoke good English, so I asked him: 'Doctor, can you ask her how she's feeling?'

He translated. 'She says she's feeling fine.'

'Did she feel any pain?'

'No, no pain at all. When the knife went in, she says she felt it but it was as if someone was stroking her stomach with a feather. When I removed the tumour, she felt it. She says she had a feeling of relief but no pain.'

A few minutes later, as they wheeled her away, she sat up, smiled brightly and thanked the surgeon. I do not know if she had been told to do it for the cameras, but it looked completely spontaneous.

Afterwards, the surgeon said that she was a simple peasant and had taken a lot of reassuring that she would feel no pain.

'Psychological preparation of the patient before the operation is essential,' the surgeon said. 'But the benefits are considerable. Anaesthesia by acupuncture is much safer than by drugs, and post-operative shock is much less. I would not however recommend it for foreigners.' Chinese doctors have used acupuncture for centuries to cure all manner of ailments. They have a detailed knowledge of the nervous system and where the needles need to be inserted, since different pressure points affect different parts of the body. But the use of acupuncture as an anaesthetic in operations was still comparatively new.

I also learned that, despite his skills, the American-trained doctor was paid a pittance by Western standards – about £50 a month. But then prices were exactly the same as in 1949, in other words there was no inflation. Food was cheap and there was little else for a Chinese to spend money on. Once he had acquired a bicycle, a watch, a radio and a sewing machine, he had everything a man could have in the way of consumer goods. Television sets were in every factory and public hall, but not in private homes. And no Chinese was allowed to own a car. Just how educated Chinese put up with this spartan society was a mystery to me. After all, as a race, the Chinese are just as greedy and acquisitive as anyone else. Hong Kong is full of Chinese millionaires. There are no millionaires in China now, but equally, the Communists boast, there are no beggars either. Where once on the Bund, in Shanghai, the Rolls Royces jostled one another between the rickshaws, the poster on the front of the old British Consulate now proclaimed 'Workers of the World Unite'. The great banks had a shuttered, desolate air and the crowd shuffled past in boiler-suited uniformity. But the eyes were sharp and they fastened immediately on us Westerners, noting our clothes, our shoes, our watches and above all our cameras. One man sidled up to me, stared at my camera and spat out one word: 'Pentax'. He looked me hard in the eye and then drifted away. He and others looked as if they would have liked to have spoken to us, but they did not dare. So they just stared and the Chinese can stare harder and longer than anyone else.

But they have the same appetites as other men. They are simply contained by the straitjacket that Mao, the peasant Emperor, imposed on them. One of the senior officials of the Foreign Ministry's Press Department was called Mr Chih. There were two Mr Chihs and to differentiate them they were known as Oxford Chih and Harvard Chih. Oxford Chih was rumoured to be the man who killed Anthony Grey's cat when the unfortunate Reuters correspondent was held prisoner in his own house in Peking during the Cultural Revolution.

Oxford Chih used to drop into my hotel room in the evening to talk about this and that in his excellent English and to have a glass of whisky. I soon discovered that, while he liked to talk, Mr Chih really came for the whisky. He said he had acquired the habit during his long spell of duty in London. After a couple of whiskies, he would become quite loquacious and I would press him for filming opportunities. I particularly wanted to visit the People's Liberation Army, last seen in action against the Indians in 1962 and before that more memorably against the Americans, the British and the rest of the United Nations forces in Korea ten years before.

But Mr Chih simply drank my whisky and said it was very difficult. Very, very difficult. I plied him with more whisky until my supply ran out, but all Mr Chih would say that to film the Army was very, very difficult. Several times I was tempted to ask him if he had in fact killed Anthony Grey's cat, but there was a hint of controlled violence about him that gave me pause. I could imagine him killing the poor cat with fiendish satisfaction.

The head of Mr Chih's department was called Mr Ma. He appeared only occasionally and seemed a model civil servant. But, when he went to Paris a few months later on an official visit, Mr Ma apparently enjoyed himself so much that he missed his plane back to Peking. The Chinese do not send people to the salt mines. Backsliders are dispatched for 're-education' to the paddy fields in the middle of nowhere and I imagine that is what happened to Mr Ma.

CHAPTER XIII

A Guest of General Amin in the Execution Cell. Bob Astles and the Richest Man in Uganda

In August 1972, President Amin, a figure of fun to readers of *Punch* but not to the unfortunately people of Uganda, ordered the expulsion of all Asians holding British passports – about 40,000 people. He later extended this to virtually all Asians, even those who held Ugandan citizenship, accusing them of sabotaging the economy and encouraging corruption. He claimed he had received divine guidance. God had appeared to him in a dream and told him that he must 'act immediately' to save the nation.

Politically speaking, Amin was on solid ground. Most Africans resented what they felt had been a long history of exploitation by Asian traders, the descendants of those labourers who were brought from India originally to build the railway from the coast. The Asians are the shop-keepers of Africa and every East African village had its Asian *duka*. It was often the only shop in the vicinity and so the Africans had no choice but to trade there. In time many Asians grew wealthy and, knowing that one day Kenya, Uganda and Tanzania would become independent and the British leave, they took the precaution of sending their money out of the country – to India, Switzerland or elsewhere.

Amin's expulsion order was followed by the forced sale of Asian shops and property, which only Ugandan Africans were allowed to buy. The British Government described Amin's decision as 'inhumane', but there was little they could do about it.

ITN sent Richard Lindley and a crew out to cover the story, but after a couple of weeks Lindley informed the Foreign Desk that he wanted to come home to get married. One night at the beginning of September, when I was newscasting, the duty foreign editor, Mike Morris, said to me: 'Sandy, how would you like to go to Uganda?' Since there were many places I would rather have gone to, I replied: 'Not much.' Mike explained about Richard's impending marriage, and then he played his trump card. 'The trouble is,' he said, 'there's no one else I can send. Everyone's on holiday or away.'

Put like that, I was trapped. The only way out of it would be to refuse the assignment and that was one thing I had never done and would never do.

'All right,' I said crossly. 'It's bloody inconvenient but, if you're absolutely stuck, I'll go.'

'Thanks very much, Sandy,' Mike said. 'There's a plane on Sunday.'

It was a British Caledonian flight from Gatwick direct to Entebbe and the tartan-clad hostesses plied me so assiduously with champagne in the first-class cabin that the flight passed in a pleasant haze. Next morning, after breakfast, I looked out of the window to see Victoria Nyanza, the second largest lake in the world, gleaming blue and silver below us. We banked and came in to land at Entebbe, three miles north of the Equator, the old British capital and still distinguished by the splendid Government House the British built overlooking the lake.

My Italian crew, Mario Rosetti and his soundman and nephew, Fiori, were waiting to drive me into town. Mario was as always full of smiles and Italian bonhomie, although I knew from past experience that after a day or two the yearning for Roma and his wife's pasta would soon over-power him. Fiori was an unsmiling youth and, because Mario treated him more as a pack horse than a sound recordist, Donald Wise had christened him the Donkey.

It is a pleasant twenty-mile drive along the lake to Kampala, the capital, which stands in a cluster of low green hills. We were staying not at the old Imperial, now renamed the Grand, but at a new hotel called the International, standing on the edge of a public park. Kampala was still an attractive city with some big colonial houses set high up on the hillside, their gardens ablaze with purple, red, pink, orange and white bougainvillea, cascading over trellises and climbing thirty to forty feet into the trees. The centre of the city was full of Indian-owned shops, which normally sold silks, ivory and other tourist goods. Now, half of them were closed and the rest were selling off their goods for the best price they could get.

Outside the Bank of Uganda, where we filmed next day, hundreds of Asian men had formed a long queue that wound round the outside of the building and down the steps to the street. Under new regulations, they had to get clearance from the Bank before leaving and could only take £50 per family with them. We went down the long line interviewing people at random. One man was wearing a T-shirt with Idi Amin's picture on it. Those not too frightened to talk said they were worried about what would happen if they failed to meet the ninety-day deadline. President Amin had spoken about the possibility of transit camps. 'They will beat us up there,' one young man said, looking round nervously.

At the British High Commission, they gave the impression that they were sitting underneath a volcano about to erupt. They had already completed formalities for 7,000 Asians to emigrate to Britain and were hoping to clear another 1,000 families a week. But there was no chance of shipping them all out before Amin's deadline expired.

I asked to see the British High Commissioner, Richard Slater, but I was told he was too busy. He was under-standably overwhelmed by events. Normally a foreign correspondent can rely on considerable help from British

Embassies and missions abroad, depending on the calibre of the staff, but, in Uganda, the High Commission gave us no help at all.

There were a score of other correspondents and photographers in Kampala, mostly British, including Donald Wise and Don McCullin. Donald Wise was a brave man to be there at all, I thought. The correspondent from the *Sunday Mirror* had written a scathing piece about Amin, which the paper had splashed on its front page with the headline: Is Amin Really Mad? Sensibly, the correspondent had left the country before the paper appeared and was in no hurry to come back. The *Daily Mirror*, which has a separate staff, thereupon summoned Donald from his base in Hong Kong to Nairobi. He had taken soundings there and decided it was safe to continue to Uganda. He was wrong but did not know it yet. I went to have a drink with him in the Grand: it had hardly changed since the first time I had stayed there in the days of the Kabaka, sixteen years before. Over a glass of beer, Donald said he did not blame Amin for wanting to break the Asian stranglehold on local commerce, but he disagreed totally with the way he was doing it.

We talked about the dark rumours that were circulating about Amin. There was evidence that, since his overthrow of President Milton Obote eighteen months before, Amin had liquidated many of his tribal opponents in the Army. Amin himself was a Kakwa from the banks of the Nile near the Sudan border. They were a small warrior tribe and Moslems, while most other Ugandans were nominally Christian. Amin himself was an impressive figure, about six foot five-inches tall and weighing over fifteen stone. He had been Uganda heavyweight boxing champion and the British establishment preferred him initially to Obote. He had served in the British-officered King's African Rifles and had been the first black Ugandan officer. At the Independence Day parade in 1962, Amin had carried the colour. A complaint that he had killed a number of innocent Kenya villagers while hunting Mau Mau terrorists in Kenya was conveniently glossed over. Amin was also said to be suffering from syphilis, although he looked fit enough when I saw him next day.

We were relaxing beside the pool when we heard that he was due at the hotel to give a lunch for the Olympic team. Hastily pulling on shirts and trousers, we hurried down to look for him. The team were there, standing in groups, wearing their Olympic uniform of maroon blazers and grey slacks. But there was no sign of Amin. It was only when they went inside that someone spotted him, too late to take a picture. He too was dressed in blazer and slacks and, if it had not been for his huge size, we would have missed him altogether.

We followed them in, Mario carrying the camera, and pushed our way into the banqueting room. Amin was at the top table and I went round to try and get a few words out of him but, as soon as he saw the Press and the television cameras approaching, he scowled bad-temperedly. Still, I thought it was worth a try.

'Good afternoon, President Amin,' I began, holding the microphone towards him. 'This must be a proud day for you, having all your Olympic team here.'

Instead of answering, he gave me a glare, grunted something and turned to the man beside him.

I tried again. 'I see you have your silver medallist with you, too.'

Amin looked balefully at me for a moment then turned back to the man beside him and said in a stage whisper, 'Get these people out of here.'

The aide rose and shouted, 'All you Press. Leave the room immediately.' He waved his arms dismissively. We retreated, muttering rude comments under our breath and taking a few last shots. It was the first time I had seen Amin and I was impressed by the sense of malevolence that flowed from him, like some potent and sinister witch doctor's spell.

Over a sandwich at the pool, I took stock of the situation. We had now been in Uganda for four or five days. We had already done the main story and shipped it to London. Amin was obviously not going to cooperate by holding a press conference. There seemed to be not much else to be done. When the office called that night, I told Mike Morris there was no point in staying.

'Well, just hold on over the weekend,' he said, 'and let's review things on Monday. Tell you what; you like animals. Why don't you and the crew go the Game Park for the weekend. Enjoy yourselves and we'll talk again on Monday.'

Mike knew my weakness for game parks and safaris, and I happily agreed. On Saturday we set off to drive 150 miles north to the Murchison National Park on the Nile. It was magnificent country. As we neared the Nile the vegetation grew lusher, the trees taller, and brilliantly-coloured carmine bee-eaters perched on the telegraph poles beside the road.

We stopped at the Karuma Falls to admire the Nile hurtling through a narrow gorge and then drove the last few miles beside the river, now broad and placid. We took the ferry over to Chobie Lodge, the main tourist camp.

Next day we were told we could take a paddle steamer up river to the Murchison Falls, coming back in time for lunch. It was a memorable experience and we were happy and relaxed when we got back to the Lodge. We had just sat down to lunch when the Scotsman who ran the place came bustling over to the table.

'I've just heard the local news,' he said. 'Kampala Radio says there's been an invasion by Obote supporters in the south from across the Tanzanian border. It sounds verra bad. They're talking of over a thousand men. They've occupied three towns and there's heavy fighting.'

We gulped down the rest of our lunch, paid our bill and, after an argument over a fee for filming in the park, were on our way half an hour later. We crossed the ferry and were soon on the road south, doing a steady seventy down the empty strip of tarmac, hoping no elephant or rhino would unexpectedly emerge from the bush.

On the outskirts of Kampala a long line of cars was held up at an army checkpoint. Jumping the queue, we drove to the front. A paratrooper with a red beret and an automatic in his hand flagged us down angrily. 'Press.' I brandished my card.

He made us get out and searched the boot. He was jumpy and hostile but he finally waved us through.

As we walked into the lobby of the hotel, I saw two of my colleagues, Chris Munnion of the *Daily Telegraph* and

384

David Fairhall of the *Guardian*, sitting in the middle of the room with tense expressions on their faces. An African policeman with a rifle sat opposite them.

I walked up and said to Munnion, 'Christ, what the hell's going on?'

'Don't be a bloody fool,' he hissed. 'Piss off.' I wanted to show my moral support, but I did not want to get arrested myself. As I walked away, I noticed they had overnight bags with them.

Upstairs in my room, I had a shower, changed and came down to see what was happening. Munnion and Fairhall had gone. Someone told me they had been taken away in a police van. The lobby presented a curious sight. Small groups of people stood about in twos and threes, almost whispering. Behind the main desk, it looked as if the staff were being questioned by two or three men whom I had not seen before. I guessed they were plain-clothes police.

I went back upstairs and tried to book a call to London.

'Sorry sir,' the operator said. 'But all international calls have to be taken downstairs.'

So that they can listen in more easily, I told myself, and rang off.

I went back downstairs to the bar and ordered a whisky. There were few drinkers and they were talking in low voices. A little later my name was called. London was on the line.

'Hallo, Sandy. It's Eric Stevens [a script writer on News at Ten]. How are you?'

'All right,' I said. I was in the middle of the lobby in front of the main desk and I could see secret policemen standing about in the room behind the desk.

'Can you give us a voice piece on what's happening?' Eric asked.

'It's a bit difficult now,' I said. 'I'm in rather a public place at the moment.'

'Oh,' said Eric, realising there were problems. 'Well, could you tell us anything in question and answer?'

'I'll try,' I said, 'but there are a lot of people listening.'

'I see . . . well, we've got on tape that there's been an

invasion in the south. And that they're fighting in three places. Can you give us any more details?'

'That's all I know,' I said, 'except that two of my colleagues Chris Munnion of the *Telegraph* and David Fairhall of the *Guardian* have been arrested and taken away from the hotel.'

Eric was obviously taking notes. He asked a couple more questions and then, not wanting to compromise me further, rang off.

Next morning, I listened to the news on the radio. Fighting was still going on in the south, the announcer said. The heroic Ugandan Army was rushing reinforcements to the spot. Then came the nasty bit. Britain and Tanzania were both responsible and the Uganda Government knew that there were 'many British spies' in the country, many of them military men posing as civilians. If any citizen saw these suspicious characters, he should report them to the authorities. All this was said in the name of a Ugandan army spokesman. We all knew that was how Amin described himself when he did not want to be quoted in person. I knew then exactly what would happen. Everyone in Uganda would be looking for 'British spies'. I decided that the sensible thing to do was to leave before we were all arrested.

I called Donald Wise and arranged to have lunch with him at the little Italian restaurant between our two hotels. At least he had not been arrested. Then, with Mario and Fiori, I went to the airline office in the hotel and booked seats to Nairobi on the afternoon flight. After that I went upstairs to write a script for a game park film – it was mainly about the slump in tourism, once a useful foreign currency-earner for Uganda, but now suffering like everything else from Amin's erratic policies.

I had just finished the script and was getting ready to leave for lunch with Donald when there was a knock and the door opened. A medium-sized middle-aged African with short-cropped hair came in, looked around casually and said: 'I would just like to ask you a few questions.' I wanted to say, 'who the hell are you?' but I knew immediately he was police.

He came over to the bed and picked up some of the papers

scattered on it. I cursed myself silently for leaving my sheaf of cuttings, some of them critical of Amin, in full view. I should have destroyed them as soon as I heard the radio that morning. He rummaged among them and then picked up a ticket.

'What's this?' he asked, looking at me with his mournful eyes. I decided he was ex-Special Branch and British-trained.

'A ticket.'

'It says Simba on it,' he held it up. 'Why are you interested in the Simba Battalion in Mbarara?' Mbarara, in the south, was one of the towns involved in the fighting.

For a moment I was non-plussed. Then I croaked a laugh. 'That's the name of the boat that goes up the Nile to the Murchison Falls,' I said. 'Look, it has Murchison National Park written on it. We went there for the weekend.'

He grunted, unconvinced.

'I'd like you to come to headquarters and answer some questions from my superiors.'

Again, I thought of refusing. Was he carrying a gun? I imagined so. But, in any case, I knew resistance would not only be hopeless, it would be downright stupid.

'All right.'

'Bring your things,' he said, indicating the wardrobe.

'If I'm only going to answer a few questions, what's the point?'

He shrugged.

Compromising, I packed my toothbrush and electric razor in an airline bag. He opened the door, nodding for me to go first. As we walked to the lift, I glanced quickly up the corridor in the direction of Mario's room. It was empty. The lift came, we got in and went down in silence. In the lobby, he tried to make me walk straight towards the back door but I insisted on going over to the desk to leave my key. I wanted to be sure that they would see me leaving and would know I had been arrested.

Outside, the noonday sun struck the top of my head with physical force. A white Peugeot waited in the car park. My captor opened the back door and told me to get in. There was one other European in the back, a young man I had not seen before. As I stepped into the car, my foot tripped on something and I looked down. There was a newspaper on the floor and, underneath it, now half uncovered, was the black metal of a sub-machine gun. I suddenly felt scared. Sad Eyes got in behind me and slammed the door. There were three men in the front, the driver and two other secret police. One of them wore dark glasses. The driver reversed noisily and then, racing the engine, drove fast out of the back gate.

All the Africans were talking at once.

'Hallo,' I said to the young man beside me, introducing myself.

'Hallo, I'm Nick Moore. Reuters in Nairobi.'

I felt I was looking at myself sixteen years ago. 'They just picked you up too?'

'Yes . . . They're very hostile, these people,' he said. The man with the sunglasses had twisted round in his seat and was talking volubly to Sad Eyes.

'They're saying that we are ungodly, the British. That we're not believers. They're all Moslems. They . . . I can't understand all they're saying . . . but they're very hostile and very anti-white.'

The Africans were talking Swahili. I wished I had learned it properly in Kenya. I had no idea what they were saying but perhaps that was a good thing, I thought. They were driving fast, up the hill past the old British colonial houses amid their bougainvillea. Then we were out of the city and still climbing. Suddenly the driver swung the wheel over hard, and I saw the entrance to a military camp. A sign said Makindye Military Police Barracks. The barrier was raised and the car swung in with a rasp of tyres, braking with a jolt in front of the guardroom. We were ordered out and into the guard-room under the curious gaze of passing African soldiers.

Inside it was so British that, under different circumstances, I might have laughed. Two large black MPs sat behind a desk, the senior one a corporal.

'Sit down,' he barked. I looked round. There was no chair on our side of the table.

My young colleague put it into words. 'Where? There's nowhere to sit.'

The second MP, a private, stood up, leaned past me and hit Nick Moore a stinging blow across the side of the head with his truncheon. I slid down on to the cement floor and flicked a glance at him. He was breathing sharply but there was no blood.

'Put your effects on the table,' the corporal said. 'Everything.'

We hastened to comply: passport, Press card, handkerchief, money. The corporal entered it laboriously in a ruled exercise book. Nick made a separate pile.

'Shoes and socks,' the corporal barked, and they were added to the pile.

Finally, the inventory done, we were taken outside. It must have been about 1.30 by now, the sun high overhead, the air warm, but we were on a small lawn, shaded by trees. The corporal shouted and a big soldier came forward. He was taller than me, about six foot three or four, well-built and he looked about twenty-two. He wore webbing ammunition pouches over his battle dress and carried an FN, the heavy NATO automatic rifle.

We stood together, barefoot, defenceless. The young soldier shouted something.

'He wants us to run,' Nick said.

'Where?'

I got the answer in my back. A terrific jab from the FN. The force of it threw me forward and we both started to run across the small patch of grass towards the gate at the far end. Halfway across the lawn the soldier gave me another vicious blow in the back. It was like a bayonet thrust without the bayonet. I gasped with the pain.

'He wants us to run faster.'

I did, but the thought went through my mind: if I run too fast he'll shoot me and claim that I was trying to escape. We went through a wooden gate surrounded by barbed wire and emerged on to a smooth earth road. I tried to keep a steady pace, not so fast as to give him an excuse to shoot – this thought was uppermost in my mind – but not too slow either.

He hit me again. I already knew what the pain was like but it still made me cry out.

We came to a fork and the soldier shouted something.

'Right,' Nick gasped.

We were now running up a hill. I could see a line of huts at the top and there was a big orderly room or headquarters on the right.

Halfway up the hill, I could hear the big soldier's boots pounding behind me and then, like a bullet striking the flesh, he hit me a fourth time, the same place, the same pain.

You bastard, I thought.

Someone was coming towards us, swinging a wooden club in his hand. As we ran past, not daring to slacken speed, the newcomer shouted and Nick panted, 'Stop'. As we stood there, breathing heavily, the officer, a major, walked towards us swinging his club.

'Sit down,' he ordered, in English, waving away the soldier who was holding the FN inches away from my face. He stood, swinging his club menacingly in front of us. I thought he was going to start hitting me, so I started to talk fast, willing myself to be clear and coherent.

'We're British journalists. My friend here works for Reuters news agency in Nairobi. I work for Independent Television News in London. I don't know . . . '

'Television . . . ?' The major interrupted. 'How long have you been in Uganda?'

'A week,' I said. 'I don't know why we've been arrested. We have done absolutely nothing wrong. We have been trying to report honestly on what is going on in your country . . . ' I was still panting from fear rather than the running, and my mouth was dry.

'You're both journalists?'

'Yes.'

'Get up,' he ordered, still swinging his club but with less menace now, I thought.

We stood for a moment, catching our breaths, while he talked to the guard. Then he nodded towards the line of huts and the guard jabbed his rifle, into the air this time. As we approached I saw they were numbered. After some hesitation the major chose the one marked C 19, opened the door and we were pushed inside. In a curious way, it was a relief.

Outside, I felt vulnerable, a target. Inside seemed safer. The hut was long and narrow with a smooth concrete floor and grey-white plaster walls and ceiling. There was no furniture. About half a dozen Africans sat on the floor near the door and, perhaps in a subconscious effort to get as far away from the door as possible, we walked to the far end of the room and sat down on the floor with our backs to the wall.

The door shut and we could hear the key turning. Silence descended and I examined the other prisoners. Two soldiers lay sprawled on the floor just inside the door. Next to them were three other Africans in shirts and trousers. They also lay silently, staring at us with dull, frightened eyes. Finally, in the opposite corner to where we sat, at the end of the cell, a sixth African lay without moving, as if unconscious, his fatigues completely covered in mud.

I tried to make out if the two soldiers at the far end were guards or prisoners. I decided they must be prisoners because they had no weapons and they looked so thoroughly dejected. I examined the rest of the cell. At the far end were the lavatories, washbasins and showers – what the British Army call 'ablutions'. A thin wooden skirting board ran round the edge of the floor and we were just able to sit on it, instead of on the cement. Something drew my attention to the wall behind me. I craned round and saw that it was a hole in the plaster about two inches deep and six across, the kind that a bullet makes. Then I noticed the wall to my right. A line of bullet holes started about waist high about ten feet away and climbed at evenly-spaced intervals to the top of the wall. My eyes went to the ceiling above us. It was splashed with blood. It was dry but did not look very old.

The bullet holes along the wall had been made by an FN or a sub-machine gun firing on automatic, I guessed. The bullet hole behind us could have been part of the same burst, or a separate shot. The blood on the ceiling was more puzzling. I could only speculate that the force of the bullets meeting the flesh had sprayed blood over the walls and ceiling and that they had wiped the walls but forgotten about the ceiling. Whatever the precise details, the general conclusion was unnerving: someone had been killed in this cell and not too long ago.

Nick had apparently been having identical thoughts. He turned to me and whispered urgently, 'I don't think we're going to get out of this place. I think they're going to kill us.'

The thought had also occurred to me but hearing it said aloud automatically made me reject it. I felt it was vital to refuse to give in to despair and to attempt to keep up my own morale as much as his. I said: 'It looks bad but I am sure we're going to be all right. They wouldn't dare do anything to us. It'll just take a little time until someone highup realises we are here.' All this was said in a whisper. Silence fell again. The Africans lay in a kind of stupor.

About half an hour after our arrival, I heard the key turn in the lock and a couple of armed guards stood in the doorway. One of them gave a packet of cigarettes to each of the two soldiers; the other handed out some biscuits. He did not bother to walk down the cell, but sent a couple of packets skimming along the smooth cement floor towards us. I opened the cellophane wrapping and bit into one; it was hard and tasteless. After a couple of mouthfuls I decided I was not hungry.

The arrival of the biscuits represented a very small sign of hope. If they were planning to take us out and shoot us they would not have bothered to give us biscuits, I reasoned. But I suspected that the threat did not lie in planned violence: if it came it would probably be haphazard and irrational. I recalled the murder of two young Americans, one a free-lance journalist, another a lecturer at Makerere University, who had been investigating the killing of 160 soldiers by Amin's men the year before and who had been murdered on the orders of an officer. Their bodies had never been recovered.

Another half-hour or so went by and again the key rattled in the lock. The door swung open and a guard came in, followed by four prisoners carrying a fifth man. As they put him down on the floor, I could see that the back of his shirt was covered in blood. He groaned once. As the prisoners filed out, the guard looked up the cell, straight at us. I was sitting with my arms folded on my knees and my chin resting on my hands. I pretended to be asleep, thinking that it was perhaps unwise to be seen watching. After only a second's hesitation,

392

the guard shouted something and the four prisoners came back into the room, picked up the wounded man and carried him out again. One of them came back inside with a brush and a pail and started sweeping the blood on the cement towards the ablutions. The door was locked again and after a minute or two I heard a curious thumping sound, like a hammer or a club hitting something soft. Almost immediately there came the ringing noise a shovel makes on hard ground. Then silence. The air in the room was oppressively heavy. It sounded as if they had been hitting the wounded man. I was told later that many prisoners in Makindye were beaten to death with twenty-eight pound hammers. And the shovel? I wondered at first if they had been burying the man. But that seemed implausible. Possibly they were scraping away the blood on the ground outside.

Things now looked much worse. Maybe Nick had been right. Maybe we were going to be killed. I felt sick with fear and, despite the warmth of the day, suddenly cold. I began to pray. 'Our Father which art in Heaven . . . ' I must have repeated the Lord's Prayer four or five times, trying to rally what was left of my courage and my diminishing reservoir of hope. I clung to the idea of life. I did not want to die.

The shadows were creeping round the cell walls when, about four, the key ground in the lock again. The room seemed to fill with people. Three or four officers came in first, followed by about half a dozen hefty soldiers carrying rifles and sub-machine guns. The prisoners beside the door sat up straight. So did we. The only person who did not move was the muddy soldier in the corner. Talking and laughing, they walked the length of the cell towards him. The officer in front, a major, bent forward and jabbed the recumbent figure with his swagger stick. The soldier sat up, half dazed, rubbing his eyes, and they all laughed loudly. When he got to his feet, I saw that he was tall and thin. The major continued to pin him with his swagger stick, as if he was an unpleasant insect, and then turned him round and pushed him down the cell. The guards now took over, kicking and shoving him in the direction of the ablutions, his head snapping back like a doll's. They disappeared and the shower was turned full on.

A few minutes later, the tall soldier reappeared, soaking wet, still fully clothed. Instead of muddy red, his uniform was now dark green. As he walked back to his corner, with a few kicks to help him on his way, the water ran in rivulets on to the cement floor. Having had their fun, the visitors turned to go. Then, as if he had seen us for the first time, the major with the swagger stick turned in our direction, peering at us through the gathering dusk.

I scrambled to my feet, thinking we had a better chance standing up than sitting down.

'Who are you?'

'We're British journalists,' I said. 'My friend here is from Reuters News Agency. I'm from British Independent Television News.'

He seemed surprised. They talked among themselves for a few seconds.

'Here,' the first one said. 'Write down your name and organisation.' He produced a scrap of paper and a ballpoint. I held it against the wall and tried to write, but the angle made it difficult.

'Hurry up,' the officer said impatiently. Finally we handed the paper back and they stood, in the poor light, trying to decipher who we were.

'Wait,' the major said, 'I will find out.' We sat down again as they all clumped off down the cell, slamming the door behind them.

An hour passed, the cell was quite dark now and I must have dozed off. I woke suddenly, hearing the familiar rattle at the door. Torch beams zigzagged in the darkness and boots scraped along the cement. I could see the outline of several men. It was the major again, with two or three guards. menacing in the half-light.

'You two. Come with me.'

We followed him down the room towards the door, passing the dim shapes of the three Africans and the two soldiers lying on the floor. Outside the sky had a reddish glow from the camp lights, the air was warm and velvety and the earth felt cool beneath my bare feet.

As we stood, waiting for the guard to lock the cell door,

new fears assailed me. What was going to happen to us now? Were we going to be interrogated? Beaten up? Or even shot?

'Go forward,' the major ordered and pointed down the hill we had run up so agonisingly only a few hours before. But instead of walking past the orderly hut we branched to the right. Here it was darker and the ground sloped away more steeply. Were they taking us to the killing ground, where a bullet in the back of the neck, or a blow from a hammer, would finish us off? I took a deep breath, resolving that, if these were my last moments, I would try and meet them with my head up and my courage intact.

'Stop here,' the major said. We were at the bottom of a small dark hollow. He gave an order and one of the guards started searching among his bunch of keys. I could see that there was a hut just to our right, all in darkness. After several minutes it was obvious the guard could not find the right key. The major gave another order and we walked forward again. I could see another hut beyond, silhouetted against the perimeter lights.

'Stop,' the major ordered. This time the guard found the key and, after a lot of rattling and turning, finally unlocked the door.

'Go inside.'

They were the sweetest words I had heard all day. I ducked gratefully through the doorway into the protective darkness. On the left, by the door, two Africans were sitting cross-legged, conducting some sort of religious service. I could see about half a dozen other people sitting round in a rough circle. I stumbled and a hand guided me down to a seat on the floor. Somebody waved from the other side of the room.

'Hey, Sandy. When did they pick you up?' It was Don McCullin, jaunty as ever.

'Shhh.' Someone pushed a mug of tea into my hand.

'Hallo, Sandy, I'm Bob Astles. I know you but you don't know me. I used to work for Obote. Remember when you did that interview with him? He asked me to get him the transcript afterwards. You gave him a rough ride. Remember?'

'Yes,' I said. 'I remember very well.'

One of the two Africans by the door was reading from the Bible. The other sat attentively beside him, his expression rapt, withdrawn. The first finished his reading and they both started to say the Lord's Prayer. We all joined in . . . 'for thine is the kingdom, the power and the glory, for ever and ever, Amen.'

There was a buzz of conversation. 'They have a little service every evening,' Astles explained. 'We all join in, they take it very seriously.'

'How long have they been here?' I asked.

'The one on the left was inside under Obote. Then they let him out, now he's been back inside again for about a year. He used to be a big shot at the airport. He doesn't think he'll ever get out of here alive.'

Someone grabbed my hand. I turned to find Don. 'You old bastard. I laughed when I saw you coming into the cell. Like an officer coming round to see if there were any complaints.'

'How did you get here?' I asked.

'They picked me up yesterday. I was down in the market taking pictures. This bastard hit me with his rifle butt. Then they brought me up here. Fucking awful place.'

Astles interrupted.

'They bring you straight in here?'

'No,' I said. 'They took us first to one of the cells up at the top. C19. They kept us there for about four hours.'

'C19?' Astles asked. 'Why, that's the execution cell. You're bloody lucky, mate, to come out of there alive. You'll be all right here. This is the VIP cell.'

There was a rattle at the door and two guards appeared.

'Grub's up,' Astles said.

It looked so unappetising that I could not bring myself to eat anything. I had another cup of tea.

Astles reappeared. 'You can sleep in here tonight,' he said, indicating a room on the right. 'It's Madhvani's. He's a nice chap, come and meet him.'

Manubhai Madhvani was a slim Indian of medium height, wth dark eyes and a relaxed manner. We shook hands. He had a bed alongside one wall. He pointed to a mattress and blankets on the floor.

'I'm afraid that's the best we can do.'

'Sheets,' I said, turning down the top blanket. 'Why, that's sheer luxury.'

Madhvani chuckled. 'We do the best we can.'

I just had time to clean my teeth before lights out. I got into bed gratefully, dog-tired, but feeling much happier now I was in the VIP cell.

There were nine of us in the cell: Don McCullin, Nick Moore and myself, the two Ugandans, a fat, jolly Ghanaian businessman, Madhvani, Astles and an Englishman who worked for a tea company. It was divided into six small rooms, three on each side, with a lavatory and washbasin at the far end. Astles was the unofficial head man and took it upon himself to give advice and organise things. But Madhvani was the VIP, the head of the richest Asian family in Uganda. When I asked him for a match, he held out a box with a smile: 'May I offer you one of the fourteen products of the Madhvani empire.'

The story of his arrest, as told by Astles and others, was that Amin had designs on the wealthy widow of Madhvani's late brother, Jehant. According to this version, Amin had even proposed marriage, and the family, horrified and knowing that Amin's sole purpose was to get his hands on her fortune, shipped her out of the country on the next plane. In his fury at being thwarted, Amin had promptly thrown Madhvani into jail.

Keys rattled in the lock and the guards appeared at the inner barred door. Breakfast consisted of lukewarm tea and unappetising chunks of bread.

McCullin pulled a face: 'Did you see what he was carrying the bread in?' he asked.

'No.'

'A bloody dustbin.'

Madhvani, who was standing on his head, his ritual every morning, overheard. 'Don't worry,' he said from his upside-down position, 'something better will be coming soon.'

Neither of us knew what he meant but, about a quarter of an hour later, an African appeared, dressed in immaculate white tunic and shorts, carrying an elaborate picnic basket which looked as if it might have come from Fortnum and Mason's. The basket was passed in to the cell where Madhvani undid the strap and lifted out a series of circular, stainless steel mess tins, each containing a different dish: scrambled eggs, boiled vegetables, bread, honey and yoghourt. There was also a thermos flask of tea. Madhvani waved a hand. 'Help yourselves. I told my wife there were lots of us and to send in plenty of food.'

I suddenly felt extremely hungry, having hardly eaten for twenty-four hours. As I stuffed myself with scrambled eggs and vegetables – Madhvani was a vegetarian – I asked him, 'How on earth do you manage to get your cook into a place like this?'

'Simple, really,' Madhvani said with his deprecating smile. 'You see, my cook is a Kakwa, the same tribe as General Amin comes from. Most of the soldiers here are Kakwa too. So, when he arrived at the gate and spoke to them in their own language, they let him in. Now of course they know him.

He came three times a day, always dressed in his crisp white ducks, carrying his spotless picnic basket.

Don McCullin thought as little of the prison food as I did. 'Just as well we've got Madhvani to look after us,' he said. 'Otherwise, we'd bleedin' well starve to death.'

After breakfast several of the other prisoners exercised by walking up and down the cell, and Don and I joined them. It was so small I felt like a caged animal, but at least it was better than sitting still. I counted as I walked. Fourteen paces to the end wall, turn beside the lavatory, and fourteen paces back to the door with the steel bars. Turn and fourteen paces the other way. We went up and down like that for about an hour, catching a glimpse through the bars of the sunshine beyond. Occasionally the guards would come and peer in, setting up a small tremor of fear. The first time it happened, they simply wanted Nick Moore and me, as new arrivals, to write down our names and organisations. But, the next time, they called me forward by name. The guard opened the steel door.

'Out,' he said, beckoning with a rifle. I stepped outside, barefoot, reluctant to leave the security of the cell. Why me, what have they got on me? I wondered anxiously as we marched across the dusty earth towards the guardroom. I was told to halt and sit on a bench opposite the guardroom.

An African in a suit came towards me. 'Mr. Gall?'

'Yes.'

'I'm the manager from the International.'

'Oh, really?' He was the last person I had expected to see.

'I've come about your bill.'

Christ, I thought, they never let go, do they? Then it occurred to me that perhaps I could use him to get a message to London. He seemed sympathetic.

'You see,' he went on, 'when you left yesterday, you did not settle your account.'

'I left in rather a hurry,' I said, deadpan.

'Yes, I know, Mr. Gall,' he said, equally deadpan. Then, dropping his voice, 'Are you all right?'

I glanced towards the guard. He was standing about ten paces away, not looking at us. 'Yes,' I said. 'I'm all right – at the moment.'

'Good,' he whispered. Then, raising his voice, 'I have the bill here.' He produced it. 'The full amount is 7,000 shillings.' I divided by twenty.

'About £350.' I reached into my hip pocket. I had forgotten, when we were booked in at the guardroom, that I had my traveller's cheques with me. I counted out £200 and signed them.

'You'll have to telex my office in London for more money. Can you do that?'

'Yes, I will try. If you give me the number.'

I made him write it down and he got up to go. 'Goodbye, Mr. Gall, Good luck, I hope to see you soon.' He gave my hand an extra squeeze. I walked back to the cell feeling slightly more cheerful. If he could get a message through to ITN they would at least know where I was and start putting pressure on the Foreign Office to try and secure our release.

(I was told by ITN later that they eventually got through to the hotel and spoke to the manager. They asked him for news of me. He said he had seen me and that I was all right but he could not tell them where I was being held. But, he added,

399

Mr. Gall requests you to send more money to pay his bill. John Parker, then on the Foreign Desk, laughed: 'When we heard that you were asking for more money, we knew you were all right, you old bastard.')

That evening, after the two Africans had conducted their prayer meeting, and before supper, Bob Astles came over to where Don and I were talking. Astles was a curious figure. He had been in Uganda a long time, had a Ugandan wife and ran a dairy farm outside Kampala. He had been on the fringes of Government for a long time, mainly on the Information side. But I suspected he had also been connected with the police in some way and I did not altogether trust him. Later, he was to become very close to Amin. Now, he started talking about the killing that was going on in Makindye.

'How do you know?' Don asked him.

'I've seen the bodies with my own eyes,' Astles said. 'They kill them with hammers and take them away in lorries at night. I've seen them loading the bodies on the lorries.'

Don got up. 'I don't want to hear about it,' he said. 'I just don't want to hear another bloody word. It makes me want to puke.'

I listened, though, because I suspected Astles knew what he was talking about. I thought of the sounds I had heard outside C19, after they had carried out the badly-wounded prisoner. Also, I had not heard a single shot being fired in the camp, nor did I in three days. It was possible of course that condemned prisoners were taken some distance away from Makindye and executed in the forest. But why should Astles invent such a story? I could see no point. And I knew Uganda had a history of tribal killings. Amin was simply the last of a long line of bloody tyrants.

That night I was woken by the sound of African voices just outside the window. I lay listening, alert for trouble. It sounded like two guards talking, one asking the other questions. Finally, the questioner went off into a long peal of bubbling laughter. I relaxed and went back to sleep. Next day, the Englishman who worked for one of the big tea companies told me what the conversation had been about.

'One guard was telling the other that there was a hole in the perimeter fence. Then he asked who was in this end hut, nearest the fence. The second man said it was the *Mzungu*, the white men.

' "Did the *Mzungu* have their shoes?" the first one wanted to know.

' "No," the second guard replied. "The *Mzungu* did not have their shoes."

' "Ah," said the first one, "then it's all right. Because, if the *Mzungu* don't have their shoes, they cannot possibly run away." ' Then he burst out laughing. I had to laugh too. It was true that, without shoes, I would not have run very far.

Next day, some of the guards started mending the hole in the perimeter fence in front of the cell. We watched them idly through the bars of the door. After a time, Madhvani came over.

'I wouldn't sit so near the door,' he said gently. 'They are very touchy and they might resent you watching them.'

Every time new guards came on duty, they would come over to the cell, apparently to make a routine inspection. Madhvani, who had been brought up in Uganda and spoke fluent Swahili, would go the door and discreetly slip a couple of packets of cigarettes through the bars. The guards always treated him deferentially. We, who spoke little or no Swahili, and had no cigarattes to offer, got precious little respect.

The English tea executive had apparently been arrested because he had once been in the Police Reserve. But the case of the Ghanaian was the strangest of all. He had been invited to Kampala by the Ugandan Government and had been in the middle of negotiations for a shipping contract when he had suddenly found himself being arrested in his hotel and dragged off to Makindye. His round, beaming, if rather bewildered face was in stark contrast to the other-worldly expressions of the two prayerful Ugandans.

By the third day, time began to hang heavy. Madhvani's cook arrived punctually with his picnic basket at breakfast and lunchtime, and after both meals I paced the cell, fourteen strides to the back wall, turn, fourteen strides to the door, quick glance out at the sunlight and greenery, turn and back again. Then, about five, when the light was beginning to take

on a yellowish tinge, a shadow fell across the door and a key
rattled in the lock. We stirred lethargically, imagining it was
another routine inspection. But soon it became clear that this
was different. They began to call out names – McCullin,
Moore, Gall, Astles, the tea planter, the Ghanaian. But not
the Ugandans, and not Madhvani. I shook hands with him.
His face was patient, resigned.

'Good luck,' he said. 'I'm glad they are letting you out.'

'I'm sorry you're not coming with us.'

He managed a little smile. 'I hope I'll be joining you before
too long.'

Outside, we were marched into the middle of the
compound and halted beside a table. All the belongings which
had been confiscated on arrival were laid out in neat piles. To
my surprise my watch and loose money were there as well.
And, most importantly, my desert boots.

Chris Munnion and David Fairhall, whom I had last seen
sitting under guard in the lobby of the International, now
appeared from the next-door cell looking pale and ill. They
had been less fortunate than we. They had had no Madhvani
food and their treatment had been rougher.

As we were signing for our belongings, a squad of men
came marching towards us three abreast, under guard. As
they drew level I saw they were all police officers, but their
badges of rank had been torn off, leaving their epaulettes
bare. I looked at their faces. They were almost grey with fear,
their eyes the eyes of men who have lost hope. I had an overwhelming impression that these men were being marched to
their death. I watched them march across the compound
towards the guardroom past an officer and a small group of
soldiers. The officer held out a knife and made a play of
wiping it on his sleeve. Several of the soldiers laughed,
doubling over and slapping their thighs. And then they were
out of sight, marching with heads high, to an unknown fate.

We now moved to the main gate where a tall, thin,
extremely hostile officer was waiting to make us sign our
deportation papers. He called us out one by one. 'Sign here,'
he ordered. 'And don't ever come back to Uganda.'

'Don't worry,' I said, 'I won't.'

I was halfway to my place when he snapped, 'You, come back here.' I turned and walked over to him.

'What did you say?' he demanded, his voice shrill with rage. 'What did you say just now?'

I cursed myself for being such a fool. Why hadn't I kept my damned mouth shut?

'I apologise,' I said. 'I apologise profusely. I didn't mean it. Please forgive me for what I said.'

There was a hideous pause. God, I prayed wildly, please don't let him cancel my release. I started to sweat.

'Don't ever say that again,' he finally spat out.

Not daring to utter another word, I turned and walked back to the others as calmly as I could. My mouth was dry and my heart was pumping.

'Jesus,' Don whispered, as I rejoined the little group, 'I thought we'd lost you there, mate. I moved right away. I didn't want to be seen standing next to you. Christ, you did give me a turn.'

I said nothing. I could see the thin officer still watching me, as a stoat watches a rabbit, ready for the kill.

Finally, with my heart-beat slowing down, we climbed into a waiting bus which, after a last unexplained delay, crunched into gear and drove slowly out of the gate of Makindye. Thank God, I thought, that bloody officer has stayed behind.

It was now about six and the lights were coming on in the town below. The escorting officer wanted to take us straight to the airport but I explained that I still had all my clothes at the International. Reluctantly, he agreed to the detour. When we reached the hotel, he came with me to my room and suspiciously watched me pack. One or two small things were missing, a pair of nail scissors, a bottle of aftershave. I presumed the room boy had helped himself, thinking perhaps that I would not be needing them again. Five minutes later, we were in the lobby, suitcase in one hand, typewriter in the other. The manager who had come to see me in Makindye was not about, but I asked for my bill and told them I would send them the money from London. They looked at the officer beside me and, nervously licking their lips agreed that would be quite all right.

It took an hour to get to the airport. The road was virtually empty but the Army had set up numerous roadblocks. We did not have much trouble but I heard later that it was a nightmarish journey for ordinary travellers, especially Asians, leaving the country. Many of them were dragged out of their cars and robbed and assaulted at gunpoint by soldiers.

There was a final checkpoint just before the airport. Inside, soldiers carrying rifles and sub-machine guns lounged about, watching us contemptuously. A brisk figure in a neat dark blue suit materialised and demanded, 'Which of you is Andrew Tasca?' Tasca was the Associated Press correspondent from Nairobi and had been in the cell with Munnion and Fairhall. The man asking for him was the American Chargé d'Affaires.

Tasca stepped forward and the Chargé shook his hand. 'You okay? All of you boys okay?' He gestured to two youngish men in white coats with name tabs on their chests. 'I brought two of our medical people from the Embassy along just in case any of you had been roughed up in Makindye and needed medical attention.'

While Tasca and the Chargé talked, I heard a bitter voice, which may have been mine, say, 'The American Chargé comes out to the airport with two doctors to see if Tasca is okay. There are half a dozen of us here, but you'll notice that none of the bloody Brits from the High Commission bothers to come out.'

The Chargé was busy telling Tasca, 'I've been in touch with the White House and President Nixon himself has taken a personal interest in the whole case.' I wondered if Nixon's pressure on Amin to get Tasca released had indirectly helped us. I recalled that the American Ambassador had been withdrawn in protest when the American freelance journalist and his friend had been killed by Amin's troops more than a year before.

They took us through immigration and customs around nine and, still under guard, we sat down to wait for the British Caledonian flight which was due in at ten from Nairobi. The bar was closed. We could not even get a drink.

At half past ten the handful of other passengers started boarding and finally, at about a quarter to eleven, we were told to board. I felt like cheering but I restrained myself. I would not believe we were finally free until the plane took off. As we walked out into the hot, humid, tropical night, towards the plane which stood about a hundred yards away in front of us, an extraordinary sight presented itself. At the edge of the tarmac, a great jet of naptha flame illuminated the darkness and, round it, like some mad galaxy, dived and danced a huge cloud of insects. As I walked past I could hear, above the roar of the gas flame, a terrible sizzling noise as individual beetles and moths, driven mad by the brilliance of the light, hurled themselves into the flame. The ground was littered with their singed corpses. But, for every one that perished, a hundred more jostled to take its place. It seemed that every insect in Entebbe was intent on self-immolation – all but one. He was quite small, white, ruby-eyed, and clung to my lapel all the way to the plane. I brushed him off gently into the darkness before climbing the steps. Inside, cool air and soft music greeted us, a whiff of cologne and a tartan smile of welcome. 'What would you like to drink, sir?' the glamorous hostess demanded.

'Champagne?' I asked.

'Oh, we don't normally serve champagne in economy,' she said. 'But wait a moment, let me ask the captain.' She was back in a second. 'The captain is sending down two bottles of champagne with his compliments.'

We gave a small cheer, and then we were trundling down the runway, picking up speed and lifting off smoothly. I looked down at the fast-receding lights of Entebbe, caught a last glimpse of Lake Victoria, raised my glass to Don McCullin, sitting beside me, and gave him the Scots toast.

'Here's tae us, Don, fa's like us, Deil the yin.'

CHAPTER XIV

The Fall of Saigon – I take over the Keys of the British Embassy Club

I had not been in Vietnam since 1968. Much had happened since then. The Americans had withdrawn the last of their fighting men in 1973, leaving behind only advisers. The war had been 'Vietnamised', which meant the South Vietnamese had to do all the fighting that previously had been left to the Americans. After the Americans had withdrawn, the great question that everyone debated was: would the South Vietnamese ever be able to stand up to the North Vietnamese on their own? The sceptics, among whom were most of the Saigon Press Corps, said the South was too corrupt and too soft to resist the battle-hardened war machine of the North for very long. The optimists, who naturally included the American administrators and its numerous cohorts in Saigon, argued that, if the South Koreans had turned out eventually to be as good soldiers as the North Koreans, who had over-run them in 1950, what was to prevent the South Vietnamese doing the same? As long as American aid and armaments poured in, it was just possible to believe the optimists. But then Congress began to grow tired of doling out endless grants of money and equipment, without any visible improvement in the morale or efficiency of the South Vietnamese forces, and the pessimists began to nod their heads and say I told you so. But it was not just the drying-up of American aid which tipped the scale. Indeed some American officials have said that the aid argument was just an alibi and that even at the end the South Vietnamese still had massive amounts of equipment they had stockpiled over the years and never used. No, there was a deeper reason. There was something basically wrong with the whole psyche of South Vietnam. There was a worm at the heart of the fruit. Too many politicians and too many generals – and the two were often synonymous – were either corrupt or inefficient. And many were both. What hope then was there for the poor wretched South Vietnamese infantryman who was often just as brave and as good a fighter as his Northern brother?

In the North they believed they were fighting for an ideal, however misguidedly; in the South the ordinary soldier must often have felt he was risking his life simply to keep the generals and their friends safe to grow rich in Saigon. And, while aid from America declined, the rockets and shells poured into the North from China and the Soviet Union.

Then, at the beginning of 1975, the military situation in the South began to deteriorate with alarming rapidity. After a series of lightning attacks in mid-March, North Vietnamese troops overran the key town of Ban me Thuot. Outnumbered and outmanoeuvred, the South Vietnamese withdrew, leaving the whole of the Central Highlands to fall into the Communist lap. Vietnam is a long thin country, much of it made up of a narrow coastal plain backed by mountains. The effect of this victory was to drive a wedge into the middle of President Thieu's half of the country, leaving the two ends dangerously exposed. This was bad enough, but much worse was to follow. On March 23, the North Vietnamese encircled Hue, the old Imperial capital, the city that the American Marines had fought so tenaciously to recapture in 1968. As the shells started to land, the local population, remembering the massacre that had followed the previous Communist occupation, fled in terror towards the coast. The South Vietnamese troops defending the city were caught up in this flood of panicky refugees who impeded their movement and sapped their morale.

Then, on March 30, an even bigger blow fell. Da Nang, the great northern base and once the headquarters of the Marines, was abandoned in an atmosphere of panic and confusion that must have delighted the Kremlin and the North Vietnamese high command as much as it shocked and appalled the White House and the South Vietnamese. The incredible scenes at Da Nang were seen on television round the world. The most extraordinary incident of all was the departure of the last plane from Da Nang. Edward Daly, the President of World Airways, a private company that had been evacuating refugees from Da Nang, wanted to make one last flight to the beleaguered city. Against the advice of American officials, he took off from Saigon on March 29 with two 727s. When he landed at Da Nang, thousands of South Vietnamese soldiers and civilians, waiting desperately for a plane out, made a rush to get on board. Daly tried shooting over their heads to frighten them off, but so desperate were they that they stormed the plane. Finally, 270 people crowded on board, all soldiers except for two women and one child. Daly had to knock several soldiers off the steps of the plane with his fists in order to get the steps up and the door closed. Even so, soldiers desperate to escape the advancing Communist troops jumped on to the wings and clung to the undercarriage as the jet took off. Someone threw a grenade and the flaps jammed open. Rockets started falling at one end of the runway and the pilot of the second 727 decided not to land. Eventually, Daly's 727 somehow managed to get airborne, but many of those clinging to the wings and the undercarriage fell to their deaths or were crushed as the wheels came up.

But the worst was never recorded by the television cameras. There were no Western pressmen there and few Vietnamese either, when the remnants of General Truong's shattered army started burning and looting Da Nang, South Vietnam's second largest city. There were two million refugees in Da

Nang then, about 100,000 of them soldiers, the remnants of four divisions. All of them, as one American official described it, were 'trapped like rats in a cage'.

After the fall of Da Nang, what was left of the morale and cohesion of the South Vietnamese régime seemed to collapse. President Thieu appeared to lose his grip completely. Contradictory and disastrous orders were relayed in bewildering succession to commanders in the field. Before long the whole of the north and the centre had gone, in many instances without a fight. Finally Thieu drew a line across the map north of Saigon and there, he declared, he would make his stand.

By the time we arrived in Saigon on April 3, President Thieu controlled only the southern third of the country and even there his hold was shaky. The North Vietnamese Army, aided by the local Vietcong guerrilla battalions, was within thirty or forty miles of Saigon, not only to the north and west near the Cambodian border, but to the south as well, in the Mekong Delta. Saigon was encircled. One of the first thing I did was to attend a briefing at the British Embassy given by the Defence Attaché, Colonel John Strong. It took me only a few minutes to realise that here was a man who knew what he was talking about and was also a good briefer.

He painted a gloomy picture. The North Vietnamese had eighteen divisions or 350,000 crack troops in the South, most of them around Saigon, whereas President Thieu had only six divisions or 100,000 men. So the North Vietnamese had a superiority of at least three to one. The main thrust could come from several directions, the colonel said, and it looked as if one of them would be Xuan Loc, a town about forty miles north-east of Saigon.

For the first few days, I found it hard to get my teeth into a story. After the speed of the collapse in the north and centre, the North Vietnamese Army were obviously regrouping for their next offensive. Would it be their final one? More and more people believed it would be and that it would not be long in coming.

We drove around the countryside to the west and north, finding everywhere that the scattered fragments of the South

Vietnamese Army were waiting rather hopelessly for the next attack. It was like watching a punch-drunk boxer who is still on his feet but wide open for the knockout punch.

On the 8th, we woke to hear the blast of bombs in the centre of Saigon and then the sound of an aircraft. A defecting pilot made three passes over the Presidential Palace, dropping his bombs on the third run. His aim was bad, the bombs hitting one corner of the building and injuring only one person. President Thieu was unhurt, but psychologically the attack added to the general sense of impending disaster.

A few days later, the expected Communist attack on Xuan Loc began. President Thieu gave orders for the town to be held at all costs since it lay astride the main road from the east, Route Nationale 1, the traditional invasion route to Saigon. President Thieu sent a detachment of the Airborne, his best troops, now kept in reserve for the defence of the capital, to stiffen the garrison.

We drove towards Xuan Loc in a taxi and stopped about ten miles from the town to watch the South Vietnamese air force bombing the area before the Airborne went in. We were a long way away, but we got pictures of the planes circling and the smoke from the explosions. We could not get any closer because North Vietnamese tanks were reported to be on the road about a mile ahead.

After the first strike we waited for an hour or so to see if anything else would happen. A spidery Vietnamese photographer who worked for the Associated Press came up and offered us some bananas he had found by the roadside. We munched them gratefully. I tried to strike up a conversation but he spoke very little English. Still, he was friendly, as thin as a stick-insect, with bright, almost fanatical eyes behind thick glasses. Finally, when it seemed there was going to be no more action that afternoon, we turned and drove back to Saigon. Halfway there we came round a corner to find twenty or thirty helicopters parked in the fields beside the road, busy loading up reinforcements for Xuan Loc. As we were filming by the side of the road a car drew up and Colonel Strong from the British Embassy leaned out of the window. Like us, he had been as far up the road as he could drive to see what was happening.

For the next few days, we drove up the road to Xuan Loc every morning, each time getting a little nearer the town as the South Vietnamese tried to force a way through for reinforcements. Heavy fighting was reported from the town itself, where the defenders were still holding out although heavily outnumbered and under intense shell and rocket fire. President Thieu was desperate to hold on, because he knew that, as soon as Xuan Loc fell, the road would be open to the big base at Bien Hoa just north of Saigon, and to Saigon itself.

Journalists have always gone to war by taxi and it was our only method of getting to the front. This sounds ridiculous and it was. A small fleet of dilapidated American cars used to ply for hire at exorbitant prices outside the Caravelle Hotel. Coming out in a rush in the morning, we would grab the first taxi driver available and tell him, 'Xuan Loc.' Sometimes they refused if they thought the road was too dangerous, but on the whole the temptation of a small fortune in dollars persuaded them to take the risk. The prices were high because apart from their personal safety, if their car was hit and damaged or destroyed, there would be no insurance or compensation. On the other hand they probably realised they might not be in business very much longer in any case. Installed in the decrepit old Dodge or whatever it might be, we would speed over the Newport Bridge, a huge single arch spanning the Saigon River, and drive north towards Bien Hoa, dodging between the huge American lorries. Before Bien Hoa we turned right, towards the east. Soon we were in paddy fields and banana groves. It must have been lovely country before the war, green and gentle, but it had been raped and battered by B52 strikes and countless battles, and the villages we passed were dusty, dirty and depressing. Sometimes we would meet a long line of refugees coming down the road, the women carrying their children and a few paltry possessions on their backs, their faces numb with terror and despair, another few hundred to add to the millions of refugees who were converging on the south from the rest of the country.

411

At the first sign that we were nearing the fluid and unpredictable 'front line', the driver would become agitated, and try to pull in to the side of the road. After much urging and cajoling, he might be persuaded to go a bit further. But, if he was really stubborn, we would have to get out and walk towards the action. I did not mind a walk of a mile or two up the road or through the fields, but the crew had to carry a heavy camera and sound gear and it was extremely hot. One day after we had left the driver in a village and gone on up the road with a South Vietnamese unit, a few Communist rockets or mortars dropped on the village. When we got back later, tired and thirsty and looking for our car, we found that the driver had retreated a mile or so down the road and nothing would persuade him to come back. We had to walk on down the road until we eventually found him.

'Where the hell did you get to?' I demanded crossly.

'Communist locket fall near car,' he said, recollection rekindling his fear. But my anger soon evaporated. Why should the poor man sit in the middle of a village under mortar fire just because some eccentric 'round-eyes' with cameras were risking their lives for reasons best known to themselves. I felt a certain bond between us. We were allies, in a curious way; we depended on each other. We would need a car tomorrow and he would need the money.

On one of these forages along the road to Xuan Loc, we were halted by a loud bang from just off the road. Getting out of the car to investigate, we found a South Vietnamese tank half hidden in a banana grove firing up the road at some target in another clump of banana trees. I could just see the top of a house and someone said that an advance unit of the North Vietnamese was in the house. The gun on the tank cracked like a whip, the shells whistled off through the heavy air, we heard a dull crump and saw the smoke rising among the trees. But there was no means of telling whether they were doing any real damage.

One afternoon, while ten or fifteen of us were standing on the road after some skirmish, two Communist mortar shells came over and burst in the middle of the group, spraying shrapnel around and slightly wounding a young English soundman working for the American Broadcasting Company. The other shell dug a nasty hole about six inches deep in the tarmac. We were lucky to have got off so lightly. It was becoming increasingly ovious that Xuan Loc was not going to hold out much longer. The South Vietnamese failed despite repeated attempts to open the road and the nutcracker kept tightening. A day or so later, the Army Information Office in Saigon announced that they would take a small party of correspondents to the town by helicopter. Those interested should put their names on a list. We did so and were assured that we had every chance of getting a seat. We were to report outside the office, which was near the Caravelle Hotel, at six on Sunday morning. We did. There was a slight chill in the air and the sky was grey. No one said very much. The little group grew, to include two or three American television crews, ourselves and a handful of photographers and journalists. At a quarter past six, a South Vietnamese major arrived and was immediately buttonholed by one of the Americans. A muttered conversation followed and then the major read out the names of the people who had been given seats. The American television crews were called first, then papers like the *New York Times* and finally, the photographers and news agencies. Suddenly he had come to the end of the list and our names had not been called.

'Excuse me, Major,' I said. 'But what about ITN? We put our names down and we were told we were certain to go.' The major shook his head, waved the list and said: 'Sorry, we can only take a limited number and these are the people who have been allocated seats.'

'Well, can you take one?' I said desperately, thinking that at a pinch Peter Wilkinson, the cameraman could go on his own. At least we would have some pictures and I could write a commentary afterwards.

The major shook his head. 'No, I'm sorry. It is not possible.' He walked towards an army bus and the others followed him.

'Damn,' I said in frustration and anger. 'We get up at five in the morning and then the bastards won't let us go.'

413

'You didn't bribe him enough,' said an American who had also failed to get on.

'Really?' I demanded. 'Are you kidding?'

'Nope,' he said. 'I know some of those guys gave him something to make sure their names were on.'

'God!' I fumed. 'What a way to run a war!'

Xuan Loc fell a couple of days later and the road was open to Bien Hoa. Colonel Strong's briefings became more and more pessimistic. The ring of North Vietnamese divisions round Saigon was tightening daily. It was only a matter of time. After one of his briefings, I stayed behind to chat with him. He told me that he had just been to the wedding of the son of a South Vietnamese friend, a general. 'It was a good wedding, the bride was very pretty and the proxy was a nice young man.'

'Proxy?' I asked. 'What do you mean proxy?'

'Well, you see, the general's son is in Singapore, dodging the draft. If he'd come back for the wedding, they'd have picked him up for the army. So he got married by proxy.'

'But do you mean the general connives at his son's draft-dodging?'

The colonel shrugged. 'They all do it.'

'Well,' I said, 'no wonder they're losing the war.'

'I'm afraid that's right. It just about tells you the whole story.' I realised then why he had told me the anecdote.

When the rockets started landing on the Bien Hoa runway, it was clear that the final act was about to begin.

The British Government thought so too and, despite pressure from the Americans, who still seemed to hope some sort of political deal could be struck, ordered the evacuation of the entire staff of the British Embassy. The night before, the Consul, Rex Hunt, (later Governor of the Falklands), gave a party to which he invited me. He lived in one of the old French colonial houses with a large garden and a tennis court at the back. We sat at small tables outside in the warm dusk, the air heavy with the scent of frangipani. Candles made little pools of light and we drank the last of Rex's chilled French white wine. He had an excellent Cambodian cook and the dinner was delicious. It was hard to believe that, as we ate and drank and enjoyed ourselves, the last battles of the Indochina War were being fought only a few miles away.

Next day, the British left. I went to the Embassy Club near Rex's house, to see them off. As he was giving final instructions to the Vietnamese girls who ran the club, I noticed that he was holding a huge bunch of keys. Half-jokingly, I said: 'Rex, why don't you leave the keys with me? I'll look after the place for you and we'll use it as a Press Club.'

To my astonishment, he held out the keys. 'Sandy, what a very good idea! Here, take care of the girls and my cook and his family. I'm delighted someone's going to be looking after the place.'

Still rather stunned by my own temerity, I grasped the keys and, after waving goodbye to Rex and the rest of them, went over to the bar to have a celebratory gin.

On March 21, President Thieu resigned. Frank Snepp, one of the CIA men at the American Embassy, says in his book *Decent Interval* that he drove Thieu to the airport to catch a plane to Taiwan, where his brother was Vietnamese Ambassador. The departure was kept top secret and, to avoid creating fresh panic, Thieu was made to crouch down in the back of the car, an ignominious exit for one who had been hailed for so long by the Americans as the strong man of Vietnam. Intense political manoeuvrings now followed, with a neutralist general called 'Big Minh' being tipped to take over as Thieu's successor. But to take over what? A rump of a country and a government that had virtually ceased to function. Here, as elsewhere, the Americans seem to have been bamboozled by the Communists into believing that negotiations were possible if only Thieu could be got rid of. Now Thieu was gone, but the negotiations never materialised. You cannot negotiate from utter weakness and that was the position of Saigon and the American administration.

On the Saturday before Thieu's departure, I was invited by a Vietnamese friend to play at the Saigon Golf Club. It was next to the airport and to get to it we had to drive through the heavily-fortified military compound where many top Army and Air Force generals lived. It was certainly a good area if you wanted to make a quick getaway.

The golf course was about fifty years old – it had been laid out originally by the British and French – and the fairways ran between lines of magnificent hardwood trees. Most of the caddies were women who wore conical straw hats and white cotton gloves. When you asked for, say, a five iron, the pretty young caddy would pull it out of the bag and hand it to you with a little bow and a smile. Jet fighters took off on sorties just behind the trees. I played with the Foreign Minister who told me that, a few weeks before, he had travelled back from some conference with Henry Kissinger, the Secretary of State and architect of the American withdrawal from Vietnam.

'Kissinger said we would get no more aid,' he said. 'Congress has made up its mind that there's going to be no more money for Vietnam and that's that. He could not do anything about it. He was very upset but I knew then that it was hopeless.'

I asked him if he was thinking of leaving. No, he said, he would stay and see what could be salvaged from the ruins. (As far as I know, he left near the end like the rest of them.)

The American evacuation was now in full swing. Every day giant US Airforce C141 Starlifters rolled down the runway at Tan Son Nhut and lifted off into the grey overcast with full loads of American officials and Vietnamese hangers-on – wives, mistresses and Vietnamese who had worked for the Americans in sensitive jobs such as Intelligence. It was said that the flight crews made a fortune, charging desperate Vietnamese hundreds and in some cases thousands of dollars for a seat. But thousands more wanted to get out as well. Every day the queues outside the American Embassy lengthened and the faces became more tense. Scuffles broke out as people fought to get past the guards. The news from neighbouring Cambodia was not encouraging. Phnom Penh had fallen to the Khmer Rouge on the 17th and reports were filtering out of how the victors had ordered the two million inhabitants, most of them refugees, to leave the city. What would happen when Saigon fell people asked. Would there be a bloodbath as the Communists took the city? Would they burn and loot, sack and pillage? My own fear was that, in the final stages of defeat, the discipline of the South Vietnamese forces would break and they would turn against their former allies. Anyone who looked like an American might be put up against the wall and shot.

The American evacuation plans did nothing to damp the rising wave of hysteria. They warned all journalists that, if they wanted to be included in the final evacuation, they must submit their names in advance to the American Embassy. John Pilger of the *Daily Mirror* and I were voted joint list-makers for the British and other non-American Press Corps. We completed a list of about a hundred people and took it to the Embassy. When the signal came, we were told, all of us, carrying one item of hand luggage only, should proceed to a pre-arranged rendezvous near the Caravelle, from where we would be taken to the airport. How would we know when to move, I asked. What was the signal? We'll get word to you, they said. Neither of us felt very confident about that.

Michael Nicholson, the other ITN reporter, and I both accepted that we should join the evacuation provided it came at the very end. John Mahoney, the Foreign Editor, told us that he would leave the decision to us, but he strongly advised that all of us should come out with the Americans.

On the morning of Sunday, April 27, I got word that there was fighting at Newport Bridge, on the outskirts of the city. We summoned a taxi and set off. The streets were choked with traffic, much of it the movement of refugees coming into Saigon from the surrounding countryside. By now, with the British gone, it was impossible to get a briefing on the progress of the war. The Americans were too busy with their evacuation and the South Vietnamese Command was in total disarray. We knew the Communist armies were poised for the kill all round the city, but we had no precise details.

As we neared Newport Bridge, which we had crossed every day on our way to the Xuan Loc front, we were overtaken by several Army vehicles driving fast. A minute or two later the great single span of the bridge came into view and we heard the crackle of gunfire. The driver immediately jammed on the brakes but we made him go forward to within fifty yards of the bridge where a small group of South Vietnamese soldiers and Press men were looking expectantly in the direction of the shooting. We got out, camera at the ready as always in Vietnam, and walked towards the little group. I spotted a friend from French television and one or two Vietnamese I knew by sight. But there was no sign of the BBC or, surprisingly, American television.

Being a Frenchman, Patrick ignored the shooting long enough to shake hands and wish us, *'Bon jour.'*

'What's happening?' I asked.

'The VC have set fire to a building on the other side of the river and have a machine-gun at the other end of the bridge.' This meant that the road to Bien Hoa, which had been under heavy shelling for the past day or two, was cut and that the war had moved to within only five or six miles of the centre of Saigon, closer than it had been since 1968.

The machine-gun banged and I could hear the bullets whistling harmlessly over our heads. The South Vietnamese now started to advance, moving up on both sides of the bridge, crouching to present as small a target as possible. We followed, feeling fairly safe as long as we were below the apex of the big single span. As we got near the highest point, we could see that the Vietcong, or more probably North Vietnamese, had set fire to a USAID warehouse to the left of the bridge on the far bank. The machine-gun seemed to be dug in in a swampy piece of ground on the right. They had also lowered a barrier across the road at the far end of the bridge and tied a red rag to it. The machine-gun uttered a few deep barks – single shots – and the South Vietnamese flung themselves down and returned the fire. A new sound made me look round. Two South Vietnamese Army helicopters were approaching. The first one came up level to where we were filming, hovered in mid-air and then loosed off several salvoes of rockets. They went off with an ear-splitting crack, followed by a hiss and the bang of their explosion. I stood up on the bridge, describing the action, while Peter Wilkinson filmed me and the helicopters behind and above. I could see the rockets kicking up great gouts of earth in the swampy patch where the machine-gun was supposed to be and thought: how terrifying to be on the receiving end. But, as the first helicopter wheeled away, the machine-gun started firing again. The second helicopter came up, steadied, hovered and fired. The rockets struck with a fearsome force and the white smoke drifted towards the river. This time there was no reply from the swamp. The South Vietnamese moved forward cautiously, drawing some fire, but it came from farther back and sounded like AK47 rifles. At the same time a group of South Vietnamese Rangers, who had crossed the river farther down, ran towards the road, outflanking the Communist position.

Around one, the fighting died down and the South Vietnamese started pulling back from the crown of the bridge. Newport Bridge had been saved for another day.

That night the sound of heavy shelling was audible in the centre of Saigon. We went up to the roof of the Caravelle which over the years had afforded the world's Press a grandstand view of the fighting. But this was the first time I had ever seen such heavy shelling and rocketing so close to Saigon. Most of it seemed to be directed at Tan Son Nhut airport. As we stood on the roof, twenty or thirty of us, sipping our drinks, we could hear the thump of the incoming rockets and see the orange fireballs glowing in the darkness five miles away. Watching the flashes illuminating the sky round Tan Son Nhut, we all wondered if this was the beginning of the final assault and if the advancing Communist forces were trying to halt the American evacuation by going first for the airport. By the time we went to bed, well after midnight, we still did not have the answer.

This was the day General 'Big Minh' had been sworn in as South Vietnam's new President. Few men can have inherited a more thankless task. Early next morning, April 29, an excited buzz ran round: all journalists to report to the evacuation rendezvous a few blocks from the Caravelle, near the river. Everyone had prepared his or her one piece of personal hand luggage and a long line of people started to make their way through the empty streets. The sky was overcast and grey, but there was already a stickiness to the air and later it would be hot, a clammy heat that sapped the energy.

When we reached the rendezvous point, which looked like a CIA 'safe house', there was a disconcerting lack of activity. Evidently they were not expecting us. Finally we managed to rouse an American who appeared at the window only long enough to tell us that the plans had changed and we should go instead to another building near the American Embassy. We piled our luggage in an army pick-up and set off to walk the mile or so to the new rendezvous point, a big empty warehouse. My crew and I joined the long queue outside the building and were shuffling forward slowly when Michael Nicholson came up on his own.

'Where's your crew?' I asked.

'They're not coming.'

'Christ, when did they decide that?'

'They've just told me,' Nicholson said. 'They say a lot of French are staying and they think that the BBC are as well.'

'Where are they?' I asked.

'In the hotel. In my room.'

I left Mike and the others in the queue and walked quickly the 300 yards or so to the Caravelle. When I burst into the room, sweating from my exertions, Jacques and his colleague Lucien were sitting chatting quietly. Jacques was smoking his pipe.

'What the hell's going on?' I demanded. 'We're all standing in the queue for the evacuation and you're sitting here as if there isn't a war on.'

They looked at me with maddening calm. Jacques, who spoke the better English, took the pipe out of his mouth. 'The BBC are staying, so we decided we should stay too. You know the French Embassy is remaining open. There are many, many French people here, and a lot of French journalists are staying on as well. So,' he shrugged his shoulders expressively. 'We stay too.'

'But I thought it was all arranged,' I said, trying to keep equally cool. 'We don't know what's going to happen when the North Vietnamese arrive. There could be a bloodbath. It could be bloody dangerous. We just don't know. But, quite apart from that, you can be absolutely sure that they'll cut all communications and that we won't be able to get any film out. They'll probably stop us filming as well. You know what they're like. So, is it worth it? I don't think it is. I think we should all go out on the American evacuation.'

Jacques blew out some smoke. 'It's different for us, Sandy. We're French. They know there are many French here and they don't hate us like they hate the Americans. But, for you, we quite understand. The British and the Americans, for the North Vietnamese it is the same. So why don't you go with Mike and the others, and we'll stay. After all, we're UPITN.'

There was a piece of office politics here. UPITN is a film agency in which ITN is the major shareholder. Although hired by ITN for this assignment, Jacques and Lucien were really a UPITN crew. I saw the force of their argument.

'How do you know the BBC are staying?'

'We heard one of them, the cameraman, I think, talking in the Continental. He said he was staying.'

'Shit!' I said. 'If the BBC *are* staying, that changes everything. You're no good on your own without a reporter. That means I'll have to stay as well. I'll have to become an honorary Frenchman,' I joked.

'Oui, mais vous êtes à moitié déjà,' Lucien said, his eyes laughing behind his spectacles.

I got up. 'Right, I'd better go and tell the others.'

They were still in the queue, but inside the building by now, and I repeated the conversation I had just had with Jacques and Lucien, adding that I had decided to stay. It had been tacitly agreed between Nicholson and myself that, since he had been in Vietnam several weeks longer than I had, he should be the first to leave. And we both agreed that, if there was any chance of the BBC staying, we had to stay as well. I said goodbye to Peter, Hugh and Mike and walked back to the Caravelle. I was not to know until much later that they would have a desperate time getting out. After a considerable delay they were taking to the airport in a bus. The airport was sealed off and in their attempts to get through they ran over a child. The Vietnamese troops on the gate refused to let them in and they had to drive all the way back to the American

421

Embassy. There, having pushed their way through a frantic mob of Vietnamese, who were besieging the palace, they had to climb over the wall of the Embassy, while Marine guards used their rifle butts to keep the crowds back. They were finally lifted out after dark by helicopter.

Jacques and Lucien were standing outside the hotel with their camera gear at the ready.

'What's going on?'

'A plane has crashed in Cholon.'

'Who said so?'

They pointed to a small, thin, smiling Vietnamese. 'He says he'll take us in his car,' Lucien said, indicating a white jeep parked at the kerb.

'Okay,' I said. 'Let's go.'

Toc was a good driver, threading his way skilfully through the crowded streets. As we neared Cholon, the Chinese part of Saigon, we could see thick smoke and hear the wail of sirens. We turned into a broad, tree-lined street. The plane, a C119 Flying Boxcar of the South Vietnamese Air Force, had crashed into the top of the Hong Kong Hotel, breaking up and scattering débris into the street below. The tail was still stuck in the corner of the building between the fourth and fifth floors and, just below, caught upside down in the branches of a tree, was a body, whether of a member of the crew or someone from the hotel it was impossible to say. Badly-burnt and mangled corpses were being brought out on stretchers. Several aircraft including another C119 had been shot down earlier in the day by Strela missiles and it looked as if this was also a victim of the North Vietnamese gunners. A large crowd had gathered to watch the rescue operations, but there was no sign of panic, only a rather ghoulish curiosity.

It was a very different picture at the docks which we passed on our way back. A mass of Vietnamese were pushing and scrambling frenziedly to get on board two cargo ships at the quayside. As one of them, the *Lung Ho*, prepared to cast off, the frenzy redoubled. One old lady was hoisted up over the gunwale like a stick of furniture. A baby, terrified by the commotion, screamed its head off as it was grabbed like a parcel. People were hauling their relatives over the side, all shouting at once. I asked where the boats were going. No one seemed to know, although presumably they would head downriver and hope to slip through the North Vietnamese cordon after dark.

As the *Lung Ho* swung out into midstream, a string of big American Chinook helicopters flew over our heads. The final stage of the evacuation was under way. As we turned into the square in front of the Caravelle, I noticed a commotion at the far side and told Toc to drive over to investigate. On the corner stood a big building surrounded by barbed wire known as Brinks. It had originally been an American NCOs' club and I remembered how the Vietcong had exploded a bomb outside it in the early Sixties. More recently it had become a PX for the multitude of Americans who worked in the Embassy as military advisers. Now, an astonishing sight greeted our eyes. Hundreds of Vietnamese were pouring in and out of the building, like an army of ants, carrying away everything they could remove: sheets, typewriters, chairs, fridges, lamps and every conceivable bit of bric-à-brac. One man was even managing to ride his bicycle with a wardrobe balanced on his head. The Vietnamese looted with a sort of silent ferocity that was at once despicable and yet completely understandable. The Americans had deserted them and they were taking their revenge in the only way they could.

As I stood just inside the gate, a small group of Vietnamese came up. 'Excuse me, sir,' one man said. 'We're trying to get to the airport. Can you help us please?'

'I'm not an American,' I said. 'What's the matter?'

'Well, sir, Mr . . . [I could not catch the name] told us to wait here until he came back.' He pointed to the far side of the compound where a bus was parked. It was full of Vietnamese men and women. 'But he's been gone over an hour now and we're getting worried. We're all from Voice of America,' he explained.

'I see.' I felt desperately sorry for them. Voice of America employees would get short shrift from the conquering North Vietnamese, I imagined.

'Well, since he hasn't come back, why don't you drive yourselves to the airport?'

'Mr . . . took the keys with him.'

The shit, I thought. He's left them stranded while he's buggered off to the airport himself.

'I'll tell you what,' I said, searching desperately for some sort of helpful suggestion while not getting too embroiled. 'Do you know how to jump the leads on a car?' They looked blank.

'Have you got a driver?'

'Yes, sir, over there.'

'Well, tell him to start up the bus by shorting the wires. And then drive to the airport. That's the only thing you can do.'

'Thank you, sir,' they said, moving away. I could see the growing hopelessness in their faces and I doubted if they would ever make it.

I suddenly remembered our daily radio circuit from London at six. Mike and I had taken it in turns to go to the radio station about three miles away on the far side of the city. I quickly typed out a 'voice piece' describing the day's events and asked Toc to drive me. Halfway there, just as we were crossing the big boulevard on which the American and British Embassies were situated, I heard two or three heavy explosions which could have been bombs. A few seconds later the sound of aircraft was audible above the noise of the traffic and I craned my head to see what was happening. At that moment every Vietnamese soldier in Saigon seemed to open fire. Rifles, machine-guns, automatics, they all blazed and blasted away. It sounded as if every finger was on every trigger.

At the radio station, I had to climb four flights of stairs to the control room and studios at the top. Up there, the noise of the shooting was even louder, the acoustics of the building making it almost deafening. I had to record my 'voice piece' three times, I was so rattled. When I had finished, I apologised to John Mahoney. 'I'm sorry, John, there's so much noise that I could hardly hear myself speak.' For once the cliché was absolutely true. I told him that Nicholson and the others had left on the American evacuation. (In fact they were still in the Embassy grounds, waiting for a helicopter.) I told him I had decided to stay because of the BBC and also thanks to the French crew.

'All right, Sandy, it's your decision. We respect that. You're on the spot and we can't legislate for you. We've heard incidentally that the BBC man was told to come out by his office and that he refused and they tried to pull rank on him. We don't think that's the way to play it. Here's Nigel who wants to have a word with you.'

The quality of the line was deteriorating but I could just hear Nigel Ryan, the Editor.

'Don't worry about the money now, ole boy,' he drawled, his voice distorted but still recognisable through the static. 'Good luck.' The line went dead. It was the last time I was to speak to London for almost a month.

When I got back to the hotel, I discovered what all the excitement had been about. Five A-37 fighter bombers, led by the same defector who had bombed the Presidential Palace a week before, had attacked the airport, destroying several aircraft on the ground, causing heavy damage to the military control tower and killing and wounding a number of Americans and Vietnamese.

But that night, surprisingly, the North Vietnamese did not press home their advantage. Unlike the previous evening, there was very little rocketing or shelling round Tan Son Nhut and we could only conclude that the Communist high command had decided to allow the American evacuation to run its course without further disruption.

The best French restaurant left in Saigon, the Aterbea, was just round the corner from the hotel and we usually went there for dinner. It was owned by a taciturn old Corsican with a Vietnamese wife and served marvellous seafood. They also had a good white wine from the Midi which the maître d'hôtel had selected the last time he was in Nice. The Corsican had refused to pay the exorbitant price required to obtain a licence, so the wine was described on the menu as 'tea' and served in a jug.

I took along a bottle of wine I had bought at the airport in

Paris on my way out and which I had carefully kept for a special occasion. The American evacuation, I thought, was a fitting moment. We opened it in good time and the maître d'hôtel poured it with care. It was a Château Mouton Rothschild, 1968, a good wine but a poor year. It turned out to be thin and undistinguished, a great disappointment. The joke was really on me because Nicholson had tried several times to persuade me to let him taste this supposedly high-class claret and I had always found an excuse.

The maître shook his head after sampling a glass. 'Never mind, I have something much better at home in my flat. I will bring it in for you tomorrow.'

Wednesday April 30 dawned grey and overcast. I woke early, had a shower and went up to the roof restaurant for breakfast with a sense of expectation, of great events in the making. I felt keyed-up, in anticipation of what was to come, whatever it might be, but, now that the decision to stay was irrevocable, no longer tense. Most of the night, their navigation lights flashing red and green, the big choppers had ferried the last of the evacuees out to the Gulf of Tonkin and the waiting aircraft carriers of the Sixth Fleet. Now, the sky was empty and the city quiet. I sat down and ordered the dreadful breakfast which the Caravelle had served for as long as I had stayed there: tinned orange juice, watery scrambled eggs, toast that tasted of sawdust, revolting jam and dishwater tea. Just before eight Jacques and Lucien appeared. A few minutes later we heard the sound of a helicopter and a big Marine Chinook with twin rotors settled on to the roof of the American Embassy about a quarter of a mile away.

'Quick,' I said to Jacques, 'the camera.' He got up and ran from the room to his bedroom two floors below. As the Chinook landed, a couple of Marines in flak jackets and steel helmets jumped out and took up guard positions, carbines at the ready, watching the street below. Within a minute several figures appeared and, clutching briefcases and bending low, ran towards the chopper. I wondered if it was the Ambassador, but could not tell at that distance. The helicopter lifted off, climbed vertically for a few hundred feet and then put its nose down and went speeding away towards the river and the sea. As it disappeared from sight Jacques returned clutching his camera.

'Damn it, too late,' I said crossly, cursing myself for not having foreseen such a possibility and making sure he had the camera with him.

It was the last helicopter to leave Saigon and we had missed the shot. But there was no time for recriminations. 'Let's go over to the Embassy and see what's happening,' I said. Just as we were leaving the hotel, two or three tremendous explosions went off near the river. They sounded like rockets. We went down Tu Do, turned left at the bottom and drove towards Naval Headquarters. The road was cordoned off and military police waved at us to stop. Lucien had started filming when the police pointed their automatics in the air and fired several warning bursts. Toc revved the engine. 'They tell us go away,' he said nervously.

'Okay,' Lucien said, a cigarette dangling from the corner of his mouth. 'I finish. You go.'

The American Embassy was a big white building set in a compound behind a high white wall. Until now, it had seemed, whatever the reality inside, a haven of well-ordered calm. Now it was a shambles. Thousands of documents were scattered all over the lawn in front of the building and floated soddenly in the blue water of the swimming pool. The main lifts were locked but the looters had made their way up the staircase at the side. We started to climb. On every floor, offices had been smashed open and everything moveable ripped out. What had not been looted lay sprawled in confusion. Finally we emerged on the flat roof with its chopperpad. A crowd of Vietnamese, perhaps 150 to 200 men and women, were clustered together, like frightened starlings. A lone American in a blue safari suit and white cotton gloves stood in the middle looking up at the sky.

'What are you doing here?' I asked him.

'That's a good question,' he said. 'I was hoping to get the last of my people out on a chopper but I guess they've all gone.' He said he was a contractor and had been so concerned about the evacuation of his Vietnamese employees

427

that he had missed the boat himself. Some of the Vietnamese started to leave the roof, but the majority stayed, clearly hoping that, against all the odds, a last helicopter would reach down and pluck them to safety. But for the first time in months, if not years, the sky above Saigon was empty. The black kites had it to themselves at last.

Halfway down, someone let off a tear gas grenade and immediately a choking cloud of fumes filled the narrow stairwell. My eyes filled with tears and I felt I was going to choke. Holding my handkerchief to my nose, I bolted down the stairs and out into the open, coughing and spluttering. For a few minutes I thought I was going to pass out, so violent was the effect.

Outside the Embassy, cars left by the Americans were being stripped of every moveable item. In one or two cases, the looters simply pushed them away.

As we walked over to our jeep, an attractive young Vietnamese woman came up and said in a soft sing-song accent: 'Please, you take me with you?'

'What's the matter?' I asked, moved by the appeal in her eyes.

'My man. He say he take me with him but he not come back.' It was the same pathetic story again.

'I'm not an American,' I said, disowning responsibility and feeling rather ashamed of doing so. 'I'm a British journalist.'

'Please,' she said coming closer. 'Take me with you.'

'But I'm not going anywhere.' I lapsed into pidgin in desperation. 'I stay here in Saigon. I not go away.'

She came closer, pleading, close to tears. 'Please, you take me with you. I want come with you.' She stepped forward as if to climb into the jeep. Toc said something sharply in Vietnamese and she fell back as if she had received a blow.

As the jeep moved away, she came running after it, still imploring us to take her away. To assuage my feeling of guilt, I told myself that, if I showed her any kindness, she would cling like a limpet and it would be impossible to get rid of her.

But now we had another problem. Jacques looked extremely pale and said he felt sick. I wondered if it was the

428

delayed action of the tear gas. We drove back to the hotel and took him to his room where he collapsed on his bed. I told him as kindly as possible to stay in bed, but inwardly I cursed. To have one of the team go sick on this day of all days was infuriating.

'Lucien,' I said. 'You'll have to manage on your own.'

'*Oui, oui,*' he said puffing his cigarette. 'I'll try.' Luckily he and Jacques were interchangeable, equally able to use camera and sound.

It was now about 10.30 and the lull that had set in the previous evening seemed to be continuing. There was little traffic in the city and no sounds of shelling. I decided that, in order not to miss the climax of this drama, we had to keep moving. Luckily we had Toc and his jeep. We drove back down Tu Do to the river. The scene was even more frantic than on the previous day. More ships were moored alongside and hundreds of Vietnamese, clutching bundles of food and household possessions, were fighting to get on board. On one of the boats, a small group of Airborne, once the pride of the South Vietnamese Army, had installed themselves on the bridge with their weapons. They looked sullen and dangerous.

When we had finished filming we walked back to the Majestic Hotel where we had left the jeep. Toc was standing on the pavement disconsolate.

'Soldiers take jeep,' he said. 'I tell them no, but they have gun.' He pointed down the street to where half a dozen Airborne troopers were standing round the vehicle. Lucien straightened his shoulders and strode towards them. A husky young soldier in camouflage trousers and singlet, an M16 in his hand, was standing by the driver's door.

'This is my car,' Lucien said, holding out his hand. 'You give me key, please.' The soldier looked at him and for a moment I thought he was going to turn nasty.

'Easy, Lucien,' I said.

'Please,' Lucien repeated. 'This is my car.' Reluctantly the soldier handed over the keys. Then, leaving some of their equipment on the ground, they all wandered off, irresolutely looking for another way of escape.

'Well done, Lucien,' I said.

Without the jeep, we would have been in serious trouble. On the way back to the hotel we passed another group of Airborne. They were stripping off their uniforms and putting on civilian clothes, their weapons leaning against a wall. Lucien got ready to film but then one of them looked up and glared at us. We drove on. It was too risky to take a shot.

We parked outside the Caravelle. It was now almost noon and very hot. No traffic moved. The city seemed to be waiting, hushed, expectant. My thoughts were turning to a cold gin and tonic when an open jeep with its lights flashing came towards us from the top of Tu Do. Two of the passengers were carrying a banner with a slogan in Vietnamese. A third who was waving a palm frond I recognised as my spidery photographer friend from the Xuan Loc road.

The jeep went past blowing its horn and I ran to the corner. It did a U turn and, as it came back towards us, I stepped into the road and shouted: 'Hey, what's going on?'

The jeep slowed and my friend waved at me, shouting. The words were incomprehensible but his meaning was clear.

'Come on, Lucien, they're going to give us a lift.' We scrambled over the tail-board, Lucien carrying the camera, and I the sound gear. The driver accelerated and we started to roar up To Do, horn blaring.

'What's happening?' I shouted, trying to keep my balance as the jeep braked and then shot forward again. 'NLF,' the Spider said, his face alight. The National Liberation Front was the official name of the Vietcong.

I looked up Tu Do, past the great red brick cathedral built by the French and, as if through a telescope, saw a T54 tank trundle past, going from right to left. Then another. And another. Then we were amongst them. The tanks were coming down the boulevard one after the other in line ahead. I looked the other way towards the Presidential Palace. More tanks. It looked as if they were just about to enter the gates.

'Come on, Lucien,' I shouted. 'This is it.' He scrambled out and started filming like a man possessed. I looked up at

430

the tank commanders as they roared past. Each was standing to attention, eyes front, white-gloved hands gripping the hatch in front of him as if on parade. We had just, but only just, been in time. Thanks to the Spider. We hurried towards the Presidential Palace, about 300 yards away. With the Palace in the background, I stopped to say a few words to the camera. 'This is a historic moment . . . ' I started off, and indeed it was. For this was the end of the Vietnam War which had started in 1945 and which, with a few interruptions, had ground on like a juggernaut until now, thirty years later, it was finally over. Not a shot was being fired in this last, almost ceremonial moment of the longest war in the history of the twentieth century.

In the middle of my remarks, a lorry-load of North Vietnamese infantry pulled out from the side of the road and I had to step back smartly to avoid being run over. We hurried on again through the gates of the Presidential Palace which had been smashed down by the leading tank and now lay flattened.

More tanks drove on to the lawn in front of the Palace, churning up the turf and parking with their guns trained on the building. There was no need. Resistance was already over. We saw a line of Palace guards, their hands tied behind their backs, being marched away.

The victors, in pith helmets, appeared on the balcony and looked down on the armour that was still rolling along the broad avenue towards us. People were hurrying up the steps into the Palace and Lucien and I followed. I expected to be stopped but instead we were waved on up to the first floor. It was dark inside but I could see that a crowd had gathered in the big salon and that as we arrived some ceremony was about to take place.

The tall figure of the new President, 'Big Minh', stepped forward to make a declaration. I asked him what was happening. Speaking in French, he said: 'I am handing over to people who are more worthy than me.' Flash-bulbs popped. A television light lit up his face. And then a North Vietnamese officer in a pith helmet stepped forward and, without actually pushing him, urged him out of the room and down the stairs. We followed them down and out into the open. 'Big Minh', his short-lived Presidency already over, was escorted across the lawn towards the gate where a Russian jeep waited, engine running. He was told to get in. Lucien moved round in front, still filming. 'Big Minh' climbed into the front seat beside the driver. On the windscreen was a photograph of Ho Chi Minh, the founding father of Vietnamese Communism, who had died six years earlier. He had not lived to see the final victory but April 30, more than anyone else's, was his victory.

'Out of film,' Lucien said, lowering his camera. The jeep, with 'Big Minh' looking rigidly straight ahead, drove off into the crowd. The Indochina War was truly over.

When the North Vietnamese marched into Saigon they immediately severed all communications with the outside world. Telex and telegraph links were cut, the airport sealed off and the radio station occupied. On the off chance that circuits to London were still working, I drove to the radio at five to find it full of Communist troops. One of the South Vietnamese engineers I knew stopped me and said seriously, 'No circuits. Everything closed.' The North Vietnamese soldiers looked at me without overt hostility, but I could sense their suspicion and I did not linger. As I drove back in Toc's jeep to the Caravelle, I went through all the possible ways of getting the news to London. The answer was depressingly negative: no telex nor telegraph, no telephone, no radio, no aircraft. The only possible channel was the French Embassy's radio and, as usually happens on these occasions, diplomats do not like transmitting Press reports, especially if you are not even a fellow national. I did manage to send a brief pool message via the French next day, but it simply said: 'All British Press alive and well in Saigon, able to move freely but not communicate . . . Scotch holding out.' And, to tease ITN a bit, I added: 'Send more money.'

We were, however, able to film, and next day, May Day, saw us out early with the cameras. Jacques, to my relief, had recovered from his mysterious illness although he still looked pale.

The day before we had seen the North Vietnamese tanks. Now it was the turn of the infantry. All morning they marched in from the outskirts, many of them absurdly young-looking, real footsloggers, carrying everything on their backs: AK 47s, mortars, B40 rocket launchers, belts of ammunition slung on bamboo poles. They wheeled their amazing bicycles, the cross bars hung with mortar bombs and sacks of rice and decorated with plastic flowers. To a North Vietnamese a bicycle is like a car to a Westerner. It is his main means of transport. These were North Vietnamese regular troops and they had come all the way down the Ho Chi Minh Trail, that famous series of tracks and roads that the Americans had bombed so often for so many years with so little apparent effect. The North Vietnamese always managed to repair it in record time. Looking at these young men in their Ho Chi Minh sandals, cut from the tread of an old tyre, in their green cotton uniforms and their pith helmets with the small red star, I began to realise how they had managed to stand up to the devastating firepower of the Americans and wear them down in the end. They were a guerrilla army which had mastered conventional tactics. They did not depend on the roads and on helicopters as the Americans and their South Vietnamese protégés had always done. They were mobile, they walked everywhere, using the country as only guerrillas can. And yet, at the same time, they were a highly professional army, equipped with the latest Russian and Chinese weapons that were as good as or better than the American equipment used by the South Vietnamese. In short, they were bloody good soldiers. I could read the determination on their faces and see the discipline in their ranks. They came padding down Le Loi, Saigon's Champs Elysées, past the looted and deserted American Embassy. On the opposite side of the street, the smaller British Embassy had also been looted by the South Vietnamese. Papers were strewn all over the grass and the North Vietnamese were already in occupation.

The new arrivals marched on until they reached the gates of the Presidential Palace where they halted and stood gazing at the red flag now waving from the top of the building. This, more than anything else, was the symbol of their victory.

Then they drifted off in small groups among the trees and set up camp. After a while curious Saigonese plucked up courage and began to wander among them. One soldier sat on his tank, cradling a baby in his arms while the proud father gazed up fondly. I wondered if they were brothers or cousins separated by the cruel divisions of civil war or simply fellow Vietnamese enjoying the first sweet moments of peace. Fraternisation, as they used to call it, was beginning.

There was a moment of panic when the sound of shooting was heard from the port but on inspection it turned out that one of the South Vietnamese Navy's tenders had caught fire and the ammunition on board started to explode.

On the third day we went out to the airport, which was still sealed off, and saw signs of what must have been the last fierce throes of the battle. Three North Vietnamese T54 tanks lay wrecked near the gates of Tan Son Nhut, apparently knocked out by anti-tank rockets.

We could follow the progress of the North Vietnamese as they made their final drive into the city. South Vietnamese equipment littered the streets – abandoned American armoured personnel carriers, tanks, lorries and weapons, a lot of it undamaged. North Vietnamese recovery crews were hard at work dragging it away. In some cases all a vehicle needed was a tankful of petrol to get it started again. They would hastily paint on a red and yellow star and drive it off, just as the Israelis did in the desert at the end of the Six-Day War.

In the centre of Saigon, the markets were opening for the first time. There was a rush to buy food and something else that was also deemed necessary for survival; lengths of red and blue cloth with a yellow star, the Vietcong insignia.

With that unerring instinct for survival that was always so noticeable in Saigon, people were hastily changing their colours, and soon a forest of flags was flying over the city, sometimes several on one house.

In Cholon, the pavement markets spilled over with something like their old abundance: fruit and vegetables of every description, and fish, crabs, shrimps and prawns in wriggling profusion. The roads were now open to Dalat, traditionally the market garden for Saigon, and to the Delta and the coast, from where the rice and sea food came.

Even the flower stalls were reopening and the old ladies, drawn like butterflies to a buddleia, peered and haggled and then, clutching an armful of cannas or gladioli, climbed into the pedicabs and cycled off just as if nothing had happened.

It was fascinating to see the city coming back to life, but it was also increasingly frustrating. All our film of the fall of Saigon and its aftermath was in the hotel, the pile getting bigger every day, and we had no means of shipping it out. Our only hope was somehow to get it on a plane. We discovered that one or two officials from the propaganda department of the Foreign Ministry in Hanoi had arrived on the heels of the occupation army and we started to lobby them. They were, not surprisingly, hugely non-committal. Understandably, the Western Press were low on the list of North Vietnamese priorities and planes were scarce. Alas for the days of American plenty and know-how! Instead of the optimistic 'can do', we now became accustomed to the negative; 'It is very difficult'. We quickly realised that we had to form ourselves into some sort of organised body if we were going to have any clout at all.

The British contingent was small but vocal and consisted of: Stewart Dalby of the *Financial Times*, John Edwards of the *Daily Mail*, Martin Woollacott of the *Guardian*, Colin Smith of the *Observer*, Peter Gill of the *Telegraph*, James Fenton of the *New Statesman*, Julian Manyon of LBC, Derek Wilson and Brian Barron of the BBC, and myself. There were also odd people like Neil Davis, a very funny and knowledgeable Australian who worked as a cameraman-reporter for NBC. But easily the biggest national groups were the French and the Japanese, both of them about forty-strong.

Because of their long involvement with Vietnam, the French Press Corps included several distinguished old Far East hands like Jean Lacouture, the novelist, as well as well-connected young journalists like Jean Debré, the son of the former Gaullist Prime Minister Michel Debré. As British representatives, Dalby and I would go across to the Continental for discussions with Debré.

Something of the old Indo-China atmosphere still lingered. The rooms with their high ceilings and fans were shuttered against the sun and the signs of the new order outside. Debré's tall, exotic-looking wife – only a Frenchman would bring his wife – would glance up from the sofa where she would be reading and murmur, *Bon soir.'*

The Japanese were the most clannish group and yet at the same time fiercely individualistic. They refused to nominate spokesmen who could act on their behalf and, when with Debré we drafted a joint letter to the Communist authorities asking for urgent evacuation, every Japanese insisted on reading the letter for himself. Instead of ten minutes the whole business took a couple of hours.

We finally appealed to the Japanese Consul, Mr. Watanabe, to see if he could speed things up. This he did splendidly, haranguing the assembled Japanese Press Corps and not so much asking them their opinion as giving them their instructions. They submitted meekly and we had no more trouble.

It was a neat illustration of the difference in the two national characters. British journalists would never allow themselves to be dictated to by a Foreign Office official. Any such attempt would bring out their deepest anti-Establlish-ment prejudices. Watanabe was a forceful character, so forceful that his appearance in the bar of the Caravelle became a signal for alarm. Things would start well enough, with Watanabe generously buying a round of drinks, and then another. But, very soon, as the whisky took its effect, he would start slapping reluctant drinking companions on the back and urging them to have another. Colleagues complained that Watanabe's back-slapping was so exuberant as to be painful.

One evening, I strolled into the Caravelle bar to have a drink before dinner. The Vietnamese barman, with the shiny black hair that covered his head like a beetle's carapace, and who had been there for years, greeted me with a wide smile. 'Wikky, m'sieu, wikky à l'eau?' This was the closest he could get to whisky. Watanabe introduced himself and immediately ordered a fresh round of drinks. John Edwards winked at me and muttered, 'Here we go.' True to form, friendliness soon turned to boisterous bonhomie and Watanabe caught me a stinging blow on the shoulder. I winced. 'Have another whisky, Mr. Gall.' 'No thanks.' 'One more whisky,' he told the barman. Suddenly I had a brainwave. Like anyone else I had read that respect for age is common to all oriental societies. Looking Watanabe in the eye, I said, 'Tell me, Mr. Watanabe, is it true that in Japan, as in other Eastern countries, you respect age?'

'Yes,' he said. 'It's very important in Japan.'

'In other words,' I went on, 'you listen carefully to what an older person had to say?'

'Oh, yes,' he said, 'always.'

'How old are you, Mr. Watanabe?'

'Forty-two.'

'Ah, well, I'm forty-seven, so I'm a good deal older than you, and if I tell you that I and my colleagues do not want another drink then you must respect that and not try to bully us. Do you understand, Mr. Watanabe?' For a moment I thought he would lose his temper. But he swallowed his pride.

'Yes, Mr. Gall, I'm sorry. Please accept my apologies for being rude.' With that he bowed and left. We never had any trouble with him again.

On Wednesday, May 7, the twenty-first anniversary of the battle of Dien Bien Phu, the new military government staged a big celebration, showing itself in public for the first time on the balcony of the Presidential Palace. Thousands of Saigonese were made to parade to listen to General Tran van Tra's speech. A huge idealised portrait of Ho Chi Minh smiled down on the crowd and on several hundred tough-looking North Vietnamese soldiers, who stood to attention, gripping their AK47s with spotless white gloves, staring straight ahead. The general, a gnarled little nut of a man, warned his audience, which was in effect the whole country, that anyone who attempted to sabotage the revolution would be 'eliminated'. The next day he gave a press conference, which turned out to be long on Marxist platitudes and short on facts. I asked him about the status of British and other foreign property in Saigon. Had it been confiscated or not?

437

The general would not give a straight answer.

Immediately after the press conference the telex reopened and there was a ruthless rush by the assembled Press Corps. The agency and newspaper men went wild, churning out pages of prose. I sent ITN a short message including my description of the capture of the city a week before which I had written for the radio circuit and never sent. But this did not solve my main problem, which was our pile of film that kept growing larger each day.

That evening the general threw a party to which he invited various members of the Press, including the BBC but not ITN. Presuming this was an oversight on his part, I bluffed my way in with a substitute invitation card.

Communist troops stood to attention on both sides of the steps which led to the first floor and the huge brightly-lit salon where President Thieu had given his receptions. Along both sides, tables draped with white tablecloths had been laid with a generous array of Vietnamese food and Western drink: rows of bottles of Johnny Walker Red and Black Label, French chamagne and brandy, all presumably, from President Thieu's cellar. The assembled guests were wolfing it down as if they had not had a square meal for months. At the far end of the room, surrounded by his officers, I spotted General Tran himself. On the spur of the moment, I said to John Edwards, 'Come on, let's ask him if he can help us to get a plane out.'

We made our way to the dais, climbed the steps and stepped politely through the throng of top brass, all in their Russian number ones and medals.

'General,' I said in French. 'I'm Sandy Gall of Independent Television News from London.' He frowned in the effort to understand. 'General, we have a problem. We have historic film of your arrival in Saigon. This is a great victory for you and the world waits to see it. But, since we cannot get our film out, no one has actually seen the pictures of your triumph. Can you help us with a plane so that we can fly the film out?'

The general turned to another senior officer and went off into Vietnamese. I wondered how much he had understood. Then he turned back to me and said in halting French, 'We will try.' He shook hands, bowed and edged quickly away. I felt I had at least struck a blow for freedom, but I was not sure how effective it would be.

We were now in the second week and the occupation was becoming unbearably noisy. Apart from the tramp of feet of the 'Communist cadres' who were rapidly taking over the hotel, there was the music. Every morning, at six o'clock, the loudspeakers in the square in front of the hotel would crackle and then blare forth the strains of 'The East is Red', or some such raucous melody. Sleep being impossible, I would get up and do my exercises, shower and go upstairs for breakfast. Afterwards, we would drive around the city to see what was happening – and to escape from the sound of the dreadful music. Luckily the British Press Corps had been befriended by a soft-spoken young Indian called Sammy Maideen, whose wealthy father had just been released from prison after four years as the involuntary guest of President Thieu. According to Sammy, his venerable white-haired papa had been arrested for refusing to cooperate with a Minister in a gold-smuggling racket. Sammy was looking after the property of a British bank, and staying in the deputy's manager's house with a full complement of servants. We would go there after making our daily rounds and swim and play badminton.

The Vietnamese servants, hoping that the presence of all these Britons would be some sort of protection against the Communist invasion of their city, greeted us like princes. Gins and tonics appeared as if by magic and each day a huge lunch was prepared and served with a devotion that was touching and a trifle embarrassing.

Sammy seemed to have access to unlimited amounts of gin, whisky, wine and money. When our piastres began to run out he would bring a suitcase full and dish it out like monopoly money. We nicknamed him 'The Great Gatsby'.

Our only other refuge was the British Embassy Club of which I was honorary president *ad interim*. All the British Press Corps were automatically members and could bring guests. Our only gatecrasher was a lunatic Frenchman who

439

not only insinuated himself but tried to take over the club. I had to inform him, in my most presidential manner, that he did not qualify for membership and could only come when he was invited. The poor man eventually went off his head, scattering money in the street, and was carried struggling to the French hospital where he tried to send telegrams to President Giscard.

The club was small but very pleasant. Apart from the bar, presided over by Moi, a tiny Vietnamese who could only just see over the counter, there was a ping-pong table, a paperback library, a tennis court, a small swimming pool, changing room and a barbecue. Jacques, the resident servant, kept the swimming pool clean and his wife cooked delicious alfresco meals. Whenever we wanted lunch at the club, I would give Jacques money to buy food in the market and we would buy the wine in a shop near the hotel. One day, we invited a young Reuters correspondent for lunch. As usual, we all drank wine and he seemed to enjoy his lunch. Later, when the telex reopened, among a lot of more serious matters, he wrote a light item about the Saigon Press Club. He made us sound like little Neros, enjoying ourselves while Saigon fell, swimming and eating and helping ourselves to the contents of the Consul's cellar. I was furious about the cellar bit because it implied that we were at best freeloading and, at worst, stealing. When I next saw him, I went straight into the attack. 'How dare you write lies like that!' I cried. 'A fine return for our hospitality.'

'But I saw you drinking wine,' he cheekily answered.

'Yes,' I snarled. 'But that was not the Consul's wine. It was our wine that we had bought in the shop in Tu Do.'

'Oh,' he said, 'I didn't know that.'

'Why didn't you check?' I raged at him. 'After all, you are supposed to be a Reuters correspondent.'

Four things are never forgiven a foreign correspondent. The first is to be a coward. The second is to drop his colleagues in the shit. The third is to be mean. The fourth – a long way behind – is to get things wrong. If he combines two or more he is virtually beyond the pale.

It made no difference that the Consul's house contained no

cellar. The story stuck like a burr. When I got back to London everyone in ITN had read the Reuters story and refused to believe my protestations of innocence.

But these relatively halycon days did not last long. One day when we arrived for lunch, Jacques appeared with a mournful face. 'The North Vietnamese have been here, asking questions.'

I knew immediately what that meant. Requisition teams, known as K5 and K7, were inspecting all foreign property and taking over whatever they wanted. Legal niceties, such as the fact that the club was the property of the British Government, did not concern them. I even wrote to the Ministry of Foreign Affairs asking for permission to use the club, but of course got no reply. I started to spend the odd night in the house to establish some sort of occupancy. I also escaped from the terrible music at the Caravelle. One morning, having spent a restful night in the Consular bedroom, I went down for an early dip. I had just swum my five or six lengths and was walking gently round the pool enjoying the sunshine and the stillness when the door at the far end of the compound opened and a line of purposeful-looking North Vietnamese entered, first an officer and then half a dozen heavily-armed soldiers. Entirely ignoring me, they marched in single file towards the house. I gave them a few minutes and then walked to the house. Hearing voices in the sitting-room, I strolled in, my swimming trunks still damp, to find Jacques surrounded by soldiers and being interrogated by the officer. In my politest French I said, 'Good morning. This house belongs to the British Embassy. Is there anything I can do for you?'

'Are you from the British Embassy?' the officer asked politely but pointedly.

'No,' I said, 'I'm a British journalist. But the British Consul, Monsieur Hunt, gave us permission to use the club next door.'

'I see. We are just making a few inquiries of the servant here.'

Feeling slightly ridiculous in my trunks, I withdrew and went upstairs to change. By the time I came down, they had gone. But I could see from Jacques' manner, as he served my breakfast, that he was worried. Not only had he worked for the British imperialists, but he was a Cambodian and there was no love lost between Cambodians and Vietnamese. 'They ask many questions,' he said. 'About you and Mr. Hunt. They want to take this place for themselves.'

Next afternoon, the blow fell. The same officer returned with an ultimatum. I would have to leave by six o'clock. I protested but I knew it was no use. If I refused they would simply march me out at bayonet point. So I gave in. Sammy was having his troubles too. I arrived one day to find another requisition squad occupying the sitting-room, their AK47s and B40 rocket launchers carelessly leaning against the wall. After two hours of discussion in Vietnamese and several rounds of beer, they left. Shortly afterwards they moved into the bank manager's house next door and we lost our swimming pool there.

We now made jokes about the last battle of Saigon, the battle of the swimming pools. We fought a determined but doomed rearguard action, falling back doggedly from one swimming pool to the next. The little green men, as the French called them, just as determinedly winkled us out of each successive one.

'We'll have to get out soon,' someone said. 'There's nowhere to swim and that music will drive us all mad.'

Then, two weeks and two days after the Communist 'liberation', we were told we would be flown out next day. We were to be ready to leave for the airport at six in the morning. That night we packed everything up, including the film, wondering if it would be confiscated at the last moment, just as we were about to board the plane. Next morning, we left the hotel soon after dawn and drove to the airport. It was the first time any of us had been inside since the hectic days of the evacuation. The huge American military compound, known as 'Pentagon East', was in a shambles. The roof had fallen in and the walls were blackened by fire; the Americans had blown it up before leaving. Farther on, the twisted wreckage of helicopters and South Vietnamese Air Force planes littered the tarmac, and the terminal building was filled with bullet holes. We sat down to wait for our plane. An hour passed, then two. Finally one of the North Vietnamese Press officials appeared and said without apology, 'The flight is cancelled.' There was a chorus of protest and the guards fingered their rifles nervously. 'Why has the plane been cancelled?' everyone shouted at once. But there was no explanation. We drove despondently back to the Caravelle.

A day or two later I paid a farewell visit to Jacques. The whole family, tears in their eyes, turned out to say goodbye. As we stood outside the house I could see hear the sound of North Vietnamese soldiers splashing about noisily in the pool next door. Our pool.

'That makes me really angry,' I said to Jacques. 'That's British property, they have no right to be there at all.'

'Don't worry, sir,' he said with the only smile I had seen on his face for a long time. 'I've turned off the filter. Very soon the water will go green and they will not be able to swim in it after all!'

About 40,000 French citizens were still in Vietnam, nearly all of them Vietnamese or part Vietnamese. They were all as desperate as we were to leave Saigon. Some of the French-Vietnamese women were extremely beautiful. I met one whose husband, a general in the South Vietnamese Army, had been killed in the war, leaving her with two small children. She was a French national, but vulnerable both because she was a half-caste – the Vietnamese hate anyone of mixed blood – and because she was a member of the hated ruling class. She was terrified she would be refused an exit visa. Two or three North Vietnamese 'bao dai' (soldiers) had been billeted in her house and this frightened her. 'They look at me as if I were a strange sort of animal,' she said. 'I hate having them in the house.' I never discovered whether she was finally able to leave. If not, life for her and others like her would have become intolerable.

For the North Vietnamese, who had spent years in the jungles fighting their way south, a prey to hardship, malaria and B52 bombing raids, Saigon must have outrun their wildest dreams. It was full of all the fruits forbidden or unobtainable in their own impoverished homeland: cars, motor scooters, radios, watches, television sets, washing machines, air conditioning – all the paraphernalia the Americans had introduced in such abundance. It took the 'bao dai' only a day or two to discover the black market where practically everything could be bought, from Scotch and champagne to the latest Sony portable television, from the most up-to-date digital watch to ballpoint pens and car batteries. We would see them walking through the streets in little purposeful groups, clutching their new acquisitions, usually radios.

Finally, on Friday, May 23, we were told that we would definitely be leaving the next day. I sent an urgent telex to London warning them to have the charter plane standing by to fly us from Vientiane to Bangkok.

We had a last farewell dinner in the Aterbea and rose early on Saturday. At the airport after an hour's wait, we started to shuffle towards the two officers manning the desks. As we approached with our sackful of film I prayed they would not confiscate it. The moment arrived, we heaved our cases on the counter and the North Vietnamese officer began to make a thorough search. Now the sack of film was lifted on to the table. My heart thumped. The North Vietnamese took a long look at it and then said, 'Film? Your film?' 'Yes,' we nodded. Another agonising pause. Then, 'All right,' he said, waving. 'Pass through please.'

Suddenly he noticed a large red and white sack I was carrying marked CBS. 'That your film?' he snapped.

'CBS,' I said displaying the stencil.

'You're not CBS,' he said accusingly.

'No,' I said. 'I'm ITN. I'm taking it for a friend.'

He reached out for it. 'No allowed. You give to me. You not CBS. You go through.'

The German CBS cameraman who had given it to me and who was not leaving watched impotently from behind the barrier.

I pointed him out to the officer.

'You have permit?'

The cameraman, sweating with nerves and the heat, shouted, 'What permit?'

'You need permit from Ministry of Foreign Affairs.'

Desperate now, the German disappeared at a run, but we never saw him again and I imagine CBS never saw their film either.

Over eighty of us finally crammed into an old Russian Ilyushin, flown by two North Vietnamese Air Force pilots. We took off at ten, climbing over the green rice paddies, watching the coils of the Saigon River disappear into the smoky haze. We headed north for Cambodia then, following the Mekong River, we passed into Laos and, keeping the river which forms the border with Thailand on our left, droned on for another couple of hundred miles. We touched down at Vientiane, the sleepy capital of Laos on the north bank of the Mekong, just before lunchtime. I scrambled out and looked round hopefully for our charter aircraft. Not only was it not there but, apart from our Ilyushin, there was not another single plane in sight. We strode into the terminal and demanded to know the time of the next flight to Bangkok. 'Not until Tuesday,' the pleasant young man behind the desk said. That was in three days' time.

Was there any possibility of chartering to Bangkok? I asked.

He shook his head sympathetically. There were no charter aircraft at all in Vientiane. Laos, I remembered, was virtually under North Vietnamese control.

We drove into town and made for the old French hotel on the river. Here I discovered that the BBC had taken a boat across the river to Thailand where they had a small plane waiting. They were probably now on their way to Bangkok and ahead of us in the race to get film back to London. I could not understand why our plane was not there. Surely London must have got my telex. They should have alerted Bangkok immediately, I told myself, and it was only about an hour's flight to Vientiane.

'What about the telephone?' Lucien suggested.

The hotel porter shook his head sadly. 'No telephone to Bangkok.'

'We'd better go back to the airport. He may just have come in while we've been here. And maybe we can radio to Bangkok?' I said hopefully.

But the airport lay deserted under the fierce afternoon sun, the Ilyushin gone and the tarmac empty. The same helpful young man was still on duty. I explained our dilemma. 'Come,' he said, and led the way to the control tower. There for two hours we tried to call up Bangkok on the radio.

All we got was a lot of static.

Finally at 4.30, with frustration turning to despair, we heard the throaty growl of aircraft engines and, gliding down across the tree tops from the direction of the Mekong, came an old silver-grey C46 Curtiss Commando. It waggled its wings and settled down like a fat old lady on the hot tarmac, lumbered in and coughed to a stop beside us. The door opened and a very large American in a yellow flying suit, followed by a small dark, ferrety man in a blue flying suit, came down the steps.

'Mr Gall?' The big man asked.

'Yes,' I said, 'that's me. Where've you been?'

'Hi,' he said, ignoring the question. 'I'm Hank and this is Larry. You all set to go?'

'Yes,' then looking round at the fifteen or twenty British and French colleagues who all wanted a lift to Bangkok. 'Can you take all of us?'

'Guess so,' Hank said. 'We've only got three on the manifest, but I guess it'll be all right.'

He jerked his thumb at the interior of the aircraft. 'Sorry you'll have to sit on the floor. We were dropping rice in the north yesterday and we didn't have time to put the seats back in.'

The aluminium floor was quite bare of any comfort, but I did not care. 'Doesn't matter,' I said. 'We want to get to Bangkok as soon as possible.'

An hour and a half later, the watery green plain of Bangkok swam into view out of the gathering dusk. We roared down over the klongs, the canals that run as straight as a Roman road, intersecting the paddy fields, and touched down in sight of the bright lights of Bangkok.

As we walked into the terminal building, Lou Cioffi of ABC News approached with a bottle of champagne. 'Welcome back to the world,' he shouted, pouring the champagne. 'Now, I'd just like to interview you for a couple of minutes.' Still rather dazed I drank and then spoke. Then an American I had never seen before came up and introduced himself. 'I'm from UPITN,' he said. 'It's great to see you, but I have some bad news for you, Sandy.'

Apprehension stabbed me and I wondered wildly what had happened: Was it my wife, the children?

'What?' I said.

'ITV's on strike.'

I wondered for a fraction of a second if he was trying to be funny.

'You must be joking,' I said mechanically. 'I don't believe you.'

'It's true,' he insisted. 'The technicians went on strike a week ago. The whole network is off the air.'

'Fuck,' I said, tiredness letting the anger escape easily. 'After all that, and all this bloody film and now you tell me that ITV is on strike. It makes me sick.'

'I'm sorry, Sandy,' he said. 'I'm really sorry. Can I have the film?'

'So what do we do? Satellite it all to London?'

'ITN can't take it in,' he explained. 'Since it's an ACTT strike, they won't even record incoming satellite material. UPITN, the Americans, everybody wants your stuff. It's all been arranged in London.' The film editor came forward. 'You know Jim? He'll handle it all.'

I handed it over and the pack of American television men closed in; CBS, ABC, the Japanese, they came at me like terriers after a rat. They wanted to know what was in the film, what were the best bits, where were the scripts.

I suddenly felt exhausted and sick of the whole thing. All the effort, all the risk, now seemed a waste of time. The sense of triumph in finally getting out of Vietnam with our film intact turned to bitterness.

'Do what you like with the bloody stuff,' I said. 'I'm going to bed.'

Next day I felt slightly more philosophical. Although the BBC seemed to have the field to themselves, if the strike were to end now, we might still be in the race. I caught the BA

447

Jumbo to London that night. Nigel Ryan, his deputy, David Nicholas, and the number three, Don Horobin, were at the airport to meet me.

We had lunch at the St George's Hotel beside the ITN offices. 'Well done,' they said, raising their glasses. 'It was very brave of you to stay on.'

'Not really,' I said. 'It was entirely the fault of the French crew.' They all laughed, but it was true.

'What about the strike?' I asked.

'Well,' Nigel said. 'We're hoping to be back on the air on Wednesday or Thursday. We're keeping our fingers crossed.'

It turned out to be Friday, and while we waited there was nothing I could do. Because of the strike, the editors could not touch the film. And where was the film, anyway? The Bangkok editor had slashed it to ribbons trying to meet the demands of the American networks, and since then UPITN's 'Roving Report' team had been busy making their own version. They still had it.

Finally, at ten on Friday and only after David Nicholas's forceful intervention, we got the original material back in our hands. One month after the fall of Saigon, ITN's two best film editors, Gordon Hickey and Leo Rosenberg, and I sat down in the cutting room.

There were forty tins of film, about eight hours' viewing time. 'How the hell are we going to get through all this lot by ten o'clock tonight?' Leo Rosenberg wailed in despair. 'It's impossible.' Leo is small and volatile. Gordon is big and calm.

'Like this,' he replied, taking a length of film from the bin where they had already broken out the first few rolls. 'We've got to start somewhere.'

We had filmed on a day-by-day basis and there were eight separate stories. So we decided to do it as a diary – 'Saigon Diary'. The only question was: how long could we have on 'News at Ten'.

I went to see David. 'We have two options,' he said. 'We can go for a special but the BBC have already done theirs. We probably wouldn't get a special on the air till Sunday and very late at night. Or we can hit it hard on "News at Ten" tonight, our first night back on the air. We can trail it and built it up and give it everything we've got.'

'Okay,' I said. 'Let's go for "News at Ten". How much time can I have?'

'How much do you need?'

'Twenty minutes,' I said. I reckoned there was enough material for a good half-hour, maybe more.

'I think that's a little bit unrealistic,' David said. 'How about fifteen? I'll talk to the network.' He meant that he would have to ask for an overrun on 'News at Ten'.

An hour or two later, he said: 'Sorry, the best I can do is ten minutes.' I shrugged. There was no time to argue. Gordon and Leo were at full stretch, desperately cutting their way through the enormous footage to compress into a mere ten minutes the story of how the Vietnam War ended.

A lot of material had to go, but the best of it emerged as sharp and simple as a cameo: the tanks trundling down Le Loi and driving through the gates of the Presidential Palace; the resignation of 'Big Minh'; the arrival of the infantry, carrying their rice and rockets; the last moments of the defeated South Vietnamese Army, soldiers stripping off their uniforms and using their helmets to fill up the tanks of stolen cars; the refugees clambering frantically on board the ships in the river; the roof of the American Embassy, with a hundred Vietnamese waiting for the helicopter that would never come; the girl who pleaded and pleaded to come with us. We ended on a shot of a young Communist commissar in black pyjamas drilling the youth, making them march on the spot and chant Communist slogans. My last line of commentary said that the youth of Saigon were already being indoctrinated and that their future would no doubt be one of 'spontaneous demonstration' in support of the new Communist way of life.

Afterwards there were telephone calls, congratulations, warm words and a few drinks. Gordon and Leo would have done well to get it on the air at all, but they had turned out a remarkably fluent and polished job. I went home reflecting on how ephemeral television is. Shown once and virtually gone for ever. Or do the images linger on the retina of the mind? A few do, certainly. In any case, it was good to be home.

Index